Born under Auschwitz

Studies in German Literature, Linguistics, and Culture

Born under Auschwitz

Melancholy Traditions in Postwar German Literature

Mary Cosgrove

CAMDEN HOUSE
Rochester, New York

This research project was supported by the Arts and
Humanities Research Council (AHRC).

Each year the AHRC provides funding from the Government to support research and postgraduate study in the arts and humanities. Only applications of the highest quality are funded and the range of research supported by this investment of public funds not only provides social and cultural benefits but also contributes to the economic success of the UK. For further information on the AHRC, please go to: www.ahrc.ac.uk

Copyright © 2014 Mary Cosgrove

All Rights Reserved. Except as permitted under current legislation,
no part of this work may be photocopied, stored in a retrieval system,
published, performed in public, adapted, broadcast, transmitted,
recorded, or reproduced in any form or by any means,
without the prior permission of the copyright owner.

First published 2014
by Camden House

Camden House is an imprint of Boydell & Brewer Inc.
668 Mt. Hope Avenue, Rochester, NY 14620, USA
www.camden-house.com
and of Boydell & Brewer Limited
PO Box 9, Woodbridge, Suffolk IP12 3DF, UK
www.boydellandbrewer.com

ISBN-13: 978-1-57113-556-8
ISBN-10: 1-57113-556-1

Library of Congress Cataloging-in-Publication Data

Cosgrove, Mary.
  Born under Auschwitz: melancholy traditions in postwar German literature / Mary Cosgrove.
    p. cm. — (Studies in German literature, linguistics, and culture)
  Includes bibliographical references and index.
  ISBN-13: 978-1-57113-556-8 (hardcover : alk. paper) —
  ISBN-10: 1-57113-556-1 (hardcover : alk. paper)
  1. German literature—20th century—History and criticism. 2. Melancholy in literature. I. Title.

PT405.C693 2014
830.9'353—dc23   2013048915

This publication is printed on acid-free paper.
Printed in the United States of America.

For Adrian, Sinéad, Noel†, and Michelle

Contents

Acknowledgments	ix
Introduction: In Defense of Melancholy	1
1: The Diseased Imagination: Perpetrator Melancholy in Günter Grass's *Aus dem Tagebuch einer Schnecke* and *Beim Häuten der Zwiebel*	35
2: The Disenchanted Mind: Victim Melancholy in Wolfgang Hildesheimer's *Tynset* and *Masante*	76
3: The Feminine Holocaust: Gender, Melancholy, and Memory in Peter Weiss's *Die Ästhetik des Widerstands*	110
4: From the *Weltschmerz* of the Postwar Penitent to Capitalism and the "Racial Century": Melancholy Diversity in W. G. Sebald's Work	145
Epilogue: Death of the Male Melancholy Genius: From *Vergangenheitsbewältigung* to *Vergangenheitsbewirtschaftung* in Iris Hanika's *Das Eigentliche*	185
Bibliography	201
Index	223

Acknowledgments

I WOULD LIKE TO THANK the British Academy, the Arts and Humanities Research Council, the Carnegie Trust for the Universities of Scotland, and the School of Literatures, Languages and Cultures at the University of Edinburgh for generously supporting this project. Colleagues and friends also supported me from start to finish. Anne Fuchs, Elizabeth Boa, and Linda Shortt offered great intellectual advice, feedback, and kindness at different stages of the process. I cannot thank them enough.

Rebecca Braun made very useful and detailed suggestions for the chapter on Günter Grass, Hugh Ridley read a very early version of the introduction, and Jo Catling gave me some very helpful insights into W. G. Sebald's library. I would like to thank these friends and colleagues for their support and generosity.

Thank you also to Jim Walker at Camden House—who has been, as ever, an outstanding editor—and to his editorial team. This book has benefited in myriad ways from their suggestions.

I would like to thank the staff at the Akademie der Künste in Berlin, in particular Professor Jürgen Schütte, who made time to talk to me about Peter Weiss. Thanks also go to the staff at the Deutsches Literaturarchiv in Marbach, where I was able to work in the W. G. Sebald archive.

My friends also offered great moral support and company during this project. Thank you to Niamh, Aidan, Deirdre Gleeson, Fiona, my cousin Deirdre Murphy, Cath, Corinna, and the exceptionally kind Helen Doherty. Thanks also to my in-laws Fiona, Gordon, and Ollie, for their hospitality, sanity, and good humor. Although they don't know it yet, as true antidotes to melancholy in every sense, Calvin, Liv, Billy, Mae, and Mathilda have been a very rewarding part of the journey (and they're really good at reading, too). I also have to mention good old Scooby.

Lastly, I'd like to thank Mum and Dad for always believing in me.

Some of the material in this book has been published, in somewhat different form, in the following chapters: "From Nobility to Sloth: Melancholy Self-Fashioning and the Hamlet Motif in Wolfgang Hildesheimer's *Tynset* and *Masante*," in *Wolfgang Hildesheimer und England: Zur Topologie eines literarischen Transfers*, edited by Rüdiger

Görner and Isabel Wagner (Bern: Peter Lang, 2012), 79–101; and "Sebald for Our Time: The Politics of Melancholy and the Critique of Capitalism in His Work," in *W. G. Sebald and the Writing of History*, edited by Anne Fuchs and J. J. Long (Würzburg: Königshausen & Neumann, 2007), 91–110. I am grateful to the editors concerned for their permission to republish this material.

Introduction: In Defense of Melancholy

The "Genius" of *Vergangenheitsbewältigung*

IN 1963 WALTER JENS PUBLISHED a short work, *Herr Meister: Dialog über einen Roman* (Mr. Meister: Dialogue about a Novel), that, in the form of an exchange of letters between a novelist (called A) and a literary critic (called B), considered the usefulness of melancholy traditions for the contemporary novel concerned with the memory of the Holocaust.[1] The letters are not fictional but showcase an intellectual exchange that took place between Jens and the German-Jewish writer Wolfgang Hildesheimer in the years 1961 and 1962 (*HM*, 11).[2] Hildesheimer, correspondent A, was interested in melancholy discourses at this time, as his fascination with Shakespeare's *Hamlet* and his later novels *Tynset* (1965) and *Masante* (1973) demonstrate.[3]

Despite the fact that *Herr Meister* commemorates Jews in the Holocaust, it is a minor text that has not been accorded much attention in discussions of postwar German literature.[4] However, its scholarly focus on the aesthetic possibilities of different melancholy traditions for developing a literary discourse of *Vergangenheitsbewältigung*—a problematic appellation that delineates the task of coming to terms with the Nazi past and the Holocaust and that for all its inadequacy will be used throughout this book to designate questions of remembrance—renders it an appropriate starting point for the present study.[5] *Born under Auschwitz* examines melancholy self-fashioning in works by Günter Grass, Wolfgang Hildesheimer, Peter Weiss, W. G. Sebald, and Iris Hanika, all of whom, in their reflections on the poetics of remembrance after the Holocaust, revive and subvert European melancholy traditions. In *Herr Meister* Jens and Hildesheimer identify these traditions as a fecund source for the development of a literary language of commemoration. In so doing they query the still-pervasive concept of a caesura in representative and aesthetic practices after Auschwitz. A recent study, for example, asks the pertinent question whether "it is possible to talk about postwar poetics in terms of creativity rather than merely in terms of the destruction of traditions."[6] In their theoretical reflections the authors return to the concept of a gap in representation, however, which reinforces the idea of destruction and under-theorizes how creativity may beguile the problem of representation. Axel Dunker's study of literature after Auschwitz also emphasizes the moment of silence and absence in representation—the idea of the unrepresentable—embracing a negative aesthetics that, as he points out, approaches the sacred.[7] From a different angle, Dominick LaCapra argues that to frame historical events in terms of silence and the unrepresentable constitutes "negative sacralization," which substitutes mythical for historical understanding and blurs the boundaries in postwar memory culture between victims and others.[8]

By focusing on how different writers commemorate the Holocaust by placing themselves in a noble and masculine cultural lineage, *Born under Auschwitz* opens up a middle ground between the positions outlined by Dunker and LaCapra, emphasizing the creativity of postwar German writing as well as its embeddedness in established cultural and intellectual traditions. This is not to deny the idea of caesura and the problem of representation after the Holocaust. Indeed, the idea of melancholy as performative, which I develop in the next section, allows for the kind of "modernist" or deconstructionist strategies of signification that Dunker identifies in commemorative aesthetics after Auschwitz.[9] Rather, the focus in this study on dynamic engagement with tradition illuminates the ways in which the writers featured self-consciously imagine themselves as creative artists whose melancholy pedigree, simultaneously verbose and inarticulate, is the signature of their postwar literary commemoration.

The idea that art after the Holocaust must be anti-redemptory and non-representational has been attributed to Frankfurt School intellectual Theodor W. Adorno's famous "dictum" that to write poetry after Auschwitz is barbaric.[10] Adorno's dictum, written in 1949 and first published in 1951, was not intended to establish a prohibition on artistic representation.[11] Rather than asserting that the impossibility of representation was a problem immanent to the postwar work of art and therefore inescapable, Adorno addressed the "unknowability" of the Holocaust as an *epistemological* problem that post-Auschwitz literary writing should aporetically reflect.[12] In other words, the language of the postwar text should thematize its limitations.

Jens's and Hildesheimer's dialogue about literary melancholy in the postwar context is an example of this kind of creative engagement. Their use of time-honored European melancholy traditions that are often anchored in optimistic humanist periods, such as the Renaissance, suggests that aesthetic practice, in order to be ethical, must not exhaustively showcase caesura and destruction. They do not suppress the idea of the unspeakable (*HM*, 139); however, their invention of a melancholy postwar personality in the character Herr Meister both confirms and questions the intellectual paradigm that renders language insufficient in the face of traumatic historical events deemed to exceed representation. This paradigm announces, to paraphrase historian Dan Diner, a "Zivilisationsbruch" (rupture in civilization), a radical break with the pre-Holocaust world and its culture, and it insists that language must reinvent itself in order to address the legacy of Auschwitz.[13]

Challenging this idea of rupture, Jens and Hildesheimer return to established melancholy traditions in order to conceptualize Herr Meister, a German scholar whose eye-witness account provides the postwar reader with a window on the era of National Socialism, as an embodiment of the remorse that, a few years later, Alexander and Margarete Mitscherlich would claim was missing from the "autistic" West German collective.[14] The text is thus not only a phenomenon of the shift, in the 1960s, toward the acknowledgement of Jewish victim experience.[15] It is also a belated product of the immediate postwar period, when Karl Jaspers produced his famous text on the question of German guilt.[16] Hildesheimer's revival of Hamlet as a kind of detective who, obsessed with finding out the truth, returns to the scene of the crime, acknowledges Jaspers's earlier mobilization of the same character as an ethical role model for the postwar German collective. Shortly after the war Jaspers suggested this melancholy investigator of the past as the ideal embodiment of the ethical memory necessary for a collective that acknowledges its crimes.[17] Hildesheimer's intertextual reference to Jaspers in the early 1960s revives the schematic outlines of a self-reflexive perpetrator consciousness that had retreated behind the "war stories" of German suffering that dominated West German society in the 1950s.[18] Crucially, his creative use of Hamlet to convey this key idea demonstrates the ethical possibilities of cultural traditions after 1945, not their bankruptcy.

A kind of witness-genius whose melancholy perspicacity enables him to investigate the past, Herr Meister is the modern incarnation of melancholy traditions that go back to Renaissance humanism. Accompanying the image of the pained witness who is committed to the ethical memory of the dead Holocaust victims is his simultaneous glorification under the sign of Saturn, the planet that during the Renaissance came to be associated with the creative brilliance of artists and thinkers (*HM*, 53).[19] Through references to Albrecht Dürer's famous engraving *Melencolia I* (1514), the authors codify Herr Meister as a noble melancholy type who, consistent with the idea of German remorse, is also a *Beichtkind* (a penitent, *HM*, 63). Yet shimmering through the earnestness of one who testifies to historical atrocity is also the mannered specter of the dandy (*HM*, 85). While highly gifted, Herr Meister is vain, lazy, and a hypochondriac, features that cast doubt on his ability to remain focused on the victim other and that suggest that any effort on his part to remember the suffering of others will of necessity take a long time to come to fruition (*HM*, 88–89).[20] Far from perfect, this particular *homo melancholicus* of the early 1960s is a quirky, mixed creation whose composite parts occasionally expose him to parody and the absurd (*HM*, 27). His iconic pedigree renders him a kind of "genius" of literary *Vergangenheitsbewältigung*, clad in the noble apparel of tradition that in its very pomp risks ridicule. In this way, Jens and Hildesheimer creatively allude to the ongoing effort that must be invested in remembering the Holocaust dead: the ethical effort to think past the self in order to empathize with the other. Moreover, his very iconicity means that Herr Meister challenges the assumption, influenced by Sigmund Freud's famous essay of 1917, that melancholy signifies a pathological, even unethical, response to the crimes of National Socialism and the Holocaust, a point that receives attention in the final section of this introduction.[21] Like Jens and Hildesheimer, in *Born under Auschwitz* I approach melancholy discourse as a *performative* system of signs and icons and not primarily as a disturbing pathology of the individual or collective psyche. Viewed as a performative discourse, melancholy offers the postwar German writer concerned with ethical memory many possibilities for creating a varied and self-reflexive literary language of remembrance.

Melancholy as Performative

A hybrid of different melancholy icons, Herr Meister expresses in typological fashion a universal sadness about the Holocaust. Yet this means that he also *performs* this sadness, which is to say that Jens and Hildesheimer, in creating him, cite established melancholy traditions.

The concept of "performativity" or "the performative" has had a complex history since the English philosopher J. L. Austin began to theorize it in the 1950s.[22] Austin argued that our utterances are performative; that is, they are not merely the linguistic descriptions of events in the nonlinguistic world. Rather, utterances such as bets, promises, and threats, for example, constitute actions that are "performed." As James Loxley puts it, these utterances, "are actions *in themselves*, actions of a distinctively linguistic kind."[23] Viewed from this angle, language does not just reflect our world; it also helps to create it. Austin argued further that performative utterances are conventional—ritual or ceremonial—in nature. This means that they are both inherently repeatable and, perhaps somewhat counterintuitively, creative linguistic acts. In his deconstructionist treatment of the performative, Jacques Derrida emphasizes Austin's insistence on the conventional character of performative utterances. He develops the idea of conventionality further, however, to encompass the deconstructionist view of language as characterized by a constitutive lack or absence. For Derrida, the conventionality and citationality of the performative, what he terms its "iterability," continually evokes this fundamental condition of language.[24] From a deconstructionist angle, literary language that uses established melancholy tradition points to its own deficits and it does this through the very conventionality of melancholy discourses. To take this one step further: melancholy understood as performative in the deconstructionist sense offers a stylized expression of the problems of lack, deferral, and surplus that deconstruction asserts as central problems of language and signification.

Derrida's view of the performative is thus interesting for my discussion. In the case of Herr Meister, who is a medley of melancholy icons, we can observe the performative at work. Jens and Hildesheimer cite established melancholy types, which is a form of repetition as well as a creative act. Creativity is evident in the combination of the old with the new, namely their citation of pre-twentieth century traditions in the new post-Holocaust context. The iconic plenitude of melancholy discourses, which hark back to pre-Holocaust epochs, subtly thematizes the limitations of language and representation since 1945. These limitations come to the fore when we consider, for example, that melancholy to some degree should symbolize mood and affect. And yet, as Thomas Pfau argues, melancholy as performative "unravels the project of an authentically expressive poetics," which points to the gap between signifier and signified and suggests that distance constitutes the representation of sadness.[25] While this performative aspect to melancholy discourse means that it has often been regarded as inauthentic, *Born under Auschwitz* seeks to introduce a more differentiated view.[26] The objective is to show, through the analysis of an exemplary set of texts, how melancholy discourses help develop a literary language of *Vergangenheitsbewältigung* in this period.

Derrida's theory of iterability is founded on the repeatability of all linguistic signs within language. He argues that the same sign can be repeated in different contexts, which underscores both its sameness and its difference. This in turn suggests that a sign is never quite identical with itself: it is permanently iterable or repeatable. In his study of performativity, Loxley reasons as follows:

> Insofar as a mark is iterable, it cannot be said to belong ultimately or originally in any particular context. If it is essentially repeatable, it can be extracted from any set of linguistic or social circumstances and grafted onto another, remaining in some way the same as it is repeated. It can, in other words, be redeployed, quoted, or cited, in principle ad infinitum. And this capability also ensures that its use in any particular context carries the trace of the other contexts in which it features: the examples of quoting and citing reveal this particularly starkly.[27]

One prominent example of a melancholy icon that displays this kind of iterability is Dürer's engraving *Melencolia I*. While the writers who engage with this image in the current study follow art historian Erwin Panofsky's influential humanist interpretation of Dürer, reviving *Melencolia I* in a positive way as a kind of "Renaissance episteme" that functions in the postwar context as short-hand for ethical memory, other writers of this period, such as Wolfgang Koeppen and the Austro-Jewish Holocaust survivor Jean Améry, were inclined to see in the image evidence of Germany's demonic pact with National Socialism.[28] Améry and Koeppen follow a line of interpretation that Thomas Mann advanced in his postwar novel *Doktor Faustus* (1947), which tells the story of artist Adrian Leverkühn's pact with the devil, an allegory for Germany's descent into National Socialism.[29] Instead of stressing Dürer's humanist background, Mann associates the artist "with the Gothic, backward, diabolical sphere," a negative reassessment, as Martin A. Ruehl points out, "that may have been conditioned by [Mann's] awareness of the artist's positive reception in the Third Reich."[30] In his hybrid text *Aus dem Tagebuch einer Schnecke* (From the diary of a snail, 1972), Grass reverses this trend. In an effort to recast the postwar German artist as a politically engaged democrat who feels remorse for the Nazi past, he endorses Panofsky's reading of Dürer's image as the eloquent expression of Renaissance humanism, and states that he is "putting in a good word for melancholy."[31]

These examples show how the same image may be cited in different contexts by different writers, who invest it with very different meanings.[32] The polarization between, for instance, Renaissance and Gothic interpretations of Dürer destabilizes the idea that humanism constitutes the original meaning of *Melencolia I*. We might view this from a deconstructionist angle in terms of the performative that indicates a lack of original, unitary meaning at the heart of the icon.[33] The heterogeneity of meaning that emerges in this space of ambivalence is the general condition of language, according to Derrida.[34] The broad term "melancholy" signifies not only different and often contradictory cultural traditions but also loosely names an obscure mood and emotion; this points to ambivalence as a fundamental condition of language: the discontinuity between signifier and signified that characterizes the performative. Interestingly, this kind of obscurity also informs medical accounts of melancholy.[35] As distinct from other kinds of sadness that can boast a clear trigger, melancholy is usually described as sadness with insufficient or no cause: the subject struggles to identify and name the lost object that caused her/his sadness.[36] Some theories propose that in melancholy the subject laments not so much the loss of a specific object as a far greater constitutive absence, "the real that does not lend itself to signification," in Julia Kristeva's words.[37] As Pfau suggests, "the language of melancholy thus bespeaks the subject's grasp of a permanent insufficiency in . . . the signifier."[38] From this viewpoint, the rich arsenal of motifs and icons in melancholy traditions testify, in their efforts to express the cause of melancholy, to the insufficiency of signification. The epistemological problem that surfaces in this quest to understand the nature of sadness leads Hartmut Böhme to conclude that Dürer's *Melencolia I* is the allegory of an allegory that tautologically signifies the overdetermined quality of the melancholy signifier.[39] Similarly,

Pfau argues that this performative quality of the "damaged" melancholy signifier characterizes much of the historical writing on melancholy:[40]

> As early as [Robert] Burton's *Anatomy of Melancholy*, melancholy is understood as thoroughly rhetorical in its constitution and as a conscious articulation of that very fact. Thus it unfolds as a recurrent, monotonous, indeed, serial, reenactment of the *vanitas* or futility not only of symbolic signification but of the very creation that the symbolic seeks to capture and, by that very means, redeem.[41]

This body of writing, in its efforts to name an absence, is peculiarly verbose. Burton's famous early modern tome with its deference, through extensive citation, to the scholastic fathers of the medieval period and the intellectuals of antiquity is another good example of the performative quality of writing on melancholy.[42] He cites the established authorities *ad nauseum* and produces endless lists of causes, symptoms, and remedies, but arguably this does not bring him any closer to solving the mystery of melancholy.

The self-reflexive focus on the limitations of language in discourses on and about melancholy suggests a certain structural kinship between the age-old task of writing about melancholy and the more recent task of writing about the Holocaust. In both cases, the effort to find words that capture the object without distorting it raises the issues of knowing and representation and determines that these are the central concerns of the signifying process.

In the works featured in this study, the historical event of the Holocaust is a prominent cause of the melancholy depicted. However, the writers use the longstanding ambiguity around what causes melancholy to point up the insufficiency of language and rational explanation after the Holocaust. The very performativity of melancholy—the fact that conventional icons appear in very different works—plays an important role in this endeavor. Grass and Hildesheimer, for example, cite the "Renaissance episteme" of melancholy genius in their respective works on Holocaust memory, *Aus dem Tagebuch einer Schnecke*, and *Tynset* and *Masante*. Yet Grass belongs to the German perpetrator collective, while Hildesheimer is a member of the Jewish victim collective. Both adapt the humanist melancholy icon to address the legacy of Auschwitz, but the contexts into which they transfer this icon—the moral worlds of the perpetrator and the victim—vary significantly. Consequently, they encode the "Renaissance episteme" differently, as chapters 1 and 2 demonstrate. While Grass insists that the remorseful German is by definition a melancholy genius, Hildesheimer's novels document survivor guilt as the ruinous slide from genial nobility into the sin of sloth. Self-congratulation is the dominant tone in Grass, while self-recrimination permeates Hildesheimer's poetics. This comparison highlights the ethical effects of the performative quality of the image of melancholy genius. That the central protagonists of two morally very different worlds may be channeled through this common "mark" points to the impersonal, insufficient, and—worse still—perhaps even inauthentic nature of language—to quote Loxley "the disturbing thought that something technical or mechanical haunts our purposes and meanings at their origins."[43] In the context of postwar German literature, this issue is particularly acute, as Adorno's dictum showed. To expose the conventional quality of language, however, is also to expose its struggle to say anything meaningful about atrocity and its aftermath. And yet this struggle, borne of catastrophe, may blaze a creative trail. The performativity of melancholy traditions in the post-Holocaust literary text goes right to the heart of this matter, demonstrating the inventive potential of any conventional structure, including those deemed insufficient. The revival of melancholy traditions in the post-1945 German literary context is a moment of inventiveness in this sense. Against the one-dimensional notion of melancholy as a pathological affliction of the psyche, understanding melancholy discourse as performative illuminates how writers navigate their way through a new moral universe by citing and combining established icons to create a literary language of remembrance.

Herr Meister demonstrates this performative quality of melancholy discourse in the post-Holocaust world. To be melancholy in *Herr Meister* is not only to lay bare the suffering of the damaged psyche. It is just as much to perform penitence, to strike a pose, according to literary and cultural conventions. To subvert what Hamlet says to his mother, Gertrude, who complains that he wears too much black: to be melancholy is not just to suffer the internal crisis of the soul. It is also to don the trappings and the suits of woe.[44] Rather than being merely a naive expression of emotion, then, melancholy discourse enables critical investigation of cultural norms and values and offers an arsenal of motifs and figures of shifting import that transmit the effort to grasp what exceeds ordinary understanding.

Terminology

The word "melancholy" can describe very different emotional and psychological states. In one sense, it denotes the experience of sadness that might linger for an indefinite period and that may or may not have a clear cause. Since the late nineteenth century this condition has been referred to as "depression," a medical term that does not connote the rich cultural and intellectual legacy of melancholy from antiquity to the present.[45] For "melancholy" also describes a state of cultural attainment. Within the body of writing on melancholy, images of illness and despair thus alternate with the image of heroic, genial melancholy or *melancholia generosa* that originated with Aristotle, came to prominence in the Florentine

Neoplatonism of the Renaissance, and made an emphatic reappearance during Romanticism.[46] In recognition of such rich traditions, "melancholy" is understood here as a shifting cultural representation that reflects historical changes in the evaluation of sadness and not as an anthropological constant. In this spirit, *Born under Auschwitz* acknowledges the breadth and diversity of melancholy in some cultural discourses as "good" sadness, a creative blessing, and in others as "bad" sadness, a debilitating condition. Important to note is that both variants are cultural constructs that may have little resonance with any individual's experience of sadness.

The term "sadness" is more general than the term "melancholy," which has an established, if varied, cultural legacy. "Sadness" is a broad enough category to encompass both "melancholy" and "depression," although these nouns do not always describe the same phenomenon. I occasionally use the term "sadness," usually qualified as a "good" kind (genial melancholy, for example) or "bad" kind (spiritual sloth), as a synonym for melancholy. In this study "melancholy" and "sadness" refer to a contemplative response to recent history that is embedded in the ancient cultural traditions of writing about and depicting the universal human experience of sorrow.[47] In the interest of clarity, I avoid the alternative term "melancholia"; while it was a synonym for "melancholy" during the Renaissance, its application, in other epochs, has often been restricted to descriptions of disease.[48]

Title, Authors, and Gender

The title *Born under Auschwitz* is inspired by Rudolf and Margot Wittkower's iconological work, *Born under Saturn* (1963), which examines the self-stylization and popular image of the artist as an eccentric, noble genius from antiquity to the French Revolution. The Saturn of their title references the recasting, during the Renaissance, of this planet as the astral mentor of the gifted intellectual and is thus a positive marker of identity. By contrast, the intertextual reference to astrology in *Born under Auschwitz* is nominal only and is not intended to convey astrological fatalism in the face of major historical events. Rather, it signals the coming of age after 1945 of literary authors who use melancholy as a means of crafting an ethical discourse of literary commemoration. New readings of literary texts that were published in the period since the 1960s, the decade in which the concept of *Vergangenheitsbewältigung* was critically expanded to include the perspective of Jewish victims, highlight how the writers engage with diverse melancholy traditions to convey a particular interpretation of the past.[49] Establishing the literary effect of each author's efforts to combine the old with the new—how they create a literary language for the present that embeds the legacy of the Holocaust in a particular intellectual tradition—the treatment of each writer looks back to earlier centuries at the same time that it considers postwar literary discourses on memory.

While there are other postwar German writers whose works could be considered melancholy, the writers featured in this study have in common the explicit engagement, as a means of addressing the Nazi past, with melancholy traditions since antiquity.[50] *Born under Auschwitz* examines four male writers and one female writer, which raises the question of gender. As Julia Schiesari argues, melancholy is a predominantly masculine discourse that, from Aristotle to Giorgio Agamben, has been expressed, diagnosed, and described mainly by male thinkers.[51] Ever since the thinker referred to as "pseudo-Aristotle"—one of Aristotle's pupils whose thoughts on melancholy were published under Aristotle's name—asked why it was that all great *male* heroes suffered from melancholy, women have largely been excluded from the image of the manic-melancholy creative genius.[52] According to this perspective, great melancholics are men, and their pathological sense of loss has, in the Western canon, acquired a cultural status denied to woman's more mundane experience of sadness. Freud exemplifies this exclusion of women from the great melancholy canon when he refers to Hamlet—one of the male stars of Renaissance humanism—as melancholic.[53] Sad women Freud dismisses as "mere hysterics" or "just depressed."[54] According to Schiesari, Kristeva also assigns an essentially depressive status to women, separating out "some superior, implicitly male, aesthetic or cultural possibility" from the more "prosaic grief" of the sick woman.[55]

Clark Lawlor argues, however, that women writers have contributed more to the cultural genesis of melancholy than they are given credit for historically.[56] In the postwar German context, Ingeborg Bachmann, for example, could be regarded in this light.[57] An analysis of the ways in which women writers appropriate an explicitly masculine tradition of melancholy, while intrinsically worthwhile, would exceed the objective of this book, which is, broadly speaking, to trace the rise and decline of a *masculine* type in the context of postwar German literature. *Born under Auschwitz* thus examines how male writers engage with melancholy discourses, illuminating how they position themselves in a noble and overwhelmingly masculine European lineage. The inclusion of Hanika, the only female author in this study, is not intended to address a gender imbalance in the selection of authors. Her deeply satirical novel, *Das Eigentliche* (Authenticity, 2010) offers a pithy counterpoint to the other writers featured here: she announces the death of the male melancholy genius of *Vergangenheitsbewältigung* and the end of Holocaust memory in the Berlin Republic. Peter Weiss is the only other writer in this study who ponders in a critical way the question of melancholy, gender, and postwar ethical memory.

By contrast, the texts by Grass, Hildesheimer, and Sebald use the patriarchal tradition of melancholy, which marks male loss as singularly worthwhile, to lend a sense of moral greatness to the task of working through the past. This reinforces the sense that serious memory work and ethically endowed "Trauerarbeit" (mourning work) are the business of perspicacious menfolk. Gisela Ecker argues that, historically speaking, mourning work, in the gendered division of cultural labor, has always been a second-rate task assigned to women.[58] However, the exceptional German situation after 1945 demonstrates how in some historical epochs the public expression of loss has a high cultural and ethical value that recodifies mourning and melancholy as legitimate *masculine* tasks. Thus in investigating how the texts in this study establish the male genius of *Vergangenheitsbewältigung*, we must take into consideration gender and the abject status of women in discourses about melancholy. Jennifer Radden points out that historically "the category of genius had no more place for women than had the category of melancholy," even though women in Renaissance and baroque representations of melancholy often embodied a female figure known as Dame Melancholy.[59] When feminized, the melancholy figure was often deemed to have lost its positive Aristotelian attributes, becoming old, deadly, and contaminating (*SM*, 329).

Melancholy: The Field of Research

Contemporary scholarly sources on melancholy feature in the personal archives and libraries of the individual authors of the texts under scrutiny here, revealing the authors' knowledge of melancholy traditions and suggesting their awareness of what I term melancholy as performative. In *Herr Meister* one of the letters mentions how Jens has sent Hildesheimer a parcel containing reading material, including Panofsky's and Fritz Saxl's groundbreaking iconological study of Dürer's engraving (*HM*, 102). Grass also mentions this source in *Aus dem Tagebuch einer Schnecke* and in the archival material for the diary. Weiss's archive contains a clipping of *Melencolia I*, which is reproduced in his notebooks. Sebald refers to the same image in *Die Ringe des Saturn* (The Rings of Saturn, 1997), and notes he made in his copy of Walter Benjamin's work on baroque tragic drama reveal close engagement with Benjamin's interpretation of the engraving.[60] Alongside the thematization of melancholy as a vessel for ethical Holocaust memory, the authors' engagement with this rich phenomenon is intriguing in another respect. The earlier works by Grass, Hildesheimer, and Jens coincide with a wave of scholarly output on the topic of melancholy in the 1960s. Studies from many different disciplines were published throughout the decade, many of which still belong to the canon of scholarly works on melancholy today.[61] Together they provide sources and inspiration for subsequent literary treatments of melancholy within the field of German Studies.[62]

When one reviews this field of scholarly research, two questions arise: first, why melancholy enjoyed such prominence in the early 1960s; second, how this scholarship was absorbed by German writers with an interest in the literary representation of the Holocaust and the Nazi past.

It is beyond the scope of the present study to answer the first question exhaustively. Indeed, one would need to embed such an investigation within an intellectual history of the 1960s. However, one feature of melancholy as a subject of academic enquiry is difficult to overlook when considering its popularity at this time: its interdisciplinarity within the context of the burgeoning field of Cultural Studies.[63] The versatility of melancholy as an object of study makes it an attractive topic for scholars interested in intellectual milieus beyond their immediate field. No single study on melancholy exemplifies this principle as convincingly as the ground-breaking work by Klibansky, Panofsky, and Saxl. Arguably still the most influential study on melancholy within the Humanities, *Saturn und Melancholie* (Saturn and Melancholy, 1964) is a product of the Aby Warburg school of thought, which developed the iconological method for research in art history, an approach that examines artworks by looking at them in their iconographic, historical, and cultural context and that transcends the high-low divide in the interpretation of visual culture.[64]

This masterful study places *Melencolia I* in its historical and iconographical context, illuminating what was new about the engraving at the dawn of the early modern period. The authors demonstrate how Dürer combined different melancholy traditions, such as those based on ancient Greek medicine, medieval astrology, and the Neoplatonic division of the soul, to articulate a new, modern subjectivity that recognized the epistemological limitations of the mind in the face of the growing complexity of the world. As well as providing the reader with a detailed overview of several melancholy discourses, this study also drives home the message of melancholic artistic genius, for the whole work propels its impressive scholarship toward the concluding section, where Dürer's startling originality as a unique intellectual of his time, as well as an outstanding painter, is revealed in irresistible splendor. It is this image of melancholy genius that exerts such magnetic influence on the male writers under examination here.

The impact of *Saturn und Melancholie* and the interdisciplinary approach to literary studies is palpable.[65] Unsurprisingly, there is no firm consensus on the question of where to establish disciplinary boundaries in the study of melancholy. Were one to write an intellectual history of melancholy in the twentieth century from a predominantly Humanities perspective, its medical reconceptualization as depression since the end of the nineteenth century would have to be traced, and beyond this, one would have to uncover the impact of this medicalization on the study of melancholy in Humanities subjects.[66] In this vein, Burkhard Meyer-Sickendieck's recent study on brooding attempts to straddle the divide between literary-cultural analysis and neuroscientific research.[67] By contrast, Martina Wagner-Egelhaaf resurrects disciplinary boundaries by dismissing the description and classification of diseases from literary scholarship.[68] These two positions reveal the difficulty of deciding where to set limits on the melancholy object of scholarly enquiry.

This is an issue affecting the present study. Rather than providing a history of the concept in its various guises across different disciplines, however, an endeavor that would swell to encyclopedic proportions, I take the literary text as a point of departure and establish, on the basis of close readings, the kind of melancholy the individual authors use in their quest to create a poetics of remembrance. This approach identifies the epochal and thematic preferences of the different authors. Often they use similar imagery; however, the melancholy "object" as it appears in the various texts can be encoded very differently, depending on what the author wishes to say about the legacy of the Nazi past and, more often than not, depending on whether the author belongs to the victim (Hildesheimer, Weiss) or perpetrator (Grass, Sebald, Hanika) collective. In this way, each chapter includes only those aspects of specific melancholy traditions that are relevant for the discussion of the texts at hand. Certain key images from the history of melancholy, such as Dürer's engraving, recur across these texts.

Despite the many studies on literary melancholy since the 1960s, melancholy as a discourse under the sign of Auschwitz has yet to be identified as a trend in postwar German literature. This oversight arises, to some degree, from the scholarly association of German melancholy traditions predominantly with the early modern period, the baroque period, Romanticism, and also the crisis of modernity, and it is perpetuated in postwar publications on melancholy in German literature, most of which stop their analysis before the twentieth century. An exception is Günter Blamberger's study, which examines the postwar German novel.[69] However, Blamberger is concerned more with the role melancholy plays in the crisis of the novel during existentialism than with its potential as a memory discourse after Auschwitz. The gap in research can also be explained through the narrowing of the term "melancholy" in psychoanalytical discourses on German memory since the 1960s. In these, melancholy demarcates an obscure, psychopathological state, while its performative potential as a literary discourse of memory is neglected.

Yet beyond psychoanalysis, traditions of melancholy have had a sustained literary afterlife in the latter half of the twentieth century. Especially prominent in post-Auschwitz literary melancholy are the figure of the Renaissance genius and the Christian view of melancholy as a sin. It is useful, therefore, to provide a brief overview of these key phases in the intellectual history of melancholy. Together they can be grouped into a "good" kind of melancholy and a "bad" kind. The German writers featured here use both "good" and "bad" images to articulate their views on the legacy of the recent past. More often than not, the images they select already contain a statement on this past, because their choices carry value judgments on the complex phenomenon of sadness that colors contemporary discussions about how to commemorate the past. To return to the question of how these writers engage with melancholy in a post-Auschwitz context, the provisional answer is: dramatically, ostentatiously, and with a flair for the performative. Nobility is a key marker of the brilliant melancholy type, so to be presented as evidently melancholy in this particular sense is to possess dignified, perhaps even ethical, postwar credentials.

"Good" and "Bad" Melancholy: An Overview

Melancholy has had many different faces throughout the millennia and also at any one period. A perplexing phenomenon, it has always been divisive, whether it is understood as the pathological disease of clinical enquiry, as an everyday transitory mood that afflicts many, as a sign of demonic possession, or as a fashionable marker of artistic creativity. In history, melancholy has been intimately connected to major upheaval and epochal intellectual shifts, such as the humanist debates of the Renaissance, the theological conflicts of the Reformation, and the emergence of modernity and with it a sense of historical crisis. In observers it has inspired a wide range of strong reactions, perhaps because no single version of melancholy exists that can harmonize its internal ambivalences and intrinsic dialectical vitality.[70] Designating a limitless terrain between illness and empowerment, the different mood states described by the term "melancholy" swing, at least since pseudo-Aristotle's association of melancholy with extraordinary ability, between the darkness of a pathological condition and the dazzling heights of genius.[71] These two poles mark out the dialectical tension that is germane to melancholy. On the one hand, it is an anthropological-medical phenomenon that describes a pathological condition or a disease. On the other, it circumscribes the nobility of the tragic outlook.

The Medical View

The dichotomy of "good" and "bad" melancholy is structured around this split between mental illness and gifted state. Both accounts of the condition have proved tenacious. As early as the fifth century B.C. the

Corpus Hippocraticum, a series of medical texts that are attributed to Hippocrates and his pupils, associated the melancholy condition with a dark bodily fluid: black bile, in classical Greek: "melaina cholè." In these writings, black bile was first described, with reference to humoral theory, as a natural constituent of the body. The idea of the humors was consistent with the Greek worldview that postulated correspondences between microcosm and macrocosm, individual and cosmos. Humoral theory identified four different bodily liquids or humors that included blood, yellow bile, black bile, and phlegm. Each humor was thought to be prevalent during one of the four seasons—respectively spring, summer, autumn, and winter. Each humor was furthermore paired with different qualities: blood with warmth and moisture, yellow bile with warmth and dryness, black bile with coldness and dryness, and phlegm with coldness and moisture. Disease occurred when a humor was thought to be in excess of its optimal levels. In this way, an excess of black bile, autumnal, viscous, cold, and dry, interfered with "the principle of equilibrium" central to the worldview of antiquity. This concept of disequilibrium on the humoral level was crucial in the etiology and pathogenesis of melancholy in antiquity.[72]

Five centuries after Hippocrates, the Greek physician Galen elaborated from humoralism the theory of the four temperaments, in each of which one particular humor dominated. These were known as the sanguine, choleric, melancholic, and phlegmatic temperaments. An excess of black bile was believed to cause the psychological and physical effects of melancholy. These included anxiety, despondency, restlessness, and a fear of death.[73] Again, central to this ancient medical understanding of melancholy was the idea that it was the consequence of deviance from an optimal balance of the humors, which, if maintained, usually meant good health.

Up to and beyond the Middle Ages medical ideas about melancholy did not change very much. Humoral theory and the ensuing theory of the four temperaments persisted from antiquity as an explanatory model for personality type and mental predisposition until the early eighteenth century, when the concepts of the central nervous and circulatory systems started to replace humoralism.[74] Yet the enduring symbol of black bile in literary texts is a notorious example of the longevity of certain metaphors, even after the scientific basis for their importance had disappeared.[75]

In medical terms, however, melancholy, which in the nineteenth century increasingly became associated with partial insanity, began to acquire more narrowly negative connotations. The perspective of modern medicine did not necessarily allow for the redeeming features that since pseudo-Aristotle had periodically been attributed to the condition. Thus in the late nineteenth century Emil Kraepelin's conviction that every psychiatric clinical disorder could be reduced to an organic substratum of the brain further consolidated the view of melancholy—by now termed manic-depressive insanity—in the field of psychiatric medicine as caused by hereditary factors and a morbid predisposition.[76] This biological view is still prevalent today with regard to clinical depression.[77] It has not gone unchallenged, however, as critics and practitioners are now identifying culture and society as the source of much individual depression.[78]

The Religious View

Medical discourses throughout the millennia have not been alone in regarding melancholy as an impairment rather than as a sign of exceptional ability. It was viewed darkly in the medieval period when the church fathers began to apply Christian morality to humoral pathology, transforming melancholy into sloth or *acedia*, a sign of demonic possession. Sloth, originally a monk's affliction, was a sign of waning faith in God. This danger was personified in the apparition of the noonday demon; after hours of prayer and fasting hermits were by midday at their most vulnerable to temptation away from the ascetic life. *Acedia* is a withdrawal from the divine good, which is followed by the individual's descent into spiritual torpor and *taedium vitae*.[79] The wandering mind that accompanies this deviance from the right spiritual path is precisely that hypertrophy of the imagination that connects *acedia* to melancholy as a disease of the corrupt imagination that has been invaded by demonic forces.[80]

The Middle Ages were not the only time that melancholy was associated with religious world views. Seventeenth-century baroque culture again linked it to Christianity, but now the melancholy perspective on the world could penetrate earthly materiality and recognize its transience, as symbolized in the traditions of *vanitas* and *memento mori*.[81] Thus melancholy acquired a positive aspect as a virtuous perspective that recognized the vanity of the material world.[82]

The View of Antiquity and the Renaissance

The most dramatic contradiction of the negative view of melancholy issues from its reputation as the symptom of an exceptional state of insight. This view of melancholy as a trait of genius begins with the revival, during the Florentine Renaissance, of the Aristotelian text on melancholy. The opening line from the thirtieth book of pseudo-Aristotle's *Problemata* famously formulates this perspective:

> Why is it that all those who have become eminent in philosophy or politics or poetry or the arts are so clearly of an atrabilious temperament, and some of them to such an extent as to be affected by diseases caused by black bile, as is said to have happened to Heracles among the heroes?[83]

While pseudo-Aristotle identifies extraordinary ability as a component of the melancholy condition, he explains it in natural terms by describing greatness as the outcome of a balanced black bile that was neither too hot nor too cold. In either one of those extreme states, corrupted black bile can provoke mania or torpor respectively. The man of genius thus represents normality within abnormality. Embodying a state of health within an anomaly, his is a unique constitution that allows his gifts to emerge (*SM*, 91).

The association of melancholy with greatness was relatively short-lived in antiquity. The view of melancholy as caused by excess of black bile was more prominent from this point in time until the Renaissance—described by Jean Starobinski as the golden age of melancholy—reinvented melancholy under the sign of Saturn.[84] The concept of melancholy genius, largely attributed to the work of the Neoplatonic Florentine scholar Marsilio Ficino, came about as a result of the fusion of classical sources with astrological theories, an initiative of Arabic philosophers in the ninth century. The Aristotelian understanding of melancholy as an exceptional state was thus imbued with occult saturnine imagery, which drew on astrology at the same time that it harked back to the Olympian deities, merging the cannibalistic Greek god of time, Chronos, with the more benign Roman god of the harvest, Saturn, to reanimate and expand the genial type. While humoral and temperamental theory still prevailed, the origin of melancholy now shifted to the planet Saturn, which was believed to cause those born under its influence to be melancholy and gifted.[85] Renaissance melancholy became a kind of heroic melancholy, as it gave expression to burgeoning humanist ideas of subjectivity at the dawn of the early modern period. The idea of genius falls within this context of a new subjectivity, and arguably it is in the image of the melancholy Renaissance genius that the dialectical tension germane to melancholy is at its most dramatic. As depicted in Dürer's engraving, to quote Max Pensky, "the dialectics of affliction and empowerment" are intrinsic to this divided figure.[86] Shifting incessantly between the poles of inspiration and listlessness, the genius continually encounters the epistemological limits of her/his finite mind.[87] This figure risks falling prey to the baleful influence of Saturn that could, at other times, also prove a source of creative inspiration.[88] Thus Ficino, like Burton after him, devises detailed programs of self-management concerning diet and other external factors which, if adhered to, can lessen exposure to negative saturnine forces.[89] The other high points of melancholy include Elizabethan England, when melancholy, as an aristocratic fashion imported from Italy, was *en vogue*, and European Romanticism, when the figure of the solitary thinker enjoyed prominence.[90] Radden suggests that today, despite the reductive effects of the clinical term "depression," a kind of neo-Romantic melancholy is currently on the rise, as depression sufferers take recourse to creative melancholy as a way of recasting the condition positively.[91]

In Defense of Melancholy

As we have seen, "good" and "bad" versions of melancholy have been defined differently and according to historical epoch since writing on the condition began. In this final section I examine how the understanding of melancholy fares in psychoanalytical studies of postwar German memory. Freud's seminal essay from 1917, which distinguishes mourning from melancholy, is very influential in this context, thus a brief exposé of his analysis is necessary. However, it is also important to place Freud in the intellectual history of melancholy, and to do this we must return to a central theme of writings on melancholy: the problem that the cause of melancholy is insufficient to justify the sadness it unleashes, and the suspicion that it has no cause at all.[92] Radden observes that Western writing about melancholy has always struggled to explain this matter and furthermore that it uses the question of cause/causelessness to distinguish between "normal" sadness and the "abnormal." Abnormal suffering is frequently described as sadness with insufficient or no cause, while appropriate forms of sadness are understood to be the clear response to an identifiable loss, such as bereavement. Arguing that cultural and medical ideas about feelings are normative, she states that "To be human is to suffer, certainly; but to suffer in the right way, in response to one's life experience, . . ., is to possess the preconditions for character and right action."[93] The way we distinguish between suffering that marks us as human and suffering that is pathological—both of which may appear similar in behavioral terms—has important implications for how feelings are linked to the moral life. Behind the judgment of pathological sadness as an excessive—because causeless—mood-state is a cultural evaluation of emotional appropriateness that rests, as Radden argues, "on rationality and moral norms."[94]

The problem with melancholy, understood as sadness without cause, is that it fails to produce the alibi of a convincing lost object and thus defies rational explanation. In the modern era melancholy has often been described as an objectless, moody affect as, for example, Kraepelin's use in the late nineteenth century of the term "endogenous depression" demonstrates, implying that depression without a clear external trigger, is "hypothetical," at best attributable to "elusive pre-dispositions."[95] Against the Kraepelinian psychiatry of his day, Freud's originality was to introduce a loss analysis of melancholy based on his theory of the unconscious mind. For him the problem is not that melancholy does not have a cause. Rather, it appears to be causeless only because it is exceedingly difficult, given the power of unconscious repression, cognitively to identify the loss that gave rise to the melancholy condition in the first place.[96] Furthermore, Freud's essay does not distinguish clearly between mourning and melancholy. However, some critics who write on post-Holocaust memory extrapolate out of his essay a dichotomy that postulates mourning, as opposed to melancholy, as a model for the ideal emotional afterlife—that is, the collective ethical memory—of the post-Holocaust world.

At first glance Freud's essay appears to suggest an absolute difference between melancholy and mourning. In truth, he regularly draws our attention to the similarities between the two. Initially he argues that in mourning it is possible to discern the external causes that brought about the period of grief (*TM*, 428–29). At times, however, it is also possible to discern the external cause of melancholy (*TM*, 430). Yet frequently in the case of melancholy the cause remains obscure, and so Freud must theorize the paradox of a loss without a lost object. He does so by introducing the concepts of narcissistic identification and unconscious repression (*TM*, 436, 443–44). In refusing to give up—that is, acknowledge—the lost object, the melancholic internalizes this object to preserve it. This process of introjection is an intense form of unconscious identification with the lost object, to the extent that the ego merges with the object.[97] Thus the ambivalence—an unresolved mix of love and hate—felt toward the elusive object is redirected toward the self (*TM*, 437). This explains why Freud suggests that a distinguishing feature of melancholy, as distinct from mourning, is the lowering of self-esteem and a tendency to self-destruction (*TM*, 438–39).

Freud seems to posit a clear difference between the two modes here, yet he also points out that profound mourning has similar traits to melancholy, including that of self-reproach. However, he suggests that self-reproach in mourning cannot be pathological, as in melancholy, because its cause is clear and legible. By contrast, the uncertain status of the loss endured in melancholy must be, deduces Freud, of an unconscious kind (*TM*, 443–44). The concept of the unconscious helps to explain the obscurity that surrounds the original cause of melancholy and its propensity to pathological manifestations. The repressed character of the lost object, incorporated in the ego and converted into an unspeakable secret, corresponds to a gesture of withdrawal into the self, a turning away from the world and from other objects that could, as in a successful work of mourning, potentially become cathected in new attachments (*TM*, 430).[98]

The way melancholy passes off after a certain time without leaving traces of any major change is another feature it shares with mourning (*TM*, 439). Hinting at a further similarity, Freud ponders the obscurity of mourning work: all that can be ascertained is the slowness of the process, as the ego learns gradually to give up the attachment to the lost object, symbolize that loss, and then after a time form new attachments (*TM*, 442). Melancholy and mourning thus share key features, such as ambivalence toward the lost object, some features of narcissistic object desire due to unconscious incorporation, and self-reproach. Where they differ is on the nature of the lost object. In melancholy it is obscured in the unconscious mind while the loss manifests itself in outer symptoms, some of which may be deemed pathological. In the case of mourning, the loss is cognitively identified and as a result can be worked through.

In the negative assessment of melancholy as a post-Holocaust affective disposition that produces a problematic memory culture, narcissistic pathologies that arise in the original constitution of the subject feature prominently. I now focus on three works that produce this analysis of melancholy: the Mitscherlichs' *Unfähigkeit zu trauern* (1967), Eric Santner's *Stranded Objects* (1990), and LaCapra's *Writing History, Writing Trauma* (2001).[99] In the Mitscherlichs' work we read that the West German collective exhibits no traits of melancholy or mourning, hence this collective is autistic. The Mitscherlichs argue that melancholic breakdown—the result of a traumatic narcissistic crisis—is the first step toward mourning work. Breakdown forces acknowledgement of the narcissistic ruin of postwar West German identity. The mourning work that emerges from melancholic breakdown is a coming-to-terms with the loss of the love-object, Hitler, and from this wreckage of the collective self, acknowledging guilt and responsibility for the war and the Holocaust (37).

The position of melancholy in the Mitscherlichs' reading is ambivalent and reflects the vicissitudes of Freud's text. Initially, the Mitscherlichs seem to be saying that there can be no mourning work without the preliminary phase of a more primitive mourning work, that is, the breakdown that heralds the end of melancholic introjection and the onslaught of a narcissistic crisis. Melancholy here is sequentially positioned before mourning as an indispensable step in the grieving process. While this appears to be a positive appraisal, the feature of narcissism ensures a simultaneous negative assessment: the pathologically melancholy narcissist cannot empathize with the other. To drive this home in no uncertain terms, the Mitscherlichs propose Hitler as the original melancholy megalomaniac (39). Thus while they suggest that melancholy is a pathological intensification of mourning, they also introduce a qualitative difference between the two, and "Hitler," as the symbolic instance that underpins the intrinsic narcissistic pathology of melancholy, rhetorically safeguards this distinction. The manic-melancholic moment is also negative—in the form of the economic miracle it is merely the external sign of repression.

Santner, who draws on Freud and the Mitscherlichs, describes adult melancholics as secondary narcissists who love the object only insofar as they can repress its difference. Such narcissism inhibits the work of mourning and "people's capacities to assume post-modern, post-Holocaust lives" (26). For melancholy to come to an end, the adult melancholic must work through the loss of the fantasy of omnipotence typical of the narcissist (6–7). However, this they must do with a degree of affective investment. Santner argues that it is not enough merely to mime the motions of "a-pathetic discourse," an empty linguistic operation that is "unreal, even inhuman, dissociated from the drama of human subjectivity," a kind of "structural" mourning work (28). In the postwar context, this denial of the victim other's difference facilitates the German self-understanding as victim, a central finding of the Mitscherlichs' analysis. "Structural mourning" is more the sign of the persistence of a melancholy, narcissistic disorder than the process of working through loss. Returning to the idea of melancholy as "sadness without cause," the empty "structural mourning" that Santner identifies could be regarded as a melancholy discourse of original *absence*, as opposed to historically situated *loss*, an absence that, by virtue of its uncertain origins, "unravels the project of an authentically expressive poetics."[100] In positing an absence—as opposed to loss—analysis of melancholy, Santner deviates from Freud. But what is most striking about his critique is the demand for discursive presence—signifying authenticity—in the form of appropriate affect (26). The "structural mourning-work" of the melancholy narcissist reveals the highly conventionalized quality of the performance of sadness. This absence of authentic affect is what renders structural mourning work ethically suspect: where we might expect some expression of authenticity, we encounter only the divergence between words and interior affective states. To some degree, Santner's critique calls for a return of affect in post-1945 discourses of mourning and melancholy. Yet postwar German literary discourses seem to prioritize emotional distance over expressions of pathos.[101]

LaCapra's study on post-Holocaust affect and the dangers of identification also equates melancholy with foundational absence, as opposed to loss. As an affective state that presupposes a fundamental existential absence or lack, melancholy is timeless and non-specific, a kind of "negative sublime." Stressing the binary of "good" versus "bad" sadness, LaCapra argues that melancholy, as opposed to mourning, demonstrates "a compulsive preoccupation with aporia, an . . . impossible mourning, and a resistance to working through." Melancholy is no less than a "secularized displacement of the sacred" and produces foundational myths of absence which, after 1945, make everyone a potential victim (23). This leads to identity politics and destabilizes the historical specificity of victim experiences. While LaCapra rhetorically mentions the interrelatedness of melancholy and mourning, his analysis consistently asserts a binary understanding of the two modes (65, 142–44). Melancholy emerges as vicarious, ahistorical, and unempathetic. It manifests the same narcissistic fixation or "vicarious identification" we encounter in the other two analyses (47). Melancholy, as the excessive performance of affect, becomes ethically and politically suspect, because it elides the difference between victims and individuals who are not victims. Mourning is the positive alternative in LaCapra's vision of post-Holocaust Western emotional life (65–66). As a solution to the impasse of melancholy and vicarious acting-out—as exemplified by Binjamin Wilkomirski, whose fake memoir of a childhood in the concentration camps convinced many that he was a victim-survivor—LaCapra proposes that individuals must come to terms with absence as absence: an existential void that marks out the human condition (57–58).[102] In other words, absence—and not just historically specific losses, such as the Holocaust—must be worked through. This might help prevent the vicarious, or to paraphrase Slavoj Žižek, "deceitful" conversion of absence into loss typical for the melancholic and, in LaCapra's context, the wrongful appropriation of victim identity.[103]

This brief overview shows how the lack of a convincing lost object in the case of melancholy renders it problematic in a post-Holocaust context. These studies underscore the pathological abnormality and ethical insufficiency of melancholy by rhetorically employing the notion of a "good" sadness in mourning.[104] However, thinkers such as Kristeva, Agamben, and Benjamin regard the ghostliness of the lost melancholy object, in line with the humanist tradition of the Renaissance, as the site of imagination and cultural production.[105] In Agamben's analysis, for instance, melancholy is a creative way of managing the terrifying prospect of potential loss. The melancholy subject mobilizes the sense of an existential void—foundational absence—to act as the lost object. In this way, the subject never has to fear the shock of loss. In the disguised form of a foundational absence, a kind of pseudo-loss has become the universal norm. LaCapra's analysis critiques the melancholy position for doing the opposite. In a bid to deny the existential emptiness that always threatens to engulf the self, the melancholy individual of his scenario treats foundational absence as a concrete loss that is usually someone else's experience. While the two analyses stand at different ends of a spectrum that moves, in respect of the lost object, from ghostly abstraction to material concretion, both identify an elaborate signification practice in melancholy discourse. Agamben argues in a positive sense for melancholy as a mode of cultural production, while LaCapra and the others view as ethically dubious its ostentatious choreography around the phantasm of the lost object.

The irony of some of these theoretical studies is that even while they do not engage with a longer tradition of writing on melancholy, their assessment of melancholy itself stands in a long tradition of negative writing on melancholy. The association of melancholy in the medieval period with the sin of sloth or *acedia* is one example of this dubious past. Hans-Jürgen Schings demonstrates how melancholy came to represent the negative irrational other of the orderly world of reason in the rational discourses of the Enlightenment.[106] Benjamin's attack on the affected melancholy posing of those left-leaning intellectuals who are content to lament the status quo but who remain complacent and inactive connects to the idea of melancholy as wallowing.[107] Pitching memory against history, historian Charles S. Maier explicitly links post-1989 Western identity politics to a surfeit of emotive memory that he calls "sweet melancholy," less a rational faculty for recovering the past than "an exercise pleasurable in its own right."[108] To invoke Susan Sontag's concept of illness as metaphor, in these post-Holocaust theoretical discussions of memory, melancholy—ever the flexible foil in discourses that require a negative other—is a metaphor for the wrong kind of behaviour, attitude, emotion, and memory.[109] Viewed in this way, melancholy is stripped of its manifold positive attributes.

By contrast, German writers of the postwar era embrace melancholy as a mannered discourse through which to address the Holocaust and its legacy. This body of writing delivers a more comprehensive picture of melancholy traditions than the theoretical discourse allows. In the literary texts, melancholy alternates between suffering, creativity, resistance, capitulation, despondency, and so on. The dialectical tension between despair and inspiration germane to genial melancholy exemplifies the ongoing struggle to feel and understand what eludes the mind. In the figure of the genius we encounter not just exceptional creativity but also the effort to grasp more of the world: in Pensky's phrase, melancholy as "a meta-subjective form of disclosure."[110] This type lends itself well to the task of performative remembrance, which, in its ideal form, continually reveals the struggle to understand and take responsibility for the past. Remembrance in this sense is an open-ended process that replaces closure with an ethical openness that connects past, present, and future. In this way, the melancholy performance of remembrance in literary texts can be aligned with a central feature of "memory contests": the critical investigation of cultural norms and values.[111]

In the following chapters I try to reflect the breadth and depth of each writer's engagement with melancholy traditions. In chapter 1 I examine the apologetic function of melancholy from the perspective of Grass, a member of the perpetrator collective. To this end I discuss *Aus dem Tagebuch einer Schnecke* and, to a lesser extent, the later confessional text where Grass belatedly mentions his Waffen-SS membership, *Beim Häuten der Zwiebel* (Peeling the Onion, 2006).[112] In chapter 2 I identify melancholy, as seen from the perspective of Hildesheimer, a member of the victim collective, as a discourse of self-accusation and survivor guilt in the novels *Tynset* and *Masante*. In chapter 3 I consider melancholy in Weiss's seminal work *Die Ästhetik des Widerstands* (The Aesthetics of Resistance, 1983) as a gendered image of post-Holocaust ethical memory and also as part of a thoughtful commentary on the ambivalent place of emotion in ethical memory. In chapter 4 I demonstrate, with reference to several of Sebald's works, how melancholy in the era of postmemory is a language shared between members of victim and perpetrator collectives alike. I also illustrate how Sebald uses different melancholy discourses to talk about globalization, environmental concerns, and genocide. Finally, in the epilogue I examine how Iris Hanika in *Das Eigentliche* pitches different melancholy traditions against each other in order to announce the decline of *Vergangenheitsbewältigung* in the Berlin Republic of the twenty-first century.

While some of the works also present melancholy as an inner mood-state and a psychopathological affliction, my analysis is framed by the idea of melancholy as performative, precisely the dimension that the metapsychological accounts suppress. Understood in this way, "melancholy appears to reflect the subject's acute knowledge of the inherently transactional nature of cultural production; it reflects the subject's full knowledge of the inescapably social and conventional character of speech."[113] In other words, melancholy, as the conventionalized expression of subjectivity, offers the possibility of a literary discourse that aesthetically thematizes the problems of insufficient representation after Auschwitz raised by Adorno. The "damaged signifier" of the melancholy performative communicates the insight that the melancholy condition is "no longer an expressive origin but a recognizably 'literary' product."[114] Postwar German melancholy literature performs this self-conscious aesthetic reflection that ponders the gap in representation and the limits of knowledge by reanimating the cultural traditions of a pre-Holocaust world.

Notes

[1] Walter Jens, *Herr Meister: Dialog über einen Roman* (Munich: Piper, 1963). Hereafter cited in text as *HM*.

[2] Jens points out that their discussions began in 1951; *Herr Meister* focuses on the exchange of the early 1960s, however (Jens, *Herr Meister*, 9).

[3] Wolfgang Hildesheimer, *Tynset* (Frankfurt am Main: Suhrkamp, 1965); *Masante* (Frankfurt am Main: Suhrkamp, 1973). For other examples of Hamlet in Hildesheimer's work see "Hamlet," in *Exerzitien mit Papst Johannes* (Frankfurt am Main: Suhrkamp, 1979), 9–25, and *Vergebliche Aufzeichnungen* (Frankfurt am Main: Suhrkamp, 1962). On the Hamlet motif in Hildesheimer's work see Franz Loquai, *Hamlet und Deutschland: Zur literarischen Shakespeare-Rezeption im 20. Jahrhundert* (Stuttgart: Metzler, 1993), 192–213, esp. 197; Volker Jehle, *Wolfgang Hildesheimer: Werkgeschichte* (Frankfurt am Main: Suhrkamp, 1990), 84–110; and also Mary Cosgrove, "From Nobility to Sloth: Melancholy Self-Fashioning and the Hamlet Motif in Wolfgang Hildesheimer's *Tynset* and *Masante*," in *Wolfgang Hildesheimer und England: Zur Topologie eines literarischen Transfers*, ed. Rüdiger Görner and Isabel Wagner (Bern: Peter Lang, 2012), 79–101.

[4] In his study of melancholy in postwar West German literature, Günter Blamberger mentions *Herr Meister* in an endnote. *Versuch über den deutschen Gegenwartsroman: Krisenbewußtsein und Neubegründung im Zeichen der Melancholie* (Stuttgart: J. B. Metzler, 1985), 145–46.

⁵ On the term's semantic history see Thorsten Eitz and Georg Stötzel, *Wörterbuch der Vergangenheitsbewältigung: Die NS-Vergangenheit im öffentlichen Sprachgebrauch* (Hildesheim: Georg Olms, 2007), 601–17. For a more detailed overview see Torben Fischer and Matthias N. Lorenz, eds., *Lexikon der "Vergangenheitsbewältigung" in Deutschland: Debatten- und Diskursgeschichte des Nationalsozialismus nach 1945* (Bielefeld: transcript, 2007).

⁶ See Gert Hofmann, Rachel MagShamhráin, Marko Pajević, and Michael Shields, eds., *German and European Poetics after the Holocaust: Crisis and Creativity* (Rochester, NY: Camden House, 2011), 8.

⁷ Dunker, *Die anwesende Abwesenheit: Literatur im Schatten von Auschwitz* (Munich: Fink, 2003), 23.

⁸ LaCapra, *Writing History: Writing Trauma* (Baltimore, MD: Johns Hopkins University Press, 2001), 23.

⁹ Dunker, *Die anwesende Abwesenheit*, 15, 18.

¹⁰ Adorno, "Kulturkritik und Gesellschaft (1951)," in *Gesammelte Schriften*, ed. Rolf Tiedemann, 20 vols. (Frankfurt am Main: Suhrkamp, 1977), 30.

¹¹ Adorno's position on his "dictum" changed, which has helped fuel the debate about its original meaning. For a brief overview see Dunker, *Die anwesende Abwesenheit*, 9–12. See also Stefan Krankenhagen, *Auschwitz darstellen: Ästhetische Positionen zwischen Adorno, Spielberg und Walser* (Cologne: Böhlau, 2001), 83–120, and Petra Kiedaisch, ed., *Lyrik nach Auschwitz: Adorno und die Dichter* (Stuttgart: Reclam, 1995).

¹² Krankenhagen, *Auschwitz darstellen*, 56.

¹³ Diner, ed., *Zivilisationsbruch: Denken nach Auschwitz* (Frankfurt am Main: Fischer, 1996).

¹⁴ Alexander Mitscherlich and Margarete Mitscherlich, *Die Unfähigkeit zu trauern: Grundlagen kollektiven Verhaltens* (Munich: Piper, 2007), 38.

¹⁵ This shift is evidenced by Adolf Eichmann's trial in Jerusalem (February–December 1961), the Auschwitz trials in Frankfurt am Main (December 1963–August 1965), and the translation into German of influential Holocaust testimonies by Primo Levi and others that publicly underscored Jewish victimization in the Holocaust. For an overview of the 1960s see Fischer and Lorenz, *Lexikon der "Vergangenheitsbewältigung,"* 125–85.

¹⁶ Karl Jaspers, *Die Schuldfrage* (Zurich: Artemis, 1946).

¹⁷ Karl Jaspers, *Philosophische Logik I: Von der Wahrheit* (Munich: Piper, 1947), 936–43, esp. 937.

¹⁸ See Robert G. Moeller, *War Stories: The Search for a Usable Past in the Federal Republic of Germany* (Berkeley: University of California Press, 2001).

¹⁹ See Raymond Klibansky, Erwin Panofsky, and Fritz Saxl, *Saturn und Melancholie: Studien zur Geschichte der Naturphilosophie und Medizin, der Religion und der Kunst*, trans. Christa Buschendorf (Frankfurt am Main: Suhrkamp, 1992). Hereafter cited in text as *SM*. Also Rudolf and Margot Wittkower, *Born under Saturn: The Character and Conduct of Artists; A Documented History from Antiquity to the French Revolution* (London: Weidenfeld & Nicolson, 1963).

20 On laziness as an attribute of the artist-genius see Wittkower and Wittkower, *Born under Saturn*, 59. On the dandy of the nineteenth century as a melancholy figure see Wolfgang Lepenies, *Melancholie und Gesellschaft: Mit einer neuen Einleitung; Das Ende der Utopie und die Wiederkehr der Melancholie* (Frankfurt am Main: Suhrkamp, 1998).

21 Sigmund Freud, "Trauer und Melancholie," in *Gesammelte Werke: Chronologisch geordnet*, 18 vols., ed. Anna Freud, E. Bibring, W. Offer, E. Kris, and O. Isakower with the collaboration of Marie Bonaparte (Frankfurt am Main: Fischer, 1963), 10:428–46. For an example of a recent theoretical account of cultural memory after the Holocaust that shows the influence of Freud's concept of melancholy, see LaCapra, *Writing History, Writing Trauma*.

22 Austin, *How to Do Things with Words*, ed. J. O. Urmson, Marina Sbisa (Oxford: Clarendon, 1975 [1962]). For an overview of the concept and the debates surrounding it see James Loxley, *Performativity* (London: Routledge, 2007).

23 Loxley, *Performativity*, 2.

24 See Jacques Derrida, *Limited Inc*, trans. S. Weber (Evanston, ILL: Chicago University Press, 1988). Also Derrida, *Without Alibi*, trans. P. Kamuf (Stanford, CA: Stanford University Press, 2002).

25 Pfau, *Romantic Moods: Paranoia, Trauma and Melancholy, 1790–1840* (Baltimore, MD: Johns Hopkins University Press, 2005), 326.

26 Some of the scholarship on W. G. Sebald reflects this tendency. See, for example, Thomas Wirtz, "Schwarze Zuckerwatte: Anmerkungen zu W. G. Sebald," *Merkur* 6 (2001): 530–34.

27 Loxley, *Performativity*, 78.

28 See Mary Cosgrove, "Erinnerungsethik und Dürerdiskurs im Werk von W. G. Sebald, Peter Weiss, Günter Grass und Jean Améry," in *W. G. Sebald: Intertextualität und Topographie*, ed. Irene Heidelberger-Leonard and Mireille Tabah (Berlin: LIT, 2008), 153–68. The term "Renaissance episteme" comes from Henning Mehnert's study, *Melancholie und Inspiration: Begriffs- und wissenschaftsgeschichtliche Untersuchungen zur poetischen "Psychologie" Baudelaires, Flauberts, und Mallarmés* (Heidelberg: Winter, 1978), 82–83.

29 Thomas Mann, *Doktor Faustus: Das Leben des deutschen Tonsetzers Adrian Leverkühn, erzählt von einem Freunde* (Frankfurt am Main: Fischer, 2007).

30 Martin Ruehl, "A Master from Germany: Thomas Mann, Albrecht Dürer, and the Making of a National Icon," *Oxford German Studies* 38, no. 1 (2009): 101.

31 Günter Grass, *Aus dem Tagebuch einer Schnecke* (Munich: Deutscher Taschenbuch Verlag, 1998), 325. Stephen Brockmann gives an overview of Dürer's changing national legacy in the nineteenth and twentieth centuries, arguing that in postwar West German cultural memory *Melencolia I*, rather than Dürer's engraving *Ritter, Tod und Teufel* (1513) which Hitler favored, became a more prominent and positive image. Brockmann, *Nuremberg: The Imaginary Capital* (Rochester, NY: Camden House, 2006), 242–44. For a detailed discussion of the reception of *Ritter, Tod und Teufel* before and during National Socialism see Ruehl, "A Master from Germany," 102. In a different context, Wolfgang Emmerich imagines the betrayed GDR artist, both

before and after the *Wende*, in Dürer's melancholy pose, suggesting that the artist is a noble, if disappointed, utopian thinker cast adrift in a chaotic world. Emmerich, *Kleine Literaturgeschichte der DDR: Erweiterte Neuausgabe* (Leipzig: Gustav Kiepenhauer, 1997), 460.

[32] See, for example, the wide range of poems that have been inspired by Dürer's engraving. Ludwig Völker, ed., *"Komm, heilige Melancholie": Eine Anthologie deutscher Melancholie-Gedichte* (Stuttgart: Reclam, 1983), 445–81.

[33] Hartmut Böhme traces the engraving's reception history in Europe, arguing that by the twentieth century it could no longer be naively received by literary authors, as it had been during the nineteenth century. Böhme, "Zur literarischen Rezeption von Albrecht Dürers Kupferstich *Melencolia I*," in *Polyperspektivik in der literarischen Moderne: Studien zur Theorie, Geschichte und Wirkung der Literatur*, ed. Jörg Schönert and Harro Segeberg (Frankfurt am Main: Peter Lang, 1988), 83–123.

[34] Derrida, *Limited Inc*, 119.

[35] For example, Allan V. Horwitz and Jerome C. Wakefield argue that contemporary psychiatry has pathologized normal sadness, rendering it extremely difficult to make "a conceptually coherent diagnostic distinction between depressive disorders and normal intense sadness responses." Horwitz and Wakefield, *The Loss of Sadness: How Psychiatry Transformed Normal Sorrow into Depressive Disorder* (Oxford: Oxford University Press, 2007), 19. This insight is confirmed in *DSM-5*, the most recent edition of the American Psychiatric Association's influential *Diagnostic and Statistical Manual of Mental Disorders* (Washington, DC: American Psychiatric Publishing, 2013), in which the "bereavement exclusion" has been controversially removed from the definition of major depressive disorder. This means that where the previous edition, *DSM-IV—4th ed., text revision* (Washington, DC: American Psychiatric Association, 2000), advised clinicians to exclude bereaved persons from the diagnosis of major depressive disorder for the first two months after bereavement, now bereaved persons can also be diagnosed as suffering from a major depressive disorder within that time frame. See http://www.dsm5.org/Documents/Bereavement%20Exclusion%20Fact%20 Sheet.pdf, accessed Aug. 2, 2013.

[36] On the idea of "sadness without cause," see Stanley W. Jackson, *Melancholia and Depression: From Hippocratic Times to Modern Times* (New Haven, CN: Yale University Press, 1986), 315–17.

[37] Julia Kristeva, *Black Sun: Depression and Melancholia*, trans. Leon S. Roudiez (New York: Columbia University Press, 1989), 42.

[38] Pfau, *Romantic Moods*, 323.

[39] Hartmut Böhme, *Albrecht Dürer: Melencolia I; Im Labyrinth der Deutung* (Frankfurt am Main: Fischer, 1989).

[40] Pfau, *Romantic Moods*, 337.

[41] Ibid., 322.

[42] Burton, *The Anatomy of Melancholy*, ed. Thomas C. Faulkner, Nicolas K. Kiessling, and Rhonda L. Blair, 3 vols. (Oxford: Clarendon, 1997).

[43] Loxley, *Performativity*, 90.

⁴⁴ HAMLET: Tis not alone my inky cloak, good mother,
Nor customary suits of solemn black,
Nor windy suspiration of forced breath,
No, nor the fruitful river in the eye,
Nor the dejected 'haviour of the visage,
Together with all forms, moods, shows of grief,
That can denote me truly: these indeed seem,
For they are actions that a man might play,
But I have that within which passeth show;
These but the trappings and the suits of woe. (Hamlet, act 1, scene 2).

⁴⁵ *DSM-IV* regards melancholy only as a specifier that describes features of a current or recent depressive episode, for example, Major Depressive Episode, with Melancholic Features, 419–20. On the shift from "melancholy" to "depression" in the nineteenth and twentieth centuries, see Clark Lawlor, *From Melancholia to Depression: A History of Depression* (Oxford: Oxford University Press, 2012), chapters 4 and 5.

⁴⁶ Wittkower and Wittkower, *Born under Saturn: The Character and Conduct of Artists*, 42–66, 93, 106. On melancholy in Aristotle, Florentine Neo-Platonism, and Romanticism see *SM*, respectively 55–92, 351–94, 347.

⁴⁷ See also Mary Cosgrove, "Introduction: Sadness and Melancholy in German-Language Literature from the Seventeenth Century to the Present; An Overview," in *Edinburgh German Yearbook 6: Sadness and Melancholy in German-Language Literature and Culture*, ed. Mary Cosgrove and Anna Richards (Rochester, NY: Camden House, 2012), 1–17.

⁴⁸ Jackson, *Melancholia and Depression*, 5.

⁴⁹ See Fischer and Lorenz, *Lexikon der "Vergangenheitsbewältigung,"* 125–85.

⁵⁰ Thomas Bernhard and Ingeborg Bachmann, for example, are recognized as melancholy writers but do not feature here. See Markus Scheffler, *Kunsthaß im Grunde: Über Melancholie bei Arthur Schopenhauer und deren Verwendung in Thomas Bernhards Prosa* (Heidelberg: Winter, 2008), and Katja Krylova, "Melancholy, Topography and the Search for Origin in Ingeborg Bachmann's "'Drei Wege zum See,'" *German Life and Letters* 62, no. 2 (2009): 157–73. Other novels, such as Heinrich Böll's *Ansichten eines Clowns* (Cologne: Kiepenhauer & Witsch, 1963), draw on melancholy traditions to address problems in the Bonn Republic and not the memory of the Holocaust. See Blamberger, *Versuch über den deutschen Gegenwartsroman*, 101–34. Other writers of the 1950s and 1960s who are often associated with melancholy, but whose main focus is not Holocaust memory, include Wolfgang Koeppen, Max Frisch, and Günter Eich. On Koeppen and melancholy see Walter Jens's speech on the occasion of Koeppen's winning the Georg-Büchner Prize for literature in 1962: Jens, "Melancholie und Moral," in Jens, *Von deutscher Rede* (Munich: Piper, 1983), 200–213. On melancholy in Frisch's work see Bettina Jaques-Bosch, *Kritik und Melancholie im Werk Max Frischs: Zur Entwicklung einer für die Schweizer Literatur typischen Dichotomie* (Bern: Peter Lang, 1984). On Günter Eich and melancholy see Susanne Schulte, *Standpunkt Ohnmacht: Studien zur Melancholie bei Günter Eich* (Hamburg: LIT, 1993).

⁵¹ Schiesari, *The Gendering of Melancholia: Feminism, Psychoanalysis, and the Symbolics of Loss in Renaissance Literature* (Ithaca, NY: Cornell University Press, 1992).

⁵² Aristotle, *Aristotle: Problems II, Books XXII–XXXVIII*, trans. W. S. Hett (Cambridge, MA: Harvard University Press, 1957), 30.155. The text on melancholy is widely attributed to a follower of Aristotle, Theophrastus or "pseudo-Aristotle." See Hellmut Flashar, *Melancholie und Melancholiker in den medizinischen Theorien der Antike* (Berlin: de Gruyter, 1966), 61.

⁵³ Freud, "Trauer und Melancholie," 10: 432.

⁵⁴ Schiesari, *The Gendering of Melancholia*, 61.

⁵⁵ Ibid., 77–83.

⁵⁶ Clark Lawlor, "Fashionable Melancholy," in *Melancholy Experience in Literature of the Long Eighteenth Century: Before Depression, 1660–1800*, ed. Allan Ingram et al. (Basingstoke, UK: Palgrave Macmillan, 2011), 44–46.

⁵⁷ One could revisit, for example, the *Todesarten* project from this angle. Ingeborg Bachmann, *Das Buch Franza / Requiem für Fanny Goldmann: Texte des Todesarten-Projekts*, ed. Dirk Göttsche and Monika Albrecht (Munich: Piper, 2004). Other women writers who would also be interesting in this context include Anna Seghers, Ilse Aichinger, and Christa Wolf. Contemporary women writers who engage with melancholy discourses, albeit mainly to commemorate the demise of the GDR, include Monika Maron, Jenny Erpenbeck, and Julia Schoch.

⁵⁸ Ecker, "Trauer zeigen: Inszenierung und die Sorge um den Anderen," in *Trauer tragen—Trauer zeigen: Inszenierungen der Geschlechter* (Munich: Fink, 1999), 11–12.

⁵⁹ Radden, *Moody Minds Distempered: Essays on Melancholy and Depression* (Oxford: Oxford University Press, 2009), 47.

⁶⁰ Panofsky and Saxl, *Dürers Melencolia I: Eine quellen- und typengeschichtliche Untersuchung*. Studien der Bibliothek Warburg 2 (Leipzig: B. G. Teubner, 1923). See Grass, *Aus dem Tagebuch einer Schnecke*, 305, and Günter Grass Archiv, Stiftung Archiv der Akademie der Künste, Berlin, no. 178. See also Peter Weiss Archiv, Stiftung Archiv der Akademie der Künste, Berlin, no. 3014, and Weiss, *Notizbücher, 1971–1980*, 2 vols. (Frankfurt am Main: Suhrkamp,1981), 2:863–66; Sebald, *Die Ringe des Saturn: Eine englische Wallfahrt* (Frankfurt am Main: Fischer, 1997), 16; and Sebald's copy of Benjamin's *Ursprung des deutschen Trauerspiels*, ed. Rolf Tiedemann (Frankfurt am Main: Suhrkamp, 1963), in W. G.-Sebald-Bibliothek, Deutsches Literaturarchiv Marbach, 149–73.

⁶¹ Of particular note is the study by Klibansky, Panofsky, and Saxl, *SM*. For approaches that challenge their interpretation of *Melencolia I* see Martin Büchsel, *Albrecht Dürers Stich Melencolia I: Zeichen und Emotion; Logik einer kunsthistorischen Debatte* (Munich: Fink, 2010), and Peter-Klaus Schuster, "Das Bild der Bilder: Zur Wirkungsgeschichte von Dürers Melancholiekupferstich," *Idea: Jahrbuch der Hamburger Kunsthalle* 1 (1982): 72–134. Other works on melancholy from the 1960s include the art historical works by Günter Bandmann, *Melancholie und Musik: Ikonographische Studien* (Cologne: Westdeutscher Verlag, 1960), and the Wittkowers' *Born under Saturn*; Lepenies's sociological

study of melancholy and utopia, *Melancholie und Gesellschaft*; Jean Starobinski's cultural-historical treatments of melancholy in medical and philosophical contexts throughout the ages, *Histoire du traitement de la mélancolie des origines à 1900* (Basel: Actapsychosomatica, 1960); and Flashar, *Melancholie und Melancholiker*; from the perspective of clinical psychiatry, the phenomenological-anthropological studies by Hubertus Tellenbach, *Melancholie: Problemgeschichte, Endogenität, Typologie, Pathogenese, Klinik* (Berlin, Göttingen, Heidelberg: Springer 1961), and Ludwig Binswanger, *Melancholie und Manie: Phänomenologische Studien* (Pfullingen, Germany: Günther Neske, 1960).

[62] For example: Gert Mattenklott, *Melancholie in der Dramatik des Sturm und Drangs* (Stuttgart: J. B. Metzlersche, 1968); Klara Obermüller, *Studien zur Melancholie in der deutschen Lyrik des Barock* (Bonn: Bouvier, 1974); Hans-Jürgen Schings, *Melancholie und Aufklärung: Melancholie und ihre Kritiker in Erfahrungsseelenkunde des 18. Jahrhunderts* (Stuttgart: Metzler, 1977); Helen Watanabe-O'Kelly, *Melancholie und die melancholische Landschaft* (Bern: Francke, 1978); Ludwig Völker, *Muse Melancholie—Therapeutikum Poesie: Studien zum Melancholie-Problem in der deutschen Lyrik von Hölty bis Benn* (Munich: Fink, 1978); Mehnert, *Melancholie und Inspiration*; Franz Loquai, *Künstler und Melancholie in der Romantik* (Frankfurt am Main: Peter Lang, 1984); Günter Blamberger, *Versuch über den deutschen Gegenwartsroman*; Anette Schwarz, *Melancholie: Figuren und Orte einer Stimmung* (Vienna: Passagen, 1996); Martina Wagner-Egelhaaf, *Die Melancholie der Literatur: Diskursgeschichte und Textfiguration* (Stuttgart: Metzler, 1997); Edgar J. Foster, *Unmännliche Männlichkeit: Melancholie—Geschlecht—Verausgabung* (Vienna: Böhlau, 1998); Burkhard Meyer-Sickendiek, *Tiefe: Über die Faszination des Grübelns* (Munich: Fink, 2010); and Anna O'Driscoll, *Constructions of Melancholy in Contemporary German and Austrian Literature* (Oxford: Peter Lang, 2013). Edited volumes, readers, and anthologies include Ludwig Völker, ed., *"Komm, heilige Melancholie"*; Joachim S. Hohmann, ed., *Melancholie: Ein deutsches Gefühl* (Trier: editions trèves, 1989); Dietrich von Engelhardt, Horst-Jürgen Gerigk, Guido Pressler, and Wolfram Schmitt, eds., *Melancholie in Literatur und Kunst* (Hürtgenwald, Germany: Guido Pressler, 1990); Peter Sillem, ed., *Melancholie oder vom Glück, unglücklich zu sein: Ein Lesebuch* (Munich: DTV, 1997); Heidbrink, *Melancholie und Moderne: Zur Kritik der historischen Verzweiflung* (Munich: Fink, 1994); Lutz Walter, ed., *Melancholie* (Leipzig: Reclam, 1999); Dieter Borchmeyer, ed., *Melancholie und Heiterkeit* (Heidelberg: Winter, 2007). More recently Benjamin's work on baroque tragic drama has enjoyed a revival in the context of memory studies in the Humanities. Benjamin, *Ursprung des deutschen Trauerspiels*. See Max Pensky, *Melancholy Dialectics: Walter Benjamin and the Play of Mourning* (Amherst: University of Massachusetts Press, 1993), and Wolfgang Bock, *Walter Benjamin—Die Rettung der Nacht: Sterne, Melancholie und Messianismus* (Bielefeld: Aisthesis, 2000).

[63] Cultural Studies in the UK academic sector began with the inauguration of the Marxist Centre for Contemporary Cultural Studies (CCCS) at the University of Birmingham in 1964. In the German context, "Kulturwissenschaft," which denotes a novel approach to the study of literature and culture that can be traced back to the early twentieth century and the influence of modern thinkers such

as Walter Benjamin and the Berlin sociologist Georg Simmel, did not become established as a subject on the curriculum of German universities until the 1980s. However, these thinkers were already influencing literary scholarship in the 1960s, as can be seen in the case of Mattenklott's monograph, *Melancholie in der Dramatik des Sturm und Drangs*. On Cultural Studies see, for example, Graham Turner, *British Cultural Studies: An Introduction* (London: Routledge, 2002), and on "Kulturwissenschaften" see Hartmut Böhme, Peter Matussek, and Lothar Müller, *Orientierung Kulturwissenschaften: Was sie kann, was sie will* (Hamburg: Rowohlt, 2000).

[64] See Ernst Gombrich, *Aby Warburg: An Intellectual Biography with a Memoir on the History of the Library by F. Saxl* (Oxford: Phaidon, 1986). Klibansky, Panofsky, and Saxl, *Saturn and Melancholy: Studies in the History of Natural Philosophy, Religion, and Art* (London: Nelson, 1964). This work's production history is quite complex. It is the expanded version of the much earlier study that was cowritten by Panofsky and Saxl: *Dürers Melencolia I*, which was influenced by Karl Giehlow's work on the engraving: "Dürers Stich 'Melencolia I' und der maximilianische Humanistenkreis," *Mitteilungen der Gesellschaft für vervielfältigende Kunst* 26, no. 2 (1903): 29–41; 27, no. 3 (1904): 6–18; 27, no. 4 (1904): 57–78. The foreword of the English version from 1964 explains how the authors had to leave Germany in the 1930s as a result of National Socialism, but continued to work on an expanded version of the project in England. They sent the completed manuscript to the publisher in 1939, but later discovered that it had been destroyed during the Second World War. The authors rewrote the study in English, and it was published in 1964. This version was then translated into German in 1992. For the simple reason that it is still in print, I refer to the later German translation: *Saturn und Melancholie*, trans. Christa Buschendorf.

[65] Helen Watanabe-O'Kelly's analysis of seventeenth-century melancholy landscape in literature testifies to the visual heritage of melancholy, while Martina Wagner-Egelhaaf begins her treatment of melancholy in German literature of the eighteenth and nineteenth centuries with an interdisciplinary discourse analysis of the phenomenon since antiquity. Franz Loquai's monograph on melancholy and Romanticism places literature in the context of medical developments of the period; Schings's intellectual history of melancholy during the Enlightenment insists, along the lines suggested in *Saturn und Melancholie*, that any significant study of melancholy must include its evolution in the fields of medicine and psychology of the epoch under consideration. Watanabe O'Kelly, *Melancholie und die melancholische Landschaft*, ch. 5; Wagner-Egelhaaf, *Die Melancholie der Literatur*, 31–214; Loquai, *Künstler und Melancholie in der Romantik*, 19–57; Schings, *Melancholie und Aufklärung*, 2.

[66] Jennifer Radden's work goes some way down this path. See her *Moody Minds Distempered* (Oxford: Oxford University Press, 2009). For a similar approach see also Lawlor, *From Melancholia to Depression*; and Ingram et al., *Melancholy Experience in Literature of the Long Eighteenth Century*.

[67] Meyer-Sickendieck, *Tiefe*.

[68] Martina Wagner-Egelhaaf, *Die Melancholie der Literatur*, 7–8.

[69] Blamberger, *Versuch über den deutschen Gegenwartsroman*.

⁷⁰ Pensky, *Melancholy Dialectics*, 21.

⁷¹ Aristotle, *Aristotle: Problems II*, 30.155.

⁷² Jackson, *Melancholia and Depression*, 390. On melancholy in the Hippocratic writings see Flashar, *Melancholie und Melancholiker*, 21–59, and *SM*, 39–54.

⁷³ Jackson, *Melancholia and Depression*, 41–45.

⁷⁴ Ibid., 387.

⁷⁵ Starobinski, *Histoire du traitement de la mélancolie des origines à 1900*, 44.

⁷⁶ Gerrit Glas, "A Conceptual History of Anxiety and Depression," in *Handbook of Depression and Anxiety: Second Edition, Revised and Expanded*, ed. Siegfried Kasper, Johan A. den Boer, and J. M. Ad Sitsen (New York: Marcel Dekker, 2003), 18. See also Jackson, *Melancholia and Depression*, 188–95.

⁷⁷ *DSM-IV* considers age, gender, cultural, and social features in its diagnostic descriptions of the different kinds of depression but also observes how depression runs in families. American Psychiatric Association, *DSM-IV*, 345–428, esp. 373, 379. In chapter 6 of his study, Lawlor provides an incisive overview of what he terms the "'New' Depression," a concept of pathological sadness that arose in the 1970s and 1980s and that "has been largely defined by a biological model." Lawlor, *From Melancholia to Depression*, 157. For a similar critique see also Darian Leader, *Strictly Bipolar* (London: Penguin, 2013).

⁷⁸ Jennifer Radden, "From Melancholic States to Clinical Depression," in *The Nature of Melancholy: From Aristotle to Kristeva*, ed. Radden (Oxford: Oxford University Press, 2000), 49. See also Darian Leader, *The New Black: Mourning, Melancholia and Depression* (London: Penguin, 2008), 11–15.

⁷⁹ On sloth and *acedia* see Siegried Wenzel, *The Sin of Sloth: Acedia in Medieval Thought and Literature* (Chapel Hill: University of North Carolina Press, 1960).

⁸⁰ Winfried Schleiner, *Melancholy, Genius and Utopia in the Renaissance* (Wiesbaden: Harrasowitz, 1991), 14.

⁸¹ See Ferdinand van Ingen, *Vanitas und Memento Mori in der deutschen Barocklyrik* (Groningen, Netherlands: J. B. Wolters, 1966).

⁸² Watanabe-O'Kelly, *Melancholie und die melancholische Landschaft*, 56.

⁸³ Aristotle, *Aristotle: Problems II*, 30.155.

⁸⁴ Starobinski, *Histoire du traitement de la mélancolie des origines à 1900*, 38.

⁸⁵ On the genesis of saturnine melancholy see *SM*, 203–315.

⁸⁶ Pensky, *Melancholy Dialectics*, 31.

⁸⁷ Agamben, *Stanzas: Word and Phantasm in Western Culture*, trans. Ronald L. Martinez (Minneapolis: University of Minnesota Press, 1993), 26. On the explicitly male identity of this Renaissance figure see Schiesari, *The Gendering of Melancholia*, 7.

⁸⁸ On Saturn's dangerous polarity in this regard see *SM*, 376.

⁸⁹ *Marsilio Ficino: Three Books on Life*, trans. Carol Kaske and John Clark (Binghamton, NY: Center of Medieval and Renaissance Studies, 1989), Book 1, chs. 3–5. On Ficino's influence see *SM*, 367–94. Burton, *The Anatomy of Melancholy*, 1:220–33.

⁹⁰ See Lawrence Babb, *The Elizabethan Malady: A Study of Melancholia in English Literature from 1580 to 1642* (East Lansing: Michigan State College Press, 1951). See also Pfau's discussion of Byron in his *Romantic Moods*, 332–35.

⁹¹ Radden, *Moody Minds Distempered*, 190. A good example of this recent rehabilitation of melancholy against its associations with depression is Eric G. Wilson, *Against Happiness: In Praise of Melancholy* (New York: Farrar, Straus, & Giroux, 2008).

⁹² On this question of cause see Jackson, *Melancholia and Depression*, 315–17.

⁹³ Radden, *Moody Minds Distempered*, 13.

⁹⁴ Ibid., 14.

⁹⁵ Jackson, *Melancholia and Depression*, 211–12.

⁹⁶ Freud, "Trauer und Melancholie," 431. Hereafter cited in text as *TM*.

⁹⁷ Nicolas Abraham and Maria Torok would later term it "incorporation." Torok, "The Illness of Mourning and the Fantasy of the Exquisite Corpse," in *The Shell and the Kernel: Renewals of Psychoanalysis*, by Abraham and Torok, ed. and trans. Nicolas T. Rand (Chicago: University of Chicago Press, 1994), 110–12.

⁹⁸ "Inexpressible mourning erects a secret tomb inside the subject." Abraham and Torok, "Mourning *or* Melancholia: Introjection *versus* Incorporation," in Abraham and Torok, *The Shell and the Kernel*, 130.

⁹⁹ Mitscherlich and Mitscherlich, *Die Unfähigkeit zu trauern*. Santner, *Mourning, Memory, and Film in Postwar Germany* (Ithaca, NY: Cornell University Press, 1990); LaCapra, *Writing History, Writing Trauma*.

¹⁰⁰ Pfau, *Romantic Moods*, 326.

¹⁰¹ See Hans Ulrich Gumbrecht, *Stimmungen lesen: Über eine verdeckte Wirklichkeit der Literatur* (Munich: Hanser, 2011), 25.

¹⁰² On the Wilkomirski affair, where it was discovered that Swiss writer Bruno Grosjean had adopted the false Jewish identity of Binjamin Wilkomirski, see Daniel Ganzfried and Sebastian Hefti, eds., *Alias Wilkomirski: Die Holocaust Travestie; Enthüllung und Dokumentation eines literarischen Skandals* (Berlin: Jüdischer Verlag, 2002).

¹⁰³ Slavoj Žižek, "Melancholy and the Act," *Critical Inquiry* 26 (2000): 660.

¹⁰⁴ Horwitz and Wakefield's observation that contemporary psychiatry has not upheld a firm distinction between normal sadness and the pathological reveals how current psychiatric approaches to defining depression contrast with the tendency of post-Holocaust memory debates to insist on the distinction between melancholy and mourning. Horwitz and Wakefield, *The Loss of Sadness*, chs. 1–5.

¹⁰⁵ See Kristeva, *Black Sun*, 102; Agamben, *Stanzas*, 26; and Benjamin, *Ursprung des deutschen Trauerspiels*, 152.

¹⁰⁶ Schings, *Melancholie und Aufklärung*, parts 2 and 3.

¹⁰⁷ Walter Benjamin, "Linke Melancholie: Zu Erich Kästners neuem Gedichtbuch," in Benjamin, *Gesammelte Schriften*, 3:279–83.

¹⁰⁸ Charles S. Maier, "A Surfeit of Memory? Reflections on History, Melancholy and Denial," *History & Memory*, 5, no. 2 (1993): 138.

109 Sontag, *Illness as Metaphor and AIDS and Its Metaphors* (London: Penguin, 1991).

110 Pensky, *Melancholy Dialectics*, 2.

111 Anne Fuchs and Mary Cosgrove, "Introduction: Germany's Memory Contests and the Management of the Past," in *German Memory Contests: The Quest for Identity in Literature, Film, and Discourse since 1990*, ed. Anne Fuchs, Mary Cosgrove, and Georg Grote (Rochester, NY: Camden House, 2006), 4.

112 Günter Grass, *Beim Häuten der Zwiebel* (Göttingen: Steidl, 2006).

113 Pfau, *Romantic Moods*, 390–91.

114 Ibid., 337.

1: The Diseased Imagination: Perpetrator Melancholy in Günter Grass's *Aus dem Tagebuch einer Schnecke* and *Beim Häuten der Zwiebel*

Melancholy Vespers

MIDWAY THROUGH HIS AUTOBIOGRAPHY, *Beim Häuten der Zwiebel*, Günter Grass hosts an imaginary gathering. Two of his dinner guests hail from the sixteenth century: the French Renaissance thinker, Michel de Montaigne, and the French Huguenot monarch, Henri IV. To complete the circle the more recent Heinrich Mann, who wrote a two-volume biography of Henri IV in the 1930s when he was in exile from Germany, is also called forth from beyond the grave. The topics of conversation are surprising at first glance. They range from the discussion of bodily ailments— gallstones, kidney stones, and excrement—to the plight of the Huguenots, how lawyers and jurists are rascals, and the abject state of Enlightenment ideals in the twentieth century. Renaissance history, French religious conflict, and intestinal issues coexist in this evening of convivial chat, which is conducted in a good-natured and thoughtful manner.[1]

Diverse though these topics might seem, in fact they are established topoi of intersecting melancholy discourses. While *Aus dem Tagebuch einer Schnecke* is the main focus of this chapter, the banquet vignette of the later work reveals Grass's erudition in matters melancholy and thus serves as a rich starting point for discussion of how Grass performatively engages with melancholy traditions.[2] Although Robert Burton does not appear at the gathering, Grass follows his lead in the choice of conversational motifs: in the introduction to his encyclopedic work *The Anatomy of Melancholy* (1624) Burton imagines a melancholy-free society where jurists, the arbiters of excessive rules and regulations, would be marginal. Burton's vision is a response to the perceived excess of legal types in the real world, and indeed *The Anatomy of Melancholy*, which contains large amounts of information on the various manifestations, causes, and potential treatments for the melancholy disposition, often reads like an extended cautionary tale. Burton is keen to promote moderation, also one of Grass's concerns. Guided by the teachings of ancient Greek medicine,

Burton believes that excess in any area, from diet to religion, gives rise to melancholy or indeed aggravates it where it is already part of a person's basic physiognomy. For Grass, excess, as debated in the diary and in the later autobiography, always leads to political extremism.[3]

Burton is not alone in advocating a careful lifestyle. In his *Essays* Montaigne, a self-confessed melancholic, also advances the values of moderation, balance, and caution with regard to a range of topics, including the imagination. An intellectual figure Grass has invoked before, Montaigne is the first-mentioned guest at the imaginary soirée. In his speech "Über die Toleranz" (On Tolerance) given in 1974 shortly after Willy Brandt's resignation as SPD chancellor of West Germany, Grass uses Montaigne as a symbol of hope for the SPD who, he urges, despite the Cold War espionage scandal of the Guillaume Affair that brought about Brandt's resignation, must not give up hope. He refers to Montaigne's thought, his reasoned tolerance of others, and his belief in the individual as an independent thinker who questions social forms, as the embodiment of the best Enlightenment values.[4]

In an earlier speech, "Die melancholische Koalition" (The Melancholy Coalition), Grass cites an established melancholy image of the slumped brooding self, Albrecht Dürer's famous early modern engraving, *Melencolia I*, in order to capture the sense of challenge issued to the Social Democrats, who in 1965 were just about to enter the Grand Coalition government with their Christian Democrat rivals. The image subsequently plays a key conceptual role in Grass's documentation of his time as a speaker on the SPD election campaign trail from March to September 1969. The diary or "Sudelbuch" (scrapbook), as Grass calls it, evolved into the hybrid literary work of the *Tagebuch*. Grass included a third speech, held in Nuremberg in 1971 as part of the celebrations commemorating Dürer's birth in 1471, at the end of the *Tagebuch*. Here he adapts the painter's image of brooding genius to convey the problems of contemporary German society and the need to reform politics. The speech also pulls together, under the rubric of Dürer's engraving, several themes that are addressed in the *Tagebuch*. The snail of the title is Grass's idiosyncratic translation of the image into a vernacular idiom that is intended to communicate to a younger audience complex Enlightenment ideals that should serve as a model for self-understanding in the present. In other words, Grass uses Dürer's engraving in modern variation to capture his thoughts on many matters, ranging from the politics of reform against the backdrop of late 1960s revolutionary upheaval to the responsibilities of the artistic imagination in sociopolitical contexts.[5]

These essays and speeches reveal Grass's long-term interest in the intellectual history and iconography of melancholy. Indeed, the scholar is spoiled for choice when it comes to deciding which work of Grass's most deserves detailed treatment under the sign of melancholy.[6] This chapter focuses on the *Tagebuch* because this work was written "under Auschwitz" and demonstrates a performative approach to the literary treatment of melancholy in the postwar period. Conceptualizing ethical memory for the West German collective, Grass goes beyond psychoanalysis to put in a good word for melancholy (*TB*, 325). Melancholy is thus a kind of ethical performance, via erudite citation, of a nuanced articulation of *Vergangenheitsbewältigung* structured around the memory of the Jewish victims of the Holocaust. Yet at the same time that he commemorates the victims, Grass also compromises his ethical project. A former perpetrator, he mobilizes different melancholy traditions to don the flattering apparel of tempered melancholy genius, a conundrum that has gone largely unnoticed in the secondary literature.[7]

Grass also does not limit his adaptation of melancholy discourses in the *Tagebuch* to a canny modern translation of the major themes identified in Dürer's image by Raymond Klibansky, Erwin Panofsky, and Fritz Saxl in their seminal work of 1964, the earlier version of which features as a prominent source both in the archival material for the *Tagebuch* and in the *Tagebuch* itself (*TB*, 305).[8] While Grass, following Klibansky et al., situates his understanding of the melancholy type between prudent warning and recuperative consolation, his engagement with melancholy discourses goes beyond Dürer's image and is more nuanced than most critics have recognized. In the archival material for the *Tagebuch* one sheet of notes entitled "Über die Melancholie" (On Melancholy) shows the breadth of Grass's knowledge. Dürer is mentioned only briefly at the top of the page: in the *Tagebuch* his biography is not central (*TB*, 100, 309). The page lists instead a range of established melancholy topics, such as night melancholy, graveyard melancholy, autumnal melancholy, love melancholy, and food melancholy. Of these, food and love melancholy are particularly important in the *Tagebuch*.[9] This chapter shows how Grass uses one set of melancholy images, those that concern bodily functions—digestion and erotic love—to produce a reflective discourse on another set of melancholy images: creative genius and the powers of the imagination.[10] Melancholy in this work is not just a symbol for SPD political reform and enlightened historical progress. It is more fundamentally a key discourse in the author's self-stylization as intellectual role-model and ethically conscientious member of the generation of thinkers who in the 1960s reexamined intellectual traditions in light of their experiences of the rupture of 1945. Many of these intellectuals, like Grass, had, by the end of the war, been members of the Waffen-SS, the Hitler Youth, or the army. As such, what might initially seem to be antiquated melancholy traditions in fact constitute a dynamic but sometimes disingenuous discourse on the failure of *Vergangenheitsbewältigung* in West Germany of the late 1960s.[11]

Grass's commentary on the postwar West German imagination is the main focus of the diary. He playfully encodes his contemporary concerns with reference to early modern intellectual and theological discussions concerning the melancholy imagination. Accordingly, Montaigne and Burton loom larger in this chapter than Georg Christoph Lichtenberg, the eighteenth-century Enlightenment scientist and philosopher whose notebooks provide a prototype for Grass's diary-scrapbook (*TB*, 7, 305).[12] Grass draws in particular on contentious debates about the damaged melancholy imagination that started to emerge in Montaigne's time. Citation of these debates, in the performative sense, provides a distancing and at times ironic commentary on German society and the German artist in the late 1960s. This is particularly evident in Grass's plea for moderation in a world of extremes (*TB*, 349).[13]

This ornate framework, constituted by a sense of national belonging and grand universal intellectual identity, is also the literary expression of the author's self-understanding as both a German and international writer.[14] Grass's mobilization of the Western traditions of melancholy as a marker of the great intellectual helps to cement his identity as a public figure on the national stage of the 1960s and 1970s. In this respect, his adaptation of melancholy traditions in the *Tagebuch* is self-serving: citing the positive traditions of melancholy in the postwar context helps to glamorize and ennoble the never-ending labor of *Vergangenheitsbewältigung*. Given Grass's belated confession in the autobiographical work *Beim Häuten der Zwiebel* of his membership in the Waffen-SS, the use of melancholy as a discourse of *Vergangenheitsbewältigung* in the earlier *Tagebuch* looks apologetic. Andrew Weber points out that Grass uses the baroque melancholy motif of *vanitas* to critique the vanities of the artist.[15] Yet this critique of the artistic imagination and personality does not always convince. Indeed, it is often overshadowed by the self-aggrandizing role of melancholy artistic identity in works that explicitly thematize the National Socialist past and allude to the author's role in this past.

More than three decades later the author as moderate melancholy genius returns in the dinner-table scene of *Beim Häuten der Zwiebel*. As in the *Tagebuch*, this imaginative citation performatively casts the writer and former perpetrator in an attractive light, even though he has, just a few pages earlier, confessed for the first time his past membership of the Waffen-SS. As antidote to this proof of youthful extremism, Grass's imaginary dinner table reflects the value of moderation he so prizes. The staged amplification, via association with his noble guests, of positive traits shows how strategic citation softens the confession of perpetration and puts distance between the wise old man of the present and his bygone SS self. Thus Montaigne's idea of moderation in life is mirrored in Henri IV, the Huguenot king who established the Edict of Nantes in 1598, an act of tolerance for the protection of France's Huguenot population. Like his fellow guest, Montaigne, Henri IV assumes in this episode an allegorical function as the historical embodiment of tolerance, compromise, and moderation.[16]

The mention of the persecution of a religious minority in an autobiography, the first half of which is a strategic confessional of Grass's SS membership, raises the specter of the fate of Europe's Jews in the twentieth century and the failure of the European Enlightenment. Grass blames this failure on the abstraction of German idealism, pointing the finger at Hegel's concept of history as teleological progress. For Grass, Hegelianism is ideology, because it preaches abstraction, a view of historical progress that envisages eventual salvation from what Grass himself regards as a worthwhile struggle in the small-scale, everyday environment of lived historical conflict. As a novelist, essayist, and political activist, Grass views abstraction in this form as a denial of reality that can have disastrous consequences in the real world. Thus one of the main strands of his hybrid diary is a sustained critique of Hegelianism, which he holds responsible for the extremism of the 1968 student generation (*TB*, 25, 209). As part of this anti-ideology position, he includes a narrative strand that documents the fate of the Jews of Danzig under National Socialism. Readers should make the connection between Hegelianism and German idealism, the doomed salvation of the German nation in the *telos* of the Third Reich, the catastrophic failure of the Enlightenment in the Holocaust, and student unrest in West Germany of the late 1960s. In this context of grand historical catastrophe, melancholy in the mode of Montaigne, who bases his essays on close observations of himself and his environment, represents a desirably modest alternative to the potential exaltations of abstraction.[17]

At the international dinner table of the new millennium, Grass serves his guests a fish soup, followed by a mushroom delicacy alongside breaded veal thymus, unusual fare that is not all that surprising given his interest in characters who love to cook and eat and his self-stylization as a chef and host.[18] The position of this scene in the autobiography is worthy of note, however, because it precedes Grass's extended reconstruction of his time as a POW in Oberpfalz shortly after the end of the Second World War. He remembers how in order to distract themselves from hunger the German POWs organized themselves into teaching and learning groups. Grass opted to attend a cookery course and regales his readers with an account of a particular recipe he learned at these sessions: the "Schweinekopfsülze" (pork aspic, literally: brawn of pig's head). The irony is that there is no food available in the POW camp. Inadvertently, the cookery course becomes a series of sessions in exercising the imagination of those attending. In the absence of the requisite ingredients to prepare the "Schweinekopfsülze," language and its creative possibilities substitute the missing sensual reality. The cookery lessons are part of a cloaked commentary on the necessary benign influencing of young minds and also on the humble beginnings of the artist's imagination in the half-profane, half-abstract context of a cookery course that, for want of real fodder, somehow never was.[19]

Alongside the cozy discussion of bowel movements with his chosen intellectual companions from different centuries, the discourse on food here is connected to a melancholy scheme concerning foodstuffs and how they can aggravate or moderate the melancholy temperament. Burton, who summarizes the classical literature on the topic, is an excellent source for this dietetics. He relates that most meat, especially dark meats, should be avoided, as they are difficult to digest. For the same reason, animal heads and feet are not recommended for consumption, and nor are internal organs and entrails. Fish are universally bad for the melancholy digestive tract because they are slimy, scaly creatures. If these foodstuffs cannot be avoided entirely, says Burton, they should be consumed only in moderation; otherwise they will cause all sorts of ailments that will either ignite or worsen the melancholy condition.[20]

On an evening when Montaigne attends an imaginary meal and the conversation covers matters alimentary, it is no coincidence that Grass includes melancholy fare on his menu: fish and a calf's thymus gland. Situated just above the heart and with the whitish color and springy consistency of brain matter, the latter gourmet delicacy belongs to the group of foodstuffs forbidden to melancholy sufferers: innards.[21] Nor is it a coincidence that brawn of pig's head is the recipe we read about in such detail shortly after this scene. Both episodes borrow from melancholy dietetics. At the same time Grass, somewhat less obviously, is making another detailed commentary that is also steeped in melancholy references: a concerned discourse on the mind, on the dangers of, in the case of the artist, the wrongly used imagination, and in the case of young, impressionable minds, a discourse on the manipulated imagination.

The Diseased Imagination

These dietary sketches communicate a contemporary articulation of an older debate on melancholy that originated in Greek philosophy in the second century BC and that acquired an urgent actuality in the context of Renaissance discussions of the imagination. While the concept of melancholy as a marker of genius reemerged during the Renaissance, critical perspectives on the condition, such as those that prevailed during the medieval period, did not entirely disappear from learned discourse. Thus the term *laesa imaginatio* (the injured imagination) was a widely acknowledged concept in the Renaissance and early modern period. It conveyed an understanding of melancholy genius in the negative terms of insanity, or from a religious viewpoint, demonic possession. Grass's borrowings from the imagery of Renaissance food melancholy entertainingly frame what could be called the diseased imagination of the twentieth century. In the *Tagebuch* he presents Hegelian abstraction and its vague but thrilling promise of salvation as a contemporary version of the diseased imagination of the Renaissance and early modern periods. Other forms of this diseased imagination include the political extremes of right and left and the attraction they hold for the middle-class student generation of Grass's representation, who wish to overthrow the existing social order.[22]

As M. A. Screech shows, Montaigne's originality as a Renaissance thinker is most evident in his thoughts on the related topics of ecstasy and genius. His essays on idleness and the imagination show a keen awareness of the dangers of a mind turned in on itself and thus predisposed to the hallucinations and madness that were typically associated with the ecstasies of divine melancholy. In the genial understanding of melancholy, ecstasy is a key moment in the inspiration of genius and the claim to infallible knowledge. In the *Essays* it is broadly applied to areas of potential excess, such as love and drunkenness, where the individuals, because of inebriation or the intense desire to merge with another person, virtually transcend themselves. Ecstasy is close to death in the Platonic sense because it describes the striving of the soul to leave the body in order to glimpse Truth, Beauty, and the Divine. Burton's reflections on the dangers of the imagination, which are influenced by Montaigne's approach to the issue of melancholy and genius, state that ecstasies of fantasy and the injured imagination can result in death. Rejecting ecstasy and genial melancholy as unrealistic ideals, Montaigne advocates an earth-bound form of wise melancholy that renders the melancholy sufferer critical instead of ecstatic or insane. Perspicacious individuals, according to this view, can harness their ecstatic tendencies to focus quietly on real phenomena that compose the fabric of everyday life, such as love and drunkenness.[23]

Grass uses these themes in his discourse on the imagination in the *Tagebuch*. He distils his concepts of the imagination and the politically active intellectual from ideas concerning two opposing temperamental types, the melancholy and sanguine personalities, that arise within the system of the four humors.[24] His depiction of the intellectual between daily political activism and artistic withdrawal follows this paradoxical scheme to produce an ideal type: the intellectual "Tatmensch" (man of action). Throughout he is critical of genial melancholy, showing himself to be a follower of Montaigne, who, when writing on ecstasy in the late sixteenth century, was heir to a good century of critical reflection on the Renaissance concept of genial melancholy. Grass does not, however, demonize melancholy as a diabolical force of the imagination. If anything, he resists this demonization, just as he refrains from exalting genial melancholy. Both perspectives veer toward abstraction: in one scenario, the mind is superhuman, in the other supernatural.[25]

Rejecting both noble melancholy and melancholy as original sin, Grass proposes a nuanced concept of profane, earth-bound melancholy in a literary language that combines allegory with grotesque physiology (*TB*, 307–8, 316). This language has three main functions: first, a didactic one that aims to communicate to younger generations how important it is to maintain a skeptical distance to ideological programs; second, the playful composition of an ideal melancholy intellectual type in the *Tagebuch*'s first-person narrator; and third, the development of an ethics of memory for commemorating the Holocaust, which is intended, by engaging with the Jewish experience of persecution in one of the narrative strands, to correct the deficits of *Vergangenheitsbewältigung* in the late 1960s.

In his Dürer speech at the end of the *Tagebuch* Grass mentions how he has tried to put in a good word for melancholy, meaning that he has tried to assemble some positive elements from different melancholy traditions into a coherent representative scheme that conveys the themes that preoccupy him. As Ann L. Mason points out, this statement should also be understood as a response to Thomas Mann's demonic depiction of genial melancholy in the character of Adrian Leverkühn, the artist figure of *Doktor Faustus* (1947) whose retreat into the barbarity of aestheticism, the roots of which Mann identified in Luther's Wittenberg, parallels Germany's descent into National Socialism. In his campaign diary Grass wishes to dispel the demons of melancholy genius by fashioning the German artist, in direct contrast to Leverkühn's aristocratic contempt for reality, as a politically active citizen who, like the eponymous snail, remains obstinately attached to the ground of grass-roots politics. This alternative artist figure carefully monitors his imagination.[26]

This question of the imagination is at the forefront of the following discussion, which elaborates on Grass's engagement with melancholy traditions in his treatment of late 1960s West German society, the specter of the Nazi past, the student movement, and the position of the politically active artist-intellectual. Within this complex there emerges an aestheticized melancholy persona that exhibits elitist affectation and ironic posing, despite the focus on daily political activism, the deliberate rejection of noble melancholy, and the colloquial camaraderie that informs the tone of the diary. W. G. Sebald concludes that the *Tagebuch*'s treatment of the Jewish victim experience is unconvincing because it is driven by a sense of political correctness and personal obligation. If we add Grass's melancholy ostentation to this critique, it becomes debatable whether the issues of humorous self-stylization and greater sociocultural commentary obscure or enhance the melancholy representation of the Holocaust.[27]

The Profane Mind

In an interview with Siegfried Lenz in 1981, Grass argues that the artistic imagination must engage with social reality. This echoes an earlier speech from 1965 in which Grass, against the conventional notion of the artist as elite, states that the rightful place of the writer is in the middle of society. Genius, he goes on to say with a critical nod to late-eighteenth-century sentimental sweet melancholy—the vilified secular descendent of divine melancholy—no longer lives in "sweet madness" but in the everyday reality of consumer society.[28]

In another speech from 1965 he applies the triangle of genius, ecstasy, and aloof contemptuous behavior to the students and university professors of the time. Their passion for dangerous utopian ideologies and their "Ekel" (disgust) for reality embody the negative understanding of the intellectual who is remote from the complicated everyday world. In these two essays and in the later interview, Grass contrasts the ivory tower of the self-deluding intellectual with the grittiness of reality, which has a profane stench and obstinate materiality: the "Abgasen" (fumes) of society and the "Sumpf" (swamps) of reality. Against this, Grass, through the concept of "Mief" (stench), recasts the writer as a profane figure with exceptional olfactory powers. In the *Tagebuch* he determines that Dürer's winged genius exudes the stench of *Mief* (*TB*, 123). By contrast, the averted nostrils of students and professors convey disdain for the ordinary grind of daily political struggle. The form of imagination they exemplify is ideological. This goes against Grass's view of a socially anchored artistic imagination and constitutes a utopian flight from reality: the diseased imagination. Meanwhile, the democratic "Kleinkram" (small stuff) of grass-roots action is a less "ecstatic" form of political engagement, through which a muted genius emerges, a paradoxical figure—part jester, part genius—that negotiates its profane existence between the poles of life and art. This version of the artist as a realistic fool risks elitism in profane form, which haunts Grass in the *Tagebuch*.[29]

These opposing concepts of the imagination comment on different melancholy traditions and simultaneously reflect on the problems of the present. In one corner we have the melancholy skeptics Montaigne and Lichtenberg, and in the other we have Hegel and the tradition of German abstraction. Most revealing of all is Grass's interpretation of the depressed mood that emanates from Dürer's winged genius. Grass rejects the notion of melancholy as sadness without identifiable cause, reading the mood—and the individual—in social and historical context. For him, the figure articulates a condition of reactive melancholy at the time of humanism. Disagreeing with Hubertus Tellenbach's phenomenological-anthropological understanding of melancholy as a deeply enigmatic state, Grass refuses to read the image as an expression of purely subjective manic-depression (*TB*, 310–11).[30]

Sadness in the engraving is therefore socially explicable. While Grass uses a range of images that originally thematized the obscure origins of melancholy, he redeploys these images to express social dilemmas in the *Tagebuch*. In this vein, the depressed state of one of the characters from the fictional strand of the *Tagebuch*, Lisbeth Stomma, while framed by the atmospheric melancholy of the eighteenth-century Graveyard Poets, is a symptom of grief for the death of her small son on the very first day of the Second World War. This loss explains her obsessive visits to ivy-covered graveyards (*TB*, 142, 227).[31]

The former Nazi Augst, who plays a role in the contemporary strand of the narrative, is also presented through melancholy imagery. A pharmacist, he commits suicide by poisoning himself at the Evangelical Church Congress Day in Stuttgart in 1969 (*TB*, 172). In his reconstructions of an alternative Augst, Grass imagines him to have great knowledge of herbal remedies that can prevent bouts of depression (*TB*, 230). Augst here coincides with a further melancholy figure: the alchemist or early modern natural scientist.[32] Yet this imaginative framing of the character only underlines his guilt: Augst uses his pharmaceutical knowledge to kill, not cure himself. Grass thus suggests that Augst's suicide is the result of unresolved guilt about his Nazi past. His melancholy is partly explained by his obsessive need to belong to a greater community, which led to his SS membership during National Socialism.

Against these poetic depictions of pathological melancholy, Grass develops a further sequence of interconnected images that convey his understanding of the circumspect, balanced mind. These include the humble snail of slow historical progress that he conceives in provincial opposition to Hegel's vision of Napoleon as the embodied *Weltgeist* on horseback (*TB*, 49, 209), the character of Hermann Ott, also known as Dr Zweifel (Dr Doubt), the main protagonist of the fictional strand on the National Socialist persecution of Danzig's Jews, the discourse of love melancholy that arises in the sexual relationship between Zweifel and Lisbeth Stomma, the daughter of the Polish bicycle dealer in whose cellar Zweifel hides out for most of the war, the connection of food to a discourse of disgust that in turn connects to Friedrich Nietzsche's epistemological concept of "große Ekel" (big disgust), the curious pseudo-biological utopian discourse on the self-sufficiency of hermaphrodite snails, and the self-stylization of the artist as a melancholy figure in a new positive sense. Three interrelated melancholy themes—the imagination, food, and love—produce a multilayered discourse of literary *Vergangenheitsbewältigung* through which Grass elaborates on the controlled imagination and ethical memory.[33]

The Brotherhood of Doubt

The allegorical personality of Zweifel (Hermann Ott) is the focal point of Grass's discourse on the imagination. A biology teacher at the local Jewish high school in Danzig for part of the National Socialist dictatorship, he is described by one of his pupils as a question mark in knickerbockers, a play on the allegorical function of his nickname (*TB*, 61). While a student in the 1920s, Zweifel works part-time at a center for Jewish emigration, and his habit of questioning everything, from National Socialism to Zionism, earns him the nickname, created for him by the immigrant Jewish population of Danzig. Grass describes Ott as "das Prinzip Zweifel" (the principle of doubt), and indeed Zweifel's allegorical opposite is Augst who embodies "das Prinzip Gläubigkeit" (the principle of belief, *TB*, 224).

Both figures typify different concepts of the imagination: skepticism versus an absolute idealism that can lead to acts of political extremism. The story of Augst is based on the real Wolfgang Scheub, while Zweifel is loosely based on the Polish-Jewish literary critic Marcel Reich Ranicki. Biographical underpinning does not dilute the allegorical effect of the diary, however. Through this kind of characterization Grass, himself a complex figure in the work, demonstrates in literary-allegorical form the principles he outlines in the interview with Lenz: that the imagination, if used wisely, can enhance our understanding of reality. Insofar as Zweifel is an ideal embodiment of the artistic imagination, he also acts as an allegory of ideal behavior for the first-person narrator, who is both artist and political activist.[34]

The connections between the person Günter Grass and the narrator are palpable; however, we should remember that Grass continually exploits biographies for didactic purposes and thus distinguish between the author and the narrator. In the *Tagebuch* the creative exploitation of real-life stories, including one's own, is justified by the greater project of warning contemporary West German society about the dangers of political extremism. However, Grass's effort to create spaces of almost impenetrable artistic retreat in his writing sends out a different message, as Rebecca Braun argues, which contradicts the figure of the artist as bourgeois citizen. Alongside the self as public intellectual, the solipsistic self who longs for creative retreat in the midst of campaign stress, must also be considered a strategic self-stylization, which, as Stuart Taberner suggests, emphasizes the noble self-sacrifice of the artist who, to the detriment of his writerly existence, volunteers for public service.[35]

Zweifel is a further variation on the politically active artist we encounter in the contemporary strand of the work. Like Zweifel, this projected self is an allegory of postwar German mnemonic virtue. Grass's use of melancholy discourses as material for the task of positive self-stylization in the modes of pained contrition and noble redemption cannot be underestimated here. However, because the allegorical style complicates the equation of the writer Grass with the narrator, I refer to "the narrator" and consider the variations of the self that we encounter in this work more as literary projections of an ideal identity than as close encounters with the individual, Günter Grass. And yet these projections are an indication of how the author wishes to be viewed. Thus the final section of this chapter departs from a predominantly text-internal analysis to question Grass's self-image as a melancholic in the *Tagebuch*. These projections contain mixed messages concerning the task of how to conceive of an ethical relationship to the past. In the end, melancholy as human sadness does not fare particularly well in the *Tagebuch*, despite the effort to put in a good word for it. On the contrary, Grass reproduces the binary divide between "good" and "bad" melancholy discussed in the introduction and links this division respectively to successful and unsuccessful *Vergangenheitsbewältigung*.

In the relationship between Zweifel's creator, the first-person narrator on the campaign trail, and the character Zweifel we get an account of the artist's imagination. While informing his children about the fate of the Jews of Danzig, the narrator self-consciously tracks his creation of Zweifel. As his name suggests, Zweifel demonstrates the ability to contemplate a problem from a number of different angles. For this reason, it is almost impossible to decide on a firm physical appearance for the character—the children, and we the readers, get a running commentary on the various countenances that Zweifel could in theory have. Yet the narrator is dissatisfied with any single appearance—indeed, this would go against the allegorical principle that the character embodies (*TB*, 181). In the end, Zweifel has an awkward appearance; nothing looks right on him. It is appropriate that he, an ambassador for the principle of doubt, is untidy and misshapen (*TB*, 27).

Zweifel is not limited to the retrospective strand of the narrative; he regularly makes appearances in the contemporary strand—on the terrace of the narrator's Friedenau residence or on holiday in Brittany (*TB*, 137, 178). He is didactic in two ways. First, he represents a self-aware mode of thinking that translates into heroic action during National Socialism: he insists on continuing to teach Jews after they have been turned out of the local German schools. He also helps some Jews to escape to Palestine (*TB*, 42–43, 103–4). Second, he embodies the ideal artistic imagination in the creative process, for each time he magically appears in the narrator's contemporary world of daily political struggle, we can observe the modus operandi of the harnessed imagination.

The narrator presents Zweifel as a close acquaintance whose advice he values and whose company he mostly cherishes. He is never free of Zweifel, he tells his children, a wry acknowledgement both of his own tendency to think through doubting and of the creative process of inventing a character who occupies a fictional world in the past as well as the narrative world of the present (*TB*, 139). On the campaign trail the narrator imagines Zweifel as his scrutinizing other, who scoffs at his efforts to bluff through responses to questions concerning contemporary politics. Here the imagined imagination in the allegorical form of the fictional Zweifel acts as a controlling instance for the artist-citizen's imagination in the present (*TB*, 88). The narrator is keenly aware that when involved in the merry-go-round of political speeches, which he wearily terms

"Redenreden" (talkingtalking), he must shut out Zweifel, who annoyingly questions every statement (*TB*, 95). Later we learn that Zweifel advises the narrator to use the form of Lichtenberg's "Sudelbuch" for documenting his thoughts on the road. Zweifel points out that the non-chronological narrative form of the scrapbook, or "wastebook," will allow the narrator to write against the flow of historical time (*TB*, 135). This detail illustrates another important function of the figure Zweifel: the rejection of chronological narratives. Grass argues that these narratives deliver a reduced concept of reality that affirms a view of history as teleology.[36] Against this, the artistic imagination should communicate the temporal complexity of experience.[37]

The narrator thus fashions both himself and Zweifel as ethical characters who explore the complex simultaneity and belatedness of experience. From the perspective of large-scale narratives that document world events, the temporal confusion of lived experience is relegated to the forgotten "waste" of historical reality (*TB*, 86). Zweifel's temporal sensitivity also rejects the timelessness of utopian ideals. His connection to complex time is a further expression of the earthy profanity of the controlled imagination: if we are to imagine a utopia, it must, paradoxically, be rooted in the here and now. Indeed, Zweifel finds it nearly impossible to document anything chronologically in his "Sudelbuch," which he, mirroring the narrator in the present, continually works on while dramatic historical events unfold around him (*TB*, 155). Chronologically incompetent, Zweifel is repeatedly described as a "Zeitzerstreuer" (a time waster), which reinforces his function as an allegory of the modest, non-genial artistic imagination, for Grass equates "wasting time" with the humble artistic act of storytelling. One of Zweifel's occupations when in hiding in Stomma's cellar is to entertain his host and Lisbeth with different stories (*TB*, 156–57). Later he even starts up a "Kellertheater" (cellar theater, *TB*, 208–9). Artistic creativity becomes a means of passing the time when there is nothing else to do. It also questions the assumptions of the conventional understanding of time as chronology, such as the quasi-religious vision of history as *telos*. The war raging above ground in the name of such grand historical vision contrasts with the underground artistic destruction of the temporal understanding that is consistent with notions of salvation and final solutions to the conflicts of history.

That Zweifel becomes an artist of sorts during his war confinement should not surprise us. His career path already renders him an ideal melancholy type. He studies biology and philosophy in Berlin (*TB*, 23) and later becomes a biology teacher at a high school in Danzig. However, philosophical reflection always accompanies his interest in biology and nature: this is most apparent in his efforts to conceive philosophically of a utopia in the prototype of a self-sufficient hermaphrodite snail. Zweifel as teacher-hero thus combines the opposing traits of the so-called *Tatmensch* of the European Enlightenment: he is associated with capitalism and the world of action, a characteristic of the sanguine type, yet he withdraws from the world of action because he is able to see through it, a characteristic of the melancholy type.[38] Zweifel is also secretary of the local Schopenhauer society and acts as tour guide around Danzig, the famous philosopher's place of birth. While this interest symbolically highlights Zweifel's contemplative tendencies, his support of the Jews, which causes him to flee Danzig, makes him a man of action. Action, however, originates in critical reflection on National Socialism. In Zweifel action and contemplation merge to produce an ideal citizen who harmonizes activity and passivity: the blindness of the will, on one hand, and the tendency to asceticism, on the other. Significantly, the narrator does not endorse retreat into asceticism from the world of the will, as does Schopenhauer (*TB*, 23).[39] As Dieter Stolz points out, contemplation in Zweifel's and the narrator's worlds is always connected to a sensual world, whether it is the gastronomic world or that of snails and biology.[40] Taken with the narrator's self-description as a "heiterer Pessimist" (a cheerful pessimist), these paradoxes allegorically refer to the union of opposites visualized in *Melencolia I* at the same time that they generate an appealing public mask for the contemporary intellectual (*TB*, 103).

Perhaps Grass is sentimentally mobilizing a range of interlocking melancholy discourses in order to produce a "retrospektive Wunschfigur" (retrospective figure of desire) in Zweifel, as Sebald critically suggests. Against this view, Julian Preece argues that "the whole point about Ott . . . is that he never existed; Grass shows through him how Germans *could have* behaved in order to highlight once more their behavior in reality." In view of Grass's belated revelation of his membership in the Waffen-SS, however, Zweifel/Ott acquires a further function as an authorial alias that distinguishes between "good" and "bad" Germans, particularly forceful in the structural opposition between the heroic Zweifel and the former Nazi, Augst. These two characters are steeped in different melancholy traditions, thus the distinction between "good" and "bad" Germans is also structured around the distinction between "good" and "bad" melancholy. This schematic framework enables the narrator to downplay the human experience of sadness, despite his apparently compassionate excursions into Augst's past (*TB*, 219–34). This subtle evaluation of the different principles "Augst" and "Zweifel" suggests that Zweifel is more a retrospective figure of desire than a model of alternative German historical behavior in the past subjunctive.[41]

Of Slimy Things

The watery ways of Müggenhahl, Zweifel's home, also provide the snails he passionately collects with a damp dwelling. Their soggy habitat is prone to flooding, alluding to the watery saturnine tradition that Dürer's engraving depicts. The flooded landscape in the background of the image has been interpreted as a reference both to weather systems and seafaring, which were identified as saturnine by Arabic astronomers of the ninth century (*SM*, 457).[42] Deciphering the snail's function as a melancholy icon is not only a question of recognizing these connections, however, but of understanding its allegorical function. As Hartmut Böhme points out, Dürer's image demonstrates virtually inexhaustible allegorical sophistication: it succinctly comments on, develops, and transforms melancholy images in order to capture the sense of a new *Zeitgeist* at the dawn of the early modern period.[43] Given the allegorical nature of the engraving, the snail, as its modern translation, becomes the allegory of an allegory.[44] While the same might also be said of Zweifel, his status as an individual character who develops through the fictional narrative detracts from his purely allegorical function.

More than any other creation in the book, the snail is pure allegory. The archival material addresses this allegorical status explicitly. Here the snail occupies a surprisingly marginal position in small script at the bottom of the page alongside other objects.[45] The ruins, ivy, weeds, owls, tidal flow, and dogs Grass lists are established melancholy icons with an allegorical function, particularly in landscape melancholy of the seventeenth and eighteenth centuries.[46] The snail, an icon of *acedia* within the system of the Seven Cardinal Sins, is Grass's most significant expansion of the traditional "Hausrat der Melancholie" (melancholy household objects, *TB*, 179).[47] Fond of weeds, ivy, the night, and damp terrain, this creature fits in with the group of melancholy icons. The caricature-like quality of the snail should not deceive readers into thinking that this work is merely a didactic exercise in the instruction of younger people: there is a more considered discourse at work here that draws on the relationship between allegory and melancholy. If the melancholy perspective on the world questions the relationship between signs and objects, then allegory is its communicative medium. Allegory as a principle of representation that ponders signification makes of the diary, on the rhetorical level at any rate, an interesting, if problematic, early specimen of the kind of ethically informed language that negotiates a careful commemoration of the Holocaust.[48]

Like Zweifel, the snail is a multi-purpose entity that extends its symbolic significance throughout the entire work. A synthesis of the qualities of grounded contemplation and hard-won progress, it functions as a focal point for many of the abstract ideas that inform the book, such as doubt, political reform, and compromise. It unifies the paradoxical qualities of the winged genius into a less self-destructive and more modestly productive existence dedicated to social reality. Like Zweifel and Augst, it has allegorical significance: the politically active narrator refers to his

"Schneckenprinzip" (snail principle), which allegorically summarizes the aforementioned qualities (*TB*, 8–9). The snail is also a profane allegory of the melancholy artistic mindset that knows how to harness the positive qualities of the imagination for the greater sociopolitical good. As such, the snail is the antithesis to the diseased imagination of abstraction. In the fictional strand one particular snail even heals the depressed Lisbeth, returning her to a full physical existence by restoring the sexual ability of her body (*TB*, 264).

Grass reproduces here in literary-grotesque form the gendered history of melancholy genius. Lisbeth represents the damaged, as opposed to artistic, imagination.[49] In her grieving state she embodies the pathological side of melancholy: female depression. That only a special snail may cure her makes it explicit that the remedy for female depression comes from without. Grass thus suggests that, unlike men, melancholy women are not capable of self-transcendence. Women are not dialectically divided between illness and greatness, as is the male melancholy hero. They simply tend toward pathological illness from which they must be rescued. The *Tagebuch* implies that women, as non-dialectical, depressive creatures, are not cut out for the challenges of post-Holocaust ethical memory. Lisbeth's betrayal of Zweifel, once she is cured, and her murder of the very snail that healed her, reveal her unsuitability for the task of *Vergangenheitsbewältigung*. Instead, the ethics of postwar commemoration is a task for the moderate male literary genius.

In contrast to woman's caprice, the snail's slow trek through time—history is described as "ein schneckenbewohntes Gelände" (a snail-inhabited terrain)—communicates modesty and the realistic expectations of reform politics (*TB*, 15). While the snail is a symbol for a kind of resignation born of meditative circumspection and melancholy reflection, it also embodies the heroic attributes of tenacity and gritty earth-bound determination that deviates from the motif of the wild utopian "Sprung" (leap) into abstraction (*TB*, 37). Just like Zweifel, who before his cellar sojourn spent much of his free time close to the earth in search of snails, the narrator likes to style himself as someone with both feet obstinately on the ground (*TB*, 12). Through the snail Grass symbolically establishes an elite community of gifted menfolk, one that is threatened not just by contemporary political unrest and the burden of the Nazi past, but also by woman's caprice and obtuseness. For these intellectual men, melancholy is a "habitus of cultural empowerment," while for Lisbeth it is a debilitating disease.[50]

The Snail and Melancholy Traditions

The secondary literature on the *Tagebuch* interprets the snail, like melancholy, rather one-sidedly as the embodiment of the SPD's program of political reform and as an anti-teleological image.⁵¹ While the narrator uses the snail as a simplified motif to express these political ideas to his children, it is more complex than this and, as indicated, has links to melancholy traditions beyond Dürer. Grass uses the snail to make interventions in established traditions, which helps remodel the melancholy artistic imagination in the context of the present burdened by the not-too-distant past.

The snail enacts a carnivalesque reversal of *acedia*, the deadly sin of spiritual torpor and insufficient faith in God that was equated with immoderate grief in the Middle Ages. Unable to believe in the existence of a benevolent God, the individual—typically a monk or scholar—in a moment of spiritual weakness loses faith. Without the lofty promise of salvation in eternity, existence on earth becomes a purely creaturely affair. A vicious circle of melancholy affliction emerges in this condition, whereby the initial spiritual inertia—*acedia*—weakens the individual's faith, resulting in yet more melancholy at the prospect of an earthly existence with no respite. Certain key passages of the *Tagebuch* playfully evoke the concept of *acedia*, but only to make of this vice a virtue in the context of Grass's ongoing critique of the diseased imagination.⁵²

The most telling episode arises in the contemporary strand of the narrative, when the narrator attends the Evangelical Church Congress Day in Stuttgart, where August commits suicide after loudly greeting his former SS comrades at the end of his speech. Thousands have attended this meeting, and the narrator skeptically notes the "Theologiebedürfnis" (theological need) that drives them. In particular, the student generation is afflicted by what he terms "den paradiesischen Blick" (the gaze toward paradise), the need for a new myth or ideology that would miraculously dispel social ills. The word "paradise" scares his snail, which cowers into its shell at the mention of this word, because it remembers how it felt to be driven out of paradise (*TB*, 168–69).

The mindset—political or religious—that cannot tolerate the ambivalences of everyday sociopolitical reality is the main focus of this passage. The "principle of August" in this chapter reminds the reader of what such social malaise can lead to. The era of National Socialism might be over, but in the narrator's view the student generation of late-1960s Germany is still shaped by the principle of absolute belief and lacking skepticism that played a key role in August's blind commitment to National Socialism and, after the war, to a range of other groups, clubs, and organizations (*TB*, 223). In this context, the snail's memory of expulsion connects it to the Jewish experience of the Holocaust and renders it a symbol of Jewish victim memory.

In this scene, however, the more general reference, via *acedia*, to man's fall from paradise overshadows the thought of Jewish victimization. The understanding of melancholy as caused by original sin goes back to the twelfth-century German mystic, Hildegard of Bingen. She believed that with original sin melancholy descended on humankind: when Adam disobeyed divine orders, black bile entered his blood. Life on earth thereafter became a life of darkness and brooding without hope.[53] In this view of melancholy, bouts of *acedia* are the price humankind must pay for original sin. Melancholy is thus a fundamental feature of the human condition. Significantly, the *status corruptionis* in which humankind languishes is marked by the curse of passing time and mortality, as opposed to blessed eternity.

The narrator evokes the fall of humankind as the bane of the creaturely mortal when he describes how the people gathered in Stuttgart on a hot summer's day sweat their "theological need" out of their pores (*TB*, 168). The irony here lies in the juxtaposition of the desire for quasi-eternal absolutes and the manifest trap of the flesh. The narrator and his snail know the dangers of disdaining earthly existence. Such aloofness is a metaphor for the diseased imagination and its realization in the persecution of others: the fear of difference. References to the snail's slimy trail through history thus go beyond even the conceptual link to the humoral and planetary qualities of moisture, dryness, and slowness associated with the melancholy temperament (*TB*, 221; *SM*, 39–54). The snail's secretions epitomize its "otherness," the quality that, in a hostile world that reviles difference, exposes it to violence. Its fleshiness is a sensual reminder of the importance of committing to the idea of earthly existence in present reality instead of embarking on flights of ideological fancy in search of "paradise." With this conviction, the narrator obstinately scribbles down his "lästig irdisches Zeug" (burdensome earthy/earthly nonsense) at an event in Säckingen, while a speaker from the APO, the left-wing student extra-parliamentary opposition to the Grand Coalition, who is described as the apostle from Lörrach, makes a speech in the mode of ideological ecstasy (*TB*, 214–15). The habitat of doubting, brooding *acedia* in the real world of fallen man—the snail's habitat—appears, against the traditional understanding of *acedia* as a vice, in a positive light. In the *Tagebuch*, the snail's anti-paradise habitat is the spatial equivalent of Zweifel's chronological incompetence and the right kind of artistic imagination. It embraces reality and shuns divine genius as a form of the diseased imagination that, as the ecstasies of the apostle of Lörrach show, is the true vice.[54]

A Cautionary Romance

The *Tagebuch*'s commentary on ecstasy makes a similar intervention in another tradition: love melancholy. Using carnivalesque imagery of the body, the narrator presents the sexual relationship between Lisbeth and Zweifel as a critique of ecstasy and melancholy genius. In this constellation, woman becomes the overdetermined signifier of creatureliness. Alongside her obsession with graveyards and the dead, Lisbeth has become fleshy and inert as a result of her depression (*TB*, 145). Her slow heavy step announces her arrival in the cellar, a saturnine trait that renders her a child of this earthy, slowly rotating planet. Almost predictably, she smells of turf, which intensifies the "Mief" of *acedia* and fallen womankind that she exudes (*TB*, 196). Grass does not shift his idiosyncratic version of postwar genius—moderate, profane, well-balanced—into the feminine signifier here, however. Woman in the *Tagebuch* is merely creaturely and devoid of the intellectual and ethical talent necessary for the labor of *Vergangenheitsbewältigung*.

Her coarse father orders her to "entertain" their guest, Zweifel, who during the war is confined to the Stommas' cellar. Lisbeth is still suffering from depression as a result of her child's death and has ceased to speak. Her inability to reach orgasm during intercourse is an extension of this muteness but may also be understood as a cautionary comment on ecstatic excesses. For even though Lisbeth is eventually cured of her melancholy, regaining both the power of speech and the ability to achieve orgasm, the sequence of events informing these developments does not deliver the happy ending customary in a tale of secular salvation: romantic love.

Lisbeth's cure occurs through a unique snail that she finds in the foliage of the graveyard where her son is buried (*TB*, 255). Zweifel likes to place it on her naked body but then notices how it starts to become ever darker, as if it were sucking black bile out of her system (*TB*, 259). The snail, already a multifaceted symbol of different melancholy traditions, now becomes a purgative in the task of "evacuating" the melancholy body. Likewise, the hellebore broth consumed on the evenings of Zweifel's theater performances causes all three characters' impromptu evacuations, a reference to Burton and Hippocrates.[55] At the same time, it is also a comment, via the carnivalesque, on the therapeutic powers of art (*TB*, 205–6). During this time, Lisbeth's physical attributes of coldness and dryness disappear. Gradually she transforms into a frighteningly normal young woman who is less interested in graveyards than in perming her hair (*TB*, 263). Part of her normalization involves a growing disgust ("Ekel") for the very snail that cured her. Reviled, she treads it underfoot (*TB*, 276–77). Meanwhile, in the world outside the cellar the Russian soldiers are advancing, and Lisbeth opportunistically threatens to hand Zweifel over to them. Zweifel, who by the end of the war can go outside again, spends his time searching for a similar snail that can cure his own melancholy. He has no luck, however, and sinks into depression. Showing a lack of empathy for Zweifel's condition, Lisbeth commits him to a mental asylum, where he remains for twelve years (*TB*, 288). In so doing, she symbolizes the pathology of the West German inability to mourn: the mentality that turns away from the figure of the victim—in this case Zweifel—to the world of postwar consumerism. Once again, woman embodies impoverished and ethically suspect memory. Zweifel's depression, on the other hand, coincides with the immediate postwar period, which was slow to acknowledge the Jewish victims of the Holocaust. His pathology displays his temporally attuned antennae and superior ethical credentials. Even when clinically depressed, he is still a genius of *Vergangenheitsbewältigung*.

The tale of Lisbeth and Zweifel is a rejection of love ecstasy, especially regarding her murder of the snail that resexualizes and cures her, and her betrayal of Zweifel at the end of the war. If we return to the Platonic notion of ecstasy as the desire to transcend the limits of physical existence in order to experience Truth, Beauty, Love, and the Divine, Lisbeth's actions display a non-genial desire for a superficial status quo as opposed to a more nuanced, "genial" engagement with reality. Yet confusingly, Lisbeth's rejection of love ecstasy also constitutes a rejection of the diseased imagination as a hotbed of ideological enthrallment. On these two points she is an ambivalent figure. She functions, on one hand, as a profane critique of the diseased imagination; on the other, she embodies the undesirable state that arises as a result of no imagination at all. This ambivalence is not resolved by the end of the text.[56] Indeed, the narrator is also ambivalent on the question of genius. However, he is careful never to present himself in a non-intellectual light, instead reserving that particular role for Lisbeth.

Volker Neuhaus points out that one explanation for Lisbeth's murder of the snail lies in its messianic ability to heal. Given the anti-ideological thrust of the *Tagebuch*, it would be contradictory to allow the snail to survive. The snail has to be "crucified" in order to get across the understanding that humankind, in the postwar context more than ever, cannot afford to rely on salvation.[57] Even the doubting Zweifel ends up a convert to the powers of the messianic snail, as his efforts to find an equivalent convey. As a true skeptic he should not have been taken in by Lisbeth's cure, even if his particular conviction amounted only to a belief in the power of doubt. This could be ironic self-commentary by the author Grass, whose anti-ideological stance has often been criticized as an ideology of the middle ground. In the final analysis, doubt must also doubt itself, because the slide into unquestioning thinking is more insidious than one might think. Accordingly, even before his illness Zweifel's Achilles heel is anticipated in the intense quality of his theater performances during which he throws himself into ecstatic raptures (*TB*, 209).[58]

This last point suggests that art does not always heal perturbations of the mind. Indeed, it can even evince mercurial tendencies. The narrator makes a further informed comment on the history of melancholy here, this time concerning the practice of using theater to treat the condition, part of the so-called "moral-management" of the disease in the eighteenth and nineteenth centuries.[59] In Zweifel's case, theater does not constitute a therapeutic treatment for melancholy, and Lisbeth is also not cured by these performances. Instead, the theater episode suggests that art can function as a vessel for excesses of the injured imagination. The narrator thus emphasizes that the imagination and the work of art must engage with social reality. Even the artist as *Zeitzerstreuer* should take care not to identify too intensely with the roles he performs, for throwing oneself into a frenzy of ardent identification amounts to a loss of perspective and runs the risk of defusing the subversive potential of his art. This preoccupation with distance explains the allegorical intricacy of the entire work.

False Utopias

Just as the artist and his work of art must remain grounded, paradoxically so must utopian projections. For this reason, Zweifel's concept of utopia in the form of a hermaphrodite snail cannot work. Utopia here is a strange, biologically sexless form. The idea is that conflict between the sexes—a metaphor for conflict more generally—would end if the biological opposites they embody were combined in neutral compromise. This is an odd idea, which has not been worked out in the secondary literature, particularly in feminist readings of the text that understand the image of neutrality as a reference to a feminine utopia. For the idea of the hermaphrodite as the synthesis of opposites tends toward the very Hegelian abstraction—here symbolized in the idea of sexlessness—that the *Tagebuch* otherwise criticizes. While one might object that the "sexed" snail, too, represents a compromise position between opposing forces, significantly it is not divested of its slimy, semi-erotic physicality, as is the hermaphrodite of Zweifel's vision. The narrator always carefully counterbalances the potential abstraction of certain ideas he upholds, such as compromise, by presenting these ideas in a grotesque physiology that commits images, such as the snail, Zweifel, and even the narrator himself, to the earthly values he promotes.[60]

Two episodes criticize the hermaphrodite utopia, which suggests that Zweifel's ideas must also be questioned: the hermaphrodite is *his* utopian vision, after all. This critique reinforces the book's metanarrative skepticism: not even Zweifel is beyond scrutiny. The first criticism comes from Zweifel's Jewish pupil and friend, Fritz Gerson, who is murdered by the Nazis. Gerson is unconvinced by Zweifel's notion of a biological utopia. The objections of the future Jewish Nazi victim to this utopian vision expose the sinister biopolitical undertone that pulsates through this image of an ideal biological specimen (*TB*, 101).[61] Gerson's protests reveal that even the exemplary Zweifel can exhibit traces of the diseased imagination. The fact that the perspective of a future Jewish victim brings into question Zweifel's moral solidity suggests that reducing him to either an apologetic philosemitic or regressive antisemitic authorial mouthpiece is too hasty: the character contains an internal self-critical moment. Second, the narrator subjects the concept of the hermaphrodite and its antisocial self-sufficiency to sharp criticism when he uses it to describe the smugly selfish behavior of his conservative political opponents in the present (*TB*, 239).

On a symbolic level, then, the hermaphrodite is the negative expression of lifeless abstraction. It mirrors Lisbeth's sexlessness before her cure and goes against the "sexed" snail that heals her. Lisbeth's earlier "sick" condition is echoed in the narrator's description of Dürer's winged figure as "die mythologische Möse" (the mythological pussy), cold, dry, and also sexless (*TB*, 197). This group of images contrasts unfavorably with the more positive depictions of sexually active female genitalia, which, like the heroic snail of reform politics, are characterized by fleshiness and moisture (*TB*, 264). Grass thus delivers an odd, gendered physiology of the mind. Abstract androgyny articulates a utopian projection of the diseased imagination that has emptied reality of conflict, while images of flesh and secretions represent a truer version of reality that requires for its conceptualization and communication a socially attuned artistic imagination, however overbearingly patriarchal.

This skepticism of Zweifel's biologically neutral utopia also reinforces the rejection of paradise: just as there is no easy way out of historical reality, there is no way back to the Garden of Eden, to a mythological time before woman betrayed man. Reality consists of life after the fall, so to speak, and gender conflict is just one aspect of this reality. For this reason, we should not read Lisbeth's treacherousness as a dire reminder of the real world outside the cellar, nor should we read it only as a sexist statement on the unreliability of womankind. Rather, her capricious behavior also stands for the complex reality in which compromise must take place. From this point of view, it makes sense that she completes the transition from a cipher of abstraction to a flesh-and-blood woman who victimizes others as others victimize her. Yet just as Lisbeth is not perfect, neither is Zweifel. Their imperfection amounts to an approximation of social reality, and in the *Tagebuch*'s final analysis this grey zone is preferable to the tempting clarity offered by the strangest kinds of utopian projections.

Food Melancholy and Disgust

There is a further key moment in Lisbeth's story that runs through all levels of the book: her "Ekel" (disgust) for the snail she squashes to death. This incident adds another layer of significance to the discourse on the body and sexuality. Lisbeth, who revels in her renewed physicality, now abhors the source of her cure and the organic nature of existence represented in the snail's slime. In other words, she is reviled by life's physicality and its reminders of mortality even as she relishes her newfound sexuality.

Ironically, the imagery that comprises Lisbeth—the turf-smell, her overweight fleshy body, her vagina—associates her with the organic world of fallen humankind she abhors. Her loathing reveals a new dimension to her heretofore earthy persona: the rejection of the idea of lived reality in favor of something more abstract. Her repugnance toward the snail compares with Zweifel's search for a hermaphrodite. Both stances involve betrayal of the real in favor of imaginary worlds. Lisbeth's disgust is particularly aggressive, however. It exemplifies the primary form of disgust for earthly life that Nietzsche identifies in the Platonic and Christian message of a better realm beyond the mortal one. However, Nietzsche also argues that a yet more radical form of knowledge, "Ekel-erkenntnis" (knowledge of disgust), is possible. "Ekel-erkenntnis" comes about as a consequence of seeing through the Christian and Platonic disgust for earthly existence. This more radical knowledge about disgust for earthly existence now produces disgust for Christian and Platonic disgust. The higher knowledge of "große Ekel" (big disgust) endorses earthly existence, dispensing with the hypocritical Christian contempt for and fear of mortality. Indeed, "Ekel-erkenntnis" can amount to the Dionysian embrace of life. As a bedfellow of *acedia*, however, "Ekel-erkenntnis" may also contain a lethargic moment. Connecting disgust to the aristocratic melancholy tradition of the Elizabethan period, Nietzsche mentions Hamlet as an example of the lethargic response to "Ekel-erkenntnis," the individual who has seen through the illusory morals of the Christian worldview, but whose insights render him listless and inactive.[62]

In the *Tagebuch*, this complex of knowledge and disgust evokes the conundrum of the man of action versus the man of contemplation that is partially resolved in the compromise positions represented by Zweifel and the narrator. In particular, the narrator describes himself as suffering from "Ekel-erkenntnis" when facing his Christian Democrat political opponents (*TB*, 106–7). As an antidote to this state of mind he keeps moving on the day-to-day program of the SPD campaign, avoiding withdrawal into the melancholy shell of political *acedia*. The democratic small stuff of the everyday SPD project and the pointedly non-aristocratic activity of hard work prevent lethargy: the narrator is no hesitant Hamlet (*TB*, 26). Grass's rejection of the class associations of genial melancholy is apparent in this attitude to work. It is questionable, however, whether the artist figure in the *Tagebuch* ever really descends from the ivory tower of abstract aesthetics that he criticizes, a point I consider in the final section of this chapter.

The narrator applies Nietzsche's physiology of knowledge to embellish his discourse on food-melancholy in the *Tagebuch*. Based on a

Dionysian celebration of the taboo zone of the body's internal organs, with a special focus on digestion, this is a further reversal of another melancholy tradition. Much of what the narrator tells us about food goes against the grain of melancholy dietetics as summed up in Burton's list of prohibited foodstuffs. Ignoring Burton, the narrator often cooks entrails and other melancholy ingredients. One of the first domestic scenes of the *Tagebuch* details the preparation of entrails—the lining of a cow's stomach—for dinner (*TB*, 13). The guesthouse the narrator imagines running one day, debunkingly named "Gasthaus zum Heiligen Geist" (The Guesthouse of the Holy Spirit), features melancholy fare on its menu: fish, fowl, entrails, innards, pulses (*TB*, 83). At the Friedenau weekly market the narrator buys hare's feet, deemed to be hard on the digestion, fresh-water fish, which should be avoided because it originates in slimy stagnant waters, all sorts of herbs, and fowl (*TB*, 89). At a later point he describes how his children react with disgust to a meal of cow's udders he is preparing. To their abhorrence, the stench of boiling udders permeates the entire house. Yet for reasons of imaginative empathy, the narrator is determined that he and his repulsed family will eat this fare: in the fictional strand Zweifel, because of food shortages, gets nothing but cows' udders from Stomma for weeks. The narrator's brotherhood with his fictional creation and his commitment to the principle of doubt are here articulated in the empathetic cooking and consumption of entrails (*TB*, 192).[63]

In the *Tagebuch*, the social body throughout twentieth-century German history also suffers from digestive problems, which evokes Nietzsche's statement that the German spirit is pure indigestion. This complex is expressed in the motif of the stomach ulcer. The petit-bourgeois anti-Semites of prewar Germany suffer from a Jewish ulcer (*TB*, 18). Frustrated students of the late 1960s have a similar affliction, even if its cause is different (*TB*, 61). Augst has a stomach ulcer as a young man (*TB*, 176–77), and one of the narrator's SPD comrades, Leo Bauer, develops a stomach ulcer while a prisoner in Siberia after the war (*TB*, 240). Historical events and social conditions make these people sick to their stomachs. The narrator's answer to social upset is to get politically active. In dietary terms his reaction is, against Burton's advice, to eat melancholy foodstuffs. In other words, he refuses to be turned off reality, no matter how "disgusting" it can become. The profanity of democratic "Kleinkram" is thus mirrored in the profanity of the food he consumes. The narrator's commitment to political graft drives home how he—in the mode of a self-managing, moderate melancholy genius—always overcomes his potentially lethargic moment. Food communicates this moment of everyday self-transcendence. Ingestion of cows' udders and the like reveals a person who daily performs the "big disgust." The narrator is no languishing Hamlet, nor is he an *acedia* sufferer. True, he lives in the world of fallen humankind, but as a proponent of the "big disgust" this is exactly where he wants to be. Furthermore, his special perspicacity, his "Ekel-erkenntnis," does not lead to withdrawal into *taedium vitae* but spurs him along political and writerly paths.[64]

By contrast, those who embody the Augst principle—the principle of blind faith—suffer from constipation (*TB*, 170). On the evenings of Zweifel's cellar theatre, hellebore is consumed before the performances commence. This is a carnivalesque reversal of the fear of mortality that the constipated body symbolizes. In the world of the narrator's present, the constipated Augst represents an idealism of the body that denies its physicality. By contrast, Zweifel's body laughingly capitulates to the laxative effect of the hellebore, reveling in the body's corporeality and internal functions. Augst's constipation manifests his unwillingness to recognize reality and his questionable desire to transcend the shameful mortal self. Zweifel, however, breaks the hygienic taboo of idealism in order to revel in "life," here represented in the carnivalesque trope of the scatological.

There is a further reason why, when it comes to matters of the stomach, the narrator opts ultimately for Nietzsche as "food guide" instead of Burton. It also explains why he is so insistent that his children should consume, as he does, the "waste parts" of the animal. This concerns the search for an ethics of memory that commemorates the Holocaust without succumbing to the false illusion of success contained in the myth of the West German economic miracle. In the first food reference, the narrator mentions how, during family conversation at the table, his stomach regurgitates the entrails he has just consumed, coating his teeth in tallow (*TB*, 15). Tellingly, his children have started to ask him in detail about the Jews and the Holocaust. The past that will not go away and the question of how to represent it ethically are symbolized in the vomit of regurgitating innards. This is not an image of "Ekel," however, for it has none of Lisbeth's repressive contempt. Instead, it is an image of "Ekel-erkenntnis" or "große Ekel" in a deliberately Nietzschean mode that borrows from his work the symbolic action of "wiederkäuen" (chewing over) in order to express, from a postwar West German viewpoint, an ethical attitude to the memory of the distasteful past. The activity of chewing regurgitated stomach contents that consist of the stomach of a cow, an animal that often regurgitates its stomach contents, expresses an attitude that fearlessly embraces the past as inseparable from the present. Let us not forget that the snail, also a symbol of "Ekel-erkenntnis," is associated with German guilt and shame (*TB*, 17). It too is connected to an ethics of memory that cuts through the shiny surface of economic success—the surface that imposes "Vergangenheitsekel" (disgust for the past) in the form of insufficient *Vergangenheitsbewältigung*—to reveal in the slime of its trail a deeper more inclusive acknowledgement of what lies beneath. The refrain "wir sind wieder wer" (we are someone again) is exposed as illusory by the "disgustingness" of the snail's slimy and temporally sensitive trail: it refuses to bracket off the past from present concerns (*TB*, 119–20).[65]

The snail that recoils at the mention of the word "paradise" is thus also an allegory for the ethically correct utopia that should prevail in contemporary West Germany: the utopia of regret (*TB*, 317). The regurgitated tallow that coats the narrator's teeth is a physical image of regret and thus a paradoxical anti-utopian image of utopia: he chews on (must live with) the regurgitated fat of the past, an ethical gesture in the mode of big disgust. The close relationship between reality and imagination is once again configured in this image of chewing over manifestly unpleasant things: the imagination must endure this focus on reality and not turn away from it toward some utopian projection. These images reinforce the *non sequitur* of the hermaphrodite snail as an ethical utopia. Its ideal physical self-sufficiency is an image of closure that suggests it is not physical in Nietzsche's sense: one could argue that the hermaphrodite snail of the *Tagebuch* does not eat, it cannot regurgitate, it has nothing to evacuate. Far from being the positive image of a better world, it portrays the memory politics of postwar West German society because it is an image of willful amnesia.

Allegory and Melancholy

The *Tagebuch* self-consciously uses allegory to comment on melancholy traditions, the diseased imagination, and Germany's Nazi past. At one point in the narrative, the narrator ponders whether his snail creation reflects Walter Benjamin's theory of baroque allegory (*TB*, 100). He does not confirm this, however, ending the query with a question mark that lingers over the snail and its associated allegorical bedfellows. Ever erudite, the narrator is choosy in his reception of Benjamin, engaging with his theory only to alter it for didactic purposes, as with melancholy food and love imagery.[66]

The narrator's choice of a general allegorical mode of representation converges with Benjamin's work on baroque tragic drama, which marked a major turn in the fate of allegory as a literary figure. Since the late eighteenth century and the beginnings of Romanticism, allegory, a traditional form of rhetoric, was regarded unfavorably as too abstract a mode of representation. Compared with the symbol, it constituted an impoverished and unnatural literary language that was ill-equipped to convey emotion and subjective truth. For Benjamin, allegory is not just the convention of expression. More profoundly, it is the expression of convention; it signals "the descent from metaphysical expectancy into the lapsed finitude of history," where writing is the damaged repository of "invariant and profane signs and conventions."[67] The connection to convention reveals the performative quality of allegory and connects it to melancholy: in theoretical terms allegory, like the language and rhetoric of melancholy, is a damaged signifier marked by a lack of unitary meaning.

The intricacies of the complex debate concerning symbol and allegory cannot be covered here, thus my summary of how they were viewed until Benjamin altered the figural landscape is brief and general. The symbol operates through a unifying and organic relationship between the part and the whole: it works through analogy, substitution, and resemblance. A poet writing in the symbolic mode sees the general in the particular. The part will always represent the whole in this kind of figural language, because the whole is contained in the part. Paul de Man regards this preference for the symbol as part of the development of a new subjective vocabulary in the nineteenth century, while Hans Georg Gadamer argues that the valorization of the symbol at the expense of allegory coincides with the emergence of an aesthetic system that refuses to distinguish between experience and the representation of experience. In the Romantic vision of poetic language, thus, the world is made up of symbols that lead to a single, universal meaning. For de Man, it is "this appeal to the infinity of a totality" that accounts for the main attraction of the symbol. The symbol, then, is the proper figure of the language of individual poetic genius.[68]

Allegory, by contrast, refers to a meaning that it does not itself constitute. This is because it starts with an abstract idea that it then seeks to cloak in an image to which the idea does not "organically" belong. The symbol exemplifies the intimate relationship between part and whole, while allegory replaces this special connection with a more arbitrary relationship between the allegorical image and the idea it is meant to represent. Classical theory recognized allegory as an ambivalent mode of representation, because it normally contains two conflicting meanings. It cannot constitute an organic micro-system of correspondences that flow between its harmonious parts, like the symbol. Instead, it is a transmitter of dissimilarity and difference. Hence the reputation of allegory as a cold, cerebral mode of representation that is ill-equipped to convey subjective truth and experience. For Benjamin, and later for de Man, it is precisely this undermining of the "natural" correspondence between signifier and signified that renders allegory the more interesting literary figure. This is mainly because allegory, as a trope that is discontinuous with itself, is a more historical mode of signification. Its discontinuity makes it capable of communicating temporal complexity without the comfort of an ultimate transcendent goal or meaning.[69]

It makes sense that allegory should be the dominant mode of representation in a work that tries to portray the complexity of historical and social experience. It is also clear that in order to critique the poetic language of genius and its attendant quasi-religious values—transcendence, totality, eternity—Grass opts for a literary language that conveys the opposite. Rhetorically speaking, allegory is thus the best mode for a sustained discourse on the diseased imagination. Its historical misfortune in the aesthetic debates of the late eighteenth century and its dissociation from nineteenth-century Romantic genius further enhance its suitability for the *Tagebuch*. From this viewpoint, the narrator's description of himself straining to imagine what Zweifel might look like as a person is an arch display of the allegorical imagination at work. Starting from the idea of "doubt" this imagination flails about in search of a body that will convey the sense of doubt. In the end, Zweifel ends up with a body that dangles about and looks awkward. His body is not an organic totality that coincides wonderfully with itself. Indeed, he is not even really an image of doubt. His person is the allegorical principle itself at work, the epitome of the tenuous relationship between signifier (Zweifel's body) and signified (the idea of doubt) that characterizes allegory. The artificial nature of such constructs is perhaps what Sebald does not recognize in his judgment that the characters of the *Tagebuch* are superficial.[70]

While the snail has many evident "organic" connections to the qualities of slowness and persistence that it embodies, its status as a "symbol" for the SPD and as an anti-Hegelian motif is arbitrary. The odd utopian projection of the hermaphrodite snail can also be accounted for within an allegorical discourse that favors discontinuous relations between signifiers and signifieds. The hermaphrodite snail, an abstract utopian ideal, is an allegorical parody of the smugness of symbolic language. Thus the rejection of unrealistic utopias that the snail's "murder" suggests is not only a reference to Nietzsche's "Ekel." On the meta-narrative level it also announces the end of the symbol and the diseased imagination it conveys. In this way, the allegorical mode represents the controlled and ethical artistic imagination in process.

The narrator converges most clearly with Benjamin's figure of the melancholy allegorist in his demonstration of the allegorical imagination. In his study of German tragic drama Benjamin describes allegory as the proper mode of articulation for the melancholy mindset. This is because the melancholy gaze, as it surveys the flotsam and jetsam of creaturely existence in the world of fallen humankind, fragments and destroys all objects it alights upon, tearing these objects out of their original semantic contexts and reconfiguring them in new, "unnatural" contexts: hence the fragmentary nature of the allegorical object. The arbitrariness of the new meanings these objects convey originates in the arbitrary will of the melancholy allegorist, whose search for meaning in a transitory mortal world that no longer adds up to a totality crowned by projections of eternity makes of her/him an incessantly brooding, destructive-creative interpreter of the dead objects of the profane world. In other words, arbitrariness is the marker of the melancholy mindset that has recognized the epistemological limitations of the self and the fleetingness of the world. This insight into the transitoriness of all things corresponds to a desire to rescue these objects into eternity and adds to the melancholy awareness of epistemological limitations. Any such attempts must be frustrated, unless the allegorist mysteriously awakens in God's world, as occurs at the end of Benjamin's work.[71]

There is no such awakening in Grass's work and no hope of a mysterious salvation. The snail is killed, Lisbeth "awakens" into a historical necessity (the Soviet army is approaching) that renders her a cruel opportunist, Zweifel "awakens" into an asylum for the mentally ill after the war, and the narrating "ich" can never finally settle between a space of quiet contemplation and the democratic "Kleinkram" of the election campaign but is divided between both. A world beyond complex reality never materializes for any of these allegorical figures, the damaged melancholy signifiers of the profane postwar world. The sudden appearance of such a harmonious place would amount to a failure of the socially engaged imagination. Rhetorically speaking, then, the narrator and his creations remain in the historically determined space of baroque allegory, which constantly communicates a sense of the transitory and a sense of mortality. We could say that this is the textual space of the postwar melancholy performative.

Perhaps this explains why Grass never killed off Zweifel, despite the plans to the contrary that we find in the archival material. Death would have meant Zweifel's "salvation" to an undefined place preferable to the unpleasant reality of betrayal, incarceration, and depression. This plot line would have gone against the allegorical principle of doubt. Emphasizing Zweifel's creaturely state in the world of fallen man, his death was to have been caused by choking on fish bones, a further ironic reference to Burton's warnings against the slimy, scaly creatures. Grass upheld this melancholy reference even while keeping Zweifel alive. In the book we are told that for the twelve years Zweifel spent in the asylum his fear, otherwise silent, would manifest itself whenever fish was served, because of the bones contained within (*TB*, 288).[72]

Despite her cure, Lisbeth, too, remains closely linked to her allegorical origins in *Melencolia I*. Her dead, staring eyes during intercourse with Zweifel connect her to the skull, the baroque *vanitas* symbol of the transitory nature of earthly life. Her "cure" into a terrifyingly normal woman does not reduce her allegorical significance either, for she thereafter evokes the figure of the prostitute that Benjamin examined in Baudelaire's work and that retains the blank, staring eyes of the baroque skull. The narrator also imagines the winged figure as a capitalist whore who tries to sell her wares. No one is interested in buying her or her "Trödel" (junk), however, a reference to the contemporary world's categorization of melancholy as an illness with no positive qualities (*TB*, 179). Böhme argues that Dürer's engraving consists of conventional signs cast in a new, obscure relationship to each other. As such, it is an allegory of the allegorical process and demonstrates pure signification more than it expresses an obscure mood. In the *Tagebuch*, Grass mimics this play with and on allegory, breathing life into convention by introducing new allegorical forms, such as the snail.[73]

This process is interesting because it again demonstrates the workings of the allegorical imagination. In terms of plot, Lisbeth is no more a Parisian prostitute than she is a baroque skull. However, in the narrator's obsessively interpreting mind, this twentieth-century, rural Cassubian woman acquires a touch of seventeenth- and nineteenth-century significance. In so doing, she embodies the very temporality that de Man sees as allegory's strength. He argues that allegory weakens the relationship between signified and signifier, because it emphasizes the relationship of signifiers to other signifiers. This conveys a greater sense of passing time and transitoriness—historical reality—than do signifying systems that promote an illusorily close relationship between signifiers and their signifieds. In a relationship of anteriority and convention, thus, signifiers refer to other signifiers that precede them. This reinforces the close connections between allegory and the performative because it also points to the temporal quality of iterability. Allegory is thus an exemplary mode of intertextuality through which one can critique and reverse established traditions. As a signifier, Lisbeth refers to many other signifiers that predate her existence as a character in this text, as do Zweifel (Schopenhauerian pessimism), the snail (*Melencolia I*), and the narrator (melancholy dietetics).[74] The creation of an idiosyncratic world of signifiers that make sense only within the explicitly choreographed semantics of this world is further evidence of the hermeneutic activity of the melancholy allegorist. For while all allegorical signifiers in the work reflect and amplify one another, which could suggest that the *Tagebuch* is a signifying totality in the symbolic mode, the pronounced arbitrariness of the allegorical imagery frustrates this reading of the book. Allegory is evident in the strangeness of the snail as a reference to *Melencolia I* at the same time that it is a reference to the Holocaust and to the SPD. To put it another way, we can advance the argument that the work is an organic whole of self-reflecting melancholy images only if we first recognize the fundamental arbitrariness of the imagery. This reading departs from the biographical approach, which understands individual motifs as the Romantic fragments of a greater confessional whole.[75] Indeed, the allegorical qualities of the *Tagebuch* and its set of characters run counter to any expressive poetics of affect we might expect to encounter in a work steeped in melancholy. Through his adaptation of melancholy traditions and his play with allegory, Grass demonstrates the difficulty of finding a literary register for the expression of affect. In the postwar context, intellectual activity and not sentiment must be the cornerstone of an ethical literary poetics. Rhetorically speaking, then, the book remains within the snail-inhabited terrain of history: the fragmentary baroque landscape full of objects that empty and fill with meaning, depending on the allegorist's objectives.

And yet the eccentricity of the carefully choreographed allegorical connections is also an emphatic authorial stamp—inexorably they all lead back to the narrator-author—as well as a careful self-fashioning of this figure as a textual creation: the profane melancholy allegorist. Despite autobiographical flourishes such as the portrayal of domestic life with children and a disintegrating marriage, however, the narrator is not altogether consistent with the person Grass. This is because the narrator performs the author's evaporation in a cloud of arbitrary signifiers, such as the snail and Zweifel, transforming himself and the historical person he is meant to represent into fictional creations that assume a position marked as arbitrary in relation to a host of other signifiers.[76]

Der Übermensch (aber kleinbürgerlich)

The stylization of the narrator, however, is often very self-focused, a solipsism that reneges on the project of allegory and that lends itself rather awkwardly to the conceptualization of ethical memory for the West German collective. While we can interpret self-descriptions such as the human-become-snail and refrains of "ich ich ich" as ironic references, in bombastic, baroque style, to the apocryphal nature of identity, these descriptions also communicate the sense of a brooding lump of a self who cannot always see beyond himself and for whom the world is a room of mirrors that reflect only versions of himself in the form of his creations (*TB*, 70, 240–41). At such moments, it is as if the relationship between signifier (first person narrator) and signified (the person Günter Grass) is strengthened ("ich ich ich") at the expense of the work's allegorical, ethical message. Chapter 8 of the diary is dedicated to the narrator-author's navel-gazing, for example. The reader is justified in asking what this work is really about: German positions on the recent past, or the author-narrator who is still working out his own position on this past. Or perhaps we are meant to conclude that the two are indistinguishable: Günter Grass as person and textual effect thus comes to represent the trials and tribulations of postwar West German history writ large.

Such moments, however, do not entirely undermine the interpretation of the text as an early specimen of ethical memory politics in sophisticated literary translation that tries to consider the experience of the persecuted other. First, the insight that author and narrator are not necessarily continuous with each other must remain more or less speculative. As readers we cannot arrive at any final conclusion on this matter. We can only observe the text-internal degrees of playfulness the narrator employs to consider the author and must establish their interaction on that basis.

As Braun points out, the answer to this conundrum is to be found neither in a naive understanding of autobiography nor in a view of the text as pure fiction. Projections of the self are produced somewhere between the two poles, a mix of both autobiographical and fictional elements.[77]

Second, it is clear that the seminal essays published in 1966 by the Austro-Jewish victim survivor of Nazi persecution, Jean Améry, influenced the conceptualization of time as discontinuous in the *Tagebuch*. Améry's insight that for the victims of National Socialism the past never ends is paraphrased midway through the book (*TB*, 147). Zweifel as "Zeiterstreuer" embodies this discontinuity, as does the diary's negotiation of different time levels and the choice of allegorical representation, which also foregrounds temporal complexity. These subtle tactics demonstrate the author's earnestness. Moreover, allegory puts forward a message of difference. It is not just that time is discontinuous in the work; individuals also have contradictory identities, as we have seen. Perhaps Grass might have tried to focus more concretely on the difference of the Jewish other by making Zweifel a Jewish character. However, the work is fundamentally about Germans in the late 1960s, how they evade or embrace the task of *Vergangenheitsbewältigung*, and what this evasion might mean in terms of contemporary political extremism.[78]

Sebald accuses Grass of adding Jewish content to the book merely because it was politically correct to do so at the time. In his view, the work does not dedicate enough space to Jewish victimization and does not develop a convincing ethical language for conveying this experience. Given the growing international status of the Holocaust as a traumatic event in history throughout the 1980s and particularly after German unification, it is unsurprising that Sebald finds fault with the representative style of this earlier work. Locating the Holocaust within the representative apparatus of the book means, however, recognizing that it was written at an earlier evolutionary point in West Germany's developing memory politics, between 1971 and 1972. The point of including this narrative strand is to tell the story to Germans—represented by the narrator's children—so that they do not forget the crimes committed in their name. The story of Jewish victimization is therefore the cornerstone of West German *Vergangenheitsbewältigung*. From this perspective, the book is more concerned with the West German inability to mourn than with the Jewish memory of the Holocaust. In contrast to Sebald, I would argue that this is not a reason to deem the work superficial.[79]

In my view, a neglected aspect of this work is the representation of the perpetrator, August, and the judgment of melancholy that we encounter therein. Jürgen Rothenberg observes that the many reasons suggested by the narrator for August's depressive tendencies are ultimately ironic, because they amount to nothing specific. No cause or event in the outside world can fully explain this individual's ruinous sadness. Instead, the implication is that Augst must look to himself to understand why he is a "bad" melancholic. Contradicting the message of his speech, which attempts to regard melancholy both as a collective and an individual phenomenon, Grass seems to be suggesting through Augst that there is a limit to sociopolitical explanations for melancholy. If one cannot transform one's immoderate sadness into something productive, such as SPD reform politics, then one is a bad melancholic; disaster in the form of political extremism and suicide will be the consequence, as Augst's tragic biography shows. With Augst, Grass retreats from his play with melancholy allegory and its artificial, skeptical qualities. Instead, he slips into a reading of the former Nazi's negative melancholy affect as authentic and knowable. Augst ceases to be just a "principle" in this assessment and becomes a figure of recent historical catastrophe.[80]

Indeed, Augst embodies the thesis of the inability to mourn. He personifies on an individual level the failure of the West German collective to engage properly with the legacy of the Nazi past and provides a flattering foil for the narrator, whose brand of melancholy—enlightened, critical, and reformist—is a "good" form of melancholy. The "good" melancholic also tries to be one of the common people, rejects elitist, genial modes of melancholy, and stresses his hard-work ethic in the labor of *Vergangenheitsbewältigung*. He is made up of the superhuman ability constantly to transcend oneself— the *Übermensch*—but in a petit-bourgeois manner that demonstrably shuns the life of aristocratic contemplation, no matter how much his artistic soul might yearn for Epicurean retreat from troubled society. By contrast, Augst represents the diseased imagination of the late-twentieth century. He cannot transcend himself in an ongoing process of self-improvement that might lead to a more ethical perspective on the past.[81]

This is a strange moment in the judgment of Augst. It reinstates the ethical elitism of artistic melancholy while distancing the author-narrator, also a former perpetrator, from the "bad" melancholic and his festering perpetrator issues. Augst cannot transcend himself in Nietzsche's sense, that is, go beyond himself to create something new.[82] He remains inhibited by a melancholy that is difficult to explain because it has no identifiable cause. When the narrator ponders the question of why Augst became an SS officer, no clear answer emerges. In the final analysis the reasons must lie within the individual and his endogenous melancholy (*TB*, 252). Further, Augst did not get this sadness under control but channeled it into questionable social organizations between 1933 and 1945, an activity he continued after the war. Here Grass appears to suggest that "bad" melancholy—melancholy without identifiable cause that seems to be part of a person's character—led to the rise of National Socialism as much as it characterizes the inability to mourn after the war.

Quite apart from the strangeness of the historical picture here, Grass also appears to turn on his perpetrator creation, despite stating in an interview that the writer must lovingly embrace these problematic characters and all of their imperfections. The very prohibition of melancholy that Grass in his speech regards critically as a product of Western civilization's vision of success as happiness and that he tries to overturn in the diary resurfaces in the characterization of Augst and the "bad" version of melancholy as inexplicable sadness. Augst is not just a failure because he is a perpetrator who has not come to terms with his past. More fundamentally he is a failure because he has been sad his whole life. Indeed, this sadness is the context within which to understand his support of National Socialism. In this contradictory assessment of melancholy, the author-narrator distances himself, the "cheerful pessimist," from his fellow-perpetrator.[83]

Despite his self-stylization as earnest, his brow furrowed in perplexity, the narrator's outlook and person embody the success story of "good" melancholy and the right kind of *Vergangenheitsbewältigung*. At this meta-semantic level of the text we encounter not the humble human-become-snail artist figure but rather the elite artist as paradoxical moderate melancholy leading the people, providing the West German collective with an affective model of behavior and the right kind of work ethic for the labor of post-Holocaust memory. Indeed, the subjective experience of sadness plays a minor role in this work. If anything, sadness becomes an abstract, political-artistic ideal where it, as "good" melancholy, acquires positive traits. Is this not also an instance of reinstated idealism, despite the rhetoric of smallness that runs through the book? By contrast, immoderate sadness on the personal level is presented as sinister and pathetic: "bad" melancholy. Ultimately, the individual is to blame for not getting it under control and for unleashing it into the historical arena. The following chapter elucidates a different perspective on melancholy, however, one that allows for the dark side of melancholy at the same time that it also provides a historical context for sadness after 1945.

Notes

[1] Grass, *Beim Häuten der Zwiebel*, 195–96. Heinrich Mann, *Die Jugend des Königs Henri Quatre* (Reinbek bei Hamburg: Rowohlt, 1994), and *Die Vollendung des Königs Henri Quatre* (Reinbek bei Hamburg: Rowohlt, 1994).

[2] Grass, *Aus dem Tagebuch einer Schnecke*, 7. Hereafter cited in text as *TB*.

[3] Burton, *The Anatomy of Melancholy*, 1:91, 69. Wolfgang Lepenies points out that this view of jurists was widespread in the sixteenth and seventeenth centuries. Lepenies, *Melancholie und Gesellschaft*, 19–34, esp. 23–24. On melancholy in antiquity see Hellmut Flashar, *Melancholie und Melancholiker*, 21–59.

[4] Günter Grass, "Über die Toleranz," in *Günter Grass: Werkausgabe in zehn Bänden*, ed. Volker Neuhaus, Daniela Hermes (Berlin: Luchterhand, 1987), 9:654.

See in particular "On Sadness," "On Idleness," "On the Power of the Imagination," "On Moderation," in Michel de Montaigne, *The Essays of Michel de Montaigne*, trans. and ed. by M. A. Screech (London: Penguin, 1991), respectively 7–10, 30–31, 109–20, and 222–27.

5 Günter Grass, "Die melancholische Koalition," in *Günter Grass: Werkausgabe in zehn Bänden*, 9:176, and *Aus dem Tagebuch einer Schnecke*, 7. On Grass and the SPD see Merle Curtis Krueger, *Authors and the Opposition: West German Writers and the Social Democratic Party from 1945 to 1969* (Stuttgart: Heinz, 1982), ch. 3; also Timm Niklas Pietsch, *"Wer hört noch zu?": Günter Grass als politischer Redner und Essayist* (Essen: Klartext, 2006), 85–162. Grass's Dürer speech, held in Nuremberg on May 7, 1971, appeared in an early publication: "Vom Stillstand im Fortschritt," in *Am Beispiel Dürers: Reden von Jean Améry, Günter Grass, Richard Friedenthal, Hartmut von Hentig, Wilhelm Fucks, Adolf Portmann, Arnold Gehlen, Carlo Schmid*, ed. Hermann Glaser (Munich: Bruckmann, 1972), 82–97.

6 Other works by Grass that show an interest in melancholy, food, and the baroque period include *Der Butt* (Darmstadt, Neuwied: Luchterhand, 1987); *Das Treffen in Telgte: Eine Erzählung* (Göttingen: Steidl, 2007); and *Die bösen Köche: Ein Drama in fünf Akten* (Darmstadt: Luchterhand, 1982). On Grass's affinity with the baroque, especially in *Der Butt* and *Das Treffen in Telgte*, see Andrew Weber, *Günter Grass's Use of Baroque Literature* (London: W. S. Maney & Son, 1995), 81–82, 163–64.

7 One view regards the engraving and melancholy as a critique of teleology. See, for example, Michael Hollington, *Günter Grass: The Writer in a Pluralist Society* (London: Marion Boyars, 1980), 151–52, and Dieter Stolz, *Vom privaten Motivkomplex zum poetischen Weltentwurf: Konstanten und Entwicklungen im literarischen Werk von Günter Grass (1956–1986)* (Würzburg: Königshausen & Neumann, 1994), 292, 306. Another view regards the the image as a symbol for SPD reform politics. See Jürgen Rothenberg, *Günter Grass: Das Chaos in verbesserter Ausführung; Zeitgeschichte als Thema und Aufgabe des Prosawerks* (Heidelberg: Carl Winter, 1976), 142. Ann L. Mason and W. G. Sebald have produced the most probing analyses of melancholy in the *Tagebuch*. Mason links melancholy to Grass's discourse on the mind: "The Artist and Politics in Günter Grass' *Aus dem Tagebuch einer Schnecke*," in *Critical Essays on Günter Grass*, ed. Patrick O' Neill (Boston, MA: Hall, 1987), 70–71. Sebald questions Grass's use of melancholy as a representative mode for coming to terms with the Nazi past: Sebald, "Konstruktionen der Trauer: Günter Grass und Wolfgang Hildesheimer," in *Campo Santo*, ed. Sven Meyer (Munich: Hanser, 2003), 118–19.

8 Panofsky and Saxl, *Dürers Melencolia I*.

9 I refer to the Günter Grass Archiv, Stiftung Archiv der Akademie der Künste, Berlin, no. 178. For an overview of the significance of food in Grass's work see Volker Neuhaus and Anselm Weyer, eds., *Küchenzettel: Essen und Trinken im Werk von Günter Grass*. None of the contributions discuss food and melancholy, although Julian Preece, with reference to the baroque, places Grass's treatment of food in its literary-historical context: "Kann die Nahrung Sünde sein? Schonkost und Festessen im Barock: Von Grimmelshausen zu Grass," in Neuhaus and Weyer, *Küchenzettel*, 95–107. Rothenberg connects cooking to melancholy but does not

explore this in the *Tagebuch*. Rothenberg, *Günter Grass: Das Chaos in verbesserter Ausführung*, 159.

[10] SAdK, Günter Grass Archiv, no. 170. Stolz's analysis of love in the work also does not consider melancholy and love. Stolz, *Vom privaten Motivkomplex*, 299. On love melancholy see Stanley W. Jackson, *Melancholia and Depression*, 352–72; Eleanor M. Sickels, *The Gloomy Egoist: Moods and Themes of Melancholy from Gray to Keats* (New York: Columbia University Press, 1932), chapter 5. On melancholy and digestion see Michael Schoenfeldt, *Bodies and Selves in Early Modern England: Physiology and Inwardness in Spenser, Shakespeare, Herbert, and Milton* (Cambridge: Cambridge University Press, 1999), 96–131.

[11] On the 1945 generation see A. Dirk Moses, *German Intellectuals and the Nazi Past* (Cambridge: Cambridge University Press, 2007), 9.

[12] Klaus Stallmann points out that in Grass's understanding of the Enlightenment, Lichtenberg is the inheritor of Montaigne's thought. Stallmann, "'Von der Beschaffenheit des Abgrunds': Nachwort zu den Gesprächen mit Günter Grass," in *Günter Grass: Werkausgabe in zehn Bänden*, 378.

[13] Winfried Schleiner's study on Renaissance genius and utopian thought provides an excellent way into these debates. Schleiner, *Melancholy, Genius, and Utopia*.

[14] On Grass as both a national and international writer see Rebecca Braun and Frank Brunssen, eds., *Changing the Nation: Günter Grass in International Perspective* (Würzburg: Königshausen & Neumann, 2008).

[15] Weber, *Günter Grass's Use of Baroque Literature*, 164–65.

[16] In a different context Rebecca Braun observes that Grass develops his self-conception as a socially significant world author "with reference to a grand list of intellectual forefathers." Braun, "Günter Grass as a World Author," in Braun and Brunssen, *Changing the Nation*, 200. For a summary of the intellectual melancholy traditions in which Grass can be placed see Hartmut Böhme, "Zur literarischen Rezeption von Albrecht Dürers Kupferstich *Melencolia I*," 106–8.

[17] See Grass, "Unser Grundübel ist der Idealismus," in *Günter Grass: Werkausgabe in zehn Bänden*, 9:392–94. Gertrude Cepl-Kaufmann points out the weakness of Grass's Hegel critique: Cepl-Kaufmann, *Günter Grass: Eine Analyse des Gesamtwerkes unter dem Aspekt von Literatur und Politik* (Kronberg: Scriptor, 1975), 115–18, while Hollington describes him as a fanatical moderate: *Günter Grass: The Writer in a Pluralist Society*, 131.

[18] *Der Butt* is a good example of this interest in cuisine and delivers on Grass's ambition, expressed in the *Tagebuch*, to write a narrative cookbook (*TB*, 53). See Markus Wallenborn, "Tell us what the children eat. . . Kinderlose Mütter und mutterlose Kinder im *Butt*," in Neuhaus and Weyer, *Küchenzettel*, 109–21.

[19] Grass, *Beim Häuten der Zwiebel*, 195–206. On the relationship between cooking and the artistic imagination see Neuhaus, ". . .über Menschen als Tiere, die kochen können: Kulinaristik bei Günter Grass," in *Küchenzettel*, ed. Neuhaus, Weyer, 9–19.

[20] Burton, *Anatomy of Melancholy*, 1:211–33.

[21] Ibid., 1:213.

²² See Schleiner, *Melancholy, Genius, and Utopia*, 98–100.

²³ Screech, *Montaigne and Melancholy: The Wisdom of the Essays* (London: Duckworth, 1983), 9–10. See also Schleiner, *Melancholy, Genius, and Utopia*, 178–81. Montaigne, "On the Power of the Imagination," in *The Essays of Michel de Montaigne*, 110. Burton, *Anatomy of Melancholy*, 1:253.

²⁴ The other two are the choleric and the phlegmatic types. On temperament theory see *SM*, 165–99.

²⁵ Weber argues along similar lines when he observes that the Stoic outlook and disposition are central to Grass's ideal conception of the artist. Weber, *Günter Grass's Use of Baroque Literature*, 83.

²⁶ Mason, "The Artist and Politics in Günter Grass' *Aus dem Tagebuch einer Schnecke*," 70–71. For more detail on Grass's reception of Mann see Hannelore Mundt, *Doktor Faustus und die Folgen: Kunstkritik als Gesellschaftskritik in deutschen Romanen seit 1947* (Bonn: Bouvier, 1989).

²⁷ Sebald, "Konstruktionen der Trauer, 114. Günter Blamberger makes the same point in his *Versuch über den deutschen Gegenwartsroman*, 138. Sebald's article was first published in an academic journal and is part of a divided critical discourse, which gained momentum through the 1980s, on the status of Grass's Jewish figures. Sebald, "Konstruktionen der Trauer," *Der Deutschunterricht* 35, no. 5 (1983): 32–46. See Julian Preece, "Günter Grass, His Jews and Their Critics: From Klüger and Gilman to Sebald and Prawer," in "Jews in German Literature since 1945: German-Jewish Literature?," ed. Pól O'Dochartaigh, special issue, *German Monitor* 53 (2000): 609–24.

²⁸ Günter Grass, "Phantasie als Existenznotwendigkeit," in *Günter Grass: Werkausgabe in zehn Bänden*, 10:256–57, and "Des Kaisers neue Kleider," ibid., 10:113. Hans-Jürgen Schings traces the secularization of the image of melancholy from religious enthusiasm to the sentimentality and *Weltschmerz* of *Sturm und Drang* and early Romanticism. Schings, *Melancholie und Aufklärung*, 246–48.

²⁹ Günter Grass, "Rede über das Selbstverständliche," in *Günter Grass: Werkausgabe in zehn Bänden*, 9:144, 150, and "Vom mangelnden Selbstvertrauen des schreibenden Hofnarren unter Berücksichtigung nicht vorhandener Höfe," ibid., 9:157–58.

³⁰ See Tellenbach, *Melancholy*, 17–18.

³¹ On the Graveyard Poets see Sickels, *The Gloomy Egoist*, 32–33. Also Amy Louise Reed, *The Background of Gray's Elegy: A Study in the Taste for Melancholy Poetry, 1700–1751* (New York: Russell & Russell, 1962).

³² On alchemy and melancholy see Schleiner, *Melancholy, Genius, and Utopia*, 91–92.

³³ Friedrich Hegel, Letter to Friedrich Immanuel Niethammer, Oct. 13, 1806, in *Briefe von und an Hegel, 1785–1812*, 3 vols., ed. Johannes Hofmeister (Hamburg: Felix Meiner, 1961), 1:120. Nietzsche, *Zur Genealogie der Moral*, in *Werke in drei Bänden*, ed. Karl Schlechta (Munich: Carl Hanser, 1966), 2:866. On Nietzsche's concepts of disgust see Winfried Menninghaus, *Ekel: Theorie und Gefühl einer starken Empfindung* (Frankfurt am Main: Suhrkamp, 1999), 225–74.

³⁴ See Stuart Taberner, *Distorted Reflections: The Public and Private Uses of the Author in the Work of Uwe Johnson, Günther Grass, and Martin Walser, 1965–1975* (Amsterdam: Rodopi, 1998), 79.

³⁵ Rebecca Braun, *Constructing Authorship in the Work of Günter Grass* (Oxford: Oxford University Press, 2008), 126–27. Taberner, *Distorted Reflections*, 78, 83.

³⁶ Günter Grass, "Phantasie als Existenznotwendigkeit," in *Günter Grass: Werkausgabe*, 10:256.

³⁷ The "Prinzip Zweifel" has much in common with the principle of "Vergegenkunft" (pastpresentfuture) that features as an ethical memory concept for the post-Holocaust world in Grass's Frankfurt lecture of 1990. Günter Grass, *Schreiben nach Auschwitz: Frankfurter Poetik-Vorlesung* (Frankfurt am Main: Luchterhand, 1990), 33–34. Grass mentions "Vergegenkunft" for the first time in the novel of 1980, *Kopfgeburten oder die Deutschen sterben aus* (Göttingen, Steidl: 2003), 127.

³⁸ On the *Tatmensch* see Lepenies, "Introduction," in *Melancholie und Gesellschaft*, xvii–iii.

³⁹ Schopenhauer, *Die Welt als Wille und Vorstellung in zwei Teilbänden*, ed. Arthur Hübscher (Zurich: Diogenes, 1977), 2:489.

⁴⁰ Stolz, *Vom privaten Motivkomplex zum poetischen Weltentwurf*, 310–11.

⁴¹ Sebald, "Konstruktionen der Trauer," 113. Preece, "Günter Grass, His Jews and Their Critics," *German Monitor* 53 (2000): 619.

⁴² Grass uses many melancholy references to water: the concentration camp Stutthof is built on watery land between an estuary and a lagoon; many of Danzig's Jews escape to Palestine by boat, which captures the melancholy motifs of seafaring and travel; water and tidal flow are the backdrop to a conversation about *Melencolia I* between the narrator and Zweifel in the contemporary part of the diary. Grass, *Tagebuch*, respectively 117, 124, 176–80.

⁴³ Böhme, *Albrecht Dürer*, 9–11.

⁴⁴ See Willem van Reijen, "Einleitung," in *Allegorie und Melancholie*, ed. Willem van Reijen (Frankfurt am Main: Suhrkamp, 1992), 7–16.

⁴⁵ SAdK, Günter Grass Archiv, no. 170.

⁴⁶ On landscape melancholy see Helen Watanabe-O' Kelly, *Melancholie und die melancholische Landschaft*, 80; Reed, *The Background of Gray's Elegy*, 177.

⁴⁷ Morton W. Bloomfield, *The Seven Deadly Sins: An Introduction to the History of a Religious Concept with Special Reference to Medieval English Literature* (Ann Arbor: Michigan State College Press, 1952), 248.

⁴⁸ Volker Neuhaus argues that Grass's allegorical style invites over-interpretation; however, Neuhaus's reading of the *Tagebuch* is underpinned by a biographical approach that does not consider the mediating function of allegory and that reduces the role of the snail to Grass's political message. Neuhaus, *Günter Grass* (Stuttgart: Metzler, 1993), 23.

⁴⁹ See Schiesari, *The Gendering of Melancholia*, 1–32.

⁵⁰ Braun points to the snail's autobiographical significance: the narrator describes himself (*Tagebuch*, 70) as "der Mensch gewordene Schnecke." Braun, *Constructing Authorship*, 112–17. Schiesari, *The Gendering of Melancholia*, 15, 32.

51 Neuhaus's analysis is representative for this tendency. Neuhaus, *Günter Grass*, 124. See also Stolz, *Vom privaten Motivkomplex zum poetischen Weltentwurf*, 299–300.

52 Wenzel, *The Sin of Sloth*, 47–52. On the connection between melancholy and carnival see Peter Sillem, "'der du gedeihen läßt und zerstörst': Melancholie, Karneval und die zwei Gesichter des Saturn," in "Saturns Spuren: Aspekte des Wechselspiels von Melancholie und Volkskultur in der Frühen Neuzeit," special issue, *Zeitsprünge: Forschungen zur Frühen Neuzeit* 5, no. 1/2 (2001): 9–23. Mikhail Bakhtin, *Rabelais and his World*, trans. Hélène Iswolsky (Bloomington, IN: Indiana University Press, 1984).

53 Hildegard of Bingen, "Melancholia in Men and Women," in Radden, *The Nature of Melancholy*, 81.

54 My reading concurs with Weber's interpretation of the snail as a Stoic emblem of the ideal artist between "inner tranquillity and public political commitment." Weber, *Günter Grass's Use of Baroque Literature*, 36.

55 Burton, *Anatomy of Melancholy*, 1:232.

56 Mason singles out *örtlich betäubt* (Göttingen: Steidl, 1969) as the work in which Grass comes closest to conducting a Platonic critique of the imagination as something disruptive to the social order. Ann L. Mason, *The Skeptical Muse: A Study of Günter Grass' Conception of the Artist* (Bern: Lang, 1974), 123.

57 Neuhaus, *Günter Grass*, 125.

58 Hollington, *Günter Grass: The Writer in a Pluralist Society*, 131.

59 Thorsten Valk, *Melancholie im Werk Goethes: Genese—Symptomatik—Therapie* (Tübingen: Niemeyer, 2002), 47. My reading of the cellar theatre in this mode contradicts Keith Miles, who argues that art brings out the best in all three characters. Miles, *Günter Grass* (London: Vision, 1975), 21.

60 See Claudia Mayer-Iswandy, *"Vom Glück der Zwitter": Geschlechterrolle und Geschlechtsverhältnis bei Günter Grass* (Frankfurt am Main: Lang, 1991), 15; Barbara Garde, "'Die Frauengasse ist eine Gasse, durch die man lebenslang geht': Frauen in den Romanen von Günter Grass," *Text + Kritik* 1 (1978): 105. See also Stolz, *Vom privaten Motivkomplex zum poetischen Weltentwurf*, 299.

61 On biopolitics and National Socialist eugenics see Giorgio Agamben, *Homo Sacer: Sovereign Power and Bare Life*, trans. Daniel Heller-Rozen (Stanford, CA: Stanford University Press, 1998).

62 On the "big disgust" see Nietzsche, *Zur Genealogie der Moral* 2:866; on "Erkenntnis" see his *Jenseits von Gut und Böse*, 2:591–92; on Hamlet see his *Die Geburt der Tragödie*, 1:48–49.

63 Burton, *Anatomy of Melancholy*, 1:213–14. Nietzsche describes German idealism in terms of poor cuisine. Nietzsche, *Ecce Homo*, 2:1082–85.

64 Nietzsche, *Ecce Homo*, 2:1083; also *Jenseits von Gut und Böse*, 2:711. The fictitious meeting in *Der Butt* between baroque poets Andreas Gryphius and Martin Opitz brings out these oppositional tendencies of the artistic temperament: Gryphius embodies creative ecstasy, Opitz a tendency to unproductive introspection and sloth. Grass, *Der Butt* (Göttingen: Steidl, 2007), 282.

⁶⁵ Nietzsche, *Also sprach Zarathustra*, 2:506, and *Zur Genealogie der Moral*, 2:770. The motif of regurgitation crops up in Grass's description of the eternal return of the Nazi past as a blocked toilet in *Im Krebsgang* (Göttingen: Steidl, 2002), 116.

⁶⁶ Benjamin, *Ursprung des deutschen Trauerspiels*.

⁶⁷ Thomas Pfau, *Romantic Moods*, 327. Benjamin, *Ursprung des deutschen Trauerspiels*, 194. On allegory more generally see Jesse M. Gellrich, "Allegory and Materiality: Medieval Foundations of the Modern Debate," in "Reformulating Allegory: Literature, Theory, Film," ed. Susanne Knaller, special issue, *Germanic Review* 77, no. 2 (2002): 146–59. See also Northrop Frye, *The Anatomy of Criticism: Four Essays* (Princeton, NJ: Princeton University Press, 1957), 89–91.

⁶⁸ De Man, "The Rhetoric of Temporality," in *Interpretation: Theory and Practice*, ed. Charles S. Singleton (Baltimore, MD: Johns Hopkins University Press, 1969), 173–209; Gadamer, *Wahrheit und Methode: Grundzüge einer philosophischen Hermeneutik* (Tübingen: Mohr, 1960), 66–76. See also Angus Fletcher, *Allegory: The Theory of a Symbolic Mode* (Ithaca, NY, Cornell University Press, 1964), 1–23.

⁶⁹ See Burkhardt Lindner, "Allegorie," in *Benjamins Begriffe*, 2 vols., ed. Michael Opitz and Erdmut Wizisla (Frankfurt am Main: Suhrkamp, 2000), 53. De Man, "The Rhetoric of Temporality," 174.

⁷⁰ See Kathleen Wheeler, ed., *German Aesthetic and Literary Criticism: The Romantic Ironists and Goethe* (Cambridge: Cambridge University Press, 1984), 9–11; Cyrus Hamlin, *Hermeneutics of Form: Romantic Poetics in Theory and Practice* (New Haven, CN: Schwab, 1998), 275–87. Sebald, "Konstruktionen der Trauer," 114. On the function of baroque allegory as a distancing medium for historical complexity in Grass's work see Weber, *Günter Grass's Use of Baroque Literature*, 89–98.

⁷¹ Benjamin, *Urprsung des deutschen Trauerpiels*, 171, 268.

⁷² SAdK, Günter Grass Archiv, no. 172. The murderous potential of fish recalls Agnes Matzerath's infamous death by fish consumption in Grass's *Die Blechtrommel* (Darmstadt: Luchterhand, 1959), 190–91.

⁷³ Benjamin, *Das Passagenwerk*, 2 vols., ed. Rolf Tiedemann (Frankfurt am Main: Suhrkamp, 1982), 1:614–5. Böhme, *Albrecht Dürer*, 44. See also Lindner, "Allegorie," 78–81.

⁷⁴ De Man, "The Rhetoric of Temporality," 190–91. See also Michael Kahl, "Der Begriff der Allegorie in Benjamins Trauerspielbuch und im Werk Paul de Mans," in van Reijen, *Melancholie und Allegorie*, 299–300, 305.

⁷⁵ Stolz, *Vom privaten Motivkomplex*, 20.

⁷⁶ Stuart Taberner points out that Grass exploits the raw material of his person, both public and private, in order to achieve this constructed self-image. Taberner, *Distorted Reflections*, 28. Similarly, Rebecca Braun argues that we cannot truly speak of autobiography in the *Tagebuch*. Braun, *Constructing Authorship*, 109.

⁷⁷ Braun, *Constructing Authorship*, 110–12.

⁷⁸ Améry, "Ressentiments," in *Jenseits von Schuld und Sühne: Bewältigungsversuche eines Überwältigten* (Stuttgart: Klett-Cotta, 1977), 114.

[79] Sebald, "Konstruktionen der Trauer," 111–12.
[80] Rothenberg, *Günter Grass: Das Chaos in verbesserter Ausführung*, 158.
[81] Mitscherlich and Mitscherlich, *Die Unfähigkeit zu trauern*.
[82] Nietzsche, *Also sprach Zarathustra*, 2:279–85.
[83] Heinz Ludwig Arnold, "Gespräche mit Günter Grass," in *Text + Kritik* 1 (1978): 5.

2: The Disenchanted Mind: Victim Melancholy in Wolfgang Hildesheimer's *Tynset* and *Masante*

From Genius to Sloth

Toward the end of Wolfgang Hildesheimer's novel *Tynset* (1965), the insomniac first-person narrator ponders the contents of his kitchen cupboard as he teeters between wakefulness and fitful bursts of sleep.[1] Mentally listing different combinations of mixed dried herbs, he concludes that a specific assortment containing rosemary would never sell in Germany. A herb that Shakespeare's Ophelia links to the power of memory, rosemary is simply not a German affair.[2] Nor is garlic, the narrator muses, for "deutsche Esser" (German eaters) prefer to have pure breath. From an unidentified place of self-elected exile he remembers the German man who imparted this to him, someone he once met arbitrarily on a train and who subsequently became famous for his surgical skill. During the war this random acquaintance transplanted the hip bones of "a few" Danes to "a few" Germans. Whether the Danes in question were alive or dead at the time remains open to speculation. Having thus implied that this perhaps pioneering medical procedure was, in fact, an exercise in butchery, the narrator interrupts his disturbing train of thought and returns to his mixed herbs, concluding that there is certainly no question of *his* forgetting anything. Some punctuation—a dash—then indicates that he has drifted off to sleep, but by the next paragraph he is abruptly awake, convinced that a murderer lurks outside his bedroom window. This local projection of evil swiftly assumes cosmic dimensions as the apprehension of a far greater omnipresent evil. The narrator's response to this sense of vague but certain terror is a terrible passivity: he can do nothing to prevent the proliferation of obscure but pernicious forces. Lying flat on his back and staring with unseeing eyes at his bedroom ceiling, he exhaustedly accepts his future fate at the mercy of whatever awaits him.

This passage appears at an advanced stage in a narrative that tells the tale of a single night of insomniac wandering and pondering in a remote, mountainous region where winter seems to reign permanently. The narrator's meandering mind, which moves between imaginative escapism and the oppressive bonds of memory, is both the subject and medium of this monologue novel. Although the style of narration is fragmentary and tends toward abstraction, from an early point the reader is given a clear motivation for his flight into obscurity from postwar West Germany. Reviled by the presence of unrepentant former Nazi perpetrators, he left the country eleven years before the point in time when the narrative commences, 1963 or 1964 (*T*, 10). The image of clean breath along with the symbolic absence of rosemary from German cuisine is, from the viewpoint of an individual whose father, we later learn, was murdered by the Nazis, a bitter assessment of the paucity of *Vergangenheitsbewältigung* in the West German state (*T*, 156).[3] As a memory image that evokes collective repression and denial, odorless breath could not be further removed from the tallow-covered teeth of Günter Grass's chewing narrator in *Aus dem Tagebuch einer Schnecke*. This figure embodies an ideal of ethical memory determined to ingest—and remember—the unpleasantness of the German past. In *Tynset* there is no sense that West German memory culture will take Grass's cue and start to chew thoughtfully over the damaged past. Instead, the bitter taste of the past is the *victim*'s lot.

Tynset and its sequel, *Masante* (1973), are narrated from the perspective of the Holocaust victim-survivor. Accordingly, melancholy discourse in both novels is fundamentally different from the melancholy of Grass's *Tagebuch*.[4] Grass subverts images from genial melancholy to create for collective consumption an ideal memory model for ethical *Vergangenheitsbewältigung* based on a sober concept of the imagination. His narrator, as palatable artistic-intellectual persona and dedicated citizen, embodies these qualities. Putting in a good word for melancholy, to paraphrase the narrator, also means doing public-relations work for a certain concept of *Vergangenheitsbewältigung* and for the public intellectual who has perpetrator skeletons in his personal closet, but who despite or because of this wishes to pioneer a better way of thinking about guilt and responsibility. The dialectics of melancholy between action and inaction circumscribe this attempt at ethical memory. Divided between political activism and artistic reflection, the narrator repeatedly tries to transcend himself, demonstrating the idea of melancholy *Vergangenheitsbewältigung* as an open-ended process in the genial mode.[5]

The melancholy performative has a fundamentally different resonance in Hildesheimer's work. His adaptation of melancholy traditions for the postwar context evokes, from the *victim* perspective, the victim experience and creates an alternative intellectual identity of poetic nihilism. We encounter this figure in the passage discussed above, which invokes details from *Hamlet* in order to convey a sense of the victim's trauma. Moreover, this figure pursues, as Isabel Wagner observes, a deathly aesthetic or "Thanatapoetik," that nihilistically reflects on the redundancy of literary language after the Holocaust.[6] This chapter examines how Hildesheimer uses different melancholy traditions to voice the victim perspective and to convey a sense of caesura in literary representation after the Holocaust.

Hildesheimer was, like Grass, well versed in melancholy traditions. A study from the year 1966 that explores melancholy motifs in baroque poetry, for example, singles Hildesheimer out as the contemporary German master of *vanitas* and *memento mori*.[7] From an early point in his writerly career he was interested in the development of a postwar literary discourse that draws on existing forms of melancholy. As discussed in the introduction, he is the writer featured in Walter Jens's prose work *Herr Meister: Dialog über einen Roman*, which explores the possibilities of melancholy for developing an ethical literary discourse after the Holocaust. Alongside the fact that he had plans to write a Hamlet novel, *Herr Meister* provides us with further insight into the kind of material Hildesheimer was reading in the early 1960s.[8] Erwin Panofsky and Fritz Saxl's original iconographical study features as a source, as does George Cheynes's eighteenth-century work, *The English Malady* (1733).[9] Hildesheimer's erudition shows in the diversity of melancholy icons he invokes across the two novels, which account for the doleful atmosphere. These include references to weather systems, especially snow, coldness, and dryness, as well as autumn, which draw on stock qualities of the melancholy temperament (*T*, 50–51, 220, 236, 255–57; *M*, 11, 234–37), references to aging that evoke the four ages of man and the melancholy sufferer's position as an aging type within this scheme (*T*, 73; *M*, 135), the narrator's fondness for red wine, a typical melancholy beverage (*T*, 220–21; *M*, 45), and connotations of the black bile in the narrator's favorite painting, an image of blackness (*T*, 87). Others can be found in the depictions of instruments of measurement and astronomical references to the Renaissance genius in Albrecht Dürer's engraving of 1514, *Melencolia I* (*T*, 141–42, 177; *M*, 17); the narrator as a gardener who grows herbs, an activity typical for those born under the melancholy planet, Saturn (*T*, 9, 51, 160, 216; *M*, 230–31, 265); and references in both works to objects from the baroque *vanitas* and *memento mori* traditions (*T*, 133, 151, 175, 240; *M*, 252–54, 267, 376; *SM*, 48–49, 76–77, 212–13, 223, 232–33, 468).[10]

As indicated in the references to rosemary and Ophelia, Shakespeare's Hamlet, one of the most prominent embodiments of genial Renaissance melancholy and also a theme in *Herr Meister*, is a thread that runs through both *Tynset* and *Masante* (*T*, 20, 107, 146, 151, 155–60, 186; *M*, 218–24, 240–44).[11] Like Grass, Hildesheimer is interested in adapting genial melancholy as a template for ethical post-Holocaust memory. Consider that in act 1 of Shakespeare's play the ghost of Hamlet's father commands Hamlet to remember him, the victim of the evil deeds of others.[12] In many respects, *Hamlet* tells the story of the obligation of those who survive to commemorate and avenge the victim other, and the tragic consequences of this obligation. In *Tynset* and *Masante* the narrator, a Hamlet type, is also plagued by the regular appearance of the ghost of Hamlet's murdered father, an Elizabethan incarnation of the dead Holocaust victim. Hildesheimer thus draws on the "Renaissance episteme" of genial melancholy first and foremost to signal, from the victim survivor's perspective, an ethics of memory dedicated to the dead victims of the Holocaust. Second, while the narrator is an intellectual and an aesthete—Hamlet, too, is a scholar, having recently returned from a period of study in Luther's Wittenberg—Hildesheimer's adaptation emphasizes the passivity of this character, his lethargic and depressive moments, which reinforces the negative dimension of the melancholy dialectic between illness and empowerment and conveys the pathological consequences of victim trauma.[13] Significantly, he further darkens the "Renaissance episteme" of Hamlet by codifying the narrator as a sinner: both novels contain several images of *acedia*, the religious melancholy of the medieval period that looks back to the desert hermits of early Christian monasticism.[14] Through this combination of genial melancholy with *acedia*, the accolades of nobility, intellect, and artistic sensibility ultimately give way to the guilt and self-recrimination of the slothful melancholy sinner. In this highly original way, Hildesheimer conveys the torment of the Holocaust victim survivor.

Hildesheimer's codification of Hamlet's sloth and passivity through the image of the forsaken Christian sinner might seem unusual in novels that treat the experience of German-Jewish victimization during and after the Holocaust. However, the melancholy tradition of *acedia* describes an almost unbearable state of human existence without hope of redemption, which renders it a powerful icon for the representation of Holocaust survivor guilt. The idea of the absent God and ensuing existential void comes across strongly in *acedia*, which foreshadows the motif of the *deus absconditus* in German baroque poetry and also the literature of the absurd in the twentieth century.[15] Wagner points out that Hildesheimer's interest in the representation of nothingness must be read not just within the context of post-Holocaust language crisis but also within the broader context of the language skepticism of literary modernism.[16] However, the concept of the melancholy performative illuminates the extent to which his renderings of a caesura in representation after the Holocaust are indebted to much older discourses. Hildesheimer's use of the imagery of melancholy sin combined with genial melancholy radicalizes negativity into an uncompromising ethical commemoration of the Holocaust victims, which occurs through repeated contemplation of death and nothingness. He thus seems to favor melancholy over mourning as the appropriate mode for Holocaust memory, as if the incorporation of the lost object, symbolized, for example, by the restless specter, is the only means of honoring the dead other. It is this refusal to give up the lost object and to deny the existential void at the heart of postwar existence that lends his melancholy texts their radical tone. Like Grass, Hildesheimer strikes a melancholy pose and cites established traditions in order to do so. However, his message is one of tormented radicalism as opposed to redemptive compromise.

Ressentiment of the Melancholy Victim

Tynset and *Masante* are part of an emerging public discourse on the inner life of the victim subject, a discourse that thematized the failure of *Vergangenheitsbewältigung* in the 1950s and 1960s. In both novels the narrator's brooding perspective on the injustice of history has more in common with Austro-Jewish writer Jean Améry's concept of *ressentiment* (resentment) than with Grass's articulation of *Vergangenheitsbewältigung*. One year after the publication of *Tynset*, the term appeared in Améry's groundbreaking essay collection, *Jenseits von Schuld und Sühne: Bewältigungsversuch eines Überwältigten* (English title: *At the Mind's Limits: Contemplations by a Survivor on Auschwitz and Its Realities*).[17] Friedrich Nietzsche's theory of *ressentiment* provides the backdrop for Améry's development of the concept as a means of articulating the perspective of the forgotten victim in a post-conflict society. Nietzsche presents *ressentiment* as the pathological emotion of the weak, who blame others for their shortcomings.[18] *Ressentiment* in his thought conveys brooding, bitterness, and vengefulness, which, as Michael Ure puts it, "compels individuals to invent agents responsible for their suffering, and to magnify injuries beyond all proportion." For Nietzsche, it is a pathological disease that results from obsessive rumination about the past and ends in the scapegoating of others perceived to be stronger than the resentful self. Ure points out that Améry reverses this order, identifying "a monstrous crime as the cause and *ressentiment* as the effect" of the pathological position.[19] Here disease is the justified outcome of a wrong inflicted on the individual. In Améry's thought, moreover, *ressentiment* testifies to a moral truth about the past: victimization in the Holocaust and the evil of National Socialism. *Ressentiment* also expresses the victim's outrage at the brutality of a second victimization in the amnesiac post-conflict world. In the mode of *ressentiment*, the forgotten victim of history speaks about how she/he has had to witness the ascendance of former perpetrators in the era of Cold War global politics, where their crimes during National Socialism, for reasons of political expediency, are deliberately downplayed.

Améry's concept of the *ressentiment* of the Holocaust victim survivor provides the political context for the *Tynset* narrator's decision to leave West Germany in the early 1950s. Yet his existence in exile brings him little peace of mind: he broods continually about the Nazi criminals who literally got away with murder. In contrast to Nietzsche's outlook, where it is a sign of moral weakness, the narrator's *ressentiment* is ethically justified, and yet he exhibits the spleen of Nietzsche's bitter man of *ressentiment*. At first glance, this acerbity might seem to compromise his ethical standpoint. His identity as a ruminating, vengeful Hamlet also suggests further links to Nietzsche's version of the concept. According to Nietzsche, passive and overly contemplative individuals are more likely to develop *ressentiment* than the man of action.[20] The character of Hamlet, a brooding intellectual who notoriously hesitates to act, lends itself to the resenting mode. My discussion shows, however, that Hildesheimer's blending of Améry, Shakespeare, and *acedia* ultimately articulates an uncompromising and justifiably resentful ethical position. The narrator's *ressentiment*, moreover, does not blind him to his own flaws. As the Christian sinner of *acedia*, he internalizes the festering wound of *ressentiment* and, at the end of *Masante*, turns it on himself in an act of self-destruction.

In the world beyond the text, the West German intellectual milieu of the 1960s often failed to perceive the victim's discourse in the literary work and, in Hildesheimer's case, did not grasp the ethical importance of his poetics of melancholy *ressentiment*. Stephan Braese describes this as a "Verschiebungsdruck" (displacement impulse), articulated in many politically charged public misunderstandings of Jewish writers of the period.[21] At the time of their publication, *Tynset* and *Masante*, for example, were deemed esoteric and ahistorical, of little use for the discussion of postwar German society. West German literary critics did not recognize the "forensic moment" intrinsic to both works, their historical "facticity." Braese argues that this perspective trivializes, perhaps even denies, the voice of the victim in both works.[22] The "displacement impulse" of the West German literary milieu thus revealed the failure of this cohort to acknowledge that Hildesheimer's poetics of abstraction and *ressentiment* should be regarded as a groundbreaking and necessary political reflection on the victim experience and the possibilities of poetic language after Auschwitz. Instead, the blind spot reproduced in the literary sphere the widespread precedence over victim memory of German sensitivities concerning the memory of the war, despite the rhetoric of reconciliation with the victim other central to the project of *Vergangenheitsbewältigung*.[23]

Consistent with this general misreading, melancholy discourse in both works was judged by many critics to be pathological, decadent, and sick, a perspective that negatively acknowledges the importance of melancholy in Hildesheimer's work. In a review from 1965, Reinhard Baumgart, for example, accuses *Tynset* of self-indulgence. The title of his piece, "Schlaflos schluchzend" (sleeplessly sniveling), could hardly be clearer.[24] In a manner that anticipates some reactions to W. G. Sebald's later novel, *Die Ringe des Saturn*, Baumgart dismisses Hildesheimer's literary style as *Weltschmerz* rhetoric.[25] Worse still, he views the narrator as an unconvincing aesthetic creation, assembled from clichés, whose plaintive thoughts do not appear to be based in real experience. As Braese observes, this kind of reading passes over the juridical precision that Hildesheimer, who worked as an interpreter at the Nuremberg trials, demonstrates in describing Nazi crimes and in painting an image of the perpetrators.[26] Thus critics did not link Hildesheimer's brand of melancholy to historical experience, which marginalizes the victim's lament in his works.

The substantial field of scholarship on melancholy in Hildesheimer's work often reinforces the perspective of the early critics. Günter Blamberger, for example, regards Hildesheimer's melancholy as the expression of an anthropological constant. This view also does not make the connection between melancholy and recent history: the experience of victimization in the Holocaust and after. Instead, melancholy is the expression of a universal absurdity.[27] From a different angle, Dieter Goll-Bickmann argues that images of artistic creativity in both works modify the negativity of Hildesheimer's melancholy discourse. In this reading, the therapeutic act of creativity transcends the positions of failure and withdrawal, and mourning triumphs over melancholy nihilism.[28] Wagner's more nuanced reading identifies the ambivalence of *Tynset* and *Masante*, both of which are marked simultaneously by Thanatos, the narrator's desire for death and a space of nothingness beyond language, and Eros, his imaginative musings on music and other alternative forms of expression.[29] The tension between death and life instincts in the literary text mirrors the tension between the psychoanalytical concepts of melancholy as negation and mourning as working-through, but where Wagner argues that the world of the artistic imagination (Eros) rescues the narrator from the sociopolitical present (Thanatos), I suggest that his imaginative flights of fancy often reinforce his sense of entrapment. *Tynset* and *Masante* display the disenchanted mind, the impression that after the Holocaust language and the powers of the imagination have fallen into a crisis that ends in silence. That Hildesheimer combines Hamlet and the sinner of *acedia* supports this reading, for in so doing he questions both the concept of genius as a form of exceptional self-overcoming and, with that, the project of remembrance conceived as the success story of "mourning work."

This chapter shows how Hildesheimer draws on melancholy traditions to get across the "resenting" perspective of the victim. For *Tynset* and *Masante* remind us that post-1945 West German memory culture was still morally defective in the 1960s, the continuing existence of untried perpetrators in this society just one instance of this failure. Through the melancholy mindset of *acedia*, *ressentiment*, and aristocratic sloth, we encounter the ongoing trauma and quiet rage of the Jewish other. The narrator is an aging misanthropist, of family there is little mention, and past relationships have become fuzzy outgrowths of a memory fixated on the transitory. This morose figure is alone in the world, and the monologic structure, in particular of *Tynset*, communicates his solipsism. In a pattern that suggests a lack of healing, the narrator's retreatism has, by *Masante*, become yet more radical: he exchanges his dwelling in the lofty heights of the remote alpine region in *Tynset* for the vast expanse of the desert into which he disappears at the end of *Masante*.[30] Thus Hildesheimer's solution to the problem of history, as it strikes the victim psyche, is an act of self-effacement, which points to the other function that melancholy discourse has in both novels: to thematize the problem of literary poetics and the representation of caesura in the post-Holocaust work.

The final scene of *Masante* was intended as a statement on the exhaustion of literary fiction after the Holocaust. Hildesheimer describes this scene, where the narrator wanders into the desert, never to return, in terms of the end of fiction.[31] After *Masante*, he ceased to write fiction, experimenting instead with the genre of biography, which ultimately also revealed the limitations of language's ability to convey truth.[32] His reason for announcing the end of fiction was his view that the absurdity of an increasingly apocalyptic reality in the late twentieth century had exceeded the representative terms of fiction to the extent that the writer's imagination faced a serious challenge in trying to identify, through "transposition," Hildesheimer's term for artistic transformation, some truth about this reality.[33] Taken as a whole, *Tynset* and *Masante* narrate the end of fictional narration, the limitations and redundancy of language in the face of historical experience that cannot be made sense of and overcome. A metadiscourse on the literary representation of caesura is thus inseparable from Hildesheimer's combination of genial with religious melancholy.

Beyond Consolation: Dimension Auschwitz

Hildesheimer once described the challenge faced by poetic language and representation after the Holocaust as the "Dimension Auschwitz."[34] Through melancholy, he engages with Theodor W. Adorno's "dictum" that poetry after Auschwitz is barbaric and debates, in *poetic* fashion, the tension between literary language and historical representation.[35] The novel's self-reflexive prose communicates that literature, in view of the challenges issued to cultural representation after the Holocaust, must rethink the relationship between aesthetics and political-ethical engagement. Reflecting on Adorno, Hildesheimer observes that his interest in literary abstraction and "Phantasieprodukte" (products of the imagination) is a critical response to, and not a denial of, these challenges. From this viewpoint, the melancholy "pathology" of the *Tynset* and *Masante* narrator should be understood with reference to the problem of language and reality that is rooted in the historical precedent of the Holocaust. As the symptom of a greater problem that it tries to articulate, the narrator's "decadence," or "sickness" is historically founded.[36] In this political sense, we might say that Hildesheimer's use of melancholy, as well as expressing the trauma of the marginalized victim, also signals circumspection, on the meta-narrative level, about the problems facing literature after Auschwitz. This circumspection is apparent in what Braese describes as the "discursive discipline" Hildesheimer imposes on the *Tynset* and *Masante* narrator who, in acknowledgement of Adorno's "dictum," does not speak directly of the Holocaust, but points continually to its unspeakability.[37] The age-old ambivalence concerning the cause of the melancholy mood is one way in which Hildesheimer evokes this caesura. Mood often overwhelms the factual basis of the narratives, and thus the narrator's pathology seems to lack the alibi of a convincing lost object, leaving him open to accusations of ahistoricism and self-indulgence. In fact, this very ambivalence is the broken signifier of caesura, as I show in my discussion of the place-name "Tynset." Both works are steeped in history, but narrate it in a fragmented and episodic fashion. Abstraction permits the evocation of history and its aftermath in an *indirect* way; this is a deliberate aesthetic-political agenda that arises from Hildesheimer's skepticism about the idea of a straightforwardly "narratable" history.[38]

Another way in which Hildesheimer addresses the caesura of representation after the Holocaust is by rejecting the consolation of teleological narratives. The concept of "poetic nihilism," developed by Karl-Heinz Bohrer to theorize a literary language that imagines death without compensation, is useful for describing this radicalism. Shunning narratives that, by virtue of their orientation toward a better future, imply a way out of cultural pessimism, the poetic nihilist abandons any attempt to console the self with narratives of historical salvation. This thinker rejects teleology and can tolerate the thought of her/his own demise without the comfort of transcendence. The poetic nihilist looks away from misleading grand historical narratives that imply progress and resolution, focusing instead on the world of small, incidental objects that constitute reality devoid of illusions. This places her/him in the absurdity of historical contingency, which marks out an ethical position different from the religious or ideological outlook, because it does not entertain illusions and untruths about the bleak nature of human existence.[39]

Hildesheimer's narrator, who distracts himself from the impossible task of solving history by focusing on smaller matters, occupies this contingent space of absurdity. Grass's *Tagebuch* offers a further point of contrast on the matter of cognitive focus: while the artist-narrator of this work occupies his mind with everyday concerns, he is not a poetic nihilist. This is principally because of the orientation toward the future of his political endeavors. Grass's future vision might be moderate, in that it shies away from extreme visions, favoring instead an idea of compromise, but even this idea of compromise is underpinned by a concept of social progress and social improvement. The same cannot be said of Hildesheimer's work, for here the space of historical contingency is always a space of death that prevents orientation toward the future.

Given this historically grounded skepticism of narrative forms, it is little wonder that the presentation of a depressed subjective state of mind with no clear cure takes center stage in both works. As a terminal melancholic, the narrator rejects consolatory narratives that provide explanations for otherwise inexplicable suffering. In line with this rejection of teleological systems, there is no evident meta-narrative on the possible causes of this suffering. The reader must piece together fragments in order to divine why the narrator has become so nihilistic. Both novels thus display a phenomenology of melancholy, a snapshot of the disturbed mind that resonates with theories of melancholy that focus especially on the psychological state of the individual subject.

Between Absence and Loss: Ambivalences of Post-Auschwitz Melancholy

Tynset and *Masante* combine the narrative of loss with the narrative of absence, which weakens the sense that the narrator's depression has a sociohistorical origin and is not the manifestation of a personal pathology. This ambivalence points to the difficulty of constructing a language that would capture the Holocaust and its traumatic consequences for the individual.

As outlined in the introduction, Dominick LaCapra argues that a melancholy position on history confuses absence and loss and invokes a mythical understanding of historical catastrophe. Drawing on Sigmund Freud, he favors mourning as the appropriate form of ethical memory for the victims of history. Melancholy, which fails to identify a concrete loss in the past, articulates a problematic language of absence that risks blurring the distinctions between the real victims of history and others who vicariously identify with the victim. By contrast, mourning, which takes place through the language of historical loss, helps to keep victim and non-victim identities distinct from one another.[40]

Hildesheimer's work cannot be fully explained by resorting to these categories. The theoretical binary opposition between melancholy and mourning breaks down in both novels. This is why the narratives articulate loss and absence simultaneously, questioning whether the work of healing can take place and communicating the subjective experience of catastrophic time.[41] The narrator does not appear to have suffered violence at the hands of the Nazis. However, he knows many individuals who did, including his father. Part of his problem with trying to conceptualize the Holocaust arises through his absence from an event that destroyed so many people close to him and that continues to affect him for what is presented as an eternity in both novels. A conflict arises between his need, on the one hand, to grasp and understand intellectually a history that he did not experience first-hand—to get a handle on the lost object, so to speak—and, on the other, his desire ultimately to repress this traumatic history. In other words, part of him prefers to treat as unidentified the lost object: Europe's dead Jews and the fact of the Holocaust. It is as if he cannot bear to look at the specific details that constitute genocide. His moroseness thus often suppresses the greater historical picture of which it is the consequence, as if the melancholy we encounter is in fact the sufferer's fault. Hildesheimer combines two registers in these works, the subjective-esoteric and the historical, to produce a dream-like narrative that confuses the narrative of loss with the narrative of absence.

The Hamlet motif eloquently conveys this complex. Hildesheimer's first-person narrator in both novels could be described as a reluctant Hamlet-type. The first time the ghost of Hamlet's father appears in *Tynset*, the narrator is at pains to avoid his gaze and wants to have nothing to do with potential demands of vengeance (*T*, 20). Here the narrator rejects the role of avenger that Shakespeare's hero assumed. Toward the end of *Masante* he is still at pains to differentiate between himself and Hamlet, stating that the name is wrong because two separate entities, father and son, cannot have the same name (*M*, 223). This is an absurd statement that only makes sense within the context of Holocaust memory. If we understand the ghost of Hamlet's father as a literary embodiment of the ghost of the narrator's murdered father—a Holocaust victim—then it becomes clear why two entities may not share the same name: in a way that evokes Primo Levi's distinction between those Holocaust victims who perished and those who survived, the narrator in *Masante* cannot share the dead victim's name because he did not die as did his father.[42]

Part of the narrator's problem with the ghost of Hamlet's father thus arises through his painful sense of his own historical absenteeism. His furtive perception and rapid disavowal of the ghost of Hamlet's father illustrates this conflict: the tragic Shakespearean murder victim mediates in a familiar-strange fashion the figure of the Holocaust victim. In this way, the ghost of Hamlet's father embodies ethical memory: the specter functions as a kind of literary mnemonic prompt in the task of attempting to imagine the unimaginable. We could say that the Renaissance episteme, "Hamlet," underscores the obligation to remember history's victims.

The guilty perspective of the German-Jewish other who was absent from the Holocaust explains further why Hildesheimer's language of melancholy is more radical than that developed by Grass. Grass transforms the negativity of melancholy into a positive model of the sober mind for the greater emotional and psychological good of West German society. In this view, melancholy, once divorced from its disturbing Romantic predecessors and the clinical idea of its unfathomable psychological motivators, does not need to be healed: melancholy itself is a healing force.[43] One could even say that in making melancholy a snail, Grass robs it of its pathological dimension and renders it harmless. Hildesheimer, on the other hand, makes the pathology of the melancholy condition the central tenet of *Tynset* and *Masante*. In this context, any notion of healing must appear trite. These narratives are dedicated to the expression of pathological disturbance. Moreover, this is what gives them their ethical substance in a position on the past that rejects healing, normalization, and compensation. The two novels narrate failure, in contrast to the *Tagebuch*, which holds to a vision of success, despite Grass's discourse to the contrary.[44]

The Absurd Temporality of *Ressentiment*

Ressentiment is absurd primarily because the anger expressed therein dictates that nothing short of turning back the clock will do to make amends for suffering inflicted. In other words, the wound cannot be healed, because the resenting victim's demand can never be met. In this sense, *ressentiment* is a wrathful version of melancholy between absence and loss. The root of the suffering is clear but it cannot be made good, and so the affected must linger indefinitely in a limbo of absurdity.[45]

In *Tynset*, the movement of the narrator's thoughts between the evocation (loss) and erasure (absence) of historical events conveys this absurdity. He appears to introduce recent history onto his narrative canvas only to blot it out. As a poetic nihilist he refuses to compromise his melancholy by translating his sense of horror into a normalizing narrative that would imply that history has been "overcome." Instead, he diverts his attention to less challenging phenomena, such as dried herbs or cloud formations (*T*, 47). Contingent objects are therefore always the indirect signifiers of absence. They express the rejection of consolation and the persistence of a sense of *ressentiment* for crimes unanswered. In this manner, objects are absurd. They reinforce the sense that the narrator is stuck in the melancholy trap of history, the time-warp of victim experience between absence and loss.

In a rare passage that addresses the Holocaust directly, the narrator remembers a Jewish woman, Doris Wiener, who underwent cosmetic surgery in order to conceal her racial origins. It could not prevent her fate, alongside her husband, in the gas chambers of the extermination camps (*T*, 62–63). Abruptly, however, the narrator changes the focus of his thoughts and for a prolonged sequence describes a vision of himself on top of the Acropolis in Athens, listening to the cockcrow dawn chorus across Attica (*T*, 63–70).[46]

Absurdity is also evident in the narrator's obsessive need to submit systems and structures—timetables, phonebooks, calendars—to rigorous examination: the verb "to test" (*prüfen*) is a refrain throughout both works (*T*, 35, 41; *M*, 24, 57, 69, 92). This activity is pointless, even masochistic, for he is always reassured, no matter what system he is testing, that unrepentant perpetrators are omnipresent. In *Masante* religious name-day calendars reveal the names of guilty individuals, as does the narrator's phonebook in *Tynset*, while train timetables evoke memories of persecution and raise the specter of deportation. The narrator's "testing" activity thus confirms the status quo: a world marked by unrepentant criminality. As such, "testing" is fundamentally a marker of the victim's experience of time as absurd. It is also a sign of defeat that leads to the narrator's permanent departure from the world at the end of *Masante*, reinforcing his identity as a poetic nihilist who can, to paraphrase Bohrer, irreversibly "take leave" of the world.[47] Even more fundamentally, the narrator's compulsion bleakly to scrutinize objects in this way is a sign of the impoverished mind, the creative capacities of which have been inhibited by recent history. In *Masante*, for example, he describes his testing mind as an "Inventarium" (inventory, *M*, 67).

The tension between focus and distraction points to a further effect of the narrative's rejection of teleological versions of recent history: the problem of epistemology after the Holocaust. The narrator's thoughts circumvent what is evoked as the unknowable lack of the Holocaust, the "Dimension Auschwitz." Hildesheimer develops a narrative that thematizes not just the limits of the imagination in the face of an event like the Holocaust, but also its redundancy, which is poignantly and bitterly captured in the image of an inventory. In *Tynset* and *Masante*, thoughts on representation, imagination, and memory are channeled through an established melancholy type whose suffering arises through the failure of genial powers: the inability to transcend the epistemological limits of the world she/he inhabits. The alignment of this type with the problem of imagining the Holocaust is the subject of the next section.

The Disenchanted Mind

In *Tynset*, the narrator's nocturnal trail takes him to a lofty room full of scientific instruments of measurement and observation. In this *mise-en-scène* Hildesheimer borrows from established melancholy stock, for the instruments of geometrical examination and astronomical enquiry are traditional iconographic signifiers of the melancholy condition. Together they articulate what Klibansky et al. term the "typus Geometriae," the geometrical type who is a bad metaphysician and remains trapped in a limited creaturely space that she/he can measure and examine, but never transcend. The instruments of knowledge and discovery are, paradoxically, also melancholy symbols of epistemological limitation. As tools for the discovery of the finite world they are ill-equipped to deliver information about worlds that escape spatiotemporal definition. Klibansky et al. argue that the winged figure in Dürer's *Melencolia I*, slumped, brooding, and surrounded by the idle instruments of geometry, articulates this conundrum: the disappointed epistemological ambition of the genius who desires to understand more but is thwarted by the limitations of the mathematical mind (*SM*, 485–512). Echoing this problem of knowledge and the unknowable, the *Tynset* narrator peers through a telescope into the night sky and tries to locate a space of nothingness between the individual stars (*T*, 180–81). Pinpointing the space of nothingness proves impossible, however, and the narrator leaves the room to continue his listless shuffle. The novel's poetics suggest that the impossible idea of nothingness corresponds to the impossible idea of the Holocaust. Here we can see how Hildesheimer's melancholy performative frames the problem of knowledge after the Holocaust through the aspect of despondency captured in Dürer's Renaissance genius, emphasizing the moment of failure in the dialectics of melancholy between illness and empowerment.

In Jens's earlier work, *Herr Meister*, Hildesheimer refers to Henry of Ghent, a thirteenth-century scholastic who identified a *mathematical* melancholy type, as an intellectual source for the character Herr Meister, a witness to the crimes of National Socialism.[48] In his study of the melancholy personality, Hubertus Tellenbach discusses how Henry of Ghent describes the *typus melancholicus* as a personality who accesses knowledge through the spatial notions on which mathematics is based: "whatever they think of must have extension, or as the geometrical point, occupy a position in space." This type can think or anticipate only "within the spatio-temporal forms of visualization." In other words, she/he is bound to physical space and finite temporality, even if she/he can apprehend, but not know, the possibility of space and time beyond known categories of existence. Despite their special gifts, these individuals cannot transcend the world they inhabit: they can sense it, but they cannot think it.[49]

Tellenbach discusses a second *metaphysical* type that Henry of Ghent identifies. This type can grasp abstract ideas, transcend the world of spatiotemporal actuality, and imagine something else beyond it. Of note for the analysis of Hildesheimer's novels is the implication that the metaphysical type, because it can mentally transcend the limitations of the creaturely world and imagine an alternative spatiotemporal existence, possesses a religious ability. It follows that the metaphysical-religious thinker, in contrast to her/his spatially determined melancholy counterpart, is able to grasp the Holocaust, even as a limit event that transcends epistemological boundaries.

Confronted with the challenge of how to conceive of the Holocaust, however, the mind of Hildesheimer's narrator meanders off in different directions, focusing on stories that he can visualize, such as the bloody tale of a sixteenth-century noble, Prince Carlo Gesualdo, a composer who in a jealous rage murdered his adulterous wife and her lover (*T*, 237). Such evasion suggests that the narrator is intent on concealing from himself the historical root of his absurd existence.[50] When on occasion historically verifiable fragments of horror infiltrate his mind, such as the extermination of Doris Wiener or the thought of lampshades made of human skin, he does not linger on these details (*T*, 62–63; *M*, 206). In a post-Holocaust world, the narrator's intellect blocks the thought of genocide. Both works thus present the limited imagination as the petrification of the mind in the face of recent history. In an absurd world the human capacity to understand has been rendered obsolete, while the thrust toward the transcendental is impossible. By *Masante*, the narrator has degenerated into a bureaucrat of his own mind. He tells us that he can organize lists—this is how he envisages the passing of his days at the edge of the desert—but he also notes that his ideas and imagination are fading (*M*, 92–93). The condition of radical disenchantment that forms the basic mood of both of these works is thus a lament on the impoverishment of the imagination in the wake of the Holocaust.

The Tynset Syndrome

Spatial imagery in both novels reflects the problem of imagination and representation after the Holocaust. Projections of infinite space and tightly demarcated enclosures alternate. What we learn of the narrator's life story can be seen in terms of the struggle against enclosure and the desire for an unrestrained existence in an indeterminate, boundless space that transcends the suffering of history. At first glance, the snowscape of the mountains represents an alternative space to a society congested with perpetrators, evoking a sense of oblivion beyond contemporary history (*T*, 50–51). The internal equivalent to this external landscape is the narrator's favorite black painting (*T*, 87). The desert also features regularly in the narrator's thoughts in *Tynset* (*T*, 40, 77–82); *Masante* takes place at the edge of the desert. While vast, these spaces paradoxically reinforce entrapment. As signifiers of blankness, they are spatial metaphors of an absurd life in contingency and can be compared to the contingent objects mentioned earlier that distract the narrator from disturbing thoughts, but that restate his entrapment in traumatic history.

Borders and boundaries interrupt these images of infinite space. In *Masante* the physical point of orientation is Meona, the desolate habitation at the edge of the desert that consists of a bar that is run by a melancholy couple, the alcoholic Maxine and her partner Alain, a former priest. The narrator's thoughts are frequently punctured by the direction of his gaze across the boundary of his bedroom window out into the infinite space of the desert. His eyes are repeatedly drawn to a border he can just make out, the outline of stakes pushed into the sand (*M*, 104, 372). Even more ominously, he can decipher a warning sign on a mast in the distance. Reproduced several times in upper case in the narrative, this sign, CHI TOCCA MUORE, translates as "who touches dies" (*M*, 208–9). His ocular attraction to this deathly object echoes how he willingly undertook this journey from his abode in Urbino, Ca Masante, to the desert graveyard of Meona, a site of skeletal human remains and, as the final scene implies, his own eventual burial site (*M*, 251–52). Toward the end of the narrative he reflects that the desert, as a congested space—meaning that it is full of death—can offer him nothing. Contrary to appearance, it cannot fulfill his love of emptiness, his *amor vacui* (*M*, 63, 366).

This insight evokes the ambivalent origin of the melancholy mood between traumatic history and personal pathology. The narrator decides shortly after arriving at Meona that he will go out into the desert with a compass, an instrument of spatial orientation that he prizes (*M*, 17). This decision contradicts his *amor vacui*. He seeks out vast spaces that seem to offer freedom, yet under his geometrical gaze, these spaces shrink away. Here he exemplifies the two conflicting traits of the mathematical-imaginative type: the desire for transcendence, articulated in the vision of space, and, by contrast, the inability to transcend anything, symbolized by the compass. In this way, Hildesheimer suggests that knowledge of the Holocaust cannot be gained through rational means. Rather, the mind must take recourse to other forms of apprehension: the language of irrationality and pathology, and the imagination of the absurd. Hildesheimer's representation of the traumatized postwar psyche self-reflexively debates its own limitations. In this way, we can observe the rigor with which he translates the message of Adorno's dictum into poetic and psychological form: that the postwar literary work should aporetically address the "unknowability" of the Holocaust as an *epistemological* problem.

References to the place "Tynset" are a further example of this intricate dance around historical catastrophe. The narrator's mind continually returns to the motif of an imagined journey to the faraway Norwegian town of Tynset, which alleviates his dark musings and provides a sense of hope (*T*, 25, 55, 73, 93, 111, 223, 257). The "Tynset" refrain reappears in *Masante*, but by the second novel it is associated only with negativity (*M*, 186, 321). This negativity is also latent in *Tynset*, however. At the end of the novel the narrator has given up all plans to travel to Tynset. Instead, he sinks back into his bed and bids farewell to this dream of escape. One of his last thoughts before this moment is of the Nazi perpetrator Kabasta—now a powerful administrator in the Bonn Republic—who, in an uncanny sequence of events, helps to drive the narrator out of West Germany in the early 1950s. On the closing page of the novel, Kabasta's fleshy blond hand reigns supreme over all other images. It embodies the ascendance of Nazi violence that has not been checked by Germany's defeat in the war and confirms the narrator's sense that flight into the mountains has not translated into escape from Kabasta and his cronies (*T*, 269). The binary structure of victim and perpetrator solidifies in *Masante*, where the narrator's reflections on perpetrators feature consistently (*M*, 142, 199, 211, 242, 259). Indeed, Kabasta reappears here, a criminal force that still looms large (*M*, 112, 119).

This juxtaposition of the perpetrator with the narrator's farewell to his fantasy of Tynset conveys the problem of the mind that the mathematical melancholy type embodies. Transcendent spaces such as the snowy mountains and the endless desert collapse into negativity because they too are contaminated by history. While these landscapes evoke a sense of inexplicable absence, they also evoke the idea of loss bound in profane time. Projections of space in both novels are always ultimately non-transcendent. The signifying ambivalence of space between absence and loss eloquently reflects the narrator's problem in the face of recent history: while he cannot conceive of the Holocaust, he also cannot conceive of a world in which the Holocaust has not occurred. Spatial imagery thus represents a disturbed relationship to history that is itself a product of the pathology of traumatic history. The non-transcendent world mirrors the narrator's disenchanted mind poised between a cosmic sense of absence and the details of historical loss. In the final analysis, space in both of these works is the expression of the impoverished mind. And in *Tynset*, the narrator's "Tynset syndrome" articulates this impoverishment.

Tynset as Dimension Auschwitz

Other manifestations of the "Tynset syndrome" and the shrinking of mental space between the alternatives of absence and loss include the narrator's reading of the Norwegian train timetable and the phonebook episode. The narrator admires the timetable booklet for its literalness and enjoys reading it at nighttime. At first glance, its pared-down depiction of departure and arrival times seems reliable. As a systematic order, it exemplifies clarity and appears to stand up to intense scrutiny (*T*, 11). It is the organization of space therein, however, and not the ordering of time, that the narrator finds so fascinating. This suggests, reflecting a life spent in absurd contingency, that the idea of chronologically ordered time has little relevance for him (*T*, 10). Highlighting the measuring function of calendars, timetables, and other time devices, as well as images of entropy, J. J. Long argues that the progress of linear time is central to both narratives. However, these objects can also be seen as indicators of baroque melancholy, which negates the idea of progress and collapses time into the space of permanent decay, the melancholy time of victim *ressentiment*. Phonebook and timetable are thus politicized *memento mori* in the context of postwar West German amnesia.[51]

Crucially, it is on the matter of *space* that the narrator's faith in the ordering capacity of the timetable most falters. On closer inspection, he notes that the printed lines that display arrivals and departures to and from the different locations merely encircle empty spaces on the page.

He attempts to think of these gaps between signs in terms of a spatial "somewhere," but only the vague term "Nirgendwo" (nowhere) occurs to him. Trying to imagine nowhere as a place that exists in the here and now exceeds his epistemological limits. In melancholy mode, he observes that whatever does not have a name cannot exist (*T*, 26). For this reason, his mind latches onto the place-name "Tynset," a psychological and linguistic compromise that comes to signify, paradoxically, the concept of "nowhere."

The strategy of avoidance mentioned earlier is thus the central idea of the novel. Through the signifier "Tynset," the narrator gives "nowhere" a name, and so the idea of nothingness becomes thinkable, if in a compromised—because signified—way. This is done in the absurd mode of the poetic nihilist, whose mind, in an effort to circumvent the fall into misleading narrative solutions to the problem of understanding history, fastens on incidental phenomena, in this case a geographically contingent Norwegian town. This implies that absurdity will tell us more about history than the grand historical narrative; it is more reliable for apprehending truth in a post-Holocaust world. "Tynset" thus functions like a screen memory in the Freudian sense: between absence and loss it conceals aspects of reality even as it evinces others. Arguably, the primordial memory at the base of this elaborate way of apprehending the world is "Auschwitz," the nowhere and nothingness that cannot be named, the unspeakable element at the heart of the word "Tynset."[52] In this way, "Tynset" is the broken signifier of traumatic caesura, which simultaneously evokes and obscures the thought of historical catastrophe. The subtle ambivalence of this place-name thus indirectly thematizes the crisis of cultural representation after the Holocaust.

The phonebook episode also conveys this problem in an indirect fashion. The narrator likes to read the phonebook on his sleepless nights; this is a habit that goes back to his last years in Germany. Just as with the timetable, he finds the orderliness of organized data very soothing. Yet the order of the phonebook also reveals itself as illusory. The rows of names, addresses, and numbers only ever signify a single identity: a sick collective that has never owned up to perpetration. One of the narrator's "resenting" activities before he leaves West Germany is anonymously to dial a local number and, when the recipient picks up, to suggest that he has been "found out." The narrator then hangs up and watches from his darkened window the effects of his phone charade: a flurry of activity in the building opposite as the owner hurriedly packs and leaves. Picking out a random name or number always reveals the guilty. Thus the phonebook, an incidental object like the train timetable, carries a single meaning: the continuing asymmetrical divide of the world into victims and perpetrators, and the shameful lack of contrition of the perpetrators for crimes committed in the name of National Socialism.

In this way, the narrator comes across Kabasta, who does not fall for the ruse and locates the source of the crank calls (*T*, 45). This is the event that causes the narrator to flee Germany. The scene is one that tells a hopeless tale: the resentful victim tries to take revenge in a small way, yet even this attempt at idiosyncratic justice backfires on him. He is driven out, as if he were the criminal, while the real criminals still wield power and will always find a victim target.

The absurdity communicated in both phonebook and timetable epitomizes the narrator's entrapment in the melancholy time warp of *ressentiment*. In both cases, passing time and distracting oneself serves only to intensify the sense of the "continual spreading of confines," as the narrator, no matter what he does, becomes increasingly enclosed in restrictive spheres of existence.[53] Yet this state of affairs is not articulated as a shocking insight or sudden gruesome revelation. Rather, the trauma of reality for victim survivors has become a monotonous normality without beginning or end.

In Praise of the Slothful Self

The narrator styles himself as a slothful sinner in the mode of *acedia*. Presenting himself, the German-Jewish victim subject, as a failed Christian ascetic reinforces the sense that he battles with guilt. It also unites him, under the sign of Christianity, with the perpetrators whom he describes as Christian family men (*T*, 156). Hildesheimer thus conveys the complexity of survivor guilt by uniting the thwarted geometrician with the slothful sinner, which suggests his knowledge of the Renaissance fascination with these originally quite separate types: the "typus Geometriae" and the "typus Acediae." Klibansky et al. suggest that Dürer combined these types in *Melencolia I*. As argued above, however, Hildesheimer emphasizes the moment of failure, passivity, and sin in his citation of Renaissance melancholy, despite the fact that it encompasses, under the "geometrical type," several artisanal activities, such as architecture, astronomy, joinery, and building (*SM*, 468–76). The narrator, a slothful Hamlet, only embodies the geometrical type to the extent that his mathematical mentality reveals the problem of epistemology in the post-Holocaust world. The "typus Acediae" then reinforces this moment of failure in a distinctly theological way. At the same time, however, Hildesheimer subverts the sin of *acedia* to criticize recent history. In this way, *acedia* is not only a symbol of guilt but also a signifier of protest.

Acedia, a Hellenistic term, originally meant "lack of care."[54] In the context of Christian desert spirituality this translates into neglect of devotion to the worship of God; a kind of carelessness has crept into the soul of the monk who is bored with religious acts (*SS*, 6). This carelessness is imagined as an evil demon that attacks the weakened ascetic at his most vulnerable moment: noon. Because of its association with the noonday devil *acedia* was regarded as the most evil of all vices, the mother of the Seven Cardinal Sins (*SS*, 17). Increasingly, however, it became secularized. In the popular confessional practices of the medieval period it became a vice between body and soul, both a spiritual sin and a sin of the flesh, manifest in laziness, idleness, slumber, and general negligence (*SS*, 176). As Klibansky et al. show, *taedium vitae* and *tristitia* (immoderate sadness) merged with melancholy in the medieval period. This helped to cast the concept of melancholy genius in an ambivalent light. The nexus of *acedia*—boredom, idleness, spiritual sloth—and melancholy as inexplicable sadness that forms one aspect of creative genius is evident in nineteenth-century decadence. The *ennui* of this period has its roots in the negativity of *acedia* and in the aristocratic flavor of melancholy genius (*SM*, 324–33).[55]

All of these types of melancholy feature in *Tynset* and *Masante*. References to Hugo von Hofmannsthal's *Ein Brief* (A Letter, 1905) populate both novels. Just as the author of this despairing letter, Lord Chandos, evokes a desolate landscape littered with paltry random objects that no longer correspond to the linguistic signs that used to represent them, so the narrator in his assessment of space, objects, and words points to the insufficiency of language to express the Holocaust and the crisis of the imagination this suggests (*T*, 92; *M*, 366).[56] These references reveal Hildesheimer's alignment of the narrator with the aristocratic decadence of the *fin-de-siècle* and *ennui*. The narrator's retreatism evokes the nineteenth-century melancholy artist who shuns and is shunned by society.[57] Hildesheimer's later pseudo-biography, *Marbot*, takes this exceptional status of the artist to its logical conclusion in the suicide of the notably aristocratic Romantic anti-hero, Lord Andrew Marbot, a pioneering intellectual but failed artist. Hildesheimer himself espoused a partly elitist understanding of the artist under the auspices of melancholy.[58] In *Tynset* and *Masante*, however, depictions of *ennui* are more profoundly linked to the theological ancestor, *acedia*, than to decadence.

The desert of *Masante* evokes the desert spirituality of early monasticism: both works mention the founder of this movement, St Anthony (*M*, 289–90; *T*, 260–61). From the outset, the narrator views his room at the inn in Meona as a cell and wonders about leaving it, presenting himself as an ascetic who is prey to temptation (*M*, 35). Consistent with the stylization of his room as a hermit's cell, his thoughts are continually drawn to the impending "böse Stunde" (evil hour), and these thoughts remain with him until the end of the narrative (*M*, 39, 58, 92, 237, 247, 263, 274, 322, 356, 377). The precise character of the evil hour is never revealed, even though the narrator associates himself with criminality and sin at the end of each novel. In *Tynset*, he cowers further into his dubious "Tatbett." In *Masante*, he becomes the slothful sinner whose defenses against the demon of noontide collapse as he wanders out of his cell into the desert.[59]

The monk motif is also present in *Tynset* in the bed fugue (*T*, 189–214). The inspiration for this nocturnal rumination is the narrator's summer bed, a baroque antique from the seventeenth century. The fugue combines seven characters or "voices" in a slothful tale of disease that features the plague from the year 1522 and is an extended allegory of the Seven Cardinal or Deadly sins. It takes its formal inspiration from the popular literature of the late medieval period that dramatized the sins and vices for popular consumption within the new confessional practices of the time (*SS*, 121).[60]

A range of characters who congregate in a tavern personify the sins of gluttony, lechery, envy, avarice, and pride, a common allegory for the medieval period (*SS*, 118). These deadly vices share what many centuries later becomes the narrator's bed. As he tells us, it sleeps seven (*T*, 189). Sloth is personified in the figure of a pilgrim monk who is attacked by the vice of lechery in the form of the succubus-seductress Anne, another stock image from the iconography of *acedia*, wherein sleep is dangerous and can end in death (*SS*, 112–13). From this encounter the plague spreads, killing all seven individuals, and moving rapidly across the land in an apocalyptic vision that drives home the message of sin and damnation. Yet the monk, who is gravely ill when he arrives at the tavern, cannot prevent his seduction. It is not for want of spiritual rigor that he capitulates to Anne. Rather, his body, already sick, makes it impossible for him to defend his ascetic way of life. Hildesheimer casts the story of the fall of man in creaturely terms here. Moreover, the state of sin has a gendered origin in a play on the Biblical story of Adam and Eve. Anne embodies fallen womankind in this scene; her lechery drags the monk from the spiritual life of prayer and contemplation into sloth. The sexual sins of the female flesh beget the spiritual sin of *acedia*. In this way, the monk is an innocent figure, yet he is judged harshly in the eyes of God and meets with the same deadly fate as the others. Thus while Hildesheimer remains within the gender parameters of the Biblical tale, God's lack of empathy eclipses even the treacherousness of woman.

Hildesheimer presents the theme of a merciless deity who has abandoned his children with reference to the biblical story of Cain and Abel. Cain is known as the principle figure of Genesis who is associated with *acedia*. He is an impenitent murderer who represents one of the gravest aspects of the vice: despair (*SS*, 101).[61] Hildesheimer subverts this story by asking why Cain's offering was rejected by God in the first place. His explanation is that God did not want to listen to Cain's prayer but wanted the flesh of Abel's sacrifice instead (*T*, 108–9). Here God appears as a carnivorous perpetrator who created and abandoned humankind to an existence of suffering and eternal damnation. God's wicked caprice, along with the incomprehensibility of historical events, is thus one of the "Rätsel" (riddles) that preoccupy the narrator throughout the narrative (*T*, 109, 178). And on this point, the narrator proves just as incapable of mustering up an eschatological perspective on the world as he was of grasping the Holocaust. Religion is thus also a space of non-transcendence.

In the absence of an eschatological perspective, Cain's despair and subsequent act becomes comprehensible. The narrator identifies with Cain. He rejects the biblical narrative, questions the version of events, especially the fall of man that in the word of God and his loyal chroniclers shapes the story of creation, and emphasizes that he bears the mark of Cain (*T*, 109–10, 77). This should not be understood as the mark of an eternally damned murderer. Rather, the narrator has subverted the tale to make Cain a victim of God's inexplicable cruelty and unpredictable appetite for violence. The mark of Cain is now the mark of victimhood. God, on the other hand, bears the mark in its original negative biblical sense (*T*, 110). As victims, the monk and Cain converge to become a point of protesting identification for the narrator, who pours scorn over foundational religious narratives.

Hildesheimer uses several other details from the vocabulary of *acedia* to convey this point and to deepen the narrator's identification with slothful sinners of weak faith. Those with *acedia* are often portrayed as suffering from paralysis that translates into an iconography of the faulty foot (*SS*, 108). The narrator tells us that his gait is lame. In the wake of his discovery that God is treacherous, he describes his path through life as one he walks along with difficulty (*T*, 108). This motif reappears at the end of *Masante*, when he finally musters up the energy to walk out of his cell into the desert: his movements are hesitant and slow as befits one who displays spiritual languor (*M*, 372). The motif of the unfruitful tree that is condemned to die appears in *Tynset*. We learn that shortly after the narrator moved to the mountains an apple tree that for years had borne no fruit suddenly started to bloom. It never produced fruit again, however, and the narrator had it felled (*T*, 242). This barrenness is associated with the state of *acedia*, the condition of spiritual dryness (*SS*, 102).[62] The slothful sinner also typically neglects religious duties (*SS*, 174). At the end of *Tynset*, the church bells start to ring for an early service, "eine böse Musik" (an evil music), as the narrator terms it, returning to his bed where he remains until the narrative's end (*T*, 260). For the desert monks, manual labor was the chief remedy against sloth (*SS*, 111). In *Tynset*, the narrator refuses all "Handwerk" (manual labor), committing himself further to an existence that contradicts the religious life on almost every point (*T*, 253–54).

The theme of work also illuminates the connection between the sin of sloth and its secular descendent, *ennui*. Analogous to the monastic system, in the nineteenth century work was often recommended as an antidote to the malaise of *ennui* that, as Wolfgang Lepenies shows, lends an aristocratic tone to the melancholy of this period.[63] Fending it off through bourgeois pragmatism and industry adds to the melancholic's decadent air. Against the committed industry of the *Tagebuch* narrator, a busy citizen-artist, Hildesheimer's narrator thus appears partly in the guise of an aristocratic idler, which emphasizes the divide between the melancholy perpetrator and the melancholy victim. The narrator's self-stylization as Hamlet and Prince Gesualdo, aristocrat and artist, reinforces his aristocratic pedigree. In *Masante*, the references to *ennui* are numerous (*M*, 25, 39, 80–81, 165–67, 177, 203, 235, 295, 356, 369).

Ennui lends the narrator an air of morose indifference, behind which he can retreat when the thought of the world causes him too much pain. His solipsism reinforces the sense that the world outside the self—the world of action—is lost to the passive subject, the melancholy *homme intérieur* (spiritual man).[64] The correspondence between his mind and spatial imagery is a further indication of passivity under the sign of *ennui*. Although the narrator presents himself as the idle contemplator of landscapes, his idleness is tinged with an air of guilt that his personal space, the monkish cell, embodies. *Ennui* and decadence thus connect to a sense of sin in *Masante*. The contemplation of vast external landscapes from a position of "sinful" confinement is the paradoxical poetic expression of the process of "Verinnerlichung" (internalization) that both Nietzsche and Freud identify in the genesis of guilt, the mark of passivity that in despair turns aggression, originally destined for the outside world, against the self.[65]

Sleep is also a traditional signifier of sin. In the context of *acedia* it symbolizes the capitulation to a corporeal need and is a sign of vice, because it weakens spiritual vigilance and exposes the sleeping person to the demon of temptation, as exemplified in the medieval-style allegory (*SS*, 171). In *Masante* the narrator speaks of sleep as something that rules over him; he could never control it in the way that others can (*M*, 320). This explains his sudden lapses throughout *Tynset*, where his mind frequently drifts in and out of uneasy slumber (*T*, 55, 82). It is a creaturely need that controls him, just as hunger in *Masante* is presented as a bodily need that undermines the ascetic life (*M*, 256, 322). Yet the narrator values sleep as an antidote to boredom; for him its true value is that it is a unique way of passing the time (*M*, 321, 357). Indeed, he complains that waking up into an absurd world is the worst part of the day; the dreary task of devising how to pass time stretches eternally in front of the one awakened (*M*, 263). Sleep thus expresses the narrator's desire for escape and death, his longing for nothingness.[66]

The soulful individuals who exist on the fringes of the narrator's stream of thought are further embodiments of the slothful sinner. In

Masante, Alain, the excommunicated priest who runs the inn in Meona, appears in his Franciscan habit and begins to pray with the Irish guard (*M*, 354–55). The narrator refuses to join in and the next morning leaves this curious failed quasi-monastic settlement to struggle into the desert. Alain's partner, the alcoholic Maxine, is also described as a fallen saint (*M*, 350–51). In *Tynset*, the narrator's housekeeper, the ironically named Celestina, mirrors his *acedia*. Referencing the tradition of nuns' melancholy, the narrator suspects that she is a runaway nun who cannot accept her own actions (*T*, 22). Like Maxine, she is an alcoholic with a taste for red wine; she prays every night in drunken desperation for the salvation of her fallen soul. In the opening pages the narrator describes the scent of incense that has descended on the house during Celestina's hour of prayer (*T*, 9). This implies that in her past she gave in to the sin of spiritual sloth, and now she is dedicated to warding off the evil demon. As a result, her view of work is the opposite of the narrator's: she needs the mindlessness of work and prayer to distract herself from the thought of eternal damnation. For this reason she balefully spurns every time-saving kitchen utensil he bought her in the early years (*T*, 216–17). At one point, he discovers a list of sins that she made and keeps in a drawer, a list of sins that, in her eyes, he has committed (*T*, 218).[67]

Celestina's sense of damnation has a negative effect on the narrator. Toward the end of the narrative she coerces him into a blasphemous situation when, drunken and desperate, she mistakes him for a priest and, on her knees, begs him to absolve her of sin. The narrator is horrified, but his sense of human empathy propels him to go through the motions of religious ritual, only to have Celestina recognize him and push him away (*T*, 231). Like the seductress Anne and the alcoholic Maxine, Celestina is the gendered creaturely embodiment of the impoverished mind, symbolic proof of an existence confined to domestic, earthly spaces. This divorces these melancholy women from the intellectual tradition that the narrator, as a Hamlet figure, partly incorporates. We get to know him as a thinker who follows many melancholy, intellectual pursuits, such as astronomy, gardening, reading, and contemplation. Most of all he is a skeptic. By contrast, Celestina exhibits pathological behavior without the compensation of intellectual merit. Her drunkenness (and also Maxine's) is a slothful caricature of ecstatic self-transcendence. Pseudo-Aristotle outlines how wine, a substance external to the melancholic's body, can produce extremes of melancholy madness, just like excesses of black bile, the internal melancholy humor.[68] The narrator, too, drinks wine, but unlike Celestina he does not descend into religious fanaticism and self-castigation. The melancholy woman is the external embodiment of the narrator's most pathological, self-acrimonious emotion: guilt. She is the extreme instance of the self-reproach Freud identifies in the melancholy sufferer.[69] We also never know why Celestina suffers so dreadfully from guilt. She merely performs its never-ending pathos in her evening wine and incense rituals. In this way, Hildesheimer does not omit pathos from his narrative entirely, despite Jens's warnings of its unsuitability for a novel concerned with the legacy of National Socialism and the Holocaust.[70] Hildesheimer's solution to the problem, however, is to heap excesses of affect into Celestina's bizarre behavior, which helps preserve the skepticism and intellectual integrity of the male narrator.

Curious in this scene is the narrator's acceptance, in contradiction of his critical position on faith and organized religion, of Celestina's view of him as a sinner. This is all the more surprising when one considers that the narrator, in the Nietzschean mode of disgust for things spiritual that assails the monk during the evil hour of noontide, makes a point of unapologetically expressing his disgust for shows of holiness and the lives of the saints. His fundamental view on religion is akin to the disgust that nearly chokes Zarathustra before he goes into the mountains: the "große Ekel" (big disgust) that sees in the ascetic life and the Christian narrative of sin, penance, and conditional salvation the subservience of the individual to an alien force (*M*, 290). From this point of view, the doctrine of original sin renders humankind alien to itself.[71]

Celestina is the most consistent embodiment of this alienation in both narratives; she is so enslaved to the idea of her original sin that she cannot exist without it (*T*, 230). Through his creation of this strange pair, the insomniac Hamlet figure and his housekeeper, Hildesheimer appears to follow Freud's lead in the gendering of melancholy. Freud writes himself into the gendered history of melancholy by mentioning Hamlet as an exalted figure with privileged access to truth and self-knowledge. Melancholy women, by contrast, are confined to the domestic sphere: they are either disappointed wives or jilted brides.[72] Yet Hildesheimer does not stay rigidly within this binary, which writes women out of the tradition of genius. Celestina's addiction to red wine is one manifestation of the sensual weaknesses of the flesh, but the saints are presented as no better than this fallen woman. We are told that Augustine's *Confessions* derive their compelling quality from his youthful orgiastic excesses, while St Simeon's highly public acts of extreme asceticism are described as stunts or acrobatics: he is little more than a "prima donna of self-castration" (*M*, 136–37, 289–91).

The narrator thus pours scorn on the hypocrisy of organized religion and continually points to the Catholic church's complicity with National Socialism. Through Celestina he presents personal religious faith as pitiful and absurd. From this point of view he boldly praises the slothful self, and his torpor, passivity, and aristocratic *ennui* can be understood as protest against the lies of Christianity, whose followers did not shy away from the crime of genocide. Yet he cannot translate this skeptical outlook into action. This explains in part his decision to opt out of society and his self-stylization as an idle aesthete who, by contrast with Grass's diligent narrator, rejects the concept of work as a model for overcoming melancholy. Instead, he cuts a strange figure somewhere between Zarathustra, whose heroic fatalism culminates in the golden midday hour that transforms the suffering of the "big disgust" and the pathology of the present into the utopianism of eternal return, and the "Zauberer" (sorcerer), singer of "Das Lied der Schwermut" (The Song of Melancholy), that exposes its singer as a weak and non-Dionysian melancholy sufferer.[73] The narrator falls short of the darkly glamorous melancholy that the name Hamlet suggests. While he may have access to a melancholy and destructive truth, as did Hamlet, he cannot transform the negativity of its message into an act of mourning that would suggest that we can extract meaningfulness from catastrophe. Instead, his apprehension of past catastrophe paralyses him, condemning him to a passive and futile resenting existence.

In this way, the narrator cannot be said to embody the ideal of a masculine self that could keep overcoming tragedy. The melancholy gender dichotomy that structures the pair narrator/Celestina is thus ambivalent. The narrator is just as much a failed figure as is Celestina. Religion does not help her overcome past trauma, just as intellectual contemplation and the outer trappings of genius do not guarantee the transcendence of trauma for him. This gendered amplification of pathological, "resenting" memory contrasts with Grass's gendered representation of melancholy, which suggests that woman (Lisbeth) is incapable of ethical memory after the Holocaust, while man (Zweifel) is incapable of forgetting the German-Jewish victims of the Holocaust. In Hildesheimer, neither man nor woman can forget, and neither has a solution for how to deal with traumatic memory. These contrasting positions on gender and melancholy reinforce the difference between the visions for an ethics of memory these two writers articulate. Hildesheimer's prose expresses a loyalty to the dead victims of the Holocaust that ends in self-destruction. This is the memory of melancholy *ressentiment* that refuses to part with the lost object in an act of narrative mourning. By contrast, Grass sticks to the fundamental principle of repeated self-transcendence in his stylization of the *Tagebuch* narrator as a hard-working member of the literary intelligentsia, a bourgeois-pragmatist posture of diligence tinged through and through with Nietzsche's superhuman melancholy. Noble-bourgeois pose notwithstanding, the *Tagebuch* narrator's melancholy is somewhat desperate; the outline of the repentant former perpetrator and his guilty conscience emerge in the Sisyphean effort continually to transcend the burden of the past. This is the position that must believe in the power of compensation and forgiveness, for it has everything to compensate: its work will never be done. Hildesheimer's rejection of religion, work, and all forms of progress marks out a completely different position. Here we have the resenting victim's melancholy that rejects compensation. From this point of view, aristocratic idleness and the spiritual sloth of man and woman bear the ethical stamp of *ressentiment* in Hildesheimer's two works. They are the masked expressions of ethical maturity that mark out for posterity the divide between victims and perpetrators.

Tynset and *Masante* articulate this superior position that ultimately rejects self-transcendence through many references to images of heaviness and lightness. Hildesheimer evokes Nietzsche's prophet, Zarathustra, in these sequences. The narrator's meteorological musings in *Tynset* alongside his obsession with the wind in *Masante* symbolize lightness, height, and distance from the world. This reminds us of Nietzsche's prophet, who assumes the form of a bird and learns how to fly. Against this motif, however, the narrator introduces many images of heaviness that in Zarathustra's world represent *acedia*: subservience to a religious outlook that locates the source of spiritual lethargy in the individual sufferer and that prevents her/him from self-realization in self-transcendence.[74] Celestina embodies this heaviness, and her continuing faith serves to intensify the theological nature of the sin. Maxine even more profoundly personifies spiritual heaviness, although she differs from Celestina in that she rejects religion (*M*, 100, 116, 138, 169, 173, 198–99, 209, 238, 271). This does not prevent her from suffering from an intense form of secular *acedia*, however. Her basic feeling about life is dread. Notably, the narrator also presents himself in similar modes of sinking into the earth's gravitational pull. As mentioned, this is the image we are left with at the end of *Tynset*, where criminality and cardinal sin converge in the victim's leaden heaviness (*T*, 46–47, 250, 269). While he envisages himself in future flight as he moves further into the desert at the end of *Masante*, this sense of mobility is compromised by his actual struggle to walk through the sandstorm and by Hildesheimer's conceptualization of this scene as the narrator's death.

A defiantly failed Christian ascetic, the narrator also presents himself as a failed Dionysian prophet. The rejection of the one does not automatically translate into the realization of the other. Freedom from the religious yoke does not result in an upsurge of heroic vitalism for the world-weary anti-hero. In this regard, Hildesheimer's understanding of melancholy cannot be located in Nietzsche's godly suffering. As a poetic nihilist, he belongs more readily in Schopenhauer's pessimistic thought. His later pseudo-biography *Marbot* works out this relationship in the issue of Andrew Marbot's suicide: his posthumous writings include a lengthy consideration of Schopenhauer's thought on suicide, going beyond the philosopher's prohibition of the act to justify it.[75]

Between the two modes of failure, Christian and Dionysian, the narrator's entrapment in history reappears. He seems to be saying that there is no solution to the problem of history. In the final analysis, his narrative of failure culminates in an intensely private mood of self-accusation that can neither be captured by the religious discourse of sin nor overcome in the manner of the prophet. The ghost of Hamlet's father embodies this bottomless guilt in *Tynset*. This specter continually appears throughout the narrative, reminding the narrator that he has a case to solve and a murder to avenge: in short, an obligation to fulfil. Franz Loquai argues that the narrator's tendency to ignore this ghost expresses his confidence that he has no guilt and no case to answer.[76] As a member of the victim collective this is, on one level, undoubtedly true. Yet Loquai's perspective does not query why the narrator can see this ghost—if guilt was not an issue then he would be impervious to its spectral reminder—and further, he does not take into account the combined affective complexity of membership in a victim group and absence from the original event—the Holocaust. In my view, the ghost of Hamlet's father is an expression of the narrator's feelings of guilt for having escaped the fate that befell so many others. His need to repeat that he has no debts to pay is an attempt to make his existence as a "fortunate" survivor bearable. Both narratives, however, expose the failure of this effort, which culminates in his final farewell to the pain of history at the end of *Masante*. This sandy space is no longer the monastic desert of early Christianity, nor is it the space into which Zarathustra affirmatively strides. Rather, it is a space of personal grief that is neither theological nor philosophical. While his often irreverent critique of *acedia* weakens the theological message of sin, a different kind of sin has lodged itself in his soul: the sin of survival that no religion or philosophy can begin to address.

It is because of this deeply personal dimension that sadness in both works is articulated somewhere between the Freudian modes of mourning and melancholy. On the one hand, the Jewish victims of the Holocaust constitute a lost object that one can at least attempt to mourn in a temporally bound process. On the other, the lost object also consists of the narrator's bad feeling and guilt, which exceed historical explanation and cannot be resolved. In this regard, Hildesheimer appropriates the symbolic figure of Hamlet for the impoverished inner life of the German-Jewish survivor, a Shakespearean figure that Karl Jaspers suggests as a model for German guilt and responsibility. Hildesheimer's use of the biblical story of Cain is similar, in that he too appropriates and reverses this established symbol of West German perpetration to express the sense of primordial abandonment—the utter loneliness as Améry described it—of the victim experience.[77]

In *Tynset* and *Masante* Hildesheimer negotiates a dysfunctional relationship to history and the Holocaust through the absurdity of original sin and the failure of Dionysian vitalism. The narrator's problem is not just the trauma of history but also his absence from an event that has subsequently determined how he feels in the world. This sense of absence is articulated in both narratives as a sin of omission against the self that has little to do with matters theological. Instead, it becomes an endless grief, at times interrupted by bitter musings and reflections on absurdity that collectively do nothing to assuage it. One could speculate that the sin of omission is the sense of having failed to save a father who met a cruel end at the hands of the Nazis: a sin of omission against the father— also represented in disguised form, again like a screen memory, in the ghost of Hamlet's father. In this post-Holocaust context, the narrative of original sin is a narrative of absence, exile, and *ennui*. We can thus say that melancholy, while a rich and varied discourse that contemplates the divide between beleaguered-theological and genial-atheistic modes in both works, ultimately becomes a bottomless personal sadness, not without cause, but without cure.

Notes

[1] Hildesheimer, *Tynset*, 245–46. Hereafter cited in text as *T*.

[2] Shakespeare, *Hamlet*, act 4, scene 5.

[3] The son of German-Jewish Zionists, Hildesheimer emigrated from Germany to Palestine in 1933 with his parents. He returned to Germany in 1946 but moved to Poschiavo in Switzerland in 1957, where he remained until his death in 1991. Although this move was prompted partly by health concerns, a strong motivation was Hildesheimer's discomfort with the continuities between National Socialist Germany and the postwar period. However, Hildesheimer's father was not killed in the Holocaust; *Tynset* is thus not strictly autobiographical. See Stephan Braese, *Die andere Erinnerung: Jüdische Autoren in der westdeutschen Nachkriegsliteratur* (Berlin: Philo, 2001), 262–65. Also Henry A. Lea, "Hildesheimers Weg zum Ende der Fiktionen," in *Wolfgang Hildesheimer*, ed. Volker Jehle (Frankfurt am Main: Suhrkamp, 1989), 50–51; Lea, "Wolfgang Hildesheimer and the German-Jewish Experience: Reflections on *Tynset* and *Masante*," *Monatshefte* 71 (1979): 19. Also Patricia H. Stanley, *Wolfgang Hildesheimer and His Critics* (Rochester, NY: Camden House, 1993), 27–28. More general biographical information can be found in Hildesheimer, "Vita," in Jehle, *Wolfgang Hildesheimer*, 17–19; Hildesheimer, "Antworten über *Tynset*," *Dichten und Trachten* 25 (1965): 7; Lea, *Wolfgang Hildesheimers Weg als Jude und Deutscher* (Stuttgart: Akademischer Verlag, 1997); Volker Jehle, *Wolfgang Hildesheimer: Werkgeschichte*; Hildesheimer, "'Ich kann über nichts schreiben als über ein potentielles Ich': Gespräch mit Wolfgang Hildesheimer," in *Gespräche über den Roman*, ed. Manfed Durzak (Frankfurt am Main: Suhrkamp, 1976), 271–72; and Hildesheimer, "Mein Judentum," in *Das Ende der Fiktionen: Reden aus fünfundzwanzig Jahren* (Frankfurt am Main: Suhrkamp, 1984), 213–28.

[4] Hildesheimer, *Masante*. Hereafter cited in text as *M*.

[5] Grass, *Aus dem Tagebuch einer Schnecke*, 325.

[6] Wagner, *Textklänge und Bildspuren: Zur musikalischen Selbstreflexivität im Werk von Wolfgang Hildesheimer* (PhD diss., Queen Mary University of London, 2012), 87.

[7] Ferdinand van Ingen, *Vanitas und Memento Mori in der deutschen Barocklyrik*, 23. Hildesheimer also suffered from depression throughout his life, as some of the archival material testifies. However, it would be speculative to suggest that his interest in melancholy was motivated by the personal experience of depression. I refer to the Wolfgang-Hildesheimer-Archiv, SAdK, Berlin, no. 127. See also Hildesheimer, "Beim Malen überwinde ich Müdigkeit und Depressionen," *Zeitmagazin*, Oct. 12, 1973.

[8] As Franz Loquai observes, the Hamlet motif is fundamental to Hildesheimer's oeuvre generally. Loquai, *Hamlet und Deutschland*, 197; see also Jehle, *Wolfgang Hildesheimer: Werkgeschichte*, 84–110. A fragment of the Hamlet novel can be found in Hildesheimer, "Hamlet," in *Exerzitien mit Papst Johannes*, 9–25. See also Hildesheimer, *Vergebliche Aufzeichnungen* for further references to Hamlet.

[9] Panofsky and Saxl, *Dürers Melencolia I*. Cheyne, *The English Malady; Or, a Treatise of Nervous Diseases of All Kinds, as Spleens, Vapours, Lowness of Spirits, Hypochondriacal, and Hysterical* (Cambridge: Cambridge Scholars, 2010).

[10] See also Helen Watanabe-O'Kelly, *Melancholie und die melancholische Landschaft*, and Klara Obermüller, *Studien zur Melancholie in der deutschen Literatur des Barock*.

[11] Jens, *Herr Meister*, 102, 104–5. On Shakespeare and melancholy see Winfried Schleiner, *Melancholy, Genius, and Utopia in the Renaissance*, 233–88; also Lawrence Babb, *The Elizabethan Malady*, 106–10.

[12] The ghost's soliloquy ends with the words: "Adieu, adieu, adieu. Remember me." *Hamlet*, act 1, scene 5.

[13] *Hamlet*, act 1, scene 2. On the melancholy dialectics of affliction and empowerment see Max Pensky, *Melancholy Dialectics*, introduction.

[14] See Siegfried Wenzel, *The Sin of Sloth*.

[15] On the motif of the *deus absconditus*, see Klara Obermüller, *Studien zur Melancholie in der deutschen Literatur des Barock*, 95–100. On the absurd in Hildesheimer's work see Hildesheimer, "Über das absurde Theater," in *Das Ende der Fiktionen*, 9–26; also Günter Blamberger, *Versuch über den deutschen Gegenwartsroman*, 74–101. Jean-Paul Sartre's philosophical novel *Nausea* is a good illustration of the connection between melancholy and twentieth-century existentialist thought on the absurd: the narrator, Antoine Roquentin, is deeply melancholy because he is devoted to the logical exploration of a world without meaning after the death of God. Sartre, *Nausea*, trans. Robert Baldick with an introduction by James Wood (London: Penguin, 2000). Sartre originally planned to entitle this work "Melencolie." See Martina Wagner-Egelhaaf, *Die Melancholie der Literatur*, 2.

[16] Wagner, *Textklänge und Bildspuren*, 11, 61, 157.

[17] Améry, "Ressentiments," 102–29. The first edition was published by Szczesny in 1966. I refer to the second edition. See Irene Heidelberger-Leonard, *Jean Améry: Revolte in der Resignation* (Stuttgart: Klett-Cotta, 2005), 204–6. A further example of emerging literature on the victim experience is Alfred Andersch's novel *Efraim* (Zurich: Diogenes, 1967), inspired by Améry, as was Ingeborg Bachmann's story "Drei Wege zum See," in *Simultan: Erzählungen* (Munich: Deutscher Taschenbuch Verlag, 1974), 94–165.

[18] Nietzsche, *Zur Genealogie der Moral*, 2:782–85.

[19] Ure, "Sympathy for the Devil," in *On Jean Améry: Philosophy of Catastrophe*, ed. Magdalena Zolkos (Plymouth: Lexington, 2011), 245.

[20] Nietzsche, *Zur Genealogie der Moral*, 2:784.

[21] Braese, *Die andere Erinnerung*, 390. Other Jewish writers he includes in the category of those misunderstood by the West German literary milieu are Edgar Hilsenrath and Grete Weil.

[22] Ibid., 246–47, 312.

[23] For a general discussion of the reception of *Tynset* and *Masante* see Braese, *Die andere Erinnerung*, 304–12 and 387–93 respectively.

[24] Baumgart, "Schlaflos schluchzend," *Der Spiegel*, Mar. 3, 1965. Other critics who misread the novel include Martin Walser, Peter Handke, and, surprisingly, Walter Jens. Braese, *Die andere Erinnerung*, 304, 425–26, 514–15. In a later review of a different publication, Baumgart seems to retract this critical stance, conceding that Hildesheimer's expression of anxiety and fear had a certain charm and grace. Baumgart, *Deutsche Literatur der Gegenwart: Kritiken—Essays—Kommentare* (Munich: Hanser, 1994), 519.

[25] Thomas Wirtz's commentary on Sebald's *Die Ringe des Saturn* provides an interesting parallel to Baumgart on Hildesheimer: Wirtz, "Schwarze Zuckerwatte."

[26] Braese, *Die andere Erinnerung*, 284–85, 294.

[27] Blamberger, *Versuch über den deutschen Gegenwartsroman*, 74–101.

[28] Goll-Bickmann, *Aspekte der Melancholie in der frühen und mittleren Prosa Wolfgang Hildesheimers* (Münster: LIT, 1989), 11–13, 17–21.

[29] Wagner's analysis investigates the role of music in both texts, arguing that it represents Eros and Thanatos simultaneously. Ultimately music confirms the Faustian core of life itself, however, and works against the deathliness of the written word. Wagner, *Textklänge und Bildspuren*, 17, 241.

[30] On retreatism see Wolfgang Hirsch, *Zwischen Wirklichkeit und erfundener Biographie: Zum Künstlerbild bei Wolfgang Hildesheimer* (Hamburg: LIT, 1997), 120–21.

[31] See Hildesheimer, "Das Ende der Fiktionen," in *Das Ende der Fiktionen*, 229–50. Hildesheimer's later pseudo-biographical work, *Marbot*, continues this motif of ultimately self-destructive retreat into a vacant space, with the suicide of the eponymous subject, Andrew Marbot, who is last sighted on his way into the Italian hills. *Marbot: Eine Biographie* (Frankfurt am Main: Suhrkamp, 1981), 313–14.

[32] Hildesheimer developed an original theory of biography that aimed to deconstruct the myths around famous people, which were often perpetuated by existing biographies. He also insisted on the subjective perspective of the biographer, thus placing the genre somewhere between the historical/objective and the personal/subjective. See Hildesheimer, "Die Subjektivität des Biographen," in *Das Ende der Fiktionen*, 123–38. His biography of Mozart is a good example of this approach. *Mozart* (Frankfurt am Main: Suhrkamp, 1977). In the pseudo-biography *Marbot* Hildesheimer again plays with the limitations of this genre's ability

to approach "truth." The character Marbot is fictional but the historical reconstruction of the European intellectual milieu was so accurate that several reviewers initially believed that Marbot was a historical figure. See Lea, "Hildesheimers Weg zum Ende der Fiktionen," 45–57.

[33] On transposition see Hildesheimer, "Über das absurde Theater," in *Das Ende der Fiktionen*, 9-26; Bernd Scheffer, "Transposition und sprachlich erzeugte Situation: Zur dichterischen Verfahrensweise Wolfgang Hildesheimers," in *Über Wolfgang Hildesheimer*, ed. Dierk Rodewald (Frankfurt am Main: Suhrkamp, 1971), 17–31.

[34] Hildesheimer, *Interpretationen: James Joyce, Georg Büchner; Zwei Frankfurter Vorlesungen* (Frankfurt am Main: Suhrkamp, 1969), 78.

[35] Adorno, "Kulturkritik und Gesellschaft (1951)," 30. For an overview of how Adorno's "dictum" was misconstrued in its first wave of reception in the late 1950s see Stefan Krankenhagen, *Auschwitz darstellen*, 90–91.

[36] Hildesheimer says in interview: "Nach Auschwitz kann man nur noch Gedichte schreiben. Die Literatur hat versagt. Sie hat den Menschen nicht so darstellen können, wie er wirklich ist, und so müssen wir uns in der Kunst auf Phantasieprodukte werfen." Ingo Hermann, ed., *Wolfgang Hildesheimer: Ich werde nun schweigen; Gespräch mit Hans Helmut Hillrichs in der Reihe "Zeugen des Jahrhunderts"* (Göttingen: Lamuv, 1995), 37.

[37] Braese, *Die andere Erinnerung*, 294.

[38] Hildesheimer expresses his skepticism of the term "Geschichte" in the appendix to his play *Mary Stuart: Eine historische Szene / Anmerkungen zu einer historischen Szene*, in *Spectaculum 14: Sechs moderne Theaterstücke* (Frankfurt am Main: Suhrkamp, 1971), 329–32. See also Peter Hanenberg, who argues, against earlier scholarship, that Hildesheimer's abstract prose represents recent history. Hanenberg, *Geschichte im Werk Wolfgang Hildesheimers* (Frankfurt am Main: Peter Lang, 1989), 7–10. Also J. J. Long, "Time and Narrative: Wolfgang Hildesheimer's *Tynset* and *Masante*," *German Life and Letters*, 4, no. 52 (1999): 457–74.

[39] Bohrer, "Möglichkeiten einer nihilistischen Ethik," in *Entzauberte Zeit: Der melancholische Geist der Moderne*, ed. Ludger Heidbrink (Munich: Hanser, 1997), 42–76.

[40] LaCapra, *Writing History, Writing Trauma*, 23. Freud, "Trauer und Melancholie," 10:428–46.

[41] See Katja Garloff, "Expanding the Canon of Holocaust Literature: Traumatic Address in Hubert Fichte and Wolfgang Hildesheimer," in "Memory and the Holocaust," special issue, *New German Critique* 96 (2005): 49–74.

[42] Levi, *The Drowned and the Saved*, trans. Raymond Rosenthal (London: Abacus, 2002), 63.

[43] Grass explicitly rejects the clinical concept of endogeneity that attributes depression to obscure forces within the individual (*Tagebuch*, 310–11), while the hypothesis of the "inability to mourn" advanced by Mitscherlich and Mitscherlich in *Die Unfähigkeit zu trauern* he terms a cliché (317).

[44] Grass, *Tagebuch*, 314–15.

45 Améry, "Ressentiments," 116.

46 From a different perspective, Wagner argues that this scene symbolizes the power of Eros as a sign of artistic creativity and omnipotence. Wagner, *Textklänge und Bildspuren*, 210.

47 See Bohrer, *Der Abschied: Theorie der Trauer; Baudelaire, Goethe, Nietzsche, Benjamin* (Frankfurt am Main: Suhrkamp), 1996.

48 Jens, *Herr Meister*, 72–73. On Henry of Ghent, melancholy, and mathematics see *SM*, 474–76.

49 Tellenbach, *Melancholy: History of the Problem, Endogeneity, Typology, Pathogenesis, Clinical Considerations*, 13–14.

50 Some critics observe the narrator's mental limitation but do not connect it to the melancholy type: Blamberger, *Versuch über den deutschen Gegenwartsroman*, 82–83; Peter Horst Neumann, "Hamlet will schlafen," in Jehle, *Wolfgang Hildesheimer*, 207; Jehle, *Wolfgang Hildesheimer: Werkgeschichte*, 104; and Thomas Koebner, "Entfremdung und Melancholie," in Rodewald, *Über Wolfgang Hildesheimer*, 40–41.

51 Long, "Time and Narrative," 457–74. On *vanitas* and *memento mori* see van Ingen, *Vanitas und Memento Mori in der deutschen Barocklyrik*; also Martina Wagner-Egelhaaf, *Die Melancholie der Literatur*, 71–73, and Watanabe-O'Kelly, *Melancholie und die melancholische Landschaft*, 84–87.

52 Freud, "Über Deckerinnerungen (1899)," in *Gesammelte Werke*, 18 vols., ed. Anna Freud (Frankfurt am Main: Fischer, 1969), 1:529–54. See also Mary Cosgrove, "Netzwerk und Erinnerung in Wolfgang Hildesheimers *Tynset*," in *Netzwerke: Ästhetiken und Techniken der Vernetzung, 1800—1900—2000*, ed. Jürgen Barkhoff, Harmut Böhme, and Jeanne Riou (Cologne: Böhlau, 2004), 251–61.

53 Tellenbach, *Melancholy*, 144.

54 Siegfried Wenzel, *The Sin of Sloth*. Hereafter cited in text as *SS*.

55 On the connection between *ennui* and *acedia* see Reinhard Kuhn, *The Demon of Noontide: Ennui in Western Literature* (Princeton, NJ: Princeton University Press, 1976), 39–64; on aristocratic boredom Lepenies, *Melancholie und Gesellschaft*, 115–58; also Peter Bürger, "Der Ursprung der ästhetischen Moderne aus dem *ennui*," in Heidbrink, *Entzauberte Zeit*, 101–19.

56 Hofmannsthal, "Ein Brief," in *Der Brief des Lord Chandos: Schriften zur Literatur, Kultur und Geschichte*, ed. Mathias Mayer (Stuttgart: Reclam, 2007), 46–59. See also Sebastian Schmitter, *Basis, Wahrnehmung und Konsequenz: Zur literarischen Präsenz des Melancholischen in den Schriften von Hugo von Hofmannsthal und Robert Musil* (Würzburg: Königshausen & Neumann, 2000).

57 Loquai, *Künstler und Melancholie in der Romantik*, 66–86.

58 Hildesheimer, *Marbot*, 313–14. Hildesheimer suggests that the true artist is brilliant, mysterious, and melancholy. See, for example, Hildesheimer, "Bleibt Dürer Dürer?" in *Das Ende der Fiktionen*, 32. Also, "Büchners Melancholie," ibid., 87–101. For more on creative genius see his "Die Subjektivität des Biographen," ibid., 123–38 and "Arbeitsprotokolle des Verfahrens 'Marbot'," ibid., 139–50. On Hildesheimer's concept of artistic genius see Wolfgang Hirsch,

Zwischen Wirklichkeit und erfundener Biographie, 203–17, and Heinz Puknus, *Wolfgang Hildesheimer* (Munich, Beck: 1978), 126–49, esp. 129–30. However, Hildesheimer's fascination with the secret of genius is balanced out by his focus on failure as a part of the artistic personality, evident in the character Marbot and also in *Tynset* and *Masante*.

[59] Kuhn, *The Demon of Noontide*, 23.

[60] See Morton W. Bloomfield, *The Seven Deadly Sins*, 42–43.

[61] From a clinical perspective, Tellenbach also emphasizes despair as a fundamental trait of melancholy. Tellenbach, *Melancholy*, 165–69.

[62] See also Bloomfield, *The Seven Deadly Sins*, 70.

[63] Lepenies, *Melancholie und Gesellschaft*, 201–6; also Bürger, "Der Ursprung der ästhetischen Moderne aus dem *ennui*," 115–17.

[64] Lepenies, *Melancholie und Gesellschaft*, 141–44.

[65] Nietzsche, *Zur Genealogie der Moral*, 2:825. Freud, "Das Unbehagen in der Kultur," in *Gesammelte Werke*, 14:419–506.

[66] This complex recalls Hamlet's famous soliloquy: "To die, to sleep; To sleep: perchance to dream: ay, there's the rub." Hamlet, act 3, scene 1.

[67] See Teresa of Avila, "Melancholy Nuns," in Radden, *The Nature of Melancholy*, 109–17.

[68] Aristotle, *Aristotle: Problems II*, 30.157–59.

[69] Freud, "Trauer und Melancholie," 10:438–39.

[70] Jens, *Herr Meister*, 50.

[71] Nietzsche, *Also sprach Zarathustra*, 2:389. Also his *Zur Genealogie der Moral*, 2:866. On Nietzsche and melancholy see Michael Theunissen, *Vorentwürfe von Moderne: Antike Melancholie und die Acedia des Mittelalters* (Berlin: de Gruyter, 1996), 39–53.

[72] Freud, "Trauer und Melancholie," 10:431–34.

[73] Nietzsche, *Also sprach Zarathustra*, 2:533–36.

[74] Nietzsche, *Also sprach Zarathustra*, 2:283, 306–7.

[75] On Schopenhauer and melancholy see Heidbrink, *Melancholie und Moderne*, 116–124; Hildesheimer, *Marbot*, 304–8.

[76] Loquai, *Hamlet und Deutschland*, 201.

[77] Jaspers, *Philosophische Logik I*, 937–40. On Cain, see A. Dirk Moses, *German Intellectuals and the Nazi Past*, 23–24, and Améry, "Ressentiments," 114.

3: The Feminine Holocaust: Gender, Melancholy, and Memory in Peter Weiss's *Die Ästhetik des Widerstands*

Between Genius and Depression: Ambivalences of Maternal Melancholy

THE THIRD AND FINAL INSTALLMENT of Peter Weiss's voluminous work on anti-fascist resistance during the Second World War, *Die Ästhetik des Widerstands*, begins with the evocation of a melancholy condition.[1] On her knees in a snowy, sandy landscape that through the imagery of coldness and dryness conveys a world in the grip of a withering melancholy paralysis, the narrator's mother, alongside several other beleaguered individuals, digs into the earth with her bare hands (3:7).[2] We only later realize that these people are Jews and are digging their own graves. The shifting narrative perspective of these initial pages subtly makes clear that this opening vision is not a direct representation of the mother's experience. Rather, it is the narrator's empathetically imagined post-memory of his mother's persecution and flight through Nazi-occupied Europe—a year of "dunklester Wanderung" (the darkest journey)—before she and his father eventually arrive in Sweden (3:7).[3] Stations along this darkest of journeys include concentrated points of extermination in Czechoslovakia and Poland, a literal topography of terror that renders the mother a traumatized witness to the unfolding of the Holocaust. Darkness and the nocturnal are closely associated with the destruction of Europe's Jews in this epilogue volume, which in its first half engages with the aesthetic problem of how to represent the Holocaust. Part of this undertaking is a nuanced consideration of how aesthetics may remain ethical in a historical epoch that issues new challenges to the artistic imagination. Weiss's reflection on the mother's condition exposes the problem not just of linguistic limitations but also of how representation risks eliding individual suffering and obliterating from memory the figure and experience of the victim.

The "mythology of night" is, in this context, a strongly allegorical system of imagery that—like black bile in ancient and medieval texts—makes the invisible visible via substitution and so lends form to that which can barely be imagined. In the medical texts of classical antiquity the barely imaginable is black bile itself, a humor that, in contrast to blood, yellow bile, or phlegm, is difficult to isolate physically and as a consequence acquires mythical and allegorical properties.[4] In *Die Ästhetik des Widerstands* darkness is a kind of prop in the effort to sketch a vague outline of the unimaginable. To this end, the melancholy figure of the mother functions allegorically like the motif of black bile in earlier contexts, lending a dark, human form to obscurity and the invisible. The nocturnal impenetrability of her inner life, which perplexes her male observers, personifies in allegorical form the problem of Holocaust representation and memory. The fact that we learn about her condition through the narrator underscores this sense of impenetrability: his efforts to glean sense and meaning from her condition emphasize that no-one can observe directly the internal workings of her soul nor see what she witnessed while on "the darkest journey." In this way, the historical event of the Holocaust, alluded to here through images of darkness and the nocturnal, acquires the status of the unimaginable, the almost fantastical in the narrative. Yet the representative mode of the night does not consign the Holocaust to a space beyond historical consideration. On the contrary, Weiss means to stress the necessity of the dark "obsessional" side of the imagination in the task of conceptualizing the Holocaust and remembering its victims. In this vein, the mother is marked out as a melancholy sufferer from an early point in the narrative. Long before her breakdown, her countenance is cast in nocturnal shadows, as the narrator ponders the nightshade of her eyes, hair, and even her voice, portentous symbols of the darkness that engulfs her in the final volume (1:133). In the first two volumes the narrator also signals her solidarity with persecuted Jews; moreover, the image from volume 2 of the mother in classic melancholy pose, with her hand propping up her chin, anticipates the explicit mention of *Melencolia I* in the third volume (1:189; 2:76). Jewish victimization, maternity, and melancholy combine to articulate an ethical commitment to the memory of the Holocaust victims, a crucial undertaking during a time that, as the narrative continually shows, would rather repress the suffering of others from consciousness.[5] As observed in the discussion of Wolfgang Hildesheimer's novels *Tynset* and *Masante*, the pathology of the individual psyche stands for the ethical memory of the Holocaust that threatens to overwhelm the melancholy individuals who are consumed by it. However, the troubled melancholy "genius" in *Die Ästhetik des Widerstands*, unlike those in Hildesheimer's works, is a woman.

We could say that the mother's imagination is "diseased," in that it has been invaded by the modern-day demons of genocide during National Socialism and now obsessively broods on the *idée fixe* of the extermination of the Jews. Despite the ethical commitment it mutely expresses, however, the mother's pathology is not presented as a solution to the problem of Holocaust representation and memory. Rather, her affliction captures an important moment in the genesis of postwar ethical memory: the memory of the victims that was so lacking in the West German world of Hildesheimer's novels. Beyond this, her muteness embodies the caesura in representation and thought after the Holocaust. While Weiss's presentation of her silent condition against the backdrop of a verbose, masculine intellectual-political milieu suggests that madness is the only possible response to traumatic history, he also explores, through the narrator figure, a means of developing an ethical memory of the victims that is not pernicious for the witness/thinker and yet that does not elide the victim other. On the meta-narrative level, this endeavor complements the position of identification with the victims that the mother represents and highlights another difference between Weiss and Hildesheimer: where Hildesheimer holds to the politically charged position of language skepticism, ultimately giving up the writing of fiction entirely, for Weiss the written word, while imperfect, provides the individual with a means of self-assertion through articulation in the face of traumatic history. The word, representing the beginnings of mourning work, becomes the always provisional solution to the quandary of melancholy incorporation of the lost object, as the narrator's laborious effort to document the events he has witnessed reveals (3:148–49). Yet Weiss does not propose, in the Freudian sense, mourning work as a better alternative to melancholy.[6] Hildesheimer's poetic negativity resists the healing mode of mourning, but in contrast, Weiss's poetics suggest that melancholy (the mother) and mourning (the narrator) each mark out a valid ethical position on the past.

In this sense aesthetics and ethics belong together. Aesthetics lend form to experience and thereby distance the observing self from the visceral level of historical events that threaten to overwhelm and annihilate the individual. Art helps to translate experience into historical insight and understanding based on cognitive distance and empathy. In this way, art and aesthetics try to resist oppression. Weiss's term for the distancing effect of aesthetic form is anesthesia: the cold, distancing gaze of the intellect and observing, analyzing consciousness that facilitates the documentation of the incomprehensible.[7] Aesthetic form is thus an anesthesia against the illnesses of the time, a kind of necessary "amoral morality" that reveals the ability of the reflecting subject to resist the threat of annihilation through aesthetic contemplation and production.[8] The intellectual, artistic, and ethical survival of the individual during National Socialism and Stalinism equates to the dogged will to keep on trying to articulate experience in language. This will elucidates the inalienable principle of all art: articulation, expression, and form as weapons of the resisting subject, *despite* the onslaught of historical events.[9] Or, as Weiss puts it in an essay in which he reflects on his own situation in Swedish exile: to be outside language is death itself, a kind of capitulation or surrender to the ravages of political violence.[10]

The mother cannot sufficiently anesthetize herself; that is, she has more or less lost the power of speech, and so wastes away. This chapter considers the significance of this situation for the image of Holocaust memory in *Die Ästhetik des Widerstands*. Metaphorically speaking, women cannot seem to "self-medicate" in the way that their intellectually active male counterparts appear to. In other words, they struggle to access the anaesthetising function of politically engaged art and aesthetics. This is not just a problem of the explicitly melancholy women in the novel, the mother and the Swedish novelist Karin Boye, who in the past had succumbed to the mass ecstasy of National Socialism and who commits suicide shortly before the mother's death (3:33, 35). The resistance fighter Marcauer also struggles to find the correct political idiom through which to critique Stalinism from a feminist perspective. Unlike the character Max Hodann, who is more careful in his critique of this destructive patriarchy, she articulates her views in a way that suggests similarities between fascism and Stalinism, which makes her suspicious to Communist Party officials. Her forthrightness leads to her arrest and execution (1:313). As this sequence of events suggests, the novel presents the difficult relationship of women to politics and art as a sociohistorical consequence of patriarchal systems of authority that capitalism and also, crucially, communism embody.[11] Women's difficult relationship to the symbolic order of political engagement and intellectual reflection often translates into their morbid overwhelming by the world of historical events.[12]

Despite the mother's inability to anesthetize herself against the evils of National Socialism, the failures of communism, and the restrictions of the patriarchal world order that harmfully constitute the Party, she nevertheless represents a significant, if virtually mute, ethical position. Her catatonic state expresses an absolute commitment to the victims of the Holocaust, and thus her particular morality consists in unflinching solidarity with the Jewish victims of National Socialism. This unwillingness to give up the lost object—incorporation—is the other side of the negative melancholy narcissism that features in Alexander and Margarete Mitscherlich's analysis of the autistic, amnesiac postwar West German collective.[13] Weiss does not present this pathology as intrinsic to perpetrators, or more broadly, the perpetrator collective, who refuse to accept the victim other's experience and difference. Rather, as a modus of intense identification and mimesis, the melancholy narcissistic incorporation of the lost object—the Jewish victim other—in the extreme circumstance of witnessing the Holocaust reveals something fundamental about the nature of the emotional tie in the first place: namely, that imitation is the basic pattern through which we engage emotionally with others.[14] From this perspective, the feminine, melancholy mimesis of the lost object is a key stage in developing an ethical memory of Holocaust victims. As an allegory of the affective dimension necessary to ethical memory, the mother cannot be considered to be cut off from the masculine sphere of political relevance. Within the novel as a whole she stands for a burgeoning affective ethics of empathy and identification that is catastrophically lacking within the resistance movement, especially among some of the male resistance fighters who, as the narrator seems elliptically to suggest, might have been able to prevent the Holocaust if their powers of empathy had been directed outward toward the real plight of others instead of narcissistically inward toward the difficulties of their own situation in Swedish exile. Their inability to envisage the Holocaust, as the mother does, is presented as a failure of the empathetic imagination. The narrator's *raison d'être* in documenting this historical period is to labor against this failure and to develop a strategy of narrative empathy: the mnemonic work of the individual who survives this epoch and whose ethical task it becomes to commit it to ongoing collective memory. Woven into this ambitious undertaking is a critical reflection on gender, resistance, and the Holocaust, through which Weiss dramatizes the problem of the role of affect in ethical memory.

The men's discussions about the mother interpret her empathetic ability as evidence of a feminine predisposition to pathological melancholy. Contrary to this medical diagnosis, however, the narrator shows the masculine assessment of his mother's state to be ambivalent. His narrative presence, which frequently calls on the prowess of the implied reader, reveals that the diagnosis of his mother takes place through an intellectualizing, masculine discourse that is itself problematic and prone to unreason. This ambivalence is expressed in the way in which, in the intense discussions of her person, she becomes an overdetermined object of cultural and medical discourse and thus a complex gendered signifier for the problem of Holocaust representation. Between the polarizing alternatives of vegetative depression, and through her association with Albrecht Dürer's engraving *Melencolia I*, she becomes a deathly yet vital feminine "hypersign," to cite Julia Kristeva, of the masculine allegorical imagination that oscillates between the excess of meaning, on one hand, and its reification, on the other.[15] Alongside her status as signifier of the problems of Holocaust representation, she is also the canvas onto which the men of the failing resistance movement project their melancholy despair and their efforts, in the self-transcending manner of the melancholy genius, to overcome despair through creative, intellectual, and political engagement.

Earthly Genius: Melancholy between Anesthesia and Affect

Before he commenced work on *Die Ästhetik des Widerstands*, Weiss wrote a journal, entitled *Rekonvaleszenz*, that documents his recovery from a heart attack he suffered in 1970. Here he explores the inner emotional landscape of the individual, systematically representing this tumultuous world in nocturnal imagery that associates the emotional life with a kind of necessary madness. Weiss reflects at this pivotal point in his artistic and political development that he has been guilty in recent years of neglecting the subjective perspective in his work, favoring instead the objective, historical, documentary, and politically engaged style that informs his dramatic output of the 1960s. His development as a writer and dramatist is often understood in terms of subjective, surrealist experimentation in the early prose followed by a decided turn away from this solipsistic approach to political engagement in and through his artwork. In *Rekonvaleszenz* he tries to bridge the divide between intellect and affect, which he recognizes in his earlier documentary-style work.[16]

It is significant that this theme preoccupied Weiss just before he began to write *Die Ästhetik des Widerstands*. In many respects this novel approaches head-on the problem of individual affect—the ability of individuals to feel or become overwhelmed by history—and the necessity to control this, which could otherwise lead to stasis and the failure of political resistance. By the same token he also raises as a problem the repression of feeling and emotion, as Hodann's efforts to explore the destructive patriarchy of communism from a psychoanalytical perspective reveal. His attempt to conceive of Communist masculinity in a manner that goes beyond ideals of steely heroism to reveal the frailty of the masculine subject meets with the hostility of other resistance fighters, such as Richard Stahlmann, who, as his underground cover name suggests, glorifies the Communist patriarch Stalin and the hard masculinity encoded in this very name (3:139).

While Weiss casts in gendered terms the problem of affect versus intellect in *Die Ästhetik des Widerstands*, this is not a straightforward process. He leaves open the question of whether a harmonious synthesis of the two—feeling and thought, subjectivity and objectivity—is possible. Men and women symbolize the rupture between the two positions, while the narrator attempts, through the written word, to establish some kind of balance between them. In this respect the entire novel documents the immense effort required of him to navigate a path between the documentary and the objective, on one hand, and the dark side of subjective experience, on the other. The scene of the mother's demise pushes this question to an extreme point that is not resolved but laid bare in all its tension.

Weiss scholars have voiced concern about declining interest in his seminal work and fear its relevance is waning in the post-1989 world.[17] A strong case for the novel's contemporaneity can be made with reference to Weiss's critical thinking about the appropriate place of emotion and intellect in ethical memory. Indeed, the novel may be regarded as an early reflection on a central question concerning the memory of victims that has informed much of the Humanities discourse on memory in recent years: the problem of over-identification with victims and the difficulty in finding a balance between cognitive historical understanding and empathy.[18] The mother's situation brings to light this problem of how surviving individuals can remember the dead victims of history. On one hand, her vegetative state articulates an intense commitment to the victims of the Holocaust. On the other, however, intense identification and her inability to anesthetize—that is, to articulate her experiences and thereby distinguish between self and victim other—kills her. The flow of events thus raises the question of whether identification of this extreme kind is an appropriate response to historical catastrophe, or whether it is an unfortunate case of "negative sublimity," the melancholy that shows no sign of ending.[19]

Die Ästhetik des Widerstands does not resolve this problem, revealing instead, on the one hand, the shortcomings of affect without anesthesia, and, on the other, anesthesia with insufficient affect. Weiss's notebooks reveal that his conceptualization of the mother figure was not straightforward. Initially he describes her condition in terms of severe depression and employs the appropriate medical vocabulary. Referring to her "vegetative" state in the notebooks—a descriptor that found its way into the novel—he describes her in an interview as an inanimate, heavy lump that gives up and dies like an animal.[20] Yet somewhat contradictorily, he also views the character's pathology as the basis for an ethical aesthetics of memory and so as the radical basis for what art should be trying to achieve after 1945.[21] This helps to explain why Weiss uses Dürer's image of Renaissance melancholy genius to elaborate the mother's condition. As the depiction of a despondent mood state as well as genius, *Melencolia I* becomes an apology for the necessity of affect in the project of developing ethical memory after 1945. The mother stands for the affective life in this regard. In contrast to the figure of Renaissance genius who is surrounded by the tools of creative production with which it might at any minute begin to reengage, however, the moment of self-transcendence so germinal to the idea of melancholy genius, and indeed to the concept of political resistance, does not apply to the mother. Unable to self-transcend—unable to speak—she withers away and dies. On this point, Weiss also raises the dangers of emotional identification that escapes the anesthetizing moment of intellectual and aesthetic consciousness. While this kind of radical identification with the Holocaust victims is distinct from the wallowing and pathos of what Weiss terms "Seelenkäse" (cheesiness of the soul), it nevertheless represents a moment of danger for the resistance movement: the collapse into stasis, the omnipresent threat of capitulation and surrender in the fight against fascism.[22] In its careful discussion of identification both as "a potent and sincere force" and as an emotion that can lead to loss of self as well as to obfuscation of victim memory, *Die Ästhetik des Widerstands* maps out a contemporary topography of post-Holocaust affective-mnemonic life.[23]

Side by side in the archival material are small reproductions of both *Melencolia I* and Dürer's other homage to Renaissance genius, *Heiliger Hieronymus im Gehäuse* (St Jerome in his study, 1514). This image, in contrast to the winged figure in *Melencolia I*, depicts the saint in scholarly activity, writing at his desk in a room flooded with light.[24] As Klibansky et al. suggest, the saintly scholar represents the contemplative genius in quiet productivity and so emphasizes a different, more positive aspect of the gifted intellect than that represented in the inactive winged figure of the other engraving (*SM*, 445). It is perhaps this ideal of steady, contemplative productivity to which the narrator of *Die Ästhetik des Widerstands* aspires. Especially the second volume of the novel tracks the beginnings of his development as a writer. By the third volume he is still wrestling with the well-nigh impossible task of how to document the historical events he has witnessed and also how to document the experiences of others, such as his mother. He conceives of himself in the infantile image of the putto of *Melencolia I*, whose scribbling industriousness represents the inverse of the despondent inactivity of the winged figure (3:135). While this comparison places the narrator in the position of infant learner, it nevertheless reinforces the sense of a gender imbalance in both directions. The mother may well be likened to the winged genius; however, she does not possess the anesthetic power of speech and must rely on the child-like male other somehow to speak for her. By the same token the narrator's imaginative affinity with the putto alongside the conceptualization of his mother through *Melencolia I* suggests that he merely stands in for her when she cannot speak, act, or produce. This implies that she is the "genial" font of truth while he is her attendant scribe. The ethical importance of his role emerges here: as attendant scribe he becomes witness to a witness and thus carries responsibility for the preservation of Holocaust memory for the future.

The figure of Dante also casts light on this complex arrangement of characters who represent gendered Holocaust memory as troubled, feminine, ambivalently genial depression (the mother and Boye) on the one hand, and, on the other, as the masculine ability to speak, write, and theorize. The importance of Dante's *Divine Comedy* for Weiss's oeuvre in general and for *Die Ästhetik des Widerstands* in particular has been well documented.[25] Weiss ponders the uses of Dante's tripartite topography—paradise, purgatory, inferno—as a representative apparatus for the world of the twentieth century. In his consideration of this literary model the three dimensions acquire individual meaning. In an ungodly world, paradise becomes the space of the dead victims of history who know no salvation and have no voice to speak about their experiences. Paradise is thus a space of silence. Inferno is the world we all inhabit, the world of violence, political dictatorship, and suffering, while purgatory demarcates a space of doubt and reflection, an intellectual space where possible alternatives to the existing infernal circumstances may be considered. Purgatory is thus the space of resistance that can produce alternative possibilities.[26] From this perspective, purgatory as the space of doubt, uncertainty, and contemplation is the natural habitat of the revolutionary intellectual who attempts to find a way through the complexities of historical situations. In Weiss's reckoning, Dante embodies this kind of earthly genius, the will to stay on course through the descent into hell, and, moreover, to return and bear witness to what he observed in Hades. This will should have the power to transcend all obstacles. As Weiss notes, the original Dante would have relied on divine inspiration to help him in these overwhelming situations. In an ungodly world, however, exceptional tenacity and the ability to transcend the dangers of the external world and the fears generated by the self can only ever be human. The exemplary tool in the creation of earthly genius is language and the written word, in a nutshell the assumption of meaningfulness in even the most traumatic situations.[27]

The mother's troubled relationship to language seems to exclude her from this concept of earthly genius. However, Weiss critically points out in his essay on Dante that the moment of witnessing, of return from paradise—the space of dead victims—to purgatory is premised on a moment of unavoidable hypocrisy: the abandonment of the dead victim. In Dante's case, Beatrice is the betrayed. Weiss notes that the only way out of the terrible ensuing guilt, which we could describe as the experience of being overwhelmed into stasis by a powerful negative affect, is to speak, write, and bear witness: to commit to collective memory the dead victims of history. In the figure of the mother, however, Weiss explores the inverse of Dante as earthly genius: the refusal to give up the dead other, the refusal to write the self out of guilt and suffering. In so doing, he problematizes in terms of gendered affect the necessary moment of hypocrisy that is central to the project of anesthesia. Dante is protected by the distancing power of the highest poetry, he says, yet this special status is premised on the abandonment of the victim.[28] The memory of the dead victim thus enters language at a high price: the necessary elision of the victim.

The same unresolved tension in this issue of language and silence can be observed in Weiss's writings on Hölderlin and also in his Laokoon essay on the representative powers of word and image. In his play *Hölderlin* Weiss presents the poet's decades-long retreat into his tower and virtual cessation of all literary output as a reaction to the failure of revolution. He insists elsewhere that Hölderlin's condition cannot be explained through the modern clinical vocabulary of mental illness, nor can it be explained by taking recourse to such simplifying and unbearable terms as "Innerlichkeit" (inwardness). Instead, Weiss suggests that we must use our powers of imaginative empathy to understand what motivated the poet's reclusiveness and silence.[29]

Here Weiss reads as a special ability what is conventionally viewed as madness. Pathology is thus an alternative way of apprehending the world. The mother figure in *Die Ästhetik des Widerstands* represents one such instance of exceptional, if inaccessible, knowing. And yet she also represents the position of mute trauma marked out by Laokoon and his youngest son. Weiss mobilizes this pair in his essay on the loss and regaining of language to convey how deathly and disastrous the descent into speechlessness is for the individual subject. As in the description of the mother, the metaphors of paralysis and stoniness in this essay combine to produce an image of muteness as social, political, and ultimately biological death.[30] Suspended between Laokoon, Hölderlin, and Dante, the mother is an allegory of, on one hand, the appropriateness of speechlessness in a radicalizing world that produces masses of victims and, on the other, of the disaster of silence for the project of resistance. In the discussion of language and representation after the Holocaust, she is thesis and antithesis simultaneously, and the divided melancholy condition between genius and depression is the allegorical vessel for the depiction of the new situation.

In a note from 1965 Weiss describes himself, despite his manifest politicization in the same year, in melancholy terms. Rereading the works of Hermann Hesse, so influential during his youth, Weiss observes anew the melancholy introspective landscape of those years, concluding that a sense of melancholy and introspection has never really left him. Instead, he has constructed a world of artistic, political engagement on top of this submerged affective chamber.[31] This small note reveals much about Weiss's understanding of melancholy as a condition of the politically engaged intellectual who is beset by doubt but who nevertheless keeps trying to transcend the world in language, articulation, empathy, and cognitive understanding. For Weiss melancholy, and the brooding doubt of which it is often the expression, is the silent basis of political engagement. Without thought, reflection, introspection, and doubt there can be no revolution: this seems to be the implication of his message. As the sign of a necessary form of contemplation that requires translation into the idiom of language, melancholy belongs in the space of resistance: the space of purgatory.

The Depressed Woman and Her Black Bile

Explorations of the mother's condition in *Die Ästhetik des Widerstands* occur through a narrative perspective that shifts between the empathetic imagination of the internal experience of woman's melancholy suffering and the verbose masculine theorization of female depression. The male participants in this theoretical discourse on the mother are the son-narrator—the self-confessed, first-person "chronicler" of the entire oeuvre (2:306)—his father, and his close friend and mentor, the psychoanalyst Dr Max Hodann, a German Communist-intellectual living in Swedish exile who develops an increasingly critical perspective on Stalinism and the Communist Party (2:241–42). In this work, which blends detailed historical research with fictional and mythological elements, the only fictional characters are the proletarian mother, father, and son, who, as convinced Communists, leave Berlin during National Socialism and eventually gain political exile in Sweden. The narrator takes a different exilic route to that of his parents, volunteering first for the Communist cause in the Spanish Civil War, before leaving Spain and travelling via Paris to Sweden. Other than the fictional proletarian family, all the characters are based on individuals whom Weiss encountered in Swedish exile or whom he researched and established as part of postwar memory by including them as complex agents of the anti-fascist resistance in *Die Ästhetik des Widerstands*.[32] The third volume inexorably leads to the harrowing depiction of the executions by the Nazis of the individuals who comprised the Berlin branch of the anti-fascist resistance movement, the "Rote Kapelle" (The Red Orchestra, 3:210–20). Those executed include the narrator's young Marxist friends, Hans Coppi and Horst Heilmann, who are based on authentic historical figures of the Berlin-based resistance group around Harro Schulze-Boysen and Arvid Harnack.[33] Weiss insists on the historical authenticity of his novel, in which fictionalization processes play a key role. The figures, while based on careful documentary research, are focalized through the prism of the first-person narrator, a fictional construct whose subjective perspective on historical events blends collective and individual history, documentary research, and literary fantasy.[34]

Before the focus turns to the executions of those individuals of the "Rote Kapelle" group who have been hunted down by the Gestapo and to the failure of the anti-fascist resistance more generally, significant space is dedicated to the crisis within the narrator's own family. The ineluctable decline of the familial unit amplifies in the domestic sphere the catastrophic political and military failure of the resistance movement: its inability to consolidate its internal tensions and resist National Socialism. When the third volume begins, the narrator, who arrives in Sweden before his parents, is shocked by the spectacle of his mother—her muteness, paralysis, and withdrawal from the world. Conversations with his father posit the genesis of her illness as the result of the traumatic year-long journey across Europe to the safety of exile in Sweden, which Weiss conveys through a number of different melancholy-apocalyptic images: the Europe the parents traverse is likened to a dismembered corpse (3:11), the waves of persecuted Jews on the road trying desperately to reach safety are visualized through the iconography of flooding (3:14), on the first morning of the war German tanks—"grey monsters"—mow down a wheat field with the same saturnine deadliness, or sleight of scythe ("Sensenschlag"), as that of the melancholy deity of medieval melancholy imagery, Saturn/Chronos (3:11, 13; *SM*, 213).

Weiss's use of this imagery in the historical situations outlined in the third and final volume reinforces a sense of creaturely apocalypse. Several other images of danger and catastrophe that are communicated through rich melancholy symbolism contribute to this impression. Initial planning for the undercover mission to Berlin of resistance fighter Lotte Bischoff takes place amid tombs in a Swedish church (3:83–92), snow and stone are persistent metaphors for death (3:7, 20, 100, 214), faces are described as death masks (3:20, 58, 87), night and darkness provide the setting for several scenes, including Bischoff's arrival in the hellish city of Bremen and Stahlmann's unsettling trip to Angkor Wat (3:77, 92–93, 99 102, 104), and the underground space of resistance is described as a crypt (3:110).[35]

While this melancholy-catastrophic imagery presents war, extermination, and dictatorship in a mythological-apocalyptic register, in their discussions father and son nevertheless identify the root of the mother's melancholy in recent historical events. In so doing, they attempt to rationalize her condition, linking her pathology to a clear external cause. However, the very imagery the father employs to describe the eastward expansion of National Socialism undermines these rationalizing efforts. He likens mounting fascism to the spread of a vicious plague that has infected the mother, stifling her voice and all but extinguishing her person (3:15). The mythical qualities of this discourse on her condition amplify the eerie quality of history as it unfolds around individuals who struggle to make sense of it, whether through the metaphor of disease or, like the father, through recourse to facts, figures, and statistics (3:16). This predominantly male discourse casts the mother, as a woman and as the sufferer of a mysterious mental state, in "the position of the melancholic woman and her black bile." Her person becomes the canvas for "the visualization of some unknown state," a perspective that is uneasily sensed by father and son in this opening scene.[36] What, they wonder, if the mother's illness is not just a traumatic reaction to the witnessing of terrible events but more crucially the sign of a groundbreaking "Umwälzung des Denkens" (revolution in thought) that cannot yet be articulated. Karin Boye later reiterates this perspective more forcefully, stating that the mother cannot be considered to be mentally ill; rather, she is—in keeping with a key quality of the Renaissance melancholy genius—a seer with unusual powers of insight (3:25, 32; *SM*, 457–58).

The symbolic ambivalence of the mother figure begins to emerge here. She is described by different individuals as a patient and a sick person but also as a melancholy seer with special insights into catastrophic history (3:9, 26, 129). Her person combines the two extremes that mark out the tension of the melancholy condition: the dullness, stupor, and paralysis of depression and the rare gift of future knowledge that is associated with the melancholy genius. The mother thus embodies a melancholy dialectics between illness and a kind of *ethical* empowerment that remains obscure to the men who watch over her. The genius of *Vergangenheitsbewältigung* in *Die Ästhetik des Widerstands* is the ethically visionary yet mentally deranged woman, the antithesis to Günter Grass's melancholy discourse on gender and postwar ethical memory in *Aus dem Tagebuch einer Schnecke*. In the *Tagebuch* the male protagonist Zweifel suffers a mental breakdown after the war, while Lisbeth, previously a melancholy sufferer because of bereavement, embodies the inability to mourn. By committing Zweifel to a mental institution for twelve years, she shows little understanding for his state and no conception of a greater obligation to remember the victims of the Holocaust. With his iconic and divided image of feminine melancholy, however, Weiss relativizes the superior masculine performance of melancholy Holocaust remembrance we encounter in Grass and, to a lesser extent, in Hildesheimer.[37] Moreover, by foregrounding the limitations of rational understanding, which he encodes as masculine, Weiss also works against traditional conceptions of the depressed woman in the cultural and medical literature on melancholy. On this point, his literary gendering of post-Holocaust ethical memory is closer politically to the melancholy poetics of Ingeborg Bachmann than to those of Grass or Hildesheimer.[38]

In her work on the intellectual history of melancholy, Jennifer Radden traces the roots of the modern association of women with depression back to eighteenth-century faculty psychology which fostered the division between disorders affecting the individual's cognitive capabilities and those affecting the feelings and passions.[39] She argues that "as melancholia came to be seen as a disorder of affection and thus the fate of women, with their perceived emotionality, affective variability, and vulnerability, it became increasingly 'gendered'" (*MMD*, 7). With the development of psychology and psychiatry in the nineteenth century, which deepened this divide, the new category of depression that gradually came to replace melancholia "lost its appealing and heroic associations" (*MMD*, 18). Following Klibansky et al., Radden observes that the heroic view of melancholy as a mark of loquacious, artistic male brilliance was most popular in the Renaissance, beginning with Marsilio Ficino's revision of the negative medieval perspective on melancholy, and it again reached a high point with European Romanticism at the end of the eighteenth and beginning of the nineteenth centuries. She notes that the links between women and depression today are both associative, that is, "entrenched as part of our cultural imagination," and epidemiological: depression appears diagnostically to be more prevalent in women than in men (*MMD*, 47).

She argues, however, that the gendered bias or "sexist ideology" that connects women to the unruly passions and men to reason is historically a form of social control that has been exerted throughout the male-dominated medical profession and that has, in part, produced the contemporary gendered slant on the condition (*MMD*, 69). By contrast, when it was fashionable to be melancholy and brilliant, as was the case in the Renaissance, melancholics were notoriously male. Somewhat ironically from today's perspective, at that time men were regarded as more susceptible to melancholy than were women. The more melancholy became dissociated from its genial legacy through modern medical discourses, the more readily it became categorized as a woman's affliction, reflecting a general tendency during the Victorian era, "to identify the feminine and women with madness" (*MMD*, 48). Part of this development was a different conception of the individual in clinical medicine. Where Romanticism placed great importance on the articulation of individual sorrow, during the same period the emerging field of psychiatry began to view and diagnose the subject-patient in terms of their behavior and not just in terms of the patient's description of inner states, moods, or feelings. In a critical assessment of this development, which confers yet more power on the medic, Radden notes that "a disorder increasingly understood in terms of its behavioral manifestations will also serve to 'silence' its sufferers" (*MMD*, 45).

The almost entirely silent figure of the mother emerges for the reader by virtue of "the endless mill of speech" that emanates from the huddle of men who consider and attempt to diagnose her condition; this reflects some of the above-mentioned problems concerning gender and depression.[40] For one, she is not just a silent figure: the attention to her behavioral manifestations—refusal to eat, slow gait, lack of speech, whimpering, staring—suggests that the external, quasi-clinical observation of the male characters also partly silences her. From this angle, one could argue that Weiss reproduces the gendered discourse of depression in this part of the novel; as mentioned earlier, one of the conceptual sources for this character is the medical terminology around depression.[41]

There are two different ways in which the mother's vegetative depression may be read. She may be viewed as yet another incarnation of nonintellectual and/or abject feminine suffering, the inert, narrowly somatic counterpart to the more profound male condition, which combines the *vita contemplativa* or reflection with the *vita activa* or heroic action, as the narrator's musings on the ideal artist spell out (3:65). From a different standpoint, however, the mother figure may be regarded as a distorted reflection of the post-1945 artistic imagination, here encoded as a limited *masculine* imagination. Her person thus symbolizes the epistemological limits of existing cultural hegemony and so presents a terrifying nothingness beyond the reach of reason, language, and patriarchy. In this respect, Weiss's melancholy performative in the postwar context overturns the gendered aspect to the "Renaissance episteme" of melancholy genius. His play on the dialectical tension between illness (the depressed woman) and empowerment (the male genius) cites the gendered tradition in a new and terrifying era in order to pinpoint the origins of contemporary suffering in violent patriarchy and to suggest the necessity of developing an alternative existential modus not based on masculine hegemony. His gendered intervention in melancholy traditions also underscores the need for a different concept of memory after the Holocaust and, through the figure of the mother, alludes to the problem of a caesura in thought, representation, and language in the postwar context.

Maternal Depression as Allegory of Masculine Crisis

The sense of a crisis of masculinity is nowhere better expressed than in the repeated references to the mother's blank, staring eyes, an established literary metaphor for castration anxiety.[42] It is perhaps not so much the spectral silence of the defeated, feminine ersatz-victim that we encounter in the mother. Rather, her pathology exposes the limitations of reason, language, and rational knowledge. The uncanny quality of the mother's staring eyes alongside the reference to castration anxiety therein presents in gendered terms the alienating newness of the Holocaust and its challenge to the male psyche (3:7, 19). Here it is men, and not women, who struggle to comprehend the genocide, just as they struggle to decode the mother's blankness.

The most naive incarnation of mindless masculinity comes across through the well-meaning figure of Dr. Bratt, a psychoanalyst friend of Hodann's who runs a clinic for mentally disturbed patients near where the narrator's parents live. Considered by some medics to be a quack and by others to be a pioneer, his therapy, which draws on the time-honored practice of treating melancholy with music, consists of singing to his patients in an effort to infect them with a sense of gaiety (3:21).[43] The narrator's father is persuaded that this treatment has a calming effect on his wife; however, the narrator's observations undermine this opinion. Any beneficial effect that emerges after the visits of the round-faced, hearty Bratt has little to do with his treatment and is more the consequence of the peculiar aura that his strange companion, Boye, exudes. Her dark features contrast with Bratt's light, open face in what could be described as the symbolic, gendered opposition of temperamental types: she is blackly melancholy while the lightness and bonhomie of his facial features associates him with sanguinity (3:21–22). In this constellation of persons around the mother, it is Boye who intuitively understands that her silence is the mute sign of an extreme form of affective solidarity with the Jewish victims of the Holocaust. To break this silence and reenter a linguistic world that is not yet equipped to convey what the mother witnessed would amount to a betrayal of the memory of the victims. The mother's silence is thus not a sign of mental illness, argues Boye, but of deep insight and radical understanding (3:25).

Boye's perspective subtly challenges Hodann's later summary of the personality types of her and the narrator's mother (3:131). Comparing the two perspectives is the work of the implied reader: the narrator does not openly evaluate the difference between these positions on the mother, but conscientiously documents them.[44] Thus we learn that Hodann believes that the ability of both women to see more widely and more deeply than others endangers them. Arguably, he devalues the gift of rare intuition, here presented as pernicious, at the same time that he draws our attention to its exceptional status. This reveals his difficulty in trying to explain female melancholy and what it symbolizes: the challenge that the Holocaust presents to language and understanding. By stating that neither woman sufficiently externalizes, that is articulates, their knowledge, he presents the silence around the Holocaust as a female malady that in time will be overcome by the male gift of language and the masculine perspective on art as an anesthetic tool. In the discussion of Dürer's *Melencolia I*, Hodann's emphasis on language as a means of rational understanding overlooks the *affective* dimension of ethical memory that the mother stands for (3:132–34). Her condition, as Boye points out, expresses the necessity of initial affective fixation on the lost object as part of a potential mourning process that may develop into ethical memory (3:32). In contrast to Hodann, the melancholy Boye grasps the importance of affect for memory whenever she is in the mother's presence.

The ethical value of the mother's affective fixation returns again indirectly in the narrator's critical observation of Stahlmann's sentimental pathos upon hearing Stalin's speech after the victory of the Red Army at Stalingrad. There is something wrong with this sentimental outpouring, the narrator's observations suggest rather than state; Stahlmann's emotion is somehow inauthentic (3:138–39). The narrative elsewhere suggests the reason for this inauthenticity: other dramatic images of Stahlmann's contempt for the maternal as the non-revolutionary, non-heroic representative of the domestic sphere connect his affective short-circuit to a denigration of the feminine and a non-critical, naive dedication to aggressive patriarchy (3:63). In this respect, Stahlmann embodies the patriarchal limitations of the mythological hero Hercules that Heilmann reflects upon in the first volume of the novel (1:314–20), a point I return to later.

Hodann is a more reflective and critical character than Stahlmann and often speaks out about the subordinate position of women within the resistance movement (3:44, 248). As indicated, he too is determined by the very patriarchal structures that he critiques. Weiss conveys this idea of a pathological inheritance via the symbolic metaphor of Hodann's asthma, an illness he receives from his father that ultimately kills him (1:216, 256–58; 3:266–67).[45] Although Weiss conceives of him as the great humanist of the novel with particularly lucid insights on the point of gender, his own gender limitation influences his analysis of the mother and Boye.[46] The negative psychiatric diagnosis that he brings to bear on the two women implies his complicity with patriarchal pathology: his diagnosis suggests a kind of hereditary, endogenous female predisposition to depression and helplessness.[47] Hodann begins by challenging the cultural causation model that explains melancholy as a consequence of having witnessed disturbing historical events first-hand. He does this by suggesting the insufficiency of the father's rationale. The father adheres to the explanatory model of cultural causation concerning his wife's melancholy, because he believes that knowledge of the cause—the trauma of "the darkest journey"—will lead to her recovery. According to this logic, the mother will recover in a calm, stable environment that is far removed from the turbulences of the journey into exile and that will encourage the memory of this journey to fade. While the father's viewpoint does not sufficiently acknowledge the extent of the mother's traumatic fixation on victim experience, Hodann critiques this explanatory model from a different angle. The father's explanation, says Hodann to the narrator, stops short at those shadowy regions of the soul that no person can penetrate (3:31). In other words, the father's reasoning does not allow for an understanding of melancholy as undefined lack, that is, melancholy as an all-pervasive mood and endogenous affective disorder that has no identifiable (historical) cause. By raising this issue of causality, Hodann seems to suggest that the two melancholy women are somehow predisposed to depression and are *therefore* endangered by the challenges that history throws up. The traumatic potential of historical situations recedes in this explanatory logic. It is not historical experience that "sickens" these two women, Hodann seems to suggest; rather, traumatic history ignites their underlying pathological condition. In a similar patriarchal vein, he also explains Boye's depression partly as a consequence of her unresolved sexual orientation, thereby relegating an aspect of her melancholy to a gay woman's problem. He concedes that existing social relations are in part to blame for her sexual confusion, but concludes that Boye did not know what she wanted sexually and thus committed suicide (3:42).

The narrator's later assessments of Boye and his mother, which take place after these extensive discussions with Hodann, introduce a different perspective that builds on, but ultimately questions, Hodann's thoughts. His striking memory of Boye after they returned from one of their walks to Bratt's clinic communicates his growing awareness, even if he has not yet verbalized it, of the deadly patriarchy that threatens to destroy difference, here codified as feminine, and that, elsewhere in the novel, emerges as one of the reasons for the implosion of the anti-fascist resistance.

Standing in the dilapidated yard of the clinic and surrounded by the strange figures of the insane, Boye cradles a chick in her hands, while to the side a robust, axe-wielding young man sidles toward her (3:34–35). Apart from his intuitive recognition of a destructive masculine impulse in this scene, the narrator frequently berates himself for his misunderstanding of both Boye and his mother (3:32, 34, 36–37).

In this way masculinity comes to be associated with forgetting the victims of the Holocaust.[48] Bratt's singing therapy, for example, which is based on the principle of distraction, could be read as a means of encouraging the mother to repress what she witnessed. It echoes how the narrator's father encourages his wife to focus on the present in the hope that this will help her to forget what she saw, overheard, and experienced while on "the darkest journey" into exile (3:18–19). The narrator also records how he tries to connect with his mother by telling her of the "ecstatic" prose of a seventeenth-century Swedish writer who travelled to Bremen and recorded his rapturous impressions of the city, the narrator's birthplace and scene of his parents' first encounter (3:19–20). Yet the ineffectualness of this naive attempt to draw her out of herself, which the narrator later wryly compares to Bratt's approach, makes itself evident in his mother's unresponsive facial expression. Her stony features gesture to the inadequacy and ethical insufficiency of these male therapeutic solutions that encourage repression of traumatic events through distraction and forgetting. If her unseeing eyes reflect a kind of disengagement or disaffection, then we cannot read this as a faithful reflection of *her* soul. Her eyes reflect the blankness of the male soul; they mirror the myopic masculine gaze of cultural hegemony that tries to suppress its mounting castration anxiety, yet that also nervously witnesses in the mother's silence the weakening of the language of the symbolic order, a linguistic symptom of events unfolding across Europe.

Returning to Stockholm later that evening, the narrator compares his mother's stony features to the face of the demon Ge, mother of the earth and one of the central stone carvings on the Pergamon Altar which so fascinates him and his young revolutionary friends at the start of volume 1. He likens his mother's face to a stony mask whose surface is marked by blind, unseeing eyes, a kind of death-mask that reappears in the masculine vision of other female characters in the book (3:20). It is significant that the narrator is reminded of Ge's dying son, Alkyoneus, in this scene. Ge is one of the few ascending female figures on the Pergamon Altar, while her son, bitten in the breast by a deadly snake, plunges catastrophically downward and away from her to his death (1:10). If we read these thoughts as the imaginative premonition of the approaching final separation, through death, of mother from son, then it is interesting to note the emphasis of the narrator's mythological reflection: Alkyoneus dies while Ge lives. Yet the narrator survives his mother in this historical period and goes on to record it in written form. The narrator's apprehension, in the guise of the mythological Alkyoneus, of his own demise, suggests that he regards his mother's illness and imminent death as a maternal abandonment of his person, which implies his own death/castration. This sense of male crisis as a reaction to the withdrawal of a necessary feminine presence is borne out in the father's terrible "Raserei" (frenzy) when he realizes that his wife's death is imminent. It is also evident in the narrator's admission that he could never have gone undercover to Berlin as part of the anti-fascist resistance: his sorrow over the separation from his ailing mother would have interfered with his ability to carry out dangerous missions (3:131, 123).

Like the narrator's memory of Boye in the yard holding a chick, the imagined reversal of mother and son positions via Ge/Alkyoneus suggests a further reading of gender relations that is contrapuntal to events happening at the level of the plot. Regarded through the signifier of the mythological Ge, the mother's condition is not so much a debilitating illness as a courageous, if catastrophic, confrontation with a formidable, destructive force. That the narrator mentally plays out this scenario implies a nascent intuition concerning the limitations of masculine reason and rationality, the need, in view of the Final Solution, for a new idiom that openly bears the mark of death, affect, and subjectivity, symbolized here through the trope of the dying but warrior-like maternal-feminine. Between readings of women figures that equate them, on one hand, with victims and, on the other—paying particular attention to mythological imagery in the work—with mindless violence, this account points to a further possibility: that women are quasi-omniscient entities where unfolding history is concerned.[49] This uncanny status confers a certain symbolic power on women characters that reveals the necessity of "feminine" knowledge for strengthening the historical perspective of the male resistance figures at the same time that such knowledge often appears to the male psyche as a disturbing and terrifying apparition.

The association of female figures with the threat of death/castration is a recurring image throughout the work. In addition to the image of Ge ascending toward life while her son descends toward death, the mother's death throes are likened to the battle between Hercules and the Hydra, the female monster of Greek mythology whose incessantly growing snake-heads make it difficult to slay her. In an inverse image of pregnancy, the narrator envisages his mother's body as the incubator for a multitude of deaths: nothing less than a figure such as Hercules can fight back against this Hydra (3:129). In the mythological tale, Hercules succeeds in killing the Hydra, whereas here the narrator's observation casts doubt on Hercules as a heroic concept for the anti-fascist resistance. In so doing, the narrator anticipates Heilmann's later insight that Hercules is not a viable role model for the young Communists. The closing pages of the book, which alight once again on the gap in the Pergamon Frieze where the figure of Hercules was originally carved, capture the realization that the ideal of a heroic male figure is but an empty cipher for forms of resistance that can, in the final analysis, only be performed by earthly individuals (3:267–68). The image of Hercules in battle against the Hydra thus symbolizes in dramatic form the failure of the Left to mount sufficient resistance to National Socialism and the Holocaust. The mother's body as Hydra becomes a kind of mass graveyard for the victims of the Holocaust and for the forces of death that prove too powerful for even a modern-day Hercules to withstand. Her dying body exudes a terrifying force and thanatic knowledge that cause father and son to quake whenever they touch her (3:130). As with the blackness of Boye's appearance and the blankness of the mother's gaze, the image of the "death-bearing woman" in the form of the Hydra exudes an undeniable power, deadly for the observing male subject, whose ability to grasp the truth of emerging historical events is limited. In a gendered discourse that consistently critiques as masculine a world understanding that struggles intuitively to imagine the nature and extent of genocide, Weiss uses archaic images from the war of the sexes to show, on the one hand, the limitations of a rational worldview that shuts itself off from the "feminine"—fantasy, intuition, subjectivity—and, on the other, the return of this repressed deadly knowledge in the symbolic form of fearsome "death-bearing women."

The Genius of Witnessing

Hodann's comparison of the mother to Dürer's winged genius is the positive counterpart to the limiting, rationalizing discourse of medicine that produces the clinical diagnosis. Yet as indicated, his "cultural diagnosis" is also not straightforward. It is embedded in gendered clinical reflection that problematizes both the image of silence about the Holocaust the mother embodies and the opposite image of attempting to speak about trauma: the effort to represent the Holocaust. Weiss attaches positive value to each position here. Indeed, silence and the language that tries to address what lies behind that silence are ambivalently intertwined in this excerpt. He uses the complex image of female melancholy to convey a sense of this ambivalence between language, silence, and the Holocaust. Moreover, the narrative technique frequently draws our attention to the ambivalence of the image of female genius by introducing meaningful discontinuities between the narrator's report of Hodann's reflections and his own observations. These gaps are left open for implied readerly contemplation and point to the possibility of a further not-yet-verbalized perspective that decenters the recorded opinions, perspectives, and insights of the narrating and narrated figures. This textual strategy alone suggests the importance, contrary to Hodann's insistence on the necessity of articulation, of the unsaid. Thus even as Hodann advances a theory of ethical art that connects it to life, memory, the female genius of Dürer's engraving, and also, at a remove, to the mother, the narrative strategy allows for a different evaluation from that of the constantly describing, analyzing, and diagnosing voice of the loquacious male intellectual.

The discussion of *Melencolia I* takes place some time after the mother's death. While Hodann compares her to the winged figure of Dürer's image who sits in quiet contemplation in an "Ort der Meditation" (place of meditation), surrounded by the tools and objects of art and architecture, the narrative does not allow the reader fully to equate the mother with the image of genius (3:133). This is because Hodann distinguishes between the reality of the mother's clinical condition, "der Aufschwung dieses Versinken im Unbennenbaren" (the upsurge of this sinking into the unnameable), and the artwork by Dürer, which, according to Hodann, can tell us more about this condition than the mother can (3:132). This scene reveals how genial art becomes the safe space into which the intellectual male retreats in the face of a depressed reality— the Holocaust—that confounds him. Hodann's description of the limited possibilities open to individuals who suffer from depression suggests that art is a predominantly masculine sphere of activity. In a cultural diagnosis that is damning for the mother, he states that depressed individuals have two options: either they retreat into solipsism or they sublimate their pernicious gifts through the redeeming production of art. This last possibility presupposes openness to the external world outside the subjective internal world of morose contemplation. The implication is that those individuals who are too morbidly turned in on themselves will not be able to create artworks (3:132).

The mother fits this last diagnosis, so it seems contradictory that Hodann should liken her to the winged genius. His concept of melancholy, which he connects to openness and the possibility of healing through the power of art, aligns itself with the tradition of dialectical melancholy genius between illness and empowerment. But the mother is not a producer of great art, and at the start of this conversation Hodann categorizes her as one of those unfortunate individuals who cannot translate her experience into reality (3:131). Again, despite Hodann's status as a representative of probing, humanist thought, it is difficult to ignore the gender imbalance of this *mise-en-scène*: the critical-intellectual male resistance figure announces the diagnosis of the depressed, and therefore culturally defunct, female. He then proceeds to extrapolate from her subjective suffering to an abstract level of analysis, whereby her personal condition retreats from consideration even as it provides the original basis for the male articulation of a theory of ethical art based on ethical memory.

Here Weiss raises in gendered terms the problem of how to articulate a sense of trauma—how to bear witness—through art, without betraying the individual suffering that motivates articulation in the first place. In this case, the mother's subjective "voice"—or *parole* of trauma—is smothered by Hodann's extrapolation into the abstraction of *langue*—the masculine intellectual-cultural code of interpretation. He is thus betraying the victims, exactly what the mother was trying to avoid doing by withdrawing from her environment, as Boye had intuitively sensed. Weiss exposes the linguistic and intellectual mechanism of this betrayal in Hodann's sudden discursive shift from individual female depression to the aesthetics of genius we find in *Melencolia I*.

The continually shifting narrative perspective draws our attention to such slips, however. The narrator recounts how, upon mentioning Dürer's engraving, Hodann reaches over to his shelves and picks out a book that contains a reproduction of the image (3:132). The two men are thus captured in the act of turning away from the human figure of the mother to the aesthetic figure of Melencolia, an act that paradoxically runs counter to the concept of art as intrinsically connected to life that Hodann advances toward the end of this excerpt (3:134). As if in passing, the narrator remarks briefly on this scholarly act of turning to books and high culture, which, he remembers, has happened so many times in previous years: the effort to confirm an idea or critical thought by taking recourse to tradition and learning (3:132). The precise meaning of this observation is left open, yet its very mention points to its significance. It indirectly expresses a reservation about the capacity of existing cultural artifacts to capture the nature of the mother's experience, an unspoken sense that in her case—which revolves around witnessing the Holocaust—a watershed in existing interpretative practices has been reached and that intellectuals must create a new aesthetic.

The first detail noted about the engraving is the buckled book under Melencolia's arm, which suggests that this might be the case. At this point, the narrative has moved from the subjunctive mode, which recalls Hodann's words, to the indicative, which suggests that the narrator is recalling his own impressions of the image and the discussion. As we have seen, Hodann's ambivalent diagnosis confers a dubious special status on the mother as a depressed person and ultimately denies her the ability to move toward sense, meaning, cultural production, and great art. However, the narrator's incisive documentation of this conversation suggests an evaluating as well as a recording consciousness and thereby conducts a subtle critique of Hodann's view on language, trauma, and art. The "locked" book under Melencolia's arm signals a critical limitation to powers of cultural production and interpretation, despite the lengthy abstract discussion that follows. As with the blank, staring eyes of the mother and Ge, the closed book reflects back to the male observers the limitations of patriarchal cultural hegemony. Yet what follows this signifier of illegibility is a reading of the engraving that, against the image of the closed book, confidently interprets its meaning. By the time Hodann links art to a mysterious life force and to ethical memory, it is clear that he is no longer thinking of the mother. His initial association of her with the winged figure is thus tenuous at best. The winged figure, in contrast to the mother, is in Hodann's view an earthly being, mired in activity and work, as opposed to being turned in on herself (3:134). The object of the discussion has in fact become the ethical function of art, and thus the individuality of the mother's experience recedes behind this abstract conversation. Hodann's analysis is part of a rational, reason-based patriarchal worldview that blots out, through abstraction and intellectualization, the subjective experience embodied by the "death-bearing woman." Add to this the narrator's sense, as the mother fades away, that art too is receding from him, and it becomes questionable whether Hodann's efforts to cast light on the mother's experience by referring to art actually bridge the increasing gulf between art and life that the narrator feels to be emerging during her last days (3:125). In this way Weiss leaves open the question of how to approach the Holocaust through language and art. Language and silence, represented as masculine and feminine respectively, are ultimately enunciative positions in a discursive field that attempts to address the Holocaust.[50] The critical representation of this question through gender—loquacious (male) genius and silent (female) depression—suggests the necessity of a more balanced understanding of the problem of language and Holocaust representation, one that allows, beyond prohibition and taboo, for the synchronic coexistence of silence *and* language and that also accepts the uncanny and the irrational as an irreducible part of ethical Holocaust memory. The narrator comes to this conclusion soon after his mother's death (3:148–49).

The Madness of Witnessing

The thoughts and experiences of a number of male characters, in addition to those of the mother and Boye, deepen the impression that witnessing catastrophic history, whether at first or second hand, leads to a form of madness that exceeds the limits of patriarchal reason. These characters are the father, to whom the dying mother whispers the memory of what she witnessed while they were in flight across Europe, and a Graf von Seydlitz, who claims, in reported conversation to the Swedish chemical engineer Nyman, to have witnessed through a peephole the first experiments of extermination by gas (3:119). While the Graf, a spooky, gothic figure, represents the irrational, nocturnal side of existence, the father is, by contrast, focused on the rational interpretation of history, through facts, figures, and statistics (3:16). Nyman occupies a midway position between these two positions on current historical reality.

Through the original eyewitness accounts of the mother and the Graf, Weiss thematizes the act of witnessing as a contagion that infects with madness those who carry out the original act of seeing and/or hearing and those who are open to listening to the verbal accounts of these witnessed events. While in flight across Europe, the mother overhears whispered plans for the Final Solution. As the narrator says, she became a witness, even if this witnessing is initially limited to the act of seeing the soldiers in whispered discussion and overhearing their hissed words (3:130). Shortly after that, however, she sees how the soldiers murder a small family and she also falls into a mass grave of dead Jewish bodies. Her witnessing of the Final Solution thus consists of seeing, hearing, and feeling the imminent or actual destruction of Jewish others.

These are the accounts of witnessing that she passes on to her husband. In conversation with his son, the father can no longer tell clearly whether these thoughts were his or his wife's (3:30). On this point of mental confusion, Weiss raises the problem of bearing testimony as a form of madness that registers the threat for the individual's psyche that the Holocaust presents. The father tells of how he asks his wife why she only volunteers this information now, on her deathbed, but no answer is forthcoming. In a way that suggests the radical newness of what the mother heard and saw, there is no contextualizing discussion that can make sense of the information, and the father is left to grapple with the bare facts of what she is able to communicate to him. His inability to understand how this experience can have such a permanently drastic effect on her comes out in his own moment of insane frenzy when, in desperation, he screams at her and violently shakes her (3:131). As the narrator notes, this episode serves only to widen the gulf between the men of the family and the mother, as if whispered, muttered, half-articulated accounts along the testimonial chain infect each individual with a form of madness or incomprehension that, in the absence of contextualized understanding, alienates individuals from each other. Thus through the father's frenzy Weiss records as a moment of masculine crisis the pernicious effects of emerging knowledge about the Holocaust.

Underscoring the challenge this knowledge presents to language, the act of articulation is depicted as an arduous physical task that saps the speaker of energy. The mother's hoarse whispers recount the overheard soldiers' whispers, but she can say only so much and then sinks back into her deathbed. The narrator notes how his father can barely verbalize this exchange to him. In turn, the narrator struggles to muster up the strength to retell Hodann the account of what his mother witnessed (3:130–31). The chain of witnessing, from soldiers to mother to father to son to Hodann, thus adds to the surreal quality, extreme secrecy, and tabooed nature of the fact of extermination that the mother's account first recognizes as a new scene of violence. Language is sufficient only to cover the basic information in a way that occludes sense-making and that emphasizes the growing gap between experience and the reflection on experience. Reason and the intellectual mastery of art collapse in the face of what the mother witnesses and what nobody can retell without opening up the chasm between art and life, as the narrator reflects (3:131).

Against this backdrop, Hodann's attempt to view the mother through *Melencolia I* becomes the effort to bridge this gap and reintroduce reason to the original madness of witnessing. However, this can only happen by altering the direction of the male gaze, that is, by suppressing the specter of the mad mother, the knowledge of what she saw/heard, and by sublimating her into the worldly-wise, abstract figure of the engraving. Between female subjectivity, madness, and witnessing, on the one hand, and male "objective" aesthetic analysis, on the other, Weiss addresses in gendered terms the process of how the uniqueness of lived historical experience risks becoming abstract once translated into a cultural or linguistic code. Yet the father's momentary madness reveals the artificiality of this gendered divide, a theme that Weiss continues to explore, with relation to witnessing, through the characters of the Graf von Seydlitz and the engineer Nyman.

Knowledge of the Graf's eyewitness account also occurs through a convoluted chain of individuals. Nyman tells the narrator, in the narrator's parental home when the mother is present, of his chance encounter in the Hotel Kempinski, Berlin, with the odd Graf (3:115). During their meal the Graf suddenly begins to tell Nyman of new plans for the systematic extermination by gas of the Jews. A kind of voyeur, he reports how he once looked through the peephole of one of the transports that was being used for these experiments and thus witnessed the agonizing death of several Jews by means of this latest technology (3:119). He is thus able to describe death by gassing in intense, graphic detail, even grotesquely miming, to Nyman's consternation, the stricken faces, moaning, and death-throes of the dying individuals he saw and heard (3:120). The Final Solution as a criminal secret that carries a deadly discursive taboo comes across in Nyman's watchfulness as he nervously glances around the Kempinski restaurant for signs of their conversation being overheard. Sitting in the narrator's parents' house, he covers his mouth with his hands, cowers, and looks about anxiously, underscoring again both the acute danger of displaying knowledge of plans for the Final Solution and the sense of taboo in verbalizing these events (3:120–21). When the narrator recounts Nyman's report of the Graf's eyewitness account to his comrades in the Swedish anti-fascist underground, Stahlmann, Rosner, and Funk, they dismiss this account as the risky, treasonous reports of a madman, "die . . . Ausgeburten eines kranken Gehirns" (the evil spewings of a sick mind, 3:122). Instead, they myopically and narcissistically turn to their own concerns, a reflex that reveals the inability of the male resistance fighters to acknowledge that the Holocaust is happening as a failure of empathy. Their "empathy exhaustion" resonates with the Mitscherlichs' description of the postwar West German collective as autistic. In this sense, their attitude of indifference in this scene anticipates the unwillingness—as opposed to the inability—to mourn. Against this, the mother's function as a symbol for the affective ethics of empathy and identification acquires critical force.[51]

The Graf is a curious literary apparition. Just as Weiss dramatizes the mother's condition with reference to Hydra, Ge, and Melencolia, he also paints the Graf in vivid detail. In passing reference to the convention of nocturnal melancholy, von Seydlitz is described as possessing an owl-like face with dark, bristly hair. A watchful creature of the night, he is not quite human and exudes an eerie aura of spectrality (3:119). Nyman is inclined to believe the tales of this peculiar apparition because his own scientific knowledge as a chemical engineer in Germany has taught him, paradoxically, that truth lies in the surreal, the unbelievable. For example, Nyman is able to report on new technological advances in the mass development of toxic gas for the purpose of extermination (3:120). In this scene, Weiss conveys the necessity of combining the scientific and the fairy-tale-like for gaining a perspective on the emerging Final Solution. More accurately, perhaps, the conversation reveals science and technology as the modern incarnation of the fairy-tale. In this vein, Nyman's retelling of the conversation pays particular attention to the grotesquery of the Graf's physical person: his already strange and distorted visage becomes yet more eerie as it redelivers the sounds and physical convulsions of death. The fairy-tale figure's other-worldly story immediately contaminates the scientist, which comes across in Nyman's own disturbed body language on the night he retells these events to the narrator. His crouched, watchful person communicates the madness of the Graf's dramatic gestures. His body thus signals that he has internalized as true the grotesque, fairy-tale-like eye-witness account.

Nyman's reaction to the Graf transcends the patriarchal discourse of near non-comprehension that characterizes the male reaction to the mother's condition. Instead of dismissing him as a madman, as do the narrator's comrades, Nyman listens to the "Märchen" (fairy tales) from what seems like another world and combines them with his scientific knowledge and his desire to write down all of his impressions so that an account of this new epoch might start to emerge (3:120). In contrast to the father, who, shortly before his wife takes a turn for the worse, starts to list the capitalist facilitators and profiteers of the Final Solution, in Nyman rational knowledge and eeriness coincide to produce a disturbing account of the Final Solution as uncanny (3:126). His account evokes the Holocaust as familiar, in the sense that it takes place within structures and systems already in place, but also as utterly strange, in that the scale, intensity, and modus of the operation is the sign of a drastic new vision. The Graf's ghostly, eccentric persona embodies this sense of the uncanny, and his account disturbingly drives home what it might feel like to be gassed to death.

This contrasts with Hodann's functionalist perspective on the history of terror. In an earlier conversation with the narrator, he makes a case for the normality of the Holocaust, the excessive numbers of victims notwithstanding, by arguing that human history has always been the history of murder. It is not so much that the persecution of the Jews is beyond comprehension, he suggests. Rather, it is indifference or "empathy exhaustion" that has allowed genocide to occur and that threatens post-Holocaust memory discourses (3:47). While this is a lucid observation that is borne out in the behavior of other characters, we have seen how even Hodann's efforts at empathetic imagination err toward a rationalization that can obscure traumatic history.

The narrator's description of empathy exhaustion finds its most apt expression in the indifference of Rosner, Stahlmann, and Funk to Nyman's report. Not all listeners are open to the "contagion" of witnessing, and in that scene, Weiss raises this issue as a problem of the masculine, anti-fascist fighter. The Graf and Nyman, alongside the mother, represent a different position. To differing degrees they are all touched by "madness," that is, by the knowledge of the Final Solution. These individuals are greatly affected by what they witness or hear about, and their very bodies—the mother's uncanny, blank gaze, the Graf's contorted owl-face, Nyman's furtiveness—bear the marks of this knowledge. Madness and melancholy thus represent the opposite of indifference and lacking empathy in the face of emerging knowledge about the Holocaust. In this sense, madness, melancholy, and affect can be aligned with Weiss's concept of purgatory: the space of doubt and uncertainty that is also the proper space of resistance beyond patriarchal restrictions.

Weiss thus subtly polemicizes, in gendered terms, the concepts of cultural amnesia and cultural memory. He raises neglect of the memory of Holocaust victims as a problem embedded in a rationalizing, objectifying masculine worldview that shuns the *vita contemplativa*. Stahlmann epitomizes this very attitude, and the text presents this willful indifference as the symptom of a myopic, self-aggrandizing masculinity that is at the root of the failure of the anti-fascist resistance.[52] Ethical memory, on the other hand, emerges as a subjective, melancholy, feminine intuition and ability that the mother performs. This dichotomy could be regarded as reinforcing existing conservative cultural concepts of gender whereby the feminine stands for affect and emotion and the masculine for reason and rationality. However, Weiss goes beyond the gender binary to critique the "masculine" idea of reason in a number of ways. Not only does he refer to mounting National Socialism as a form of excessive reason that has turned into unreason, but he also depicts several male characters of the anti-fascist resistance in the grip of mounting madness. Heilmann's efforts to reinvent Hercules as a role model for the anti-fascist fighters reveal his "Schwärmer" (enthusiast) tendencies (3:205), while Hodann, like the mother and the Graf, is depicted as a dark, nocturnal creature (1:220, 257–58).

The discussion of melancholy as a form of mania or illness extends to a number of male protagonists in the work. The mythological demigod Hercules, a key symbolic figure for the concept of masculine, heroic, anti-fascist resistance, represents this particular aspect of pathological melancholy. This figure, notably absent from the Pergamon Altar in the novel's opening and closing scenes, is an ongoing source of fascination, discussion, and potential identification for the young narrator and his male Communist friends. They try to reinvent Hercules as a positive heroic figure for the class struggle and the fight against fascism. However, Hercules's susceptibility to madness and ultimate failure is exemplified in the ambivalent underground resistance character, Stahlmann, who lives in hiding in Stockholm for most of the war. In the writings on melancholy where for the first time pseudo-Aristotle connects melancholy to genius and notes that mania is one of its manifestations, Hercules is one of the great mythological figures he mentions as an example of manic-melancholy.[53] An excessive and ambivalent figure—half-mortal, half-god—Hercules, it could be argued, represents a disastrous, insufficiently contemplative, and willfully myopic male melancholy in *Die Ästhetik des Widerstands*. In Stahlmann this myopia symbolizes his lack of empathy and represents his inability or unwillingness to participate in ethical memory. Mania is evident in the character's blind commitment to Stalinism and thus to totalitarianism, as becomes clear on his nocturnal journey to Angkor Wat (3:105). Weiss warns against the dangers of self-transcendence in dubious political convictions here. In contrast to Stahlmann, Heilmann, before his execution, bids farewell to the dream of Hercules the super-hero who can rescue the individual from the pain of history (3:169). We might say that he lays to rest his "enthusiasm" and returns to an understanding of the mortal complexity of historical events and the complicated position of the individual therein. The mania lives on in Stahlmann, however, who, in his dedication to the icon Stalin, remains committed to the extremity of totalitarianism. In this figure, Weiss obliterates the melancholy male genius of ethical remembrance. In Stahlmann's case, self-transcendence does not translate into the empathetic ability to think of the other. Rather, it is directed toward the vision of a false god that narcissistically inflates the self. Collectively thus, many of the main male figures of this work—Hodann, the narrator, Heilmann, Stahlmann—perform the crisis of Holocaust memory and with it the crisis of the melancholy male genius.

Crisis of the Male Genius of Holocaust Memory

Reading the mother as a kind of indeterminate "hypersign" of the masculine imagination equates to a reevaluation of her pathological silence and vegetative state. While her association with both melancholy genius and depression renders her ambivalent, one can argue that by presenting, in iconic terms at least, the genial melancholy figure as a female one, Weiss, in contrast to Grass and Hildesheimer, adds tension and complexity to his concept of ethical memory. Historically, mourning work has been regarded and performed as an essentially feminine task. Yet the figure of the mourning woman may also function as a repository for displaced masculine emotion, an opportunity, while surreptitiously transferring affect into a culturally acceptable female form, "to repress femininity among males."[54] Both Lisbeth and Celestina, respectively the female protagonists of Grass's *Tagebuch* and Hildesheimer's *Tynset*, could be regarded, in their pathological and largely speechless states, as feminine ciphers for the disguised affect of the intellectual male narrators. Against this backdrop, the iconoclastic quality of Weiss's melancholy mother emerges in the son's self-reflexive account of her death. What becomes clear in the discussion of the mother's condition is not just an ornately allegorical portrayal of displaced male affect via the mother as Melencolia. It is also a self-conscious critique of the limitations and vanity of the exclusive male allegorical imagination as it busies itself with the heroic task of revolutionary thought, thereby neglecting the plight of the Jews and pointing to the possibility of inadequate Holocaust memory in the future.

At first glance Hodann seems to revise the view of the mother as mutely uncommunicative when he aligns her with Renaissance genius. He codifies her condition with reference to *Melencolia I*, which, contrary to the intellectual impoverishment and psycho-motor retardation associated with the clinical condition, invests her person with excessive high-cultural meaning. This intellectual investment is one example of the sustained effort to perform the politically motivated, high-cultural interpretation of art that is a cornerstone of revolutionary thought. Such effort informs the entire work and the discussion of *Melencolia I* suggests—consistent with earlier discussions of great artworks—that ethical memory of the victims of history is an inalienable part of revolutionary thought.[55] Yet in this particular scene, revolutionary thought is an exercise of the explicitly *masculine* allegorical imagination that takes as its object the mourning, proletarian mother and, in revolutionary intellectual mode, elevates her to Dürer's noble winged genius. The interpretation of great art for the purpose of better understanding a new and traumatic historical experience takes place in this scene. Yet Hodann's imaginative transformation of the mother is problematic. It simultaneously denies yet confers upon the mother cultural and intellectual status, which raises questions about

Holocaust memory as an exclusive and gendered performance in the cultural-intellectual sphere of German memory discourses. It also demonstrates clearly the danger of amnesia, which is continually present in the cultural memory of historical catastrophe.

Notes

[1] Peter Weiss, *Die Ästhetik des Widerstands* (Frankfurt am Main: Suhrkamp, 1983). Weiss wrote this three-volume epic over a period of nearly ten years, between July 1972 and August 1980. The three volumes were first published separately, in 1975, 1978, and 1981 respectively. During this decade Weiss also produced notebooks that accompany the progress of the novel and often correspond closely to the text. These notebooks were published in 1981 at the same time that the third volume appeared. Peter Weiss, *Notizbücher, 1971–1980*. Since 2007 an expanded critical edition of Weiss's handwritten notebooks has been available on CD-Rom. *Peter Weiss: Die Notizbücher; Kritische Gesamtausgabe*, ed. Jürgen Schutte, Wiebke Amthor, and Jenny Willner (Berlin: Digitale Bibliothek, 2007).

[2] On coldness and dryness as melancholy qualities see *SM*, 48. For a discussion of the steadily pernicious metaphorical quality of sand in Weiss's work see Anja Schnabel, *"Nicht ein Tag, an dem ich nicht an den Tod denke": Todesvorstellungen und Todesdarstellungen in Peter Weiss' Bildern und Schriften* (St. Ingbert, Germany: Röhrig, 2010), 352–402.

[3] On postmemory see Marianne Hirsch, *Family Frames: Photography, Narrative and Postmemory* (Cambridge, MA: Harvard University Press, 1997), 22.

[4] Jean Starobinski, "L'encre de la mélancolie," in *Mélancolie: Génie et folie en occident*, ed. Jean Clair (Paris: Gallimard, 2005), 24.

[5] On the mother as a "Jewish" figure see Julia Hell, "From Laokoon to Ge: Resistance to Jewish Authorship in Peter Weiss's *Ästhetik des Widerstands*, in *Rethinking Peter Weiss*, ed. Jost Hermand and Marc Silberman (New York: Peter Lang, 2000), 21–44. See also Irene Heidelberger-Leonard, who argues that the mother is a kind of Jewish alter ego for the narrator. Heidelberger-Leonard, "Jüdisches Bewußtsein im Werk von Peter Weiss," in *Literatur, Ästhetik, Geschichte: Neue Zugänge zu Peter Weiss*, ed. Michael Hofmann, Karl Richter, Gerhard Sauder, and Gerhard Schmidt-Henkel (St. Ingbert, Germany: Röhrig, 1992), 57–58. Hofmann goes so far as to suggest that the mother's condition symbolizes Holocaust uniqueness: Hofmann, "Antifaschismus und poetische Erinnerung der Shoah," in *Peter Weiss Jahrbuch 3*, ed. Rainer Koch, Martin Rector, Rainer Rother, and Jochen Vogt (Opladen: Westdeutscher Verlag, 1994), 127.

[6] Sigmund Freud, "Trauer und Melancholie," 10:428–46.

[7] The concept first appears in *Ästhetik des Widerstands* 1 as part of a discussion about Dante's descent into hell. The young Marxist Horst Heilmann describes anesthesia as the protective function of the word. Instead of speechlessly succumbing to the world's palpable aggression, the writer who anesthetizes the self with language tries to understand and resist through verbal articulation the historical causes of this aggression (1:83). Weiss also explores in earlier works the idea

of a necessary emotional numbness. See Alfons Söllner, "Peter Weiss' *Die Ermittlung* in zeitgeschichtlicher Perspektive," in *Deutsche Nachkriegsliteratur und der Holocaust*, ed. Stephan Braese, Holger Gehle, Doron Kiesel, and Hanno Loewy (Frankfurt am Main: Campus, 1998), 111.

[8] Jens Birkmeyer, *Bilder des Schreckens: Dantes Spuren und die Mythosrezeption in Peter Weiss' Roman "Die Ästhetik des Widerstands"* (Wiesbaden: Deutscher Universitätsverlag, 1994), 157.

[9] See "Zwischen Pergamon und Plötzensee oder die andere Darstellung der Verläufe: Peter Weiss im Gespräch mit Burkhardt Lindner," in *Peter Weiss im Gespräch*, ed. Rainer Gerlach and Matthias Richter (Frankfurt am Main: Suhrkamp 1986), 278.

[10] "Laokoon oder Über die Grenzen der Sprache," in *Rapporte* (Frankfurt am Main: Suhrkamp, 1968), 182–83. Weiss's father was a Christianized German-Jew who married a gentile, and so Weiss had little knowledge of his own Jewish heritage until his family fled Germany in 1935. He eventually arrived in Sweden in 1939, where he died in 1982. His autobiographical texts *Abschied von den Eltern* (Frankfurt am Main: Suhrkamp, 1961) and *Fluchtpunkt* (Frankfurt am Main: Suhrkamp, 1962) tell the story of a conflicted Jewish identity that eventually developed into a strong political identity centered around a commitment to the Jewish victims of the Holocaust and, beyond that, to the victims of history generally. See *Fluchtpunkt*, 210–12. Also, the essay "Meine Ortschaft," in *Rapporte*, 113–24 and the famous documentary play, based on Weiss's notes from the Auschwitz trials, which he attended in Frankfurt am Main from 1963–65, *Die Ermittlung: Oratorium in 11 Gesängen* (Frankfurt am Main: Suhrkamp, 1965). For more information on Weiss's childhood and youth see Jochen Vogt, *Peter Weiss* (Hamburg: Rowohlt, 1987), 10–63. For an examination of his poetics of exile see Katja Garloff, *Words from Abroad: Trauma and Displacement in Postwar German Jewish Writers* (Detroit, MI: Wayne State University Press, 2005). See also Jens-Fiejte Dwars, *Und dennoch Hoffnung: Peter Weiss; Eine Biographie* (Berlin: Aufbau, 2007).

[11] The secondary literature is divided on how successful this project is in the novel. Carol Poore argues that Weiss does not fall back on images of women's nature as an explanation for their social and historical exclusion from male-dominated politics and cultural production: Hodann, who offers a feminist critique of patriarchy, is a key figure in this endeavor. Poore, "Mother Earth, Melancholia, and Mnemosyne: Women in Peter Weiss's *Die Ästhetik des Widerstands*," *German Quarterly* 58, no. 1 (1985): 83. By contrast, Renate Langer sees Hodann's feminism as the symptom of a repressed but indelible patriarchal mark. Langer, "Der Sohn als Guerillero: Imaginationen von Klassenkampf und präödipalem Drama in der *Ästhetik des Widerstands*," in *Die Bilderwelt des Peter Weiss*, ed. Alexander Honold and Ulrich Schreiber (Berlin: Argument, 1995), 70. Julia Hell conceives of the novel in terms of competing feminine and masculine discourses, concluding that the feminine discourse is defeated in the end. Hell, "Rosa oder die Sehnsucht nach einer Geschichte ohne Stalin: Zur Logik einer vergeschlechtlichten Textproduktion in der *Ästhetik des Widerstands*," in *Peter Weiss Jahrbuch 6*, ed. Martin Rector and Jochen Vogt (Opladen, Germany: Westdeutscher Verlag, 1997), 151. Birgit Feusthuber argues that even in the depiction of heroic female

figures, such as Lotte Bischoff, Weiss unsettles his critique of patriarchy because ultimately the female figures are projections of a male catastrophic or utopian fantasy. Feusthuber, "Najaden und Sirenen: Weiblichkeitsbilder in der *Ästhetik des Widerstands*," in *Peter Weiss: Neue Fragen an alte Texte*, ed. Irene Heidelberger-Leonard (Opladen: Westdeutscher Verlag, 1994), 108. Likewise, Achim Kessler argues that in the case of women Weiss deviates from his habit of presenting history from the perspective of the oppressed. Kessler, *"Schafft die Einheit!": Die Figurenkonstellation in der Ästhetik des Widerstands von Peter Weiss* (Hamburg: Argument, 1997), 115.

[12] As a heroic survivor of the anti-fascist resistance, Lotte Bischoff is the exception to this rule. See Irene Dölling, "Frauen im Klassenkampf: Klassenkampf und Geschlechterfrage in Peter Weiss' *Die Ästhetik des Widerstands*," in *"Die Ästhetik des Widerstands": Erfahrungen mit dem Roman von Peter Weiss*, ed. Norbert Krenzlin (Berlin: Akademie, 1987), 60. Also Gisela Horn and Haike Wirrmann, "Der weibliche Widerstand," *Wissenschaftliche Zeitschrift* 36, no. 3 (1987): 436–38.

[13] On melancholy incorporation see Nicolas Abraham and Maria Torok, "Mourning *or* Melancholia: Introjection *versus* Incorporation," 130. Mitscherlich and Mitscherlich, *Die Unfähigkeit zu trauern*, 39.

[14] Jonathan Flatley, *Affective Mapping: Melancholia and the Politics of Modernism* (Cambridge, MA: Harvard University Press, 2008), 52.

[15] Kristeva, *Black Sun*, 99.

[16] Weiss joined the Swedish Communist Party in 1965 and six years later published his "10 Arbeitspunkte eines Autors in der geteilten Welt," in which he announces his political affiliation with socialism, his commitment to politically engaged art, and a shift away from his earlier style. Weiss, *Rapporte 2* (Frankfurt am Main: Suhrkamp, 1971), 14–23. *Rekonvaleszenz*, which he wrote in 1970, marks a shift in Weiss's political and writerly development: a return to the inner life of the individual. *Rekonvaleszenz* (Frankfurt am Main: Suhrkamp, 1991), 7. His early prose works are often viewed as solipsistic, surrealist in style, and concerned with the inner world of the artist. I agree with Sarah Pourciau, however, that the aesthetics of resistance "shapes Weiss's literary work from the moment he sets out to write and not . . . from the moment he sets out to write about politics." She argues that even the works preceding the autobiographical texts demonstrate, on the linguistic level, a political aesthetics. Pourciau, "Infernal Poetics: Peter Weiss and the Problem of Postwar Authorship," *Germanic Review* 82, no. 2 (2007): 157.

[17] See, for example, Martin Rector, "Fünfundzwanzig Jahre *Die Ästhetik des Widerstands*: Prolegomena zu einem Forschungsbericht," in *Diese bebende, zähe, kühne Hoffnung: 25 Jahre Peter Weiss, Die Ästhetik des Widerstands*, ed. Arnd Beise, Jens Birkmeyer, Michael Hoffmann (St. Ingbert, Germany: Röhrig, 2008), 14.

[18] For a critical stance on memory discourses as overly-emotional and risking identity politics, see Charles Maier, "A Surfeit of Memory?" and Kerwin Lee Klein, "On the Emergence of Memory in Historical Discourse," *Representations* 69 (2000): 127–50.

[19] Dominick LaCapra, *Writing History, Writing Trauma*, 23.

[20] Weiss, *Notizbücher, 1971–1980*, 748. Gerlach and Richter, *Peter Weiss im Gespräch*, 295–96.

[21] Gerlach and Richter, *Peter Weiss im Gespräch*, 279.

[22] Gerlach and Richter, *Peter Weiss im Gespräch*, 213.

[23] Robert Eaglestone, *The Holocaust and the Postmodern* (Oxford: Oxford University Press, 2004), 36–37.

[24] Peter-Weiss-Archiv, SAdK, Berlin, no. 3014.

[25] Birkmeyer, *Bilder des Schreckens*, 127–222. See also Irene Heidelberger-Leonard, "'Die Kunst zu erben' oder Der Gebrauchswert der 'Divina Commedia' für Peter Weiss," in *Hinter jedem Wort die Gefahr des Verstummens: Sprachproblematik und literarische Tradition in der Ästhetik des Widerstands von Peter Weiss*, ed. Hans Höller (Stuttgart: Akademischer Verlag, 1988), 21–37; Maria C. Schmitt, *"Die Ästhetik des Widerstands": Studien zu Kontext, Struktur und Kunstverständnis* (St. Ingbert, Germany: Röhrig, 1986), 148–64.

[26] The following discussion refers to two essays Weiss wrote on the topic of Dante as a possible aesthetic model for a post-Holocaust literary work: "Vorübungen zum dreiteiligen Drama divina commedia" and "Gespräch über Dante." Both are in *Rapporte*, 125–41 and 142–69 respectively.

[27] *Rapporte*, 147–48.

[28] *Rapporte*, 145.

[29] Weiss, *Hölderlin* (Frankfurt am Main: Suhrkamp, 1971), and "Laokoon oder Über die Grenzen der Sprache," 170–86. In an article that appeared in the *Frankfurter Rundschau* in March 1973, Weiss argues against French scholar Pierre Bertaux that Hölderlin's famous decades-long withdrawal from the world into his tower in Tübingen was a sign of the poet's elevated mental state and not a sign of madness. Weiss, *Notizbücher, 1971–1980*, 803–4. See also his statement that Hölderlin's illness had its roots in the politically turbulent revolutionary society of his times *Notizbücher, 1971–1980*, 861. For a detailed comparison of Hölderlin and the mother as individuals with special powers of insight see Franz Zeller, "Hölderlin in der *Ästhetik des Widerstands*," in Höller, *"Hinter jedem Wort die Gefahr des Verstummens,"* 79–102.

[30] Weiss, "Laokoon," 180–81.

[31] *Notizbücher, 1960–1971* (Frankfurt am Main: Suhrkamp, 1982), 1:386.

[32] For example, Hodann is based on the individual whom Weiss met when he arrived in Stockholm in 1940 and features as Hoederer in the earlier autobiographical work *Fluchtpunkt*. The story of Lotte Bischoff, the heroic female antifascist resistance fighter who travels undercover from Stockholm to Berlin as part of her underground activity in support of the resistance group the "Rote Kapelle," is based on interviews Weiss carried out with Bischoff in the 1970s. For more information on the historical background of the individuals featured in the novel see Robert Cohen, *Bio-Bibliographisches Handbuch zu Peter Weiss' "Ästhetik des Widerstands"* (Hamburg: Argument, 1989).

[33] For a critical evaluation of the group see Johannes Tuchel, "Das Ende der Legenden: Die Rote Kapelle im Widerstand gegen den Nationalsozialismus," in *Der*

20. Juli: Das andere Deutschland in der Vergangenheitspolitik, ed. Gerd R. Ueberschär (Berlin: Elefanten Press, 1998), 347–65.

[34] See Weiss's description of his historical research in *Peter Weiss im Gespräch*, 209–10. Schmitt describes this narrative style as "fictional authenticity." Schmitt, *Die Ästhetik des Widerstands*, 75.

[35] For more detail on these and related symbols in vol. 3, see the "death register" in Schnabel's study *"Nicht ein Tag, an dem ich nicht an den Tod denke,"* 632–40.

[36] Sander L. Gilman, *Disease and Representation: Images of Illness from Madness to AIDS* (Ithaca, NY: Cornell University Press, 1988), 19.

[37] See the discussion of the melancholy pair, the narrator/Celestina, in chapter 2.

[38] In *Das Buch Franza*, for example, Bachmann presents Franza's mental collapse as a reaction to a postwar world still determined by violent patriarchy. While she is "ill," Franza nevertheless proves capable of terrifying the men of this world with her thoughts, behavior, and requests. Like the mother in Weiss's work, Franza represents a limit point for masculine reason. Bachmann, *Das Buch Franza*.

[39] Radden, *Moody Minds Distempered*, 7. Hereafter cited in text as *MMD*.

[40] Michel Foucault, *The History of Sexuality, Volume I: An Introduction*, trans. Robert Hurley (London: Penguin, 1990), 21.

[41] Kunibert Erbel remarks on the blinkered perspective of those who see the mother's condition only in terms of a medical diagnosis. *Sprachlose Körper, körperlose Sprache: Studien zu 'innerer' und 'äußerer' Natur in Die Ästhetik des Widerstands* (St Ingbert, Germany: Röhrig, 1991), 146. Hartmut Böhme argues that the inability of the male observers to understand the mother's melancholy constitutes a moment of masculine "Härte" (hardness) and complicity with fascism. Böhme, "Zur literarischen Rezeption von Albrecht Dürers Kupferstich *Melencolia I*," 112.

[42] See Freud, "Das Unheimliche," in *Gesammelte Werke*, 18 vols., ed Anna Freud (Frankfurt am Main: Fischer, 1966), 12:227–68. On the mother as symbol for castration anxiety in Weiss's earlier autobiographical work see Axel Dunker, *Die anwesende Abwesenheit*, 82–93.

[43] On music as an established therapy for melancholy, one that originates in the Old Testament, see Günter Bandman, *Melancholie und Musik*, 11–21. Bandmann points out, however, that music as a failed therapeutic treatment for melancholy is an equally established topos, which Weiss thematizes in the passage discussed above (47).

[44] On narrative technique in *Ästhetik des Widerstands* see Birkmeyer, *Bilder des Schreckens*, 57–104.

[45] See Langer, "Der Sohn als Guerillero," 69.

[46] Weiss states that Hodann is a kind of father figure and the most important figure in the entire novel. See Weiss, "Zwischen Pergamon und Plötzensee," 266, 269–70.

[47] This understanding of depression is attributed to Emil Kraepelin, whose nosological innovations of the late nineteenth century had a great impact on the classification and treatment of depression in the twentieth century. Stanley W.

Jackson, *Melancholia and Depression*, 192. My reading of this scene goes against Ernst Leonardy, who argues that Hodann's discussion confers heroic traits on the mother: Leonardy, "Das Sterben der Mutter und Heilmanns Abschiedsbrief: Beobachtungen zur Figurengestaltung im Epilogband der *Ästhetik des Widerstands*," in Heidelberger-Leonard, *Peter Weiss: Neue Fragen an alte Texte*, 117–18.

[48] Schmitt argues that the male Leftist denial of reality extends to disbelief in the Holocaust and brings about the failure of the resistance. Schmitt, *"Die Ästhetik des Widerstands,"* 138.

[49] See respectively Hell, "Rosa oder die Sehnsucht nach einer Geschichte ohne Stalin," in *Peter Weiss Jahrbuch 6*, ed. Martin Rector and Jochen Vogt, 138–63, and Langer, "Der Sohn als Guerillero," 64–76.

[50] Alexander Honold argues that mother and father represent two aesthetic extremes: the memory archive (father) versus the *tabula rasa* (mother): Honold, "Das Gedächtnis der Bilder: Zur Ästhetik der Memoria bei Peter Weiss," in Honold and Schreiber, *Die Bilderwelt des Peter Weiss*, 110–11.

[51] Carolyn J. Dean, *The Fragility of Empathy after the Holocaust* (Ithaca, NY: Cornell University Press, 2004). Mitscherlich and Mitscherlich, *Die Unfähigkeit zu trauern*, 38.

[52] Berthold Brunner, *Der Herakles / Stahlmann-Komplex in Peter Weiss' Ästhetik des Widerstands* (St. Ingbert, Germany: Röhrig, 1999), 365.

[53] Aristotle, *Aristotle: Problems II*, 30.155. See also Walter Benjamin, *Ursprung des deutschen Trauerspiels*, 160; László F. Földényi, *Melancholie*, trans. Nora Tahy (Berlin: Matthes & Seitz, 2004), 25–26.

[54] Nicole Loraux, *Mothers in Mourning: With the Essay "Of Amnesty and Its Opposite,"* trans. Corinne Pache (Ithaca, NY: Cornell University Press, 1998), 24.

[55] For an overview of all artworks mentioned in the novel see Nana Badenberg, "Kommentiertes Verzeichnis der in der *Ästhetik des Widerstands* erwähnten bildenden Künstler und Kunstwerke," in Honold and Schreiber, *Die Bilderwelt des Peter Weiss*, 163–230.

4: From the *Weltschmerz* of the Postwar Penitent to Capitalism and the "Racial Century": Melancholy Diversity in W. G. Sebald's Work

Sebald's Melancholy Diversity

MELANCHOLY IN SEBALD'S WORK is one of the most debated subjects. His engagement with Walter Benjamin's philosophy of history, with the melancholy writings of the seventeenth-century English thinker Thomas Browne, his play with space and perspective, and his melancholy representation of time feature prominently in this body of scholarship.[1] And yet the fundamental ambivalence of Sebald's melancholy has not been sufficiently recognized. The following chapter illuminates the complexity of melancholy in his work. Indeed, it is more accurate to speak of "melancholies" in Sebald because he, like Günter Grass, Wolfgang Hildesheimer, and Peter Weiss, adapts and combines several discursive traditions. This diversity makes it difficult to derive a single overarching message from his use of melancholy. His conflation of the Freudian terms "melancholy" and "mourning" in his essayistic work further complicates matters.[2]

As we have seen in previous chapters, melancholy, because of its long and diverse history, can become an overdetermined signifier in the literary text. Sebald, too, uses melancholy traditions to negotiate a self-conscious position on the place of affect and emotion in post-Holocaust memory. In the preface to his essay collection *Die Beschreibung des Unglücks* (Describing Unhappiness, 1985) Sebald suggests that literature often exceeds psychoanalysis in its ability to convey the nature of psychic formations and deformations. In his view, the modernism of the Austrian *fin-de-siècle* managed to express precisely the pathologies of sadness that preoccupied the psychiatric disciplines at the time. Yet Sebald also uses many images and references from different melancholy traditions in a strikingly non-psychological manner. Melancholy iconography from the Renaissance and other eras features in his work alongside and distinct from psychoanalytical references to the condition of sadness. His careful reading of key studies on melancholy by Walter Benjamin and Wolfgang

Lepenies reveals a clear interest in the iconography of melancholy. For example, in his copy of Benjamin's *Ursprung des deutschen Trauerspiels*, Sebald underlined Benjamin's observations on the "ostentatious" and theatrical aspects of the performance of sadness several times. Other notes in this book suggest that he was interested in the comical possibilities of the melancholy personality.[3]

In this chapter I debate the different assessments of sadness we encounter in Sebald's use of the terms "Trauer" (mourning) and melancholy, and also consider his engagement with older melancholy traditions, in particular his focus on sentimentality and Renaissance iconography. While many scholars view Sebald's use of melancholy either positively as a form of "Trauerarbeit" (mourning work) in the service of working through trauma, or negatively as the mouthpiece for a teleology that conveys his deep-seated historical resignation, I favor a more differentiated approach that takes account of the multifaceted quality of Sebald's engagement with melancholy. He exploits an array of images from Western writing on the condition so as to accentuate the tension between the subjective gloom of the artist-intellectual and a sense of hope that arises through a more panoramic perspective on history. A reappraisal of melancholy in Sebald thus also addresses the question of whether his representation of history takes place in a tendentious mythological, nostalgic, or sentimental register. While many critics argue that this kind of register weakens both his ethical effort to write a literary account of history's forgotten victims and the incisiveness of his critique of modernity, I suggest that Sebald represents these two perspectives in a typological, iconographic fashion: the individual-psychological microcosm of quiet devastation, shame, and wry self-deprecation, on the one hand; the non-psychological appraisal of global historical forces, on the other.[4] Especially when Sebald's narrators appear to wallow in sentimentality or to "trade in nostalgia," we should consider the function of the self-irony in these scenes.[5] As a marker of circumspection, irony conveys the understanding that individual memory work takes place within a greater collective framework. Despite the high presence of melancholy sufferers in Sebald's oeuvre, therefore, melancholy cannot be viewed as a timeless anthropological constant with insufficient historical cause, or as the sidekick to the Enlightenment's fall into barbarity.[6]

Unease concerning the potential ethical compromise of the mythological dimension to melancholy in Sebald's work is particularly evident in what Andreas Huyssen has described as "moralizing" approaches to reading Sebald.[7] The concern here is, first, that a German narrator who has not experienced first-hand the traumas of the Second World War and the Holocaust risks sentimentalizing German-Jewish relations, and second, that his nostalgic representations of the prewar past weaken the effort to understand history. This point was first made by Anne Fuchs in her incisive study on Sebald's poetics of memory.[8] Highlighting the Manichaean division between a rich prewar world of cultural plenitude, on one hand, and depleted, drab postwar reality, on the other, Fuchs argues that Sebald's narrator adopts a posthumous view on a world that is doomed to self-destruct. While Sebald's world is indeed characterized by a sharp division between a culturally rich past and a bland present, I demonstrate that he in fact uses different kinds of melancholy to emphasize the historical register over the mythological in his representation of world history.

All of Sebald's prose works share, albeit to differing degrees, this understanding of melancholy as a response to the impossible path of Western history both during and preceding the twentieth century. His historicization of the melancholy condition in the case of the postwar German artist consciously draws on the tradition of the "Renaissance episteme" of genius. In his early prose poem, *Nach der Natur* (After Nature, 1992) he aligns himself with saturnine melancholy by stating that he was born under Saturn, the planet that during the Renaissance became the astrological marker of thinkers and artists. In so doing he, like Grass and Hildesheimer, presents himself in a long-standing noble intellectual tradition. He focuses this broad and timeless tradition historically, however, by mentioning in the same excerpt his year of birth, 1944.[9]

Here we can observe a process of poetic combinations that demonstrates how Sebald uses melancholy. In the reference to Saturn he invokes an ancient, universal motif that, because of its origins in a combination of Greek and Roman mythology and Arabic astrology, casts contemporary history, the end of the Second World War, and his birth in a fatalistic light. Indeed, we might well speak of transgenerational trauma in this depiction of a postwar destiny that the individual cannot control. Yet the very allusion to the war means that mythology does not entirely elide the historical register. Adapting an old melancholy motif for situating the ethical artist after 1945, Sebald strikes a balance between mythology and history. At the same time, he self-reflexively alludes to the problems of post-Holocaust representation in this juxtaposition of mythology with contemporary history. His strategy of combination follows Weiss's impressive lead, integrating the saturnine tradition into a poetic representation that reveals the power of myth to afford insight into history and the subject's place within it.[10]

For all his reservations about Grass's melancholy poetics, Sebald's interest in melancholy iconography articulates, in the case of the artist, a similar interest in establishing an appropriate way to commemorate the historical losses of the Second World War and, more fundamentally, the Holocaust. Grass's declared intent in *Aus dem Tagebuch einer Schnecke* is to foreground the melancholy of Jewish victims. This intention, as outlined in chapter 1, however, recedes behind both the melancholy of the perpetrator collective and the solipsism of the narrator's artistic melancholy. By contrast, Hildesheimer's melancholy radicalism expresses the absurd *ressentiment* and moral stringency of the victim subject.[11] Sebald's work lies between these two positions. He emphasizes the victims' voices and their melancholy afflictions. Through the personal quirks of his narrators, however, he also allows for the roundabout expression of melancholy as the occasionally self-ridiculing *Weltschmerz* of the postwar German penitent.[12]

As discussed in the case of Weiss's *Die Ästhetik des Widerstands*, melancholy can be a tool of resistance and ethical understanding in the face of repeated historical catastrophe.[13] The ethical dimension of melancholy in Sebald's work is evident both in its symbolic usefulness for the representation of world history and in the sometimes self-mocking tone of his narrator figures. Self-irony introduces indirect self-reflection on the hysterical, even melodramatic quality that their behavior periodically displays. In these contexts, Sebald exaggerates the ability to mourn and the noble melancholy mindset that ostentatiously performs this mourning work. Often depicting his narrators in the mode of torturous self-awareness, he shows how memory work, no matter how worthy, can become an empty aesthetic gesture if it turns in on itself and ceases to try to understand the world. Self-mockery reveals how living with the keenly felt sense of a memory obligation to history's victims, in particular the Jewish victims of the Holocaust, can produce in the German narrator figures a debilitating hypersensitivity borne of the stigmatization of belonging to the perpetrator collective. Sebald's embodiment of the so-called "good German" in these figures is tinged by a comical navel-gazing *Weltschmerz* that drives home an awareness of the precariousness of memory work in this sensitive context. Finally, I show how Sebald also uses melancholy discourses to illuminate the place of genocide, including and beyond the Holocaust, in world history. Before proceeding to the literary analysis, however, I turn to the complex image of melancholy produced in Sebald's essayistic reflections on the phenomenon.[14]

The Ability to Mourn as the Marker of Melancholy

In his by now legendary essay on the Allied area bombings during the Second World War, Sebald delivers an unflattering image of German writers of the postwar period who, according to him, deliberately avoided literary engagement with the destruction of German cities. In an act of moral cowardice and downright repression of their sensory experience of death and decay in the ruins of the immediate postwar period, these writers looked the other way and failed to deliver convincing literary accounts of the devastation. A second and more disturbing omission is evident in this avoidance strategy, Sebald suggests: the German corpses in the ruined city cellars obscure the other charred Jewish corpses of the Holocaust. In his vision, these writers and the busily rebuilding German nation to which they belong are characterized by the Mitscherlichs' famous thesis concerning the inability to mourn: on one hand, their failure to admit the both savage and humiliating effects on the collective psyche of German losses in the war, and on the other, their failure to acknowledge the crimes of National Socialism and to accept responsibility for the events of the Holocaust.[15]

The view prevails that Sebald's judgment was impaired by his generational blind spot as someone who, born in 1944, had no memories of the war that nevertheless shaped his identity, and by his guilty conscience as an enlightened, post-Holocaust West German citizen.[16] Leaving biographical speculation to one side, the evaluation of sadness we encounter in his endorsement of the thesis concerning the inability to mourn reveals an interesting assessment of sadness. Here the ability to mourn— the ability to appreciate the painful experience of another, notably without usurping it—becomes the marker of ethically correct behavior. Sebald thus places a high value on a productive form of sadness as a form of commemoration and repentance. The view of sadness as a dignified, if difficult, enterprise is not confined to this essay alone. Sebald also articulates it in other literary essays, most strikingly in his collection of essays on Austrian literature, *Die Beschreibung des Unglücks*, and in his article on melancholy and mourning in the work of Günter Grass and Wolfgang Hildesheimer, "Konstruktionen der Trauer."[17]

In the preface to his first collection of essays on Austrian writers ranging from Adalbert Stifter to Ernst Herbeck, Sebald once again aligns himself with a noble tradition of melancholy. By distinguishing "good" melancholy from "bad" melancholy, he differentiates between a lesser form of melancholy—"defeatist melancholy"—and melancholy as a marker of productive contemplation (13). In this preface, "good" melancholy describes a perspective that acknowledges and confronts the unhappiness of the individual and the collective. It furthermore ponders the reasons why the world can produce such sadness. This kind of contemplation does not amount to a fatalistic desire for death, Sebald insists. Rather, it articulates a form of intellectual resistance to the imperfect state of the world. This resistance takes place through the act of writing. The literary description of unhappiness is part of the continual effort to acknowledge and overcome the disconsolate perspective in the face of history's destructiveness, even if literature cannot provide concrete solutions. In this way, the melancholy position, when articulated in the literary process, can lead to a better understanding of the self and the world.

Writing emerges as a therapeutic medium in this view and provides a prototype for the process of mourning work. Sebald thus implies that literature produced by sleight of melancholy hand is an exemplary instance of mourning work, for the melancholy sufferer registers more keenly than others personal and historical trauma (12). On this point, Uwe Schütte notes that Sebald's analysis of Herbeck's poetry as the literary product of a psychopathological condition puts forward an understanding of art as the product of radical difference, in this case of mental illness. True art, is the implication, is produced in the transformation into script of pathological melancholy insight. It is not so much that writing makes the individual melancholy. Rather, being pathologically inclined to begin with enables artistic expression, which in turn facilitates the work of mourning in written, aesthetic form. In this view, a pathological disposition is the motor that drives the production of art. Sebald here reinforces the age-old idea of Renaissance melancholy as a marker of artistic exceptionality, but does not suppress the abject image and experience of mental illness, a theme that comes up frequently in his literary works. Indeed, he endorses the basic principle of pseudo-Aristotle's seminal coupling of the pathological with genius to produce a dialectical figure between illness and empowerment.[18]

In this way, Sebald's analysis of melancholy as a psychological phenomenon endows it with grace and meaningfulness. The purported dichotomy between mourning and melancholy in Sigmund Freud's essay does not apply to Sebald. The noble mnemonic figure in his work is dialectically divided between creative mourning work and the illness of melancholy as a reaction to the destructiveness of history. This noble mode Sebald identifies in Hildesheimer's "centre of sorrow," a term Sebald uses to describe the mood of authentic sadness that permeates *Tynset*. In contrast to Grass, argues Sebald, Hildesheimer creates in this novel the appropriate emotional response to the memory of the Holocaust.[19]

Sebald also criticizes the reduced status of melancholy as illness in the discourse of modern medicine. In his view, melancholy understood as an illness can offer little in the way of insight into the workings of the mind and the truth of existence. Psychology is indifferent to the object of mental illness that it constructs from within its own scientific field, he suggests. Even psychoanalysis cannot provide a better insight into the human psyche than does the literary description of unhappiness (9–10). In sum, *Die Beschreibung des Unglücks* applies melancholy dialectics to a reading of Austrian literature. Sebald rescues the image of mental illness from its negative medical definition, transforming it into a marker of artistic creativity and resistance: a rare perspective on the world that affords insight into the nature of human derangement and that can advance our understanding of history, itself a kind of complex derangement. From this perspective, *Schwindel. Gefühle* (Vertigo. Feelings, 1990) can be regarded as an extended literary exploration of a similar artistic mania, or in Jean Paul Sartre's sense, nausea, that comes across in the narrator's recurring bouts of dizziness. Likewise, Sebald's focus on the contemplative saturnine temperament in *Die Ringe des Saturn* conveys, alongside references to vertigo and depression, the close affinity between different forms of melancholy, mental illness, and artistic creativity.[20]

The alignment of writing with therapy contrasts sharply with other images of writing in Sebald's work that associate it with physical pain and suffering. Yet common to both perspectives is the semanticization of suffering, the idea that pain can have meaning.[21] This does not necessarily point to a melancholy retreatism that transcends the historical perspective, however. Rather, it can be viewed as part of the project of noble self-stylization that draws on the melancholy iconography of tortured suffering. Ultimately, this self-stylization is more topographical than psychological: the melancholy transformation in writing constitutes a model of memory as mourning work. On the level of art, melancholy is neither reactive nor reactionary, Sebald argues. Allowing the expression of pain, it is constitutive, healing, and progressive.[22]

Sebald's logic implies that the innate ability of the melancholy artist to perform mourning work is a confirmation of the true artist's ethical nobility. In conjunction with his epochal saturnine self-staging in *Nach der Natur*, he seems to suggest that the ability to mourn is a historically specific marker of the authentic postwar artist who recognizes the seriousness of the hour and the necessity of melancholy as a form of contrite and progressive memory work. This melancholy encoding of the ethical dignity of engaged postwar writing alongside the saturnine flourish is ostentatious. Perhaps it is also vain. As Rudolf and Margot Wittkower have shown, to be born under Saturn meant, in the Renaissance, public recognition as part of an exceptional artistic cohort: a sign of difficult but brilliant creative genius, the kind that Grass is so keen to avoid in his conceptualization of memory and the imagination after 1945. Humility and self-deprecation are, however, the close companions of bombastic melancholy self-description in Sebald's case. Furthermore, he makes great use of the symbols of noble melancholy for representing world history since the dawning of the early modern period and so moves beyond the solipsism of the brooding individual subject.[23]

Against the postwar German characteristic of the inability to mourn, Sebald's special brand of sadness emerges as insightful, mnemonic, and ethically driven mourning work cross-dressed in traditional melancholy apparel. Instead of interpreting this discontinuity as further evidence of the history-versus-mythology debate in the secondary literature, I explore it as the moment where Sebald ironizes his literary alter ego. If there is a risk of undermining mourning work and the ethics of memory, it does not arise through the artistic melancholy disposition of the narrators or through borrowings from melancholy traditions. Rather, mourning work is occasionally weakened as a result of, as Julia Hell points out, the self-censorship that arises through awareness that one's efforts as a German to write about Jewish suffering take place in a particularly critical public arena. While literary self-irony is one means of maintaining balance in the work of mourning, the sense of circumspection that self-irony creates does not always apply to the essays. Sebald's exaltation of Hildesheimer's mysterious "centre of sorrow" strikes a sepulchral chord, trying to make the Jewish experience of persecution in the Holocaust visible. The centre of sorrow thus represents a suggestive moment in one of Sebald's "melancholies." This is because it tends to sentimentality in the imagination of the Jewish other's affective inner life, one of the most divisive issues around the scholarly evaluation of melancholy in Sebald's work. The question of genre is relevant in this context, however. The essay does not avail itself of the strategic narrative tools that, in literary prose, safeguard the German narrator from transgressing the boundaries of his self-imposed sense of illegitimacy. Because of its narrative possibilities, the literary work is better equipped to frustrate such sentimental lapses. As I show in the next section, Sebald often foregrounds this sense of illegitimacy in a play on a melancholy sensitive figure, the *Weltschmerzler*, in order to underscore the difference between the German narrator figure and his Jewish counterpart.[24]

Weltschmerz of the Postwar Penitent

Critics have often noted a kind of sickly melancholic excess, "schwarze Zuckerwatte" (black candyfloss) as it has been termed, in Sebald's sculpting of the gloomy narrative perspective. Greg Bond argues that Sebald's aesthetics at times operate on the basis of a stylistic *faux pas* that too readily spreads a superfluous layer of thick melancholy over all objects, as, for example, during a fish-and-chips supper in *Die Ringe des Saturn*. Bond's critique, which ignores the ironic tone of the passage in question, implies that only certain objects are worthy of melancholy significance. In a café in the unemployment black spot of Lowestoft the narrator's contemplation of the breaded fish and greasy chips on the plate in front of him indicates melancholy self-indulgence, an inappropriate excess of melancholy signification that overshoots the ridiculous signified, "what happens when the melancholic gaze has to be upheld at all costs, even when there is nothing for it to fix itself upon."[25]

Although this passage is marked by a heightened sense of irony, one can make a case for how the humble object of the fish indeed merits melancholy signification. *Die Ringe des Saturn* contains a discussion of the fate of the herring species that is under threat due to humankind's plundering of the seas. As many critics note, the destruction of the herring through over-fishing evokes the destruction of the Jews in the Holocaust. Apart from this juxtaposition, Sebald's literary strategy of association also means that one can regard the fish supper in run-down Lowestoft in the further context of what humankind does to its natural environment: exploitation and ruin for the sake of profit. Mass fishing feeds the chain of mass food production, so that the result is a disgusting meal that underscores humankind's self-imposed alienation from nature. The tartar sauce comes in a plastic packet, while the breaded fish, recently pulled out of the deep freeze, has barely thawed and carries no trace of the natural environment that once housed it. The melancholy significance of the fish becomes even more loaded when we consider the town where the narrator consumes the meal. Lowestoft once was a wealthy bathing town, but has now fallen prey to the brutal rhythms of global capitalism. It is presented as a poor and irrelevant place that has regressed to a pre-modern state, so radical have been the negative effects of globalization.[26]

Sebald thus integrates the Lowestoft fish supper into a representative apparatus that conducts a critical discourse on capitalism. From this point of view, the melancholy signifier more than justifies the melancholy signified: the pernicious consequences of global capitalism. The disgusting fish supper is the tip of an invisible iceberg, but it is one that we must strain to envisage in order to work out the complex reality we move within when we purchase such fare. As opposed to melancholy for melancholy's sake, melancholy ostentation dissects man's relationship with his natural environment here and subjects it to critical examination, conducting a critique of modernity, as Long and others suggest. Sebald also draws on Romantic melancholy in his depiction of the narrator as a man of sensibility or *Weltschmerzler* who is able to negotiate his affective existence between introversion, sentimentalism, and a more worldly perspective that enables, through imaginative projection, humanitarian empathy with the suffering of others. It is precisely this humanitarian outlook that informs Sebald's melancholy scrutiny of landscape, class, and industrialization, as the second half of this chapter shows.[27]

Criticism of Sebald's melancholy rendition of world history implies that he at times wallows in the aesthetics of affect, displaying sentimentalism or pleasurable indulgence in "sweet melancholy," which undermines his ethical project.[28] In fact, Sebald uses elements of the eighteenth-century tradition of sentimentality or "Empfindsamkeit" to create a *typologically* melancholy narrator. Thus the Sebaldian narrator does not exclusively ponder on an interior subjective state. Within this aesthetic construction of subjective feeling, there are many opportunities for self-irony, which should alert us to the fact that the narrator represents a critical engagement with the role of the artist and with modernity, alongside the ethical obligation to remember the Holocaust. The narrator's "Weltschmerz"—his grandly exaggerated melancholy—is not the sign of capitulation to a natural history of destruction and the loss of historical perspective. Rather, in Sebald's ironic transformation, *Weltschmerz* represents the ability to keep the self in perspective, a critical appraisal of the emotional life that comes through both in the narrative structure and in the self-reflexive nature of self-stylization.

Weltschmerz is closely related to sentimentality or "Empfindsamkeit," which gained ground in Europe from the middle of the eighteenth century. It represents the secularization in literary form of the cult of the individual's spiritual life that originated in Pietism, the religious movement that broke with Lutheran orthodoxy and that emphasized the relationship between the individual and God as a matter of the heart, a private matter. Hans Jürgen Schings's study shows how in the rational secularizing discourses of the time melancholy came to occupy the discursive position of the anti-modern, religious other. In the new science of anthropology, as well as moral psychology, physiology, and philosophy, melancholy increasingly became the explanatory model for irrational anti-Enlightenment tendencies. In other words, melancholy for a time became indistinguishable from what was regarded as religious fanaticism and superstition, which in turn were associated with melancholy and mental illness. Schings points out, however, that Goethe's epochal *Die Leiden des jungen Werther* (The Sorrows of Young Werther, 1774) signals a change in this negative understanding of melancholy. In the figure of Werther, the melancholy enthusiast is no longer denounced as a religious fanatic. Rather, Werther represents the shift within sentimentality from enthusiasm to genius, the moment when melancholy is "emancipated" from scientific Enlightenment discourses. As such, "Empfindsamkeit" and the related mode of enthusiasm no longer exist solely within a negative understanding of melancholy as an irrational force. Instead, sentimentality becomes the mouthpiece for a more universal, all-encompassing feeling of melancholy: *Weltschmerz*.[29]

Such a feeling of exquisite pain in the face of the world's destructiveness and suffering certainly applies to Sebald's twentieth-century analysis of catastrophes in history. His borrowings from the motifs of *Weltschmerz* are almost too many to mention: ruins and graveyards are regular landscape constituents, winter and autumn, the sea, the vertiginous experience of the abyss, friendship, childhood, a fixation on the transitory. The problem is that, historically speaking, *Weltschmerz* and sentimentality are viewed as representing a contemptible lack of moral rigor and emotional self-discipline. From this perspective, excessive focus on the melancholy state separates the affective condition from the disturbing matter that causes it, shifting focus from the external world to the enjoyable and self-affirming experience of emotion. In this context, *Weltschmerz* is a form of subjectivity that cultivates feeling for the sake of feeling in the belief that this intensity somehow represents the authenticity of the private self: "Ichschmerz." We could regard "victimology" and "negative sublimity"—respectively the terms that Aleida Assmann and Dominick LaCapra develop to describe the universalization of trauma feelings after the

Holocaust—as the contemporary counterpart to the inappropriate excess of sentiment for which *Weltschmerz* is known.[30]

In Sebald's case, this brings us back to the problem of melancholy and historical explanation: the issue of sufficient or insufficient cause for individual melancholy, particularly when the melancholy sufferer has not been subjected to a specific trauma. Sebald critiques, via melancholy ostentation, this very problem of identification, or potential usurpation, of the victim position. In this way, he turns the "deceit" of the melancholy signifier into a productive instance. In the introduction of the present study I note that some critics object to the melancholy confusion of absence with loss. Their contention is that such ambivalence means that melancholy fails to produce the alibi of a convincing lost object. Instead, the lost object is a pseudo-object, ghostly and inauthentic, hence the "melancholy deceit." With Sebald we can observe a different moment in melancholy signification: its use as a mode of cultural production that has a positive ethical value within post-Holocaust memory discourses. In Sebald "melancholy appears to reflect the subject's acute knowledge of the inherently transactional nature of cultural production; it reflects the subject's full knowledge of the inescapably social and conventional character of speech." The self-awareness of the narrator figure often communicates this knowledge, which is channeled through the performative quality of melancholy imagery.[31]

An early excerpt from *Schwindel. Gefühle* demonstrates how this critical engagement via sentimentality operates.[32] The narrator's sojourn in Venice is both magical and strange, at times bordering on terrifying. He goes on a nocturnal boat trip through the waterways with an enigmatic guide, Malachio, who ponders, in the middle of this stone and water landscape with Venice glimmering ghostly in the distance, the meaning of the resurrection. His parting words to the puzzled narrator are "Next year in Jerusalem!" (*SG*, 72). Returning to his hotel, the narrator enters into a strange state that lasts for two days. He is unable to leave his room, slipping in and out of dream, vision, and wakefulness. He considers that this strange state of physical immobility, underscored by intense mental activity, could kill him: one could think oneself to death. His limbs get colder and colder, as he imagines himself to be laid out in death repose, like a corpse, and all around him is a sense of emptiness. He is interrupted only by room service, which delivers—somewhat ironically, given Malachio's thoughts on the resurrection—bread and red wine (*SG*, 75). His mind then turns to saints and martyrs, reinforcing the sense that what he is experiencing is a form of pseudo-religious self-scrutiny that deliberately taps into sentimental matters of the heart. The melodramatic gesture of the deathlike pose ironizes the play on religious mysticism. Later references to Kafka languishing in hotel rooms suggest that the narrator is arranging himself to convey affinity with this literary forefather (*SG*, 161).

However, his desire to remain in his own company for these two days also places him within the sentimental tradition of loneliness.[33]

Sentimentality, nostalgia, and artistic self-consciousness conspire to create a slightly ridiculous narrative self in this sequence, mainly because the cause for the narrator's melancholy state is unclear. The very title of the book, *Schwindel. Gefühle*, thematizes this lack of clarity, suggesting through the ambivalence of the German word "Schwindel" the association of feelings with vertigo, dizziness, and deceit or swindle. All we can discern is a general malaise after the boat trip with Malachio, which gathers momentum with the narrator's gloomy reflections on the increasingly mechanized nature of modern existence. His thoughts about traffic result in paralysis and confine him to his bed for two whole days. The apocalyptic nature of his vision of traffic as a new ocean that is creeping over the entire world further drives home the engulfing sense of *Weltschmerz*. The narrator's melancholy imagination seems to bring about debilitation. After all, as he observes, Venice lacks the monstrous traffic his mind fixates on (*SG*, 72).

This hyperbolic melancholy—hallucinations, loneliness, morbidity, and religious reflection—is reinforced when the narrator eventually leaves his hotel room and sets out from Venice to Verona. The description of the café at the train station in Venice evokes Dante's vision of hell, as the ever-sensitive narrator absorbs to his receptive core the overwhelming horror of life on earth. The final straw is the sense that two young men are watching him (*SG*, 79). Once he arrives in Verona he beats a hasty retreat to the Giardino Giusti, where for the first time in a long period he starts to feel better (*SG*, 80–81). This should not surprise us, because the garden is fitted with the icons of sweet melancholy, conventional mirrors of the sentimental soul. He breathes in the autumnal scent of cyprus trees that, he notes, have been there for a good two hundred years, an observation that situates the garden historically in the sentimental age of the late eighteenth century. As in the hotel-room scene, Sebald also plays with motifs from the imagery of sentimental (*Selbst*)*Genuß* (self-enjoyment): the enjoyable, because intense and self-affirming, experience of the inner movements of the soul. In the first scene, these moments are apocalyptic and frightening. They ignite the soul and the imagination, however, raising experience above the banal and making it into a category of intellectual-aesthetic achievement. The garden, by contrast, has a soothing effect, but it is no less self-affirming, because as an established sentimental topos it nostalgically associates the narrator with a nature idyll. This bucolic retreat is a protected, if highly aesthetic and therefore unnatural, space that underlines his affinity with rural simplicity and moral purity— he washes his face in the fountain—in opposition to the encroaching destruction of corrupt civilization.[34]

After this short period of repose, the narrator visits the arena where his vertiginous nightmare resumes and he believes himself again to be under observation by a pair of young men. Plagued by thoughts of persecution, he must gather all his reserves of rationality to stand up and leave the arena. Yet again, coldness has entered his limbs. As he retreats, however, his persecution fear takes a decidedly sentimental turn. He imagines his very heart, his sentimental core, to be under attack. Dramatically, he envisages a single arrow flying through the air, destined to enter his body through his left shoulder, fatally piercing his heart (*SG*, 84).[35]

This "shock" focus on the heart contains a melodramatic undertone similar to that noted in Sebald's projection into Hildesheimer's "centre of sorrow." Both imply an immediacy of affect that in turn implies emotional authenticity. In the essay, the "melo-traumatic" image is not subjected to ironic reflection: the "centre of sorrow" represents the Jewish other's suffering. Sebald's reading of *Tynset* in this light accords the experience of suffering an inalienable truth status that has ethical dignity. By contrast, in *Schwindel. Gefühle*, where the narrator's melancholy affliction is presented as an existential condition and not as a reaction to trauma, Sebald seems to delight in constructing an image of the narrator in the tradition of the self-indulgent sentimentalist who cultivates feelings of melancholy in order to experience the titillation of affect. Melancholy as ethical resistance to the world's destructiveness seems to have little resonance in this context.[36]

In a wider discussion of the representation of affect in Sebald's work, however, these icons of sentimentality, hysteria, and self-indulgence serve a critical function. One of the narrator's dreams in *Schwindel. Gefühle* shows how, in a contemporary context, the literary convention of sentimentality can function as a trigger for ethical thought. While languishing on his hotel bed, the narrator dreams of a boat trip across the lagoon in Venice, imagining that he is passing by an island inhabited by the mentally ill. Their faces stare out at him from the panopticon building in which they are incarcerated, their isolation on an island in the first place a brutal message of their abject social status. The narrator's dream brings us back in time to the era of burgeoning discipline and the birth of modernity, in Michel Foucault's sense. Sebald thereby constructs an associative chain between the past and the present, for the narrator's visit with Herbeck, whom he takes out of a mental institution for a day trip, precedes his journey to Venice (*SG*, 44). The narrator's self-presentation as a nervous type further suggests that he has affinities with the mentally ill, both historically and in the present.[37]

Sebald's use of the conventional imagery of sentimentality and *Weltschmerz* conveys the broad epistemological reach of melancholy traditions. The narrator embodies many "irrational" traits that, from the perspective of the late twentieth century, go back in time to question the foundations of Enlightenment rationality. As Long shows, he is continually open to experiences of wonder that point to the existence of something else beyond the rational confines of modernity. He has the ability to feel a similar sense of wonder by immersing himself in natural landscapes. Hysteria and sentimentality mark him out as a stigmatized melancholy other in a way that resists the archival rationality of the world. Thus Sebald draws on melancholy sentimental convention to establish a narrator type that can resist, through his very embodiment of anti-modern irrational melancholy, the clutches of the modern world around him. Even if the politics of this sentimental critique ultimately convey only a limited sense of resistance to the disciplinary techniques of modernity, it nevertheless demonstrates that to view melancholy in Sebald's work as the sign of anti-Enlightenment barbarity is to miss its main function as a discourse for criticizing both the Enlightenment and modernity.[38]

In *Austerlitz* (2001) the stylization of the self as a melancholy sentimentalist also offers a critical perspective on the relationship between the penitent German narrator and his Jewish victim friend.[39] Critics regard the sentimentality of this relationship as a sign of the narrator's vicarious identification with the Jewish other and evidence of emotion that weakens the ethical project of allowing the victim others to tell the story of their suffering. However, sentimental enthusiasm for the Jewish other is also a form of exaggerated penitence that contains its own moment of self-criticism and humility. The ethical function here resides in the narrator's exaggeration of sentimentality. Rueful reflections from a German perspective on the unavoidable awkwardness of the relationship remind the reader of the legacy of a past that cannot go away, despite the outward appearance of a positive friendship that in dialogue performs the act of "working through." As the narrator frets intermittently about his own behavior, we are reminded that the relationship between German and Jew has not been normalized. Instead, his unease refers to "the occult realm of true feeling" that emerges in melodramatic narratives. In this particular situation the unspoken "negative symbiosis" of the interaction between German and Jew invokes the "moral occult"—the historical fact of the Holocaust.[40]

The melancholy narrator figure that emerges in *Austerlitz* is, in contrast to Grass's self-confident, healer-therapist figure, full of self-doubt and brooding inwardness. He is inclined to self-torment. He seems to have absorbed Hildesheimer's radical message of no forgiveness that, even if Austerlitz is open to friendship with the narrator, informs the way the narrator feels as a German who wishes to befriend a Jew. Sentimental soul-searching and self-torment become, from this perspective, the ironic behavioral markers of German self-censoring *Weltschmerz*, the sign of a continuing effort to embrace and work through the legacy of the past in a way that keeps the self in constant check.[41]

From the outset the narrator behaves like an ardent lover. He seems to be dependent on his contact with Austerlitz, even though neither of them becomes aware of the truth of Austerlitz's Jewish identity until several years later. The day after their initial encounter in Antwerp train station in 1967, the narrator positions himself in a café near the glove market with the intention of engineering a further encounter with Austerlitz (*Aus*, 32). Although this does not happen, by some stroke of fate they accidentally meet a few days later in Lüttich (*Aus*, 44). This early conniving establishes the narrator as more dependent on contact with the other than is Austerlitz. From this moment on, they stay in touch until the end of 1975, when the narrator, resident in England for the previous nine years, decides to return to Germany. They lose contact at this point. However, true to this postwar romance, German and Jew, despite the considerable odds, are destined to meet again many years later.

Their chance encounter in London, nearly two decades after they drifted out of contact in 1975, is narrated in a sentimental manner that draws on what Peter Brook terms the melodramatic aesthetics of astonishment. The narrator has failing eyesight and must undergo a procedure in London. Afterwards, plagued by nausea and unsettled by exploding points of light in his eyes, he goes into the Salon Bar of the Great Eastern Hotel in Liverpool Street, where he observes the disorienting movement of people around him. Finally, his troubled eyes settle upon a point of indisputable clarity, the almost unchanged person of Austerlitz, who here assumes for the vertiginous narrator the sentimental function of the enclosed Giardino Giusti in *Schwindel. Gefühle*. The protected space in *Schwindel. Gefühle* and the Jewish character in *Austerlitz* embody virtue and a self-evident innocence that appear all the more convincing because of the contrasting effect of a hellish environment from which they stand out (*Aus*, 60–62; *SG*, 80–81).[42]

In *Austerlitz* it is as if the two protagonists have never been separated. Their last conversation of the mid-1970s simply picks up seamlessly where it left off in a way that strongly suggests an undeniable connection. Notably, it is Austerlitz who takes the conversational lead, a pattern of interaction that repeats itself in their encounters over the next period. For the narrator always comes when summoned by Austerlitz. What is more, he clearly voices this situation in the text, making no pretense about his emotional attachment and dependency on the other (*Aus*, 173, 362). Through sentimental self-deprecation, he openly demonstrates that he owes Austerlitz, the unspoken premise of negative symbiosis that pervades all their encounters.

Sebald's sentimental representation of negative symbiosis automatically places the narrator in a painful position, because the German is depicted as if he were suffering from unrequited love. His sense of self-validation is considerably threatened when he does not hear from Austerlitz. In his anxious self-reprimands we can hear *sotto voce* the self-conscious stigmatization that surrounds the fact of belonging to the post-1945 German collective, and the fear that the negative legacy of this identity has somehow clumsily expressed itself in conversation with Austerlitz (*Aus*, 139). At the same time, however, these self-reprimands are also the sentimental signs of an ethical consciousness that wishes to know more about the victim other, to understand, and to remember his suffering.

The dual signifying function of the Jewish figure, as a victim, on one hand, and as a reflector for the troubled German self, on the other, raises a feature of postwar memory ethics that Sebald's ambivalence between identification and empathy continually thematizes: the German figure cannot ruminate on the Holocaust without some degree of identification. In this respect, Sebald's concern for the affective dimension to ethical memory likens him to Weiss who, as we saw in chapter 3, also problematizes the ambivalences of emotion and cognitive understanding in the task of commemoration. This tendency to identification does not amount to the usurpation of the victim other's experience, however. Rather, mimesis stresses that the ongoing acknowledgement of one's own sense of guilt, shame, and responsibility must occur within the context of thinking about the other's suffering also. Against Gisela Ecker's view that Sebald's narrators slide into a vicarious mimesis of the Jewish figures they interact with, I suggest that the sentimental humility of the *Austerlitz* narrator and his ability to keep himself in ironic perspective is confirmation of a melancholy ethics of memory that thematizes the gray zone of interaction in the situation of negative symbiosis: an imperfect mourning work that the iconography of melancholy sentimentality conveys. This is distinct from *Nach der Natur*, *Schwindel. Gefühle*, and *Die Ringe des Saturn*, where Sebald draws more directly on the iconography of melancholy genius in his construction of the narrators. In *Austerlitz*, the narrator is overdetermined by a self-deprecating awareness of the necessity, and danger, of his devotion. The self-awareness of "German self-hatred" provides a chink in the narrative armor; this chink prevents sentimentalization from turning in on itself and coagulating into weakened memory ethics.[43]

The effect of this wry self-mockery is to suggest that while memory work, especially from within the perpetrator collective, must continue to be carried out, standards of affective propriety nevertheless apply to the expression of German penitence and contrition. Existing scholarship on Sebald normally looks to his distinctive narrative style as proof of the ethical quality of his literary aesthetics. His narrative technique makes a point of regularly signaling the distinct identity of who is speaking. While it has not always convinced readers, this narrative strategy is intended to facilitate the emergence of victims' stories, told from their perspective. In the case of *Die Ausgewanderten* and *Austerlitz*, both of which are concerned with Jewish accounts of the Holocaust that are recorded by the German narrator, this kind of narrative signaling communicates, on the aesthetic level of the text, how the German must always respect the inalienable difference of the Jewish victim other.[44]

As well as representing the experience of Jewish victim subjects, the basic narrative situation of these works is also the literary articulation of a code of proper behavior for the penitent German. While it is well and good to desire to listen, remember, and sympathize, one must nevertheless be careful about how one conducts oneself in this situation. The languages of victimology and negative sublimity are what Sebald wishes to avoid. Elaborating the narrative position as a melancholy one thus seems like a risky venture, given that melancholy can be melodramatic. However, intermittent focus on the awkwardness of being German, which comes across in the narrators' self-reflections, tempers risk with circumspection.

A weak aspect to Sebald's sentimental melancholy discourse is the fact that it privileges male homo-social desire and male bonding. Certainly, the friendship between German and Jew in *Austerlitz* renders ethical Holocaust memory the exclusive domain of the intellectual male subject. In her reading of *Die Ausgewanderten*, Maja Barzilai critiques this gendering of memory work, pointing out that women are relegated to a marginal status. The uncanny and the queer characterize relationships between men which are premised on the abnegation of the female figure. In *Austerlitz* the moment of exaggerated melancholy emotion is a moment of privilege for the narrator: it signals access to the Jewish victim other. Thus while Sebald takes care to include the abject experience of mental illness alongside melancholy as the gift of rare insight, this circumspection and inclusiveness does not extend to the themes of gender, memory, and melancholy. Like Grass and, to a lesser extent, Hildesheimer, Sebald privileges ethical memory as a masculine ability. That the sensitive male figures in his works often succumb to the irrational, thereby acquiring "feminine" traits, does not dispel the gender imbalance in Sebald's discourse on postwar ethical memory.[45]

Thus the narrator is not an ideal embodiment of the memory politics of contrition, although the considered narrative style attempts to make this an aesthetic truth of the text. He is a fallible emotional individual who continually experiences discomfort with the task of working through the burden of the past. Despite the dialogic narrative model, the narrator's emotional insecurity conveys a secondary level of affect: the overspill of awkward feeling that goes hand in hand with the task of mourning. Sebald was painfully aware of the pitfalls of trying to represent this task in a way that did not sentimentalize suffering and that did not appropriate the experience of the victim other. His use of motifs from melancholy sentimentality, at times with a deliberately melodramatic flourish, conveys, and does not undermine, this awareness. Even though Sebald's melancholy marginalizes women, it can still be regarded as a critical discourse, in that it disciplines the confessional tendencies of the narrator, reminding him that he must steel himself against intermittent fear and wallowing and continue to focus his attention on the Jewish other. Self-ironic

Weltschmerz thus functions, to subvert Long's Foucauldian analysis, as disciplinary self-monitoring within the broader panopticon of postwar memory politics and the codes of affective behavior they endorse.[46]

The Winged Genius

As argued, sentimentality and nostalgia can be regarded as ironic markers of a critical discourse that keeps the self in historical and emotional perspective. In the following analysis, which focuses mainly on *Die Ringe des Saturn*, the work by Sebald most openly aligned with melancholy traditions in Western writing, I demonstrate how melancholy as a nonpsychological category goes beyond the individual subject to represent a historically informed discussion on global capitalism, the planet's weather systems, and genocide. This insight makes it possible to "rescue" Sebald from the antiquarian tendencies with which he has been associated and illustrates how he might be more concerned with contemporary matters than he is given credit for.[47]

My analysis begins with Sebald's early invocation in *Die Ringe des Saturn* of Albrecht Dürer's famous engraving *Melencolia I* (*RS*, 19). Significantly, he does not include a reproduction of this canonical image, merely referring selectively to certain details—the central winged figure and the instruments that surround it. The reader's task is made clear from the outset by a narrative gesture that alights upon the image but does not spell out its full thematic significance for *Die Ringe des Saturn*: she/he must fill the epistemological gap left by the image's omission and the narrator's scant ekphrasis.

As noted throughout this study, the engraving is a succinct commentary on the semantic evolution of ancient melancholy symbols during the Middle Ages and the Renaissance.[48] The pondering winged genius at the center of the image embodies in pictorial form Marsilio Ficino's humanist revival of the Aristotelian coupling of genius and depression (*SM*, 126–27).[49] The engraving is also Dürer's brilliant personal articulation of a new melancholy type that anticipates the "modern" problems of a burgeoning rationalist era at the same time that it pays tribute to the rich legacy of melancholy traditions. Teeming with semantic potential, it features in the early stages of *Die Ringe des Saturn* as a premonition of what Sebald addresses thereafter: writ large, the interdependence of human and natural history and the difficulty of developing an adequate temporal sense for grasping this "world history" intellectually. The engraving thematizes the art of accurate measurement as a trait of the new melancholy personality; the narrator's reference to it is thus not just a lament for his recently deceased colleague, Janine Dakyns. His reflection on the image points to the problem of perspective, both visual and intellectual, that runs through Sebald's work as a whole.[50]

The way that Sebald uses Dürer's engraving to represent a memory of his friend draws together several recurring themes. Dakyns was the narrator's university colleague, and his memory of her is given shape by the slumped pose of Dürer's angel: the narrator remembers her seated in the center of her office either bent over a notepad upon which she was intently scribbling or slumped listlessly in the same chair (*RS*, 18–19). Dakyns embodies the two modes of artistic and intellectual behavior Dürer captures in the winged figure and its inversion, the putto above its right shoulder: artistic reflection and contemplation ("ars") that struggles to transform the melancholy of intellectual insight into creative artistic practice ("usus").[51] The work expands the theme beyond the depressive artistic individual to foreground melancholy as a basic problem of knowledge and understanding. Dakyns is one of the first incarnations of this type. In his memory she is surrounded by what the narrator describes as the tools of destruction, the objects of academic study: books, paperwork, writing equipment (*RS*, 19). These "tools" correspond to the instruments of measurement that feature in Dürer's engraving and that are scattered at the feet of the inert winged figure. Both images thematize knowledge as elusive; while the thinker in the engraving might be able objectively to measure her/his world—or, in Dakyns's case, to write about the world—the sense of an epistemological perspective that would approximate the "truth" of how things are is always missing.

Melancholy is introduced in this early image as a problem specific to the intellectual, and *Die Ringe des Saturn* is overrun with melancholy intellectuals. They are all male, however, just as the melancholy intellectual figures of Sebald's other works are exclusively male and cultivate special relationships with other men. Dakyns appears to be an exception to the rule of male melancholy. Despite her iconic appearance in the "Renaissance episteme" of melancholy genius, however, she is a marginal figure, like most female figures in Sebald's work. She is already dead when the narrator imagines her in this iconic way, so she acquires a spectral quality that Barzilai observes as a feature of the female figures in *Die Ausgewanderten*. Barzilai argues that women mediate the process of memory retrieval in this work, producing an ambivalent feminine encoding of Holocaust memory between male castration anxiety and male desire. Sebald does not directly thematize the Holocaust through the figure of Dakyns, but he does associate her person with environmental destruction. As with Weiss, the melancholy female icon functions as a deathly canvas for the catastrophic masculine imagination. The dearth thereafter of intellectual female figures in this work dilutes the impact of this image of the melancholy woman genius. There is no sustained problematization of women, gender, and ethical memory, as there is in Weiss's *Die Ästhetik des Widerstands*.[52]

The narrator's exaggerated topophilia during his walking tour of Suffolk and East Anglia in *Die Ringe des Saturn* expresses the melancholy problem of the painful encounter with epistemological limitations. Always starting from obscure details in the landscape, he constantly attempts to weave an epistemological framework that would somehow capture the interconnectedness of persons, regions, and events across space and time and that would explain—more profoundly and truthfully than chronological historical narrative—the place of humankind in the late twentieth century (*RS*, 16). As he constantly strains to conceptualize world history as a spatiotemporal whole, this mammoth endeavor takes its toll. We learn at the start of the novel that one year after he embarks on this trip he ends up in hospital, a delayed melancholy reaction to the ubiquitous signs of destruction his topophilia and brooding archaeological imagination led him to recognize in the landscape around him. Lying in his hospital bed, gazing out of his window to a vision of celestial emptiness, he embodies the divided spirit of the melancholy sufferer. He begins to write down his account of the previous year's walking trip in an attempt to stave off the specter of depression (*RS*, 12). Artistic effort, here writing, is the other face of melancholy, paradoxically the founding premise and clear, if only ever temporary, antidote to the depressive side of the condition. Just as the year previously the narrator tried to dispel the onset of depression with the activity of a walking trip, now he attempts to overcome his melancholy paralysis through the therapeutic act of writing. Sebald's model of melancholy as resistance in writing and artistic creativity thus frames the work. Toward the end he returns to the image of writing in his discussion of the torturous labor of weaving silk (*RS*, 335).

As in *Nach der Natur*, the narrator links his depression to his astrological destiny: Saturn, patron star of melancholy sufferers (*RS*, 11). He thereby elevates himself into the company of Dürer's angel, who is stylized also as a saturnine type. In so doing, he establishes a symbolic connection of melancholy genius between his personality, the great Dürer, and the astronomical features named in the title of his therapeutic work, the rings of Saturn. And it is precisely the image of rings that captures the conceptualization of history in this book, circles that symbolize historical episodes from different periods but that do not differ from each other in kind. Whether he is describing the Opium Wars of the nineteenth century or the derelict promontory of Orford Ness in the late twentieth century, the narrator's message is constant: humankind in the modern era cannot seem to control its destructive instinct.

Sebald's reflections on the modern era are temporally bound, however. He is interested in the period that encompasses the rise and dominance of what was originally European Capitalism. While he includes references to the medieval period and to pagan times, the novel is more concerned with developments in the nineteenth and twentieth centuries

(*RS*, 37, 187). His reference to Dürer evokes the beginnings of global capitalism with the discovery of the Americas in the fifteenth century. As Benjamin points out, in the depiction of a distant coastline, sea, and ships, Dürer alludes to the—at his time—contemporary theme of long sea journeys. In this allusion we can date the starting point for Sebald's temporal framework: the beginnings, through travel, conquest, exploitation, and profit, of the Western world's expansion into a paradoxically increasingly integrated global system.[53]

Virtually all characters in *Die Ringe des Saturn* are, like the sentimental *Weltschmerzler*, performative melancholy types caught up in the web of capitalist and imperialist expansion. Sebald's engagement with weather and environment in this work should also be viewed historically, and not mythologically, as a "natural history of destruction." The history of weather systems is a further "ring of Saturn" in the epistemological construct of Sebald's spatiotemporal whole, one that intersects in places with the often destructive consequences of capitalism.

Saturn's Children I

Through erudite allusion, Sebald's sickly narrator introduces a dense framework of melancholy reference right at the start of his account. He thinks back to the late summer of 1992, when the so-called dog days of summer oppressed him, leading to his hospitalization one year later (*RS*, 11). The hottest and most humid time of year falling between July and early September, the dog days derive their name from the position of the star Sirius at this time, the Dog Star and brightest of all stars seen from earth. In Greek mythology Sirius was the dog of Orion the hunter, and the constellation Canis Major is one of several celestial groupings said to represent one of the dogs following Orion. In *Die Ringe des Saturn* we learn that included on the ornate gravestone of the narrator's saintly namesake, Saint Sebaldus, is a sculpture of Nimrod the Hunter, who in Greek writing is known as Orion (*RS*, 109).[54]

In the pre-Dürer saturnine tradition, the dog is man's fellow melancholy sufferer. Inclined to be serious and constantly hunting things out, the dog is the typical beast of Saturn. Like those who suffer from melancholy, the dog is more sensitive than other animals and can fall victim to madness. Dürer includes this companion of scholars and prophets in the engraving—a dog is curled up at the feet of the winged figure. Likewise, references to dogs abound through all of Sebald's texts: in *Schwindel. Gefühle*, for example, the hunter Hans Schlag, an embodiment of the searching melancholy figure, meets his grisly end in a winter snowscape. Schlag's dog goes mad after the death of his master and must be put down (*SG*, 268, 271). The dog is always a melancholy omen of actual or potential illness in Sebald's work. When the narrator of *Schwindel. Gefühle* takes the poet Herbeck out of the mental institution for their outing to the village of Kritzendorf, a dog crosses their path. This is echoed in Verona when another dog passes the narrator in the street (*SG*, 50, 139). In *Austerlitz* a small blue relief sculpture of a dog hangs above the doorway to Austerlitz's old Prague home, a melancholy sentinel on the threshold to his submerged past (*Aus*, 221). In *Die Ringe des Saturn*, the narrator notes that the late nineteenth-century poet, Edward Fitzgerald, is always accompanied by his black Labrador Bletsoe, while the same dog features in the narrator's disturbed dreams as he passes through the region once inhabited by Fitzgerald (*RS*, 243, 247). These signs, alongside the dizzy spells and panic attacks that consume the narrator in *Schwindel. Gefühle*, are portents of artistic susceptibility to mental illness and affirm the special connection between genius and the ability to feel the sorrow of the world (*SM*, 455–56).[55]

References to the planet Saturn further emphasize affiliation with the tradition of melancholy genius. Austerlitz repeats the saturnine astrological identity claim of *Nach der Natur* (*Aus*, 93–94). In *Die Ringe des Saturn*, the narrator paraphrases the English seventeenth-century melancholy doctor and writer Thomas Browne, who conjures up an image of nightfall over earth as the work of the ancient Roman god of crops, Saturn: the god fells humankind with his nocturnal scythe as the planet rotates into darkness (*RS*, 97).[56]

The dog/hunter complex alongside the question of astral fate are details of a larger frame of reference that pervades *Die Ringe des Saturn* and other works. As the melancholy thinker's like-minded companion, the dog/hunter reinforces the sense that melancholy is a problem of the perspicacious intellectual. However, Sebald widens the parameters of melancholy "self-indulgence" by utilizing the themes of perspective, measurement, and geometry that are central problems of the melancholy condition in Dürer's time, to explore the limits of man's historical insight—for Sebald's narrators a central problem of our time. Melancholy symbolism also includes universal qualities that are associated with the natural world, which Sebald adapts for the representation of the complex interaction between the natural and human worlds: melancholy iconicity thus conveys the literary expression of ecological concerns.[57]

Sebald repeatedly engages with the physical properties associated with melancholy during the transition from the Middle Ages to the Renaissance: coldness and dryness in the first instance, and then later humidity and moisture (*SM*, 213, 224). His landscapes also enhance the melancholy stylization, sentimental and noble, of the narrator. In *Die Ringe des Saturn*, however, these references go beyond characterization to scrutinize the relationship between humankind and nature. In this vein, Sebald uses saturnine motifs in the astrological writings of Arab philosophers of the ninth century, before Saturn became a planet. As a planet, Saturn merges with many of the characteristics of the Greek god of time, Chronos. The fusion of Saturn with Chronos makes saturnine melancholy ambivalent, for Saturn was originally the benign Roman god of crops and agriculture, patron of the earth, wood, stone, agriculture, husbandry, and also long voyages, while Chronos is a notoriously troubled god (*SM*, 211–45).[58]

Sebald constructs the majority of melancholics in his work through the benign saturnine tradition. Agricultural types feature regularly, for example in the many gardener characters. In desperation the once-wealthy Ashburys of *Die Ringe des Saturn* try their hand at farming their estate, and the narrator's unfortunate neighbor, Frederick Farrar, dies in a grotesque accident in his garden (*RS*, 64, 262). William Hazel, who reminisces about the Second World War, is the gardener at Somerleyton (*RS*, 52). Their saturnine counterparts in *Die Ausgewanderten* are two Jewish figures whose lives have been affected by the Holocaust and who both commit suicide: Henry Selwyn spends much time in his garden, while Paul Bereyter embodies the love of the outdoors associated with the German "Wandervogelbewegung" (hikers' movement, *AG*, 11, 61). In fact, in Sebald's work gardeners or ecological types often connect to the victims of history. In *Die Ringe des Saturn* Frederick Farrar dies by accidentally setting fire to himself in the garden: this work reflects constantly on the themes of heat, fire, cremation, and holocaust (in the original sense of burnt sacrificial offerings; *RS*, 37). The *Weltschmerzler* who wallows in the Giardino Giusti in *Schwindel. Gefühle* also connects, through a general sympathy for history's victims, to these others, but because of the ironic hyperbole of his self-description, is not identical with them.

The environmentally friendly victim personality contrasts with other melancholy incarnations, ones that fall under the negative side of the tradition associated with Chronos, who stands for celibacy, childlessness, orphanhood, violence, and malice. The veiled reference in *Die Ringe des Saturn* to Kurt Waldheim, the one-time United Nations Secretary-General and President of Austria who was discovered to have lied about his service as an SA officer during the Second World War, conveys the potential evil dimension to the tradition. Pernicious children of Saturn may also be traitors, which is exactly how Sebald means to portray Waldheim. A recording of Waldheim's voice went into outer space on the Voyager spacecraft launched in 1977, Sebald ironically notes, a fine ambassador for the human species intended for any intelligent extraterrestrial life form that may find it (*RS*, 122–23; *SM*, 131).

The quality of moisture that originated in the figure of Chronos is the motif that Sebald most consistently applies in *Die Ringe des Saturn*. In Greek mythology Chronos was eventually banished by his son Zeus to Tartaros, a hell even lower than Hades. Chronos is a gloomy, dethroned, and solitary god who in the *Iliad* is conceived as "dwelling at the uttermost end of land and sea," a quotation that, although it does not appear in *Die Ringe des Saturn*, aptly describes the literary evocation of the English coastline in the book (*SM*, 212). The merging of Saturn and Chronos along with the black bile associations of humoral pathology means that the melancholy condition from the Middle Ages onward bears the qualities of coldness and dryness, as well as humidity and moisture. Chronos, the god of time, is also the god of rain, sea, and tears. From this point, melancholics are prone to illnesses associated with wet, dryness, and coldness. Accordingly, we get an account of the death by dropsy, an illness caused by the melancholy temperament, of one of the last Qing Emperors (*RS*, 176). As an aside, the work shows a considerable interest in the origins of the Chinese silk industry and through an account of the nineteenth-century Opium Wars an interest in matters Asian. In the ethnic variation on the humoral temperaments, the Asiatic type is the melancholic type (*SM*, 211–12).[59]

The presence of the sea drives home a sense of melancholy vastness in *Die Ringe des Saturn*. It provides the epic backdrop to the narrator's wanderings, lending to his regional travels a cosmic dimension and connecting him, in the mode of *Weltschmerz*, to world history. At the same time, the sea features in the foreground of many of his musings, such as his reflections on the Sea Battle of Southwold (*RS*, 94–97). Dürer expresses the watery dimension to the tradition that originally had little to do with moisture by including a flooded landscape in the background of his engraving. Indeed, fascination with flooding is one of the recurring images in Sebald's work, and arguably one of the reasons why he includes an early acknowledgement of the engraving in *Die Ringe des Saturn*. From the sunken coastal medieval village of Dunwich (*RS*, 187) to Austerlitz's childhood imagination of a forgotten settlement under water (*Aus*, 80), to the description in *Schwindel. Gefühle* of England's and Venice's watery landscapes (*SG*, 56, 60), Sebald's interest in water is striking. In *Die Ringe des Saturn* the narrator relies on the aesthetics of *Melencolia I* to visualize a dream that haunts him after his experience of losing his way on Dunwich Heath. He imagines himself sitting on a raised area with a view over a flooded coastal region, rather like the winged figure in the engraving (*RS*, 207). He can see the coming flood and also witnesses its consequences, which suggests that he is a modern-day incarnation of the saturnine melancholic, who could predict weather patterns, especially flooding. In the era of accelerated global warming, Dürer's winged genius acquires an iconic actuality (*SM*, 457–58).

Sebald's representation of the weather also includes many references to coldness, dryness, and heat in this work and in others, all of which feed into a critical discourse on the earth's natural environment. Images of the encroaching desert feature throughout *Die Ringe des Saturn* from the moment where the narrator reflects on Dakyns's scholarly work on

Flaubert's preoccupation with sand. Paraphrasing his friend, the narrator remembers how she told him that Flaubert had fearful dreams of sandstorms. In a somewhat prophetic manner she mentions that Flaubert was convinced that sand would conquer everything (*RS*, 17). This is an image that the narrator cannot thereafter escape: the river Blyth is being swallowed up by sand (*RS*, 165), he loses his way in the sandy labyrinth of Dunwich Heath (*RS*, 204–5), and at Dunwich strand sand is sucking Eccles Tower back into the earth (*RS*, 188–89). He gets caught up in a vicious sandstorm on his way from Woodbridge to Orford, an experience that obliterates all markers of direction and familiar features of the landscape around him (*RS*, 272–73). Images of the desert appear in *Die Ringe des Saturn*, and also in *Die Ausgewanderten* and *Austerlitz* (*RS*, 105–6, 273; *AG*, 202–15; *Aus*, 85–88). Damaging processes of desertification as a result of deforestation crop up in *Die Ringe des Saturn*; desertification is symbolically connected to man's obsession with "Verbrennung" (burning) of the earth's natural resources in order to produce more energy (*RS*, 201–3). Interestingly, Dakyns's office is slowly being taken over by one of the "tools of destruction," the narrator observes in his allusion to Dürer's engraving: paperwork is simply flooding the place (*RS*, 17–18). And the artist Max Aurach in *Die Ausgewanderten* whittles his paintings down to ash-like dust (*AG*, 237–39). The melancholy intellectual-artistic type, no matter how perspicacious, is thus implicated, through the activities of Dakyns and Aurach, in the maltreatment of the earth. Sebald's message here concerns the inescapable web of responsibility and consequence in which we all act in a claustrophobically integrated world.

Stone is a further melancholy symbolization of dryness, as Benjamin points out in his analysis of *Melencolia I*.[60] The city of Norwich, where the narrator is hospitalized, is a grey, barren wasteland of masonry, boulders, and gravel—an urban desert (*RS*, 13). In *Schwindel. Gefühle*, Venice is a stone- and waterscape (*SG*, 71), while Manchester in *Die Ausgewanderten* consists of industrial chimneys (*AG*, 250). The colonial city of Matadi in the Congo is a hellish place of stone, the colonized natives working slavishly in the quarries for their masters (*RS*, 145). The "Belgian ugliness" upon which the narrator venomously reflects connects symbolically to this colonial past (*RS*, 150). Read against this episode in *Die Ringe des Saturn*, the magnificent stone carvings and architectural detail of Antwerp train station in *Austerlitz* becomes a dubious "cathedral" of world commerce (*Aus*, 17–21).

Snow is another melancholy incarnation of coldness, dryness, and death. The grotesque apparition of the frozen corpse of the mountain climber and close friend of Henry Selwyn, Johannes Naegeli, surfaces seventy-two years after he fell to his death in the Swiss Alps (*AG*, 36). This image recalls Schlag's frozen corpse (*SG*, 270) and the death of Austerlitz's adoptive mother, which occurs in the middle of a winter landscape (*Aus*, 96).

While all the above can be understood in terms of pathetic fallacy, the landscapes extending anthropomorphically the subjective melancholy of narrators and characters, these images are more important for their commentary on the natural world and humankind's interaction with it. Claudia Öhlschläger interprets these "white spaces" as the poetic signifier of a melancholy interest in the transitoriness of all matter, a lyrical warning against the danger of forgetting. I would add that the depiction of these natural processes also suggests the neutralization of the natural landscape to a blank canvas, a space of uniformity that can be read as an allegory for the globalization processes of world capitalism. The transformation of the world into a uniform space also corresponds to the problem of perspective in this work and others. For through his depictions of devastating winds, blankets of snow and sand, and creeping waters Sebald captures humankind's myopic inability to see itself in perspective with the surrounding world, let alone in historical perspective. The ethical effort contained in the sentimental self-irony discussed earlier contrasts with this lack of perspective.[61]

The Natural History of Capitalism

According to medieval and Renaissance concepts of melancholy, those born under the sign of Saturn manifest an inclination toward seafaring, playing a part in captaining ships, ship building, and sea travel (*SM*, 223–24). These children of Saturn abound in *Die Ringe des Saturn*: the controversial Victorian-era English poet Algernon Swinburne is a melancholy pilgrim to the sunken village of Dunwich (*RS*, 192), the nineteenth-century poet and translator Edward Fitzgerald devotes much of his later life to sailing up and down the coast of Suffolk and out onto the North Sea (*RS*, 241–42). Edmund Ashbury, a sad and eccentric remnant of the English landowner class in 1980s Ireland, spends his days building a wooden longboat that he admits he can never see himself sailing (*RS*, 251). In the same vein, the narrator's favorite place on his travels is the Sailors' Reading Room in Southwold, while the narrator of *Schwindel. Gefühle* is often near water, whether in England or Italy (*SG*, 115).

In *Die Ringe des Saturn* many of these melancholy figures are writer-intellectuals whose life stories intersect with global-capitalist history, symbolized through the image of unending saturnine rings in the work's title. An example of how the narrator goes about building up this kind of analysis is the story of Joseph Conrad, whose youthful heart's desire, we learn, was to become a sea captain (*RS*, 133). Sebald tells us how under the auspices of the Belgian colonial project in the Congo this dream came to be realized (*RS*, 141). For a time Conrad was part of an expanding colonial system of exploitation until he, like the narrator on his historical trail through Suffolk, literally became ill as a result of what he witnessed in Africa: the destruction, maltreatment, and—in economics terminology—peripheralization, still continuing today, of agrarian communities (*RS,* 147).

"Peripheralization" describes a fundamental component of the processes of the world-scale division and integration of labor in the development of global capitalism. "Peripheral" does not mean marginal in the sense of dispensable, but refers to the unequal economic relationship that exists between the centers of capitalist power ("cores") and the peripheries they need in order to sustain capitalist growth. Peripheries provide low-cost production operations for suppliers and often high-return markets for products. The workings of the core-periphery relation therefore "are always everywhere characterized . . . by the phenomenon of 'unequal exchange.'"[62] The political process of "imperium" accompanies this economic process of capitalist accumulation. To be peripheralized is to be exploited; Sebald's depiction of slave labor in the Congo is an extreme example of the two processes, economic and political.

Sebald continues his analysis of global capitalism in the critical depiction of the Opium Wars between China and Britain in the second half of the nineteenth century. These wars resulted in China's enforced entry, as an unequal trading partner, into the growing world capitalist system at that time (*RS,* 170–71). Other examples of this kind of exploitation are the Dutch East Indies Company's sugar trade in Surabaya (*RS,* 229–30), the British interference in South America (*RS,* 156), and the oppression of the Irish under British rule (*RS,* 157–63). Sebald's sophisticated understanding of the mechanisms of global capitalism is evident in his accounts of contemporary unemployment and industry black holes that have developed in Great Britain as a result of market forces. Lowestoft, the depressed town that once was a booming magnet for the wealthy at the time of imperial ascendancy, is an example of the peripheralization process come back to haunt the seat of British economic power, one of the original cores of world capitalism (*RS,* 56–57). Likewise, the sandy area between Woodbridge and Orford is the site of a similar peripheralization that began and ended locally, with sobering consequences for the region and its agrarian community. The narrator reflects on how the capitalist class of the Victorian period bought up the once aristocratic estates and devoted themselves to small-game hunting, then in vogue and a desired status symbol for this group of bourgeois arrivistes. The widespread appropriation of land for this leisure activity resulted in the disenfranchisement and eventual emigration to the Antipodes of the region's agricultural class (*RS,* 266). The local impact of capitalism on this social group and its way of life reflects, on the micro level, the impact of global capitalist forces on Lowestoft a century later. Peripheralization and its consequences within Europe thus resonate, to an extent, with the Belgian colonization of the Congo.

Bearing in mind this "global" view of the historical impact of capitalism, Sebald's analysis of the crumbling remnants of nineteenth-century British capitalist ascendancy, such as occurs on his visit to Somerleyton, becomes more than just a whimsical reflection on the passing of all things and all eras (*RS* 42–52). These kinds of analyses, while melancholy in tone, provide an informed, poetic critique of the capitalist world system, not just as it was in the past, but as it continues in the present. In this vein, Sebald attempts in *Die Ringe des Saturn* to capture the particular temporal quality of capitalism, itself a rather abstract concept. As Immanuel Wallerstein and Terence Hopkins suggest in their analysis of world systems, capitalism does not have a history so much as it *constitutes* a history. By this they mean that time in the capitalist context is not simply an external coordinate of the system. Rather, "capitalist time" operates in terms of trends and cycles that contract and expand, shifting the peripheries and affecting the cores of capitalist power according to the rules of the free market. Time understood in the form of trends and cycles is an integral part of the capitalist world system and not simply an ordering dimension through which we make observations.[63]

This is how Sebald means to represent time in *Die Ringe des Saturn*: as a natural history of capitalism that has its roots in the early sixteenth century and that continues to expand in the present, but not without stagnating periodically in several of its integrated parts. Across the reach of geographical space and chronological time, places as culturally diverse and as distant from each other as Lowestoft and Surabaya are shown, through the representative logic of the book, to be integrated elements within the shifting capitalist world system that, at different times in chronological history, impacts these two different places negatively through the process of peripheralization. It makes sense from this perspective that Sebald should describe Lowestoft as an exemplary instance of civilization's regression. He likens to a natural hazard the spread of the damage that arose through capitalism's stagnation in this town. Like a wildfire it consumed businesses, revealing their vulnerability to a system infinitely more powerful than any local, or indeed national, industry. The townspeople too follow the path of regression. A quarter of the town's population is now illiterate, a sobering fact that illustrates the interdependency of industry, finance, and Western ideas about what constitutes a civilized society (*RS*, 56). This reading of time in *Die Ringe des Saturn* expands Amir Eshel's metasemantic analysis of time in Sebald's work as a decelerating poetics of suspension. Eshel argues that the slow tempo of Sebald's prose, through the creation of text-internal time effects, constitutes a form of melancholy resistance to time's gallop. My analysis shows that it is not only this; it is also, on the level of content, a subtle mimesis of the stagnating effect of capitalist time.[64]

Understanding Sebald's representation of history as an ambitious attempt to communicate the strange tempo of capitalist expansion can further explain the ghosting effect of his prose. As mentioned, the premonition of desertification rears its head as the narrator traces his way through the sandy area from Woodbridge to Orford. This transformation of the land goes back to the same class of industrial arrivistes who had the area cleared of vegetation to better facilitate their leisure activity of hunting, a development that parallels the current plundering of rain forests in Brazil, and that, along with the book's many images of desertification processes, forms a critique of the stagnating tendencies intrinsic to Western developmentalism (*RS*, 98, 105, 145–46, 175, 182, 202–3, 273). As Wallerstein observes, capitalism "'stagnates' *in* growth; it doesn't stagnate and then grow," even though Western teleology understands capitalism—and more generally history—in terms of continuing progress. Sebald abandons this register in order to represent the complex ebb and flow of capitalism. His representation of time follows this pattern and should not be read as mythology, even if he uses images from melancholy to develop a poetic version of the history and rhythms of capitalism. Thus the image of the desert that is not confined to South America or the Middle East but also pervades the English countryside is a symbol of capitalism's "natural" history: an index of the shifting cores and peripheries of an uncomfortably interconnected world system, as well as a reminder of humankind's environmental irresponsibility.[65]

The poignant story of the Ashbury family offers a particularly personalized version of this time complex. Once a member of the British landowner class in Ireland, they have come down in the world since the dawn of Irish independence. In the present they subsist in a remote corner of the Irish countryside, where they inhabit a time warp (*RS*, 249–50). They are ghostly figures—the mother, son, and two sisters—who wander around the property in an aimless manner, vaguely searching for some activity to fill their days, remnants of an elite exploitative class who have been superseded by political events. The Ashburys no longer form a confident social group in the ascendancy but engage in menial activities, such as sewing, which symbolically associates them with the exploited weavers in the British silk industry of the nineteenth century (*RS*, 334). Clearly, the Ashbury family never knew the physical and financial hardships endured by the working class of weavers depicted toward the end of the book. However, the two socially and historically distinct groups—laborers and landowners—become linked across time, class, and space if we regard what happens to them as a consequence of the peripheralization process of world capitalism. At different times and in different ways, both groups have been washed up in the flotsam and jetsam of political and economic events, peripheralized in a manner comparable to the decline of Somerleyton House, which is now described as a veritable rubbish repository (*RS*, 48). It, too, is a location of stagnation, just as the Ashburys and their ruin of a house epitomize the stagnation of their social class and the disappearance of its wealth. The peripheralization of the English silk weavers is nowhere better captured than in the description of their de facto imprisonment in the torture instruments that are the looms. Their bodies and minds suffer as a result of their labor and they are particularly predisposed to melancholy: peripheralization made tangible in (psycho)somatic form (*RS*, 334–35). These silk weavers are further linked across time and space to China, the ancient origin of silk weaving, which, as above outlined, was forced into unequal trading relations with the West by the end of the Opium Wars.

The rings of Saturn are thus a poetic image for the inescapable circularity of global processes, natural and manmade, the curious shrinking of the world into an entity composed of ever-more interdependent parts. Sebald's poetics of association, the many links he alludes to across space and time, alerts the reader to the heightened fragility of an integrated globe. This is no easy task, however, as it requires an alternative understanding of both historical processes and physical space, which amounts to a shift away from habitual perspective. With this in mind, I now examine how Sebald animates a further aspect of the melancholy tradition, the "typus Geometriae," to foreground the problem of perspective.

Saturn's Children II

In Dürer's engraving, the symbols of Saturn or of melancholy, such as the dark face, the dog, the purse, appear alongside geometrical symbols, the tools and objects such as the compass, the molding-plane, and the set square (or triangle, as it is known in North America). The geometrical objects symbolize the art of measuring either as an end in itself or as a means to an end. The hammer, saw, nails, and pincers, and the unfinished building behind the seated figure, symbolize the application of geometry to handicraft and construction. According to Klibansky et al., this merging of two types here, the melancholy "typus Acediae" and the "typus Geometriae," suggests an inner affinity between the mathematical type and the melancholy type: this is the new message of *Melencolia I*. Melancholics and geometrical types are occupational symbols from the saturnine melancholy tradition. This explains why Saturn's children do not include just the terminally sad but also builders, joiners, carpenters, architects, mathematicians, and astronomers (*SM*, 468–76).[66]

The "typus Geometriae" dominates in Sebald's works. Alec Garrard, previously a farmer who now devotes all his time to building a model of the Temple of Jerusalem, is an incarnation of the artisanal melancholy "typus Geometriae" represented in Dürer's engraving (*RS*,

288–89). This endeavor combines architectural ability, intense study of biblical and other scholarly sources, and the geometrical imagination. In *Die Ausgewanderten*, Max Aurach tells of a dream he once had of a stranger, Herr Frohmann, who spent seven years building a similar model of the temple, in Aurach's eyes the epitome of a true work of art (*AG*, 262–63). For Garrard, the completion of his temple keeps slipping from his grasp as the periodic discovery of new biblical sources forces him to alter anew the measurements of his model, which suggests an epistemological limit, despite the instruments of precision at Garrard's fingertips. This is precisely the conundrum Dürer's winged figure faces: many instruments lie idle on the ground, impotent for procuring the knowledge the figure seeks. Austerlitz's school friend, Gerald, also embodies the "typus Geometriae": he decides to study astronomy as he is convinced that it affords one a perspective of distance and height on "die ganze Misere" (the entire misery) of the world around him (*Aus*, 164).

This yearning for a unifying perspective on the world manifests itself in the motif of heightened position. For Austerlitz, also a "typus Geometriae," the ideal place is the "Sternkammer" (Star Chamber) in the Royal Observatory at Greenwich. In this room, suspended above the world and surrounded by the measuring instruments of astral enquiry, this expert on architecture begins to expound his views on the artificial construct of chronological time (*Aus*, 148–52). The very location of this conversation suggests that historical understanding is not simply a matter for watches and clocks; it is also linked to spatial understanding. Austerlitz seems to suggest that if our temporal understanding is epistemologically narrow, our spatial knowledge is also correspondingly truncated. "History" becomes the selective master narrative of a number of events that imply certain geographical centers, but that also exclude many other affected regions and unknown individuals. For Austerlitz the main problem of master narratives is their neglect of the subjective experience of history. He goes beyond this, however, by proposing that there is a condition called "Außer-der-Zeit-Sein" (Being outside time, *Aus*, 151). This place is not just the preserve of the dead and forgotten victims of history. It also encompasses the forgotten regions of the world that have been rendered invisible to the Western mind by the course of history. Lowestoft comes to mind here, as well as far flung, impoverished, and peripheralized places overseas.

In *Die Ringe des Saturn* historical understanding is also presented as a problem of visual perspective. At several points the narrator speaks from an elevated position, as if height can somehow afford the individual a new understanding (*RS*, 12, 114, 151–52, 206, 274). When in The Hague, he ruminates admiringly on Jacob van Ruisdael's landscape painting, which calms him down considerably after the disturbing experience of viewing Rembrandt's group portrait *The Anatomy Lecture of Dr Nicolaas Tulp* (*RS*, 102–3). The temporary restoration of artificial perspective in the van Ruisdael painting soothes the narrator. He acknowledges the unifying perspective of sky and land to be artifice; however, this is less problematic than Rembrandt's deliberate play with the rules of geometrical optics in his painting—he has painted the left hand of the corpse in a way that breaks with the laws of visual perspective (*RS*, 27). Sebald reads this from an ethical perspective as Rembrandt's empathy with the criminal, Aris Kindt: Rembrandt is defying the growing Cartesian rationality of the seventeenth century by asserting the body in this way, and thereby restores a semblance of humanity to the dead man on the table. The narrator is also making a point about the relationship between seeing and knowing. In this vein, he remembers a visit to Waterloo and the experience of viewing a reconstruction of the battle through the visual device of a panorama that, unlike the van Ruisdael landscape, he finds very unsatisfying. Although one looks at the panorama from an elevated position and the events within are represented in three dimensions, the entire thing is artifice, he concludes, falsification of perspective (*RS*, 152). Just as a final version of the model of the temple eludes Garrard, there is an elusive quality to historical understanding, because it is exceedingly difficult to reverse and redevelop ways of seeing and knowing.[67]

This concern is at the heart of what Dürer tries to represent in his engraving and is what he addresses in the depiction of the polyhedron that gauges perspective: the related problems of seeing, knowing, imaginative capacity, and geometrical accuracy. Klibansky et al. propose that Dürer's combination of diverse elements from the saturnine tradition articulates a psychological theory founded on epistemology. Throughout *Die Ringe des Saturn* Sebald expands this insight beyond the purely psychological perspective, transforming melancholy into an ethical category of thoughtfulness in the contemporary world. He thus acknowledges the blind spots of established and limited epistemological frameworks—the many references across his work to the curiously aestheticized nature of what the narrators observe is not just an ironic reference to the melodramatic tendencies of the sentimental *Weltschmerzler*. It also registers the a priori way we experience the world. Our epistemological preconditioning is what makes it so easy to forget victims, to look at places and persons without recognizing what we have seen. Sebald's narrators' interest in the contingent is a concerted effort to break through the established paradigms of "reality" in the hope of accessing a different knowledge and experience of the world. His "rings of Saturn" offer an alternative epistemology that cuts through time and space, but that is aware of its limits. Melancholy is part of the new ethical epistemology; it thematizes epistemological limitations yet also suggests the possibility of altering existing epistemological frameworks (*SM*, 485–512).[68]

"Late Victorian Holocausts"

As argued above, Sebald presents us with a perspective on the world as a spatiotemporal whole. One of the most effective ways he does this is by restoring a sense of geographical space to the historical site. This spatialization of history widens his historical perspective to encompass the present day, as opposed to narrowing or freezing it. Colin Riordan alludes to this expansive feature of Sebald's work, calling it "ecocentrism": the ability to see ourselves in environmental context and to think in connective processes. He argues that nature is the ultimate context in Sebald's work, but that we cannot separate human activity from the natural world: the two are inseparably linked. Fuchs adds a historical dimension to this insight by observing that nature in *Die Ringe des Saturn* is both a force beyond human control—the ultimate context, so to speak—as Sebald's fear of flooding and other such natural hazards seems to express, and a resource that has continually been plundered by Western humankind in the pursuit of capitalist gain.[69]

This reading of nature in Sebald's work can be taken a step further and presented as the literary parallel to developments in genocide historiography. This branch of genocide research poses the question of the relationship between global warming, natural hazards, and the creation of conditions favorable to the event of genocide. In Mark Levene's vision of a post-genocide world marked by the consequences of global warming, scarcity of basic resources is seen as a factor in the worsening of inter-ethnic relations. Sebald's preoccupation with flooding, his interest in sand, aridity, and desertification also communicates an interest in the reality of scarcity. Thus he includes a description of the effects of the Chinese drought-famine of 1877 to 1879 that was caused principally by weather systems beyond the control of humankind but that, in the Indian famines of the same period, was worsened by British imperial policy (*RS*, 181–82). For Mike Davis, author of *Late Victorian Holocausts*, a study that sees a connection between the crystallization of the modern Western global economy and the dramatic crop failures brought on by severe oscillations in the global weather system at the end of the nineteenth century, these drought-famines and what preceded them are nothing less than holocausts.[70]

Davis is not subscribing to a catastrophic view of the Holocaust as a general paradigm for the understanding of history. Rather, he is pointing the finger of accusation at the one-time imperial powers of the late nineteenth century, in particular the British Empire, who have yet to acknowledge their role in facilitating the drought-famines of the 1870s in regions of the world that are still peripheralized to this day. Sebald's interest in the natural environment in *Die Ringe des Saturn*, alongside his problematization of historical perspective, pursues a similar investigative strand as this branch of historiography. Both Davis and Sebald acknowledge the natural environment as an "ultimate context": the insight that we in the Western and Westernized world do not entirely run the show on planet Earth, that nature operates in cycles and trends across an obscure temporal *longue durée* that we can hope to understand only gradually, even as we, through our profiteering activities, regularly have a hand in accelerating destructive tendencies in the global weather system. This view serves as a sobering reminder that historical understanding of the twenty-first century should expand "ecocentrically" to take account of human interaction with and exploitation of nature. There is an urgent political dimension to this reminder, moreover, that is not exclusively focused on the destruction of nature as a tragedy in itself. Taken alongside Sebald's interest in twentieth-century genocide, in particular the Holocaust, his discourse on the human exploitation of the environment during the period that A. Dirk Moses terms the "racial century" of 1850–1950, can be seen not just in the economic terms of peripheralization, but more disturbingly as a basic premise of the political struggle for more land, territory, *Lebensraum* that goes hand in hand with the perpetration of genocide.[71]

Sebald has been described as a writer who endorses the uniqueness of the Holocaust as a historical event.[72] Certainly, it is the genocide he engages with most in his work. However, *Die Ringe des Saturn* should propel us as readers of his entire oeuvre to reevaluate this view. Apart from reference to the extermination of Serbs and Jews at Jasenovac under the Nazi-supported Ustasha regime, direct references to the Holocaust are absent from the account of history's atrocities in the book. In any case, Sebald contextualizes this episode by referring not only to the struggle for Serbian self-assertion in the Balkans that acted as decisive catalyst for the First World War but also to the ongoing troubles in the region in the 1990s (*RS*, 118–22). The novel element in *Die Ringe des Saturn* is how Sebald makes both continuous natural erosion and human plundering of the environment through the imperial projects of the "racial century" a possible epistemological framework for understanding the contexts in which genocides occur. This does not depoliticize genocide, nor does it mythologize it into part of a traumatic world history. Rather, it shifts the emphasis of Sebald's historical enquiry away from individual (German) identification with the tragedy of the Holocaust to a more comparative and contemporary, if still melancholy, analysis of the interaction between global capitalism, the environment, and humans of different ethnic and class backgrounds. In literary terms, it is principally his mobilization of manifold melancholy images that achieves this comparative overview.

Notes

[1] For a detailed discussion of Sebald's treatment of Thomas Browne see Anne Fuchs, *Die Schmerzensspuren der Geschichte: Zur Poetik der Erinnerung in W. G.*

Sebalds Prosa (Cologne: Böhlau, 2004), 99–107. For other readings of melancholy in Sebald's work see Anja Lemke, "Figurationen der Melancholie: Spuren Walter Benjamins in W. G. Sebalds 'Die Ringe des Saturn,'" *Zeitschrift für deutsche Philologie* 2 (2008): 239–67; Claudia Öhlschläger, *Beschädigtes Leben: Erzählte Risse; W. G. Sebalds poetische Ordnung des Unglücks* (Berlin: Rombach, 2006), 157–91; Holger Steinmann, "Zitatruinen unterm Hundsstern: W. G. Sebalds Ansichten von der Nachtseite der Philologie," in *W. G. Sebald: Politische Archäologie und melancholische Bastelei*, ed. Michael Niehaus and Claudia Öhlschläger (Berlin: Erich Schmidt, 2006), 145–56; Bianca Theissen, "A Natural History of Destruction: W. G. Sebald's The Rings of Saturn," *Modern Language Notes* 121 (2006): 563–81; Amir Eshel, "Against the Power of Time: The Poetics of Suspension in W. G. Sebald's *Austerlitz*," *New German Critique* 88 (2003): 71–96; Peter Morgan, "The Sign of Saturn: Melancholy, Homelessness and Apocalypse in W. G. Sebald's Prose Narratives," *German Life and Letters* 58 (2005): 75–92.

[2] Freud, "Trauer und Melancholie," 10:428–46.

[3] W. G. Sebald, *Die Beschreibung des Unglücks: Zur österreichischen Literatur von Stifter bis Handke* (Vienna: Residenz, 1985), 9. Benjamin, *Ursprung des deutschen Trauerspiels*, 76, 124, 133. Lepenies, *Melancholie und Gesellschaft*. Sebald's copies of these works by Benjamin and Lepenies are held in the W. G.-Sebald-Bibliothek, Deutsches Literaturarchiv, Marbach. On Sebald's posthumous library in Marbach see Jo Catling, "*Bibliotheca abscondita*: On W. G. Sebald's Library," in *Saturn's Moons: W. G. Sebald; A Handbook*, ed. Jo Catling and Richard Hibbit (Oxford: Legenda, 2011), 265–97.

[4] For a critique of Sebald's metaphysical view of history and its ahistorical effects see Fuchs, *Schmerzensspuren der Geschichte*, 165–176. For a critical overview of the field see Bettina Mosbach, *Figurationen der Katastrophe: Ästhetische Verfahren in W. G. Sebalds Die Ringe des Saturn und Austerlitz* (Bielefeld: Aisthesis, 2008), 9–31. Early voices supporting the idea of melancholy as resistance include Sigrid Löffler, "'Melancholie ist eine Form des Widerstands': Über das Saturnische bei W. G. Sebald und seine Aufhebung in der Schrift," *Text + Kritik* 158 (2003): 103–11, and Irene Heidelberger-Leonard, "Melancholie als Widerstand," *Akzente* 48, no. 2 (2001): 122–30. For a more critical stance see Andreas Isenschmid, "Melencolia—W. G. Sebalds *Schwindel. Gefühle*," in *W. G. Sebald: Porträt*, ed. Franz Loquai (Eggingen, Germany: Isele, 1997), 70–74, and Thomas Wirtz, "Schwarze Zuckerwatte: Anmerkungen zu W. G. Sebald," *Merkur* 6 (2001): 530–34.

[5] J. J. Long, "W. G. Sebald's Miniature Histories," in *W. G. Sebald and the Writing of History*, ed. Anne Fuchs and J. J. Long (Würzburg: Königshausen & Neumann, 2007), 119.

[6] Niehaus suggests that melancholy in Sebald is a timeless constant. Niehaus, "W. G. Sebalds sentimentalische Dichtung," in Niehaus and Öhlschläger, *W. G. Sebald: Politische Archäologie und melancholische Bastelei*, 182–83; Richard Langston provides the negative reading of melancholy and Enlightenment. Langston, "Affective Affinities: Sebald and Kluge on Feeling History," special issue on W. G. Sebald, *Gegenwartsliteratur* 6 (2007): 61; Mark Ilsemann, "Going Astray: Melancholy, Natural History, and the Image of Exile in W. G. Sebald's *Austerlitz*," in

W. G. Sebald: History—Memory—Trauma, ed. Scott Denham and Mark McCulloh (Berlin: Walter de Gruyter, 2006), 302–3.

[7] Huyssen, "Gray Zones of Remembrance," in *A New History of German Literature*, ed. David E. Wellbery and Judith Ryan (Cambridge, MA: Harvard University Press, 2004), 972. See also Mosbach, *Figurationen der Katastrophe*, 22–31.

[8] See Fuchs, *Die Schmerzensspuren der Geschichte*, 165–205.

[9] W. G, Sebald, *Nach der Natur: Ein Elementargedicht* (Frankfurt am Main: Fischer, 2008), 76. See also Rudolf and Margot Wittkower, *Born under Saturn*, 98–108.

[10] On transgenerational trauma, see Sigrid Weigel, "'Generation as a Symbolic Form': On the Genealogical Discourse of Memory since 1945," *Germanic Review* 77 (2002): 269. For an analysis of this phenomenon in contemporary German family narratives see Anne Fuchs, *Phantoms of War in Contemporary German Literature, Films and Discourse: The Politics of Memory* (Basingstoke, UK: Palgrave Macmillan, 2010). On Weiss and mythology see Jens Birkmeyer, *Bilder des Schreckens*.

[11] Hildesheimer, *Tynset* and *Masante*.

[12] See Sebald's essay, "Konstruktionen der Trauer." Grass later defended the *Tagebuch* against Sebald's critique. See Fridolin Schley, *Kataloge der Wahrheit: Zur Inszenierung von Autorschaft bei W. G. Sebald* (Göttingen: Wallstein, 2012), 364.

[13] Weiss, *Die Ästhetik des Widerstands*.

[14] Zilcosky, "Lost and Found: Disorientation, Nostalgia, and Holocaust Melodrama in Sebald's *Austerlitz*," *Modern Language Notes* 121, no. 3 (2006): 679–98. Brad Prager, "The Good German as Narrator: On W. G. Sebald and the Risks of Holocaust Writing," in "Memory and the Holocaust," special issue, *New German Critique* 96 (Fall 2005): 75–102.

[15] W. G. Sebald, *Luftkrieg und Literatur: Mit einem Essay zu Alfred Andersch* (Munich: Carl Hanser, 1999), 18–21. Mitscherlich and Mitscherlich, *Die Unfähigkeit zu trauern*.

[16] See Andreas Huyssen, "On Rewritings and New Beginnings: W. G. Sebald and the Literature about the *Luftkrieg*," *Zeitschrift für Literatur und Linguistik* 31 (2001): 72–90; Winfried Wilms, "Taboo and Repression in W. G. Sebald's *On the Natural History of Destruction*," in *W. G. Sebald: A Critical Companion*, ed. J. J. Long and Anne Whitehead (Edinburgh: Edinburgh University Press, 2004), 175–89; Anne Fuchs, "A *Heimat* in Ruins and the Ruins as *Heimat*: W. G. Sebald's *Luftkrieg und Literatur*," in *German Memory Contests*, ed. Anne Fuchs, Mary Cosgrove, and Georg Grote, 287–302.

[17] W. G. Sebald, *Die Beschreibung des Unglücks*, 9–13.

[18] Schütte, "In einer wildfremden Gegend": W. G. Sebalds Essays über die österreichische Literatur," in *The Anatomist of Melancholy: Essays in Memory of W. G. Sebald*, ed. Rüdiger Görner (Munich: Iudicum, 2003), 69. Schley observes how Sebald extracts symbolic capital from melancholy discourses. Schley, *Kataloge der Wahrheit*, 17. Mosbach notes that Sebald's essay on Peter Handke also privileges the pathological perspective in literary transformation. Mosbach, *Figurationen der Katastrophe*, 139. In Sebald's works, Austerlitz suffers several breakdowns and

must be hospitalized: *Austerlitz* (Frankfurt am Main: Fischer, 2001), 331, 382; in *Die Ausgewanderten: Vier lange Erzählungen* (Frankfurt am Main: Fischer, 1994) Ambrose Adelwarth commits himself to a home for the mentally ill after his lover's death from mental illness, 150, 162–63; and *Die Ringe des Saturn* begins with a depiction of the narrator's sojourn in hospital after a mental breakdown. Sebald underlines the theme of saturnine melancholy dialectics on p. 163 of his copy of Benjamin's work on tragic drama. W. G.-Sebald-Bibliothek, Deutsches Literaturarchiv, Marbach. Aristotle, *Aristotle: Problems II*, 30.155–81.

[19] Freud, "Trauer und Melancholie," 10:428–46. Sebald, "Konstruktionen der Trauer," 119.

[20] Sebald, *Schwindel. Gefühle* (Frankfurt am Main: Fischer, 2003). Sartre, *Nausea*. As mentioned in chapter 2, Sartre originally planned to entitle *Nausea* "Melencolie." See Martina Wagner-Egelhaaf, *Die Melancholie der Literatur*, 2.

[21] For this view see Anja Maier, "'Der panische Halsknick.': Organisches und Anorganisches in W. G. Sebalds Prosa," in Niehaus and Öhlschläger, *W. G. Sebald: Politische Archäologie und melancholische Bastelei*, 124. See also Mosbach, *Figurationen der Katastrophe*, 124–32.

[22] Sebald, *Die Beschreibung des Unglücks*, 12.

[23] Wittkower and Wittkower, *Born under Saturn*, 104. See also Maya Barzilai, "Melancholia as World History: W. G. Sebald's Rewriting of Hegel in *Die Ringe des Saturn*," in Fuchs and Long, *W. G. Sebald and the Writing of History*, 73–89.

[24] Hell, "Eyes Wide Shut: German Post-Holocaust Authorship," *New German Critique* 88 (Winter 2003): 12–13.

[25] Greg Bond, "On the Misery of Nature and the Nature of Misery: W. G. Sebald's Landscapes," in Long and Whitehead, *W. G. Sebald: A Critical Companion*, 41. Thomas Wirtz, "Schwarze Zuckerwatte." Sebald, *Die Ringe des Saturn*, 58.

[26] See Lemke, "Figurationen der Melancholie," 256–59, and Öhlschläger, *Beschädigtes Leben: Erzählte Risse*, 187–89.

[27] Long, *W. G. Sebald: Image, Archive, Modernity* (Edinburgh: Edinburgh University Press, 2007), 6. See also Barzilai, "Melancholia as World History," 7–89. Wirtz, "Schwarze Zuckerwatte." Eleanor M. Sickels, *The Gloomy Egoist*, 132, 295–97.

[28] See for, example, Langston, "Affective Affinities," 61–62. See also Eric L. Santner, *On Creaturely Life: Rilke, Benjamin, Sebald* (Chicago: University of Chicago Press, 2006), 68. Ribó, "The One-Winged Angel: History and Memory in the Literary Discourse of W. G. Sebald," *Orbis Litterarum* 64, no. 3 (2009): 254–55.

[29] Schings, *Melancholie und Aufklärung*. See also Hans Georg Kemper, *Deutsche Lyrik der frühen Neuzeit 6/I: Empfindsamkeit* (Tübingen: Niemeyer, 1997), 1–16; Nikolaus Wegmann, *Diskurse der Empfindsamkeit: Zur Geschichte eines Gefühls in der Literatur des 18. Jahrhunderts* (Stuttgart: J. B. Metzler, 1984); Goethe, *Die Leiden des jungen Werther* (Ditzingen, Germany: Reclam, 2001). Karl Philipp Moritz later explores enthusiasm as a cause of melancholy in his epochal "Schwärmerroman" (enthusiast novel) which appeared in stages from 1785–90, *Anton Reiser: Ein psychologischer Roman* (Frankfurt am Main: Insel, 2006).

³⁰ For an overview of *Weltschmerz* lyrical imagery see Wolfgang Martens, *Bild und Motiv im Weltschmerz: Studien zur Dichtung Lenaus* (Cologne: Böhlau, 1957). On the negative view of *Weltschmerz* see Amy Louise Reed, *The Background of Gray's Elegy*, 203–8, and William Rose, *From Goethe to Byron: The Development of "Weltschmerz" in German Literature* (London: Routledge, 1924), 7, 55–57. For the term "victimology" see Aleida Assmann, *Der lange Schatten der Vergangenheit: Erinnerungskultur und Geschichtspolitik* (Munich: Beck, 2006), 76; for "negative sublimity" see Dominick LaCapra, *Writing History, Writing Trauma*, 23.

³¹ Slavoj Žižek, "Melancholy and the Act," 660. Thomas Pfau, *Romantic Moods*, 390–91.

³² Sebald, *Schwindel. Gefühle*. Hereafter cited in text as *SG*.

³³ Martens, *Bild und Motiv im Weltschmerz*, 71.

³⁴ On the garden as a sentimental topos see Wegmann, *Diskurse der Empfindsamkeit*, 90–92.

³⁵ On this motif see Cosgrove, "Austerlitz," in *The Novel in German since 1990*, ed. Stuart Taberner (Cambridge: Cambridge University Press, 2011), 195–210.

³⁶ Hell, "Eyes Wide Shut," 35.

³⁷ Foucault, *Discipline and Punish: The Birth of the Prison*, trans. Alan Sheridan (London: Penguin, 1991); *Madness and Civilisation: A History of Insanity in the Age of Reason*, trans. Richard Howard (London: Routledge, 1999).

³⁸ Long, *W. G. Sebald: Image, Archive, Modernity*, 99–107; Langston, "Affective Affinities," 62.

³⁹ Sebald, *Austerlitz*. Hereafter cited in text as *Aus*.

⁴⁰ Peter Brook, *The Melodramatic Imagination: Balzac, Henry James; Melodrama and the Mode of Excess* (New Haven, CN: Yale University Press, 1976), 75. Dan Diner, "Negative Symbiose: Deutsche und Juden nach 1945," in *Ist der Nationalsozialismus Geschichte? Zu Historisierung und Historikerstreit*, ed. Wolfgang Benz and Diner (Frankfurt am Main: Fischer, 1987), 185–97.

⁴¹ For a critical perspective on German-Jewish relations in the novel see Prager, "The Good German as Narrator"; Stuart Taberner, "German Nostalgia? Remembering German-Jewish Life in W. G. Sebald's *Die Ausgewanderten* and *Austerlitz*," special issue on W. G. Sebald, *Germanic Review* 3 (2004): 181–202; Cosgrove, "The Anxiety of German Influence: Affiliation, Rejection, and Jewish Identity in W.G Sebald's Work," in Fuchs, Cosgrove, and Grote, *German Memory Contests*, 229–52; Zilcosky, "Lost and Found," 698.

⁴² Brook, *The Melodramatic Imagination*, 29.

⁴³ Ecker, "'Heimat' oder die Grenzen der Bastelei," in Niehaus and Öhlschläger, *W. G. Sebald: Politische Archäologie und melancholische Bastelei*, 88.

⁴⁴ Anne Fuchs notes the tendency to identification in Sebald's narrative aesthetics but argues that the self-reflexive nature of his style prevents this identification from actually taking place. Fuchs, *Die Schmerzensspuren der Geschichte*, 28–34. For a more critical perspective see Ecker, "'Heimat' oder die Grenzen der Bastelei," 77–88.

⁴⁵ Barzilai, "Facing the Past and the Female Spectre in W. G. Sebald's *The Emigrants*," in Long and Whitehead, *W. G. Sebald: A Critical Companion*, 203–16. On male desire as a site of resistance to the destructiveness of history see Helen Finch, *Sebald's Bachelors: Queer Resistance and the Unconforming Life* (Oxford: Legenda, 2013).

⁴⁶ Sebald, interview in *Der Spiegel*, "Ich fürchte das Melodramatische," Mar. 12, 2001.

⁴⁷ Sebald, *Die Ringe des Saturn*. Hereafter cited in text as *RS*.

⁴⁸ For the authoritative discussion of this development see Klibansky, Panofsky, and Saxl, *SM*.

⁴⁹ See also chapters 1 and 6 in Radden, *The Nature of Melancholy*, 55–60, 87–93, and Hartmut Böhme, *Albrecht Dürer*, 60–73.

⁵⁰ Böhme argues that the image is semantically almost inexhaustible, such is the richness of its many symbols, but that the interpretative search instigated by this potential itself exhibits the very melancholy traits thematized in the engraving. Böhme, *Albrecht Dürer*, 9–11. See the discussion of geometry and melancholy in *SM*, 462–76.

⁵¹ *SM*, 343.

⁵² Barzilai, "Facing the Past," 203–16. Weiss, *Die Ästhetik des Widerstands*. Sebald, *Die Ausgewanderten*, hereafter cited in text as *AG*.

⁵³ Benjamin, *Ursprung des deutschen Trauerspiels*, 162. On Sebald and modernity see Long, *W. G. Sebald: Image, Archive, Modernity*.

⁵⁴ *New Larousse Encyclopaedia of Mythology* (London: Hamlyn, 1970), 144.

⁵⁵ See also Benjamin, *Ursprung des deutschen Trauerspiels*, 156. Of all the melancholy icons that Benjamin lists in his discussion of *Melencolia I*, Sebald circled the word "Hund." W. G.-Sebald-Bibliothek, Deutsches Literaturarchiv, Marbach, 166.

⁵⁶ W. G. Sebald, *Nach der Natur*, 76. For a discussion of *Melencolia I* in *Nach der Natur* see Claudia Albes, "Porträt ohne Modell: Bildbeschreibung und autobiographische Reflexion in W. G. Sebalds 'Elementargedicht' *Nach der Natur*," in Niehaus and Öhlschläger, *W. G. Sebald: Politische Archäologie und melancholische Bastelei*, 62–65.

⁵⁷ See, for example, the discussion of flooding imagery in *SM*, 457–58. For coldness, dryness, windyness, and rain see 216.

⁵⁸ See also Benjamin, *Ursprung des deutschen Trauerspiels*, 162–63.

⁵⁹ Ania Loomba, *Colonialism / Postcolonialism* (London: Routledge, 1998), 115.

⁶⁰ Benjamin, *Ursprung des deutschen Trauerspiels*, 168.

⁶¹ Öhlschläger, *Beschädigtes Leben: Erzählte Risse*, 218.

⁶² Terence K. Hopkins and Immanuel Wallerstein, *World-Systems Analysis: Theory and Methodology* (London: Sage, 1982), 21.

⁶³ Hopkins and Wallerstein, *World-Systems Analysis*, 54.

⁶⁴ Eshel, "Against the Power of Time," 73. While both John Beck and Öhlschläger thematize the connection between natural imagery and the critique of capitalism,

industry, and modern progress, neither of them conceives of capitalism as a distinct temporal field that operates according to its own laws. Öhlschläger, "Der Saturnring oder Etwas vom Eisenbau: W. G. Sebalds poetische Zivilisationskritik," in Niehaus and Öhlschläger, *W. G. Sebald: Politische Archäologie und melancholische Bastelei*, 189–204; Beck, "Reading Room: Erosion and Sedimentation in Sebald's Suffolk," in Long and Whitehead, *W. G. Sebald: A Critical Companion*, 75–88.

[65] Hopkins and Wallerstein, *World-Systems Analysis*, 55.

[66] See also Böhme, *Albrecht Dürer*, 30–35. John Beck's piece on *Die Ringe des Saturn* engages with the theme of fractal geometry in the work. Beck, "Reading Room: Erosion and Sedimentation in Sebald's Suffolk."

[67] For a detailed analysis of the significance of the two paintings see Fuchs, "'Ein Hauptkapitel der Geschichte der Unterwerfung': Representations of Nature in W. G. Sebald's *Die Ringe des Saturn*," in Fuchs and Long, *W. G. Sebald and the Writing of History*, 121–38.

[68] Sebald's narrators frequently use the word "Bühne" to describe the space they look at. Some random examples are *Schwindel. Gefühle*, 51, 57, 60; *Die Ringe des Saturn*, 151, 208.

[69] Riordan, "Ecocentrism in Sebald's '*After Nature*'," in Long and Whitehead, *W. G. Sebald: A Critical Companion*," 45–57. Fuchs, *Die Schmerzensspuren der Geschichte*, 221–31.

[70] See Mark Levene, "A Dissenting Voice: Or How Current Assumptions of Deterring and Preventing Genocide May Be Looking at the Problem through the Wrong End of the Telescope, Part I," *Journal of Genocide Research* 6 (2004): 153–166, and also Levene, "A Dissenting Voice: Part II," ibid.: 431–34. Mike Davis, *Late Victorian Holocausts: El Niño Famines and the Making of the Third World* (London: Verso, 2001), 22.

[71] A. Dirk Moses, "Conceptual Blockages and Definitional Dilemmas in the 'Racial Century': Genocides of Indigenous People and the Holocaust," *Patterns of Prejudice* 36 (2002): 7–36. For a more empirical discussion of this phenomenon see Jürgen Zimmerer's analysis of the consistencies between the German imperial project and the Nazi invasion of Poland, "The Birth of the *Ostland* out of the Spirit of Colonialism: A Postcolonial Perspective on the Nazi Policy of Conquest and Extermination," *Patterns of Prejudice* 39 (2005): 197–219.

[72] See, for example, Lemke, "Figurationen der Melancholie," 259.

Epilogue: Death of the Male Melancholy Genius: From *Vergangenheitsbewältigung* to *Vergangenheitsbewirtschaftung* in Iris Hanika's *Das Eigentliche*

Losing His Religion: Hans im Unglück

IRIS HANIKA'S SATIRICAL NOVEL *Das Eigentliche* (Authenticity, 2010) announces the decline of the project of *Vergangenheitsbewältigung* and the demise of the melancholy genius of ethical memory.[1] An employee of the "Zentrum für Vergangenheitsbewirtschaftung" (Center for the Management of the Past), the main protagonist, Hans Frambach, has fallen prey to the affliction of *acedia*, the hermit's melancholy of early Christian monasticism that in the Middle Ages became one of the Seven Cardinal Sins. Reviled by the extent to which the once noble project of *Vergangenheitsbewältigung* has been degraded in the Berlin Republic to "Shoah business," Frambach tells his only friend, the lumbering, lovelorn Graziela, that his particular *acedia* is not of a theological nature (*DE*, 123). Rather, he has lost his ability to extract joy from the good works of *Vergangenheitsbewirtschaftung* because this project, established, politically correct, and in unified Germany readily financed, has become separated from authentic feeling and ethical memory.[2]

The title of the novel, *Das Eigentliche*, announces this disaffection because it plays on Theodor W. Adorno's critical essay concerning the jargon of authenticity ("Jargon der Eigentlichkeit"). In this essay Adorno criticizes the ideology of authenticity that prevails in ontological philosophy of the twentieth century. In his view, the work of Heidegger and others gives voice to a philosophy of private virtues, authenticity, and inwardness that are presented in the guise of public virtue and political action. "Jargon" is a particularly strong kind of identity thinking in Adorno's view, a reified mentality that tries to press difference into uniformity. Jargon manifests itself in language through the choice of words that reinforce an ideology of universal humanity.[3] In *Das Eigentliche*, the language of German memory culture has become reified, disconnected from the object it is supposed to represent—the past—and the ethical memory of the past. Yet within this very disaffection the memory industry of the Berlin Republic continues to thrive.

Against this backdrop, the story of Frambach and Graziela exposes the illusory nature of the notion of an authentic connection to the past. Both characters were born in West Germany in the 1960s and were conditioned to honor the duty to remember German guilt; the gradual move away in time from the National Socialist past and the Holocaust triggers an identity crisis for them. In the normalized world of the Berlin Republic, both of them struggle to find "das Eigentliche." In the early twenty-first century, the Holocaust and German guilt are no longer reliable providers of identity. Hanika thus ironically encodes their search for authenticity through several images of the inauthentic, especially with reference to performance and role-play in the working world of *Vergangenheitsbewirtschaftung* (*DE*, 18–19, 34, 43, 51, 71, 83–84, 118, 150, 168). In so doing, she conveys the idea that these characters are nowhere less authentic than when earnestly searching for authentic meaning in their lives. Their mistake is to think in the reified terms of authenticity in the first place, and the memory of the Holocaust is a prime example of this very reification.

Frambach nostalgically believes that the capacity for remorseful and empathetic commemoration was once an intrinsic part of memory culture during his youth in West Germany of the 1980s. Part of his current disaffection stems from his sense that his ability to invest emotionally in keeping alive the guilty postmemory of Auschwitz has waned. With dawning dread he diagnoses the uneventful death of his emotional connection to the Holocaust past (*DE*, 10, 17, 24–25). His lack of feeling seems to coincide with the emergence, since unification, of an increasingly thriving "Shoah business" memory industry. The source of his unhappiness has thus subtly shifted with the sad accretion of the years, in the passage from youth to middle age and from one republic to another. Where once "das Unglück" (the misfortune) festered gratifyingly in the omnipresent fact of Auschwitz, now "Auschwitz" has lost its aura and cannot trigger, at its mere mention, the feelings of guilt and awe, and a sepulchral sense of the sacred that provide Frambach's identity (*DE*, 24). As a result, he has been beset by idleness, boredom, and an all-encompassing sense of the futility of everything (*DE*, 63, 71, 93, 118, 128, 144).

Hanika goes beyond this contemporary identity crisis, however, to raise the uncomfortable question of whether individuals such as Hans and Graziela ever had an authentic affective connection to the Holocaust in the first place. In this way, she touches on the impoverished state of Holocaust memory, both individual and collective, in the present and in the past. The distancing third-person narrative perspective ironizes the whimsical utterings of the two middle-aged friends, who have always been dedicated to the memory of Auschwitz and who, correspondingly, have invariably been keen to perform and articulate the condition of unhappiness. Hanika suggests that the memory of Auschwitz has always been a key factor in the individual emotional makeup of both these characters: it is the phantasm that reminds them that they are alive and that lends ethical gravitas to their persons (*DE*, 111). The question that Hanika poses thus concerns what happens to the emotional life of Auschwitz-dependent mnemonic man and woman when the memory of trauma itself recedes with passing time and risks becoming, on the collective level and in ever more public forms, impoverished and mechanical. She shows how this degradation of "sacred" memory to the hollow "structural mourning-work" that Eric Santner criticizes in post-Holocaust life leads to a monumental loss of faith and life purpose, an identity crisis that plays itself out in Frambach's impotent *taedium vitae* and Graziela's slothful turn to the world of carnal lust.[4]

Hanika tragic-comically dresses up this paradigm shift in German memory culture since unification in the theological hair shirt of *acedia*. In so doing she rejects the post-Holocaust ideal of a normalized collective emotional afterlife that testifies to the successful task of working through this past by means of mourning. She does this by cleverly reanimating one of the most negative motifs in the history of melancholy, the sin of *acedia*, in order to undermine the ideal of successful mourning work in the post-Holocaust present of the Berlin Republic. In contrast to Wolfgang Hildesheimer, who in his novels *Tynset* and *Masante* combines the melancholy genius of the Elizabethan era, Hamlet, with the iconography and imagery of *acedia*, Hanika's choice of source texts on *acedia* in *Das Eigentliche* explicitly argues against the cult of melancholy genius and nobility (*DE*, 96–98). The crisis in faith of the desert monks of early Christianity parallels the scandalous loss of faith in the sacred memory of Auschwitz: growing indifference, waning interest, and the precedence of bureaucracy in the management of attitudes to this past. Frambach's crisis is a secular variant on the theme of the absent God, but in the early twenty-first century this absent God is none other than the fading memory of the Holocaust. Frambach laments the absence of authentic feeling in the memory discourses of contemporary Germany, a development that he notes within his own emotional makeup (*DE*, 24). The spectral melancholy object makes a covert appearance in this scenario, for what Frambach appears to mourn is not so much the historical event of the Holocaust itself as an imagined past ability to mourn, the existence of which the novel continually questions. *Das Eigentliche* thus ironically lays bare the paradoxical situation of guilty feeling about the inability to feel guilty.[5]

The opening paragraph states in a resigned tone that there comes a time in everyone's life where youthful passion, intensity, and commitment to causes beyond oneself seem to have faded. Suddenly one finds oneself in a state of truncated emotion, the pendant to which is an empty heart, a kind of affective listlessness (*DE*, 7). Indeed, references to the cold, heavy heart are legion in this short novel, as Hanika plays on the stock melancholy motifs of advancing age, coldness, and despondency that, since antiquity, have informed the melancholy type (*DE*, 22, 24, 79, 81, 90, 97, 107–8, 116, 121–22, 144, 164).[6] W. G. Sebald's work is also replete with images of the heart, which functions as an optimistic symbol of pulsating humanity, the ethical relationship to the victim other, and caritas: it is the symbol of a heartfelt devotion to an intense, passionate, yet considered memory of the victims of the Holocaust. In *Das Eigentliche*, by contrast, the heart is a symbol of the absence of the careful affective investment we encounter in Sebald's work. The *acedia* that accompanies degraded *Vergangenheitsbewältigung* in Hanika's novel communicates the decline of Holocaust memory and its degeneration into, at best, mere politically correct governmental policy and at worst, lucrative business.

Almost exactly at the midpoint—the heart—of the novel, Hanika quotes at length from Michael Theunissen's short essay on melancholy in antiquity and the *acedia* of the Middle Ages. This section, which consists only of uncommented excerpts from Theunissen's essay and one quotation from a work by Roland Barthes, is striking for its interest in the non-dialectical quality of *acedia* (*DE*, 96–98). Here Hanika presents as secondary to *acedia* the condition of genial melancholy that, even in its darkest stages, always contains the potential to self-transcend through artistic creativity and other modes of exceptionality. We might say that Hanika explicitly cites one conventional discourse of melancholy—*acedia*—in order to undermine another conventionalized discourse: genius.[7]

Theunissen's essay challenges the standard interpretation of pseudo-Aristotle's text on melancholy. The reigning view of the classical text has been heavily influenced by its revival in the Renaissance as a document that associates melancholy genius with the ability to keep black bile in a state of ideal balance and harmony. Theunissen proposes that pseudo-Aristotle cannot have meant this, as the logic of his argument suggests that the notion of balance is entirely alien to the melancholy temperament. Demonstrating the very citationality that is a hallmark of the melancholy performative, Hanika quotes the section in which Theunissen establishes that anomaly or disharmony is the central image of melancholy in pseudo-Aristotle's text. According to this excerpt, the melancholic is anomalous unto himself and with others. Moreover, the substratum of his condition, namely black bile, is also anomalous (*DE*, 96). Thus the melancholy individual of antiquity is a doubly split person: physically his black bile is imbalanced, and as a consequence his mood-state, his sense of self, and his interaction with others also exhibit discontinuity.[8]

Having challenged the genial reading of pseudo-Aristotle's text—he suggests that it does not contain the outline of the melancholy genius but is an early sketch of what is today known as the bipolar type—Theunissen then turns to *acedia*. Hanika quotes substantially from the section of his essay that deals with this condition (*DE*, 96–98). Here Theunissen focuses his analysis on Thomas Aquinas's connection of *acedia* to sin during the Middle Ages. According to Aquinas, *acedia* is not a sin of deed but a kind of inertia—a sin—of the heart ("Trägheit des Herzens," 97). In the original Greek, "a-kédia" is the negation of the word "kédos" which means "care." *Acedia* thus means lack of care about the very thing that the faithful should care about: God (*DE*, 96). The problem is that lack of care for the divine good—the release of the self from the daily labor of prayerful, meditative striving toward the divine object—leads to listlessness and apathy, as the affected can see no purpose to earthly existence. Torpor, *taedium vitae*, and disgust thus overwhelm those who suffer from *acedia*. They continually experience existence as burdensome, because the objects of the profane world cannot compensate for the loss of the divine good.[9]

In contrast to the condition of genial melancholy, there is little or no hope for even momentary respite from this condition. *Acedia*, according to Theunissen, embodies only negativity, with no prospect of compensation through sudden creative mania. Hanika engages with this aspect of Theunissen's argument, reproducing that particular paragraph from his work in her own text (*DE*, 97). More significantly, however, she also focuses on Aquinas's understanding of *acedia* as a sin of free will. As Theunissen points out, Aquinas's argument rests on the understanding of *acedia* as a willful act of the individual who makes a choice to withdraw from the divine good. The price for the exercise of free will is the gloom and monotony of a life without meaning.[10]

These excerpts from Theunissen's essay are relevant for the present study in two respects. First, it is interesting that Hanika chooses not only to present the degeneration of *Vergangenheitsbewältigung* through the symbol of *acedia*, but that in order to do so she explicitly quotes from a scholarly work that undermines the established concept of melancholy genius in Western writing on melancholy. Against the backdrop of the texts that have been discussed throughout this study, *Das Eigentliche* marks in a parodic manner the endpoint of a development in literary commemoration, one that began in the 1960s with the emergence of melancholy as a discourse of postwar ethical memory. At the end of the first decade of the new millennium it is no longer possible, Hanika appears to be suggesting, to use melancholy for this purpose. To get this point across, she takes recourse to recent scholarship that questions the age-old idea of melancholy genius. Her particular melancholy performative thus deflates, albeit indirectly, the message of self-overcoming and self-transcendence in literary-melancholy discourses of remembrance.

Hanika may well be working against the image of patriarchal nobility that accompanies earlier forms of melancholy literary commemoration, such as that identified in Günter Grass's texts (see chapter 1). Her novel suggests that the bombastic performance of memory work has become primarily the task of the German state (*DE*, 24). In the era of post-postmemory, the state has appropriated collective memory and fashioned it into an automatized business with little space for subjective initiative: individual and collective memory are thus out of synch. In the context of state-run memory, the tragic but noble figure of *homo melancholicus* has been made redundant. In his place emerges the forlorn, flaccid figure of *homo timiditas*.

The way Hanika conveys this paradigm shift in memory from individual subject to anonymous bureaucratic collective renders even as recent a writer as Sebald, the subject of chapter 4, somewhat a relic of the past. His work makes a case for the importance of subjective memory and careful empathy for the victim other. To this end his writing explores the relationship between individual memory, on the one hand, and the material embodiments of collective memory, on the other. His melancholy narrator figures, central to these investigations, are never just going through the motions of politically correct memory. They are not without moments of self-parody, but they are also critical, attuned to the complexities of representative media, and often riddled with self-doubt. Unlike Frambach, they are believers in the project of coming to terms with the Nazi past and the Holocaust and are committed to the commemoration of the past, no matter how complex this is in the era of postmemory.

Frambach, by contrast, seems to have become trapped in the cold, empty world of mechanical "Shoah business." His place of employment, the high-rise "Center for the Management of the Past" in the middle of Berlin is the memory epicenter of the entire country (*DE*, 21). The only problem is that this center is a cold, glassy structure that houses colleagues who are full of hatred and contempt for one another and regard the past as a business opportunity to be exploited (*DE*, 88, 49–51). At the heart of the building is the computer center, a kind of meta-archival, high-tech outfit that coordinates all the archives in the land that deal with *Vergangenheitsbewirtschaftung* (*DE*, 34). However, the more old-fashioned archive where Frambach works is light years removed from this technosphere of computerized management of the past. Indeed, his work is a nostalgic nod to more old-fashioned archival methods. Undermining Frambach's dewy-eyed memory of a better memory era, however, the novel does not allow us to romanticize his antiquated, laborious, and somewhat artisanal filing of the documents of Holocaust survivors. This work, too, is presented as dull and monotonous, propelled by a mechanical reflex that fails to connect emotionally or intellectually with the contents of the documents and the individuals who produced them.

Hanika parodies this way of working by reproducing in her own text the nearly blank pages that Frambach files away with each document that he assesses, documents that are part of the archival remains of a Jewish Holocaust survivor (*DE*, 41). The symbol of the blank page—also reproduced at a more advanced point in the novel with the provisional title

"Raum für Notizen" (Space for Notes, 156–58)—is the text-internal, material embodiment of the yawning divide between individuals, bureaucratic systems, and the past. While it might be tempting to conclude that these virtually wordless pages also perform the taboo of silence around the memory of Auschwitz, in the context of a novel that builds its case around the loss of faith in the project of Holocaust memory, it is more accurate to surmise that the blank sheet testifies to the burden of growing indifference to this past. The "Space for Notes" pages are most likely Frambach's, but he has nothing more to add. There is nothing left to say. Emptiness is the sign of the decline of remembrance and not the complex signifier of a tabooed historical caesura around which archivists, writers, and thinkers must carefully tread. The empty pages ironically communicate that for Frambach's generation, which was socialized in the West Germany of the 1970s and 1980s, the burden of guilt around the past has metamorphosed into the burden of contemporary mnemonic-affective sloth, analogous to the early Christian plight of *acedia*. The once "negative sublime" has decayed into the profane boredom, indifference, and silence of the everyday.

With the disappearance of awe for a negative sublime, the genius of *Vergangenheitsbewältigung* has become stripped of his passions, playfulness, and creativity. In his stead is the apathetic figure of the alienated bureaucrat whose daily existence conducts itself in the sphere of irrelevance, as the citation from the opening lines of T. S. Eliot's poem, *The Love Song of J. Alfred Prufrock* (1915), makes clear (*DE*, 58–60). Against the tradition of gendered writing on melancholy that elevates, through the trope of genius, the experience of male loss in Western culture, Hanika introduces the banal figure of the brooding functionary who is bitter and virtually friendless, and does not with any degree of certainty even stand for a world of disappearing better values. Prufrock is an interesting figure of identification for the steady dismemberment of noble post-Holocaust memory here. In the last section of the poem Prufrock rejects the identity of Prince Hamlet, stating that he is merely an attendant lord (112), or indeed a fool (120). In tandem with the increasing mechanization and depersonalization of memory work, the melancholy genius of *Vergangenheitsbewältigung* has in Hanika's work become the slothful pencil-pusher of *Vergangenheitsbewirtschaftung*.[11]

The Topology of the Unreal

This paradigm shift from *Vergangenheitsbewältigung* to *Vergangenheitsbewirtschaftung* explains why Hanika's novel is so pertinent to the present study, which identifies the melancholy performative as a significant discourse in postwar literary commemoration. *Das Eigentliche* uses melancholy traditions to suggest, in contrast to Grass, Hildesheimer, Weiss, and Sebald, who all adapt melancholy discourses to develop an ethics of memory, that Holocaust commemoration is waning. Thus while Hanika revisits icons and motifs that feature in the works by Grass and Hildesheimer, for example, her objective is to show the end of this phase in postwar German memory. We can observe this shift in her discussion of what causes the depressed mood state, a theme that all the other writers also address.

In antiquity, imbalances of black bile cause melancholy, Hanika mentions. Yet on this point, she cites an excerpt that casts doubt on whether the anomaly of black bile causes the melancholy condition, or whether it is the individual's anomalous mental state that becomes manifest in imbalances of black bile. She then cites Theunissen's argument that melancholy in antiquity, unlike *acedia*, has a relatively clear cause in the physical makeup of the individual. As such, free will is irrelevant for the melancholic of antiquity. In the case of *acedia*, however, individuals are responsible for their melancholy condition. By willfully turning away from the divine good, these individuals bring about their slothful existence. And while the cause in this case seems to be clear—sinfulness by choice—the larger question remains unanswered of why any individual would willfully turn away from a source of joy and deliver him- or herself into a life of misery (*DE*, 97).

Hanika masterfully exploits the longstanding ambiguity around the possible causes of melancholy to suggest that Holocaust memory, even on the subjective level, is forced, inauthentic, and exploitative. She does so by reconstructing in the biographies of the two characters, Frambach and Graziela, how central Auschwitz has been to their sense of worthy identity. In this way, Auschwitz has been source of "joy" for both individuals. Hanika thus poses the question of whether the problem of inauthenticity Frambach identifies in his current work environment is not also a problem that has, paradoxically and scandalously, accompanied his own earlier heartfelt engagement with the memory of the Holocaust. There are two ways of reading his predicament. First, we can take Frambach at face value and believe his self-assessment: that he has ended up in an eternal state of apathy because he feels powerless under the weight of the memory machine of the Berlin Republic. Regarding the past, this memory machine stands for values different from his. It is not authentic but exploitative. Against this backdrop Frambach cannot fail to appear as the last bastion of authentic Holocaust memory.

The narrative is more complex than this, however. Through the *acedia* of the permanently dissatisfied characters Frambach and Graziela, Hanika profiles what I would call the phantasmal quality of the Holocaust. For both individuals, the Holocaust is a topology of the unreal that has helped to fill their empty lives with contrived meaning. The opening pages tell how Frambach has for years found it difficult to travel by train. This is because Graziela once told him about a film that features trains deporting Jews to concentration camps. Having watched the film, she has ever since been filled with self-disgust. Frambach duly watches the film and from then on also feels sick whenever he travels by train (*DE*, 8–9). The novel exposes this game for what it is: a strategy of affective self-production and positive moral self-evaluation that revolves around German self-hatred as the deliberate placing of the self in a sea of abject, even enjoyable guilt. As Frambach muses from the present point of narration, back then when the titillation of guilty feeling still worked, his "Unglück" had a concrete shape: Auschwitz (*DE*, 12–13). The comparison in all sorts of banal situations of his undeserving, West German self with the past situation of innocent Holocaust victims never failed to deliver the necessary affect of guilt that over the years helped to establish his identity. If he were to withdraw from this "Unglück"—his divine good—there would be nothing left of him (*DE*, 16).

Holocaust memory emerges in these opening pages as a crutch for the postwar West German who falls for the jargon of authenticity and constructs her/his identity around it. Frambach views himself as a kind of loyal vessel for the universal "Unglück" symbolized by the Holocaust. Were he not existent, the "Unglück" would have no earthly home (*DE*, 16). Yet by thematizing the very vastness of this unhappiness and describing the deliberate efforts Frambach must make to contrive it in his everyday life, Hanika raises the question of the origins of his unhappiness. Is his "Unglück" a phenomenon of post-Auschwitz German society that can be clearly explained via the historical fact of the Holocaust and the collective remorse that he so selflessly channels? Or is Auschwitz merely the handy phantasm that distracts, by lending dubious concrete shape to his everyday life, from his fundamental apathy?

The ironic tone of the narrative suggests the second interpretation. Hanika mocks Frambach's self-assessment as someone who has lost his "religion." She describes him instead as someone who, for subjective purposes, himself exploits the historical fact of the Holocaust. Yet he cannot see his actions in this way, convinced as he is of the authenticity of his feelings and of his moral superiority to the exploiters he sees around him. Furthermore, conversations with Graziela never really address his or her personal problems. Auschwitz is always the topic of discussion (*DE*, 75). Hanika seems to be suggesting that the Holocaust is the best excuse for not engaging with the self. It offers a kind of "jargon of authenticity," a contrived language of inwardness and emotion, for the synthetic self-realization of individuals who otherwise struggle to grasp their *raison d'être*.

This explains why Hanika introduces an excerpt by Barthes on the topic of *acedia* (*DE*, 98). He argues that *acedia* is sadness for the loss of an imaginary relation of desire and not sadness for the loss of the desired object itself. The reason why the object in *acedia* can never be lost is because it was never possessed to begin with. Loss in *acedia* is therefore imaginary and never concrete. The lost object of melancholy *acedia* is thus not really an object but a phantasm. Yet the individual who suffers from *acedia* contrives the transformation of the phantasm into a lost object. Giorgio Agamben describes this imaginative investment as a "funereal strategy . . . directed to the impossible capture of the phantasm." In *Das Eigentliche* Auschwitz occupies this very role of phantasm temporarily transformed into lost object. By effecting this transformation Frambach can explain away his ongoing despondency by means of historical causes beyond his control—the Holocaust. What is more, with German guilt as prop in his sorry affective life he can remain in the space of despair while retaining his ethical credentials. Through the Holocaust as imaginative phantasmal topology of the unreal, his melancholy acquires meaning and significance.[12]

Yet the causal logic that creates the experience of justified melancholy has broken down by the time we meet Frambach. Once upon a time he could convert his overwhelming sense of the universal absence of meaning into the significance of loss (Auschwitz). Now, however, in his openly apathetic state, he has done the reverse. He reconverts loss back into absence, using the memory machine of the Berlin Republic as justification for so doing. In this context, the Holocaust no longer has the status of concrete lost object in his imaginary topology. Rather, it has been leached of all meaning by the activities of "Shoah business." Frambach is no longer able to comfortably mourn the historical loss of the Holocaust: instead, developments in German memory culture have conspired rudely to cast him adrift in the endless "divine" absence demarcated by the condition of *acedia*. The memory of the past has become meaningless.

This is an elaborate way of bidding farewell to the project of *Vergangenheitsbewältigung*, which one has simply outgrown, as the opening paragraph on the topic of aging implies. The sad accretion of the years and the failure to establish personal happiness are not good reasons to lose interest in this most important of ongoing tasks. At all costs, this gradual slump into "lack of care" about the memory of the Holocaust, alongside the suspicion that despite one's best efforts one has never established an authentic connection to the past and possibly never really intended to do so, must remain concealed from the *acedia*-plagued psyche. Instead of facing up to his own perhaps longstanding but elaborately concealed indifference, Frambach withdraws from the "divine good" of *Vergangenheitsbewältigung*—a clever way of positing the desired object as unattainable just when he has had enough. Blaming the bureaucrats of memory for their too factual approach to the past, he gives up on the possibility of ever being able to grasp the Holocaust. It is an impossible project, rendered yet more impossible by exploiters such as his boss, Marschner (*DE*, 42, 147–50).

On this point Frambach conveniently overlooks the contrived nature of his own experiments in the artificial generation of remorseful affect. Ritually immersing himself in guilt, he cannot see his own fundamental indifference. It is not only the game of "Auschwitzvergleich" (comparison with Auschwitz) that produces this feeling (*DE*, 13). Just moving through the city of Berlin on his daily business is enough to spark a sense of the sepulchral, as when, for example, he studiously avoids stepping on the "Stolpersteine" (stumbling stones), cobble-sized memorial plaques commemorating the deported Jews of Berlin (*DE*, 58–60). Instead of looking at himself and his own behavior, Frambach blames the representatives of the memory industry of the Berlin Republic, such as his boss Marschner, for his eventual departure from the arena of so-called authentic memory.

This is the baleful mindset of *acedia* at work: blaming others for his apathy, Frambach demonstrates the imaginative capacity to make the unobtainable object—his own happiness—appear as a lost object that is intrinsically linked to the Holocaust and its failed commemoration. We might say that this is a "deceitful" way of opting out of Holocaust memory, of releasing the self from a desired heavy burden of duty that has not delivered the satisfaction it was supposed to. The problem is that in giving up on Holocaust memory Frambach has also given up on himself, for it is questionable what other sources of identity are available to him after the waning of his relationship to the Holocaust. Religious communities disgust him just as much as do his colleagues in the Center. Their tendency to explain the Holocaust in terms of original sin provokes a physical reaction of revulsion. And yet the narrative implies that Frambach is guilty of a similar falsity: in the Sühne-Christi Church of Charlottenburg he recognizes himself in the austerity of a seventeenth-century religious painting (*DE*, 106–7). Even though he has lost his faith in the secular project of post-Holocaust memory and the idea of redemption, this moment of self-recognition, which makes him a bedfellow of the religious folk who disgust him, hints at his latent hypocrisy.

Indeed, his fascination with German Chancellor Angela Merkel suggests the real contours of his post-Holocaust life: a trite existence in the bland nothingness of post-normalization and post-postmemory Germany (*DE*, 64–66). Hanika raises here the question of what happens to German identity once the project of Holocaust memory has reached saturation point. Through Frambach's biography she shows how *Vergangenheitsbewältigung* once was a significant identity-provider for individuals of a certain post-Holocaust generation. Those identity-generating powers have now begun to wane, as the nation moves in historical and biological time further and further away from the events of 1933 to 1945. The real scandal is that the generously financed industry around German Holocaust memory has now become an important provider of employment, as the novel periodically reflects, so virtually no one has an interest in trying to change it (*DE*, 21, 49).

The closing scene of the book, in which Frambach erupts into hysterical laughter and tears, captures perfectly this sense of a post-Holocaust, post-postmemory identity crisis. It is a fit borne of the sense of farce in which he lives and works. Once upon a time he could contain, via imaginative conversion into the lost historical object of Auschwitz, the unquantifiable scale of the vast universal "Unglück" he senses around him. Now, however, his overwhelming sense of the absurd announces in somatic form the revelation of the Holocaust as phantasm in the world of post-postmemory. The excessive nature of his outburst is the hysterical overflowing of affect that has no motivating object. The formulation "Es lachte ihn" (it laughed through him) conveys a sense of something alien and unquantifiable at the root of his pathological affliction (*DE*, 173). Yet just as in the case of his "Unglück," the hysterical force that now invades Frambach's body also remains obscure.

This final scene of wild affect run amok unravels the project of an authentically expressive poetics in post-Holocaust life. By undermining the clear causal relationship between object and affect, Hanika suggests that Holocaust memory has entered a new phase in contemporary German life, one in which indifference is the distinguishing feature. From this perspective, Frambach's crisis is a complex reaction to the invariable passage of time, the increasingly mediated nature of memory, and the suspicion that his personal project of *Vergangenheitsbewältigung*, premised on the simplistic notion of a clearly identifiable lost object, was ill-conceived from the start.

Saints and Sinners

While Hanika's narrative sounds the death knell for the male melancholy genius of ethical remembrance, woman does not emerge as a novel alternative for the task of commemoration. Womankind in the novel, represented by Graziela, also languishes in the world of post-post-Holocaust memory sloth. Feminine *acedia* here takes the shape of abject bodily excess and degraded concupiscence. This contrasts with the intellectual sloth of the fallen ascetic we encounter in Frambach. Hanika thus plays on the gendered history of melancholy by ironically caricaturing its contours: melancholy man is a failed ascetic-intellectual while melancholy woman embodies the fleshy world of fallen humankind. Assembling both of these characters, man and woman, through different aspects of *acedia* in this way, Hanika suggests that no one is capable of committed memory work in the Berlin Republic today.[13]

If Frambach's never-ending sojourn in "Unglück" has been for him a marker of authenticity, Graziela's version of authenticity lies in the adulterous affair she has been having for several years: the sexual relationship she conducts with a married man is what she considers to be the authentic root of her existence (*DE*, 121). Like Frambach, her interest in Holocaust memory has waned throughout her adult life in the Berlin Republic. However, her search for authentic existence takes her into the world of pure corporeality. Hanika describes her body in comic-grotesque terms as a bulky mass of living flesh that she pampers, indulges, and cultivates during the years of her adulterous affair. She slathers herself in creams and perfumes, consumes chocolate in significant quantities, and all because her lover is in thrall to her hulking body. Hanika describes this attitude to the self as a reduction to the status of a piece of flesh (*DE*, 30–31). Even if Graziela believes this creaturely existence to be an authentic form of romantic love, she is nevertheless unhappy throughout. After four years, her lover begins to talk about leaving his wife—in fact, the wife wishes to leave him—and Graziela suddenly loses interest in the relationship. Separating from him, she states that with the end of the affair her period of *acedia* has also ended (*DE*, 120). She has moved out of the world of pure carnal lust and has rediscovered a passion for music (*DE*, 121). However, this respite is short-lived. By the end of the novel, Graziela has reentered the self-same carnal relationship with the same man, who is still with his wife after all (*DE*, 144). Everything remains as it has been for years. The flash of intelligence Frambach believes to have seen in his newly single friend disappears when she reenters the world of the flesh and returns to her lover (*DE*, 122). Graziela thus takes up a stereotypical position in the gendered history of melancholy. Yet if woman is here cast out of melancholy as intellectual empowerment, the same applies to Frambach, whose hysterical outbreak at the end of the novel signs the death certificate of ethical melancholy man.[14]

The Age of Indifference

Hans Ulrich Gumbrecht has suggested the category of *Stimmung* or mood as a renewed way of reading literature. Through the course of the twentieth century the idea of literature as a repository for *Stimmung*, the aesthetic form of harmony, fell from grace. The creation of distancing effects has been the dominant tendency in literature since the mid-twentieth century, as writers attempted to respond in an appropriate aesthetic manner to catastrophic historical events. Now, however, Gumbrecht proposes that the concept of harmony should accompany the study of the literary text. After the fetishization of the idea of absence in literary language, which was promoted by the deconstructionist thought of the 1960s, now presence, in the form of the pleasurable experience of harmony or *Stimmung*, has suddenly returned to literature.[15]

A study of melancholy in postwar German literature might, reasonably enough, be expected to identify a sense of *Stimmung* as authentic affect that unfolds throughout the text. As we have seen in the different analyses of each writer, however, such immediacy and sense of affective presence remain largely absent from the literary melancholy each writer, in a unique way, produces. As argued in the introduction, the systematic use of melancholy frustrates, perhaps somewhat counterintuitively, the unbridled expression of affect. Part of this skeptical distance on feeling and emotion arises, ironically, through the rich layering of densely packed melancholy icons and motifs. If melancholy traditions offer a means for the ostentatious cultural framing of Holocaust memory, then this framing ultimately produces a sense of disharmony: the absence of consensus on how the past should be remembered, uncertainty and unease around post-Holocaust identities, and in Hanika's case, the question of whether the Holocaust will continue to be remembered in a meaningful way at all. With its dramatic cultural history of bifurcation into "good" and "bad" kinds of sadness, its profiling of the problem of cause and effect in emotional life, its dialectics between illness and empowerment, and not least its rich iconicity, melancholy is an excellent vessel for these debates.

Grass articulates unrest about the past through the ambivalence of the perpetrator's melancholy. His intention is to reverse the tradition of negative writing on the condition and put in a good word for melancholy. Despite his many erudite and playful interventions in established melancholy traditions, however, ultimately he reinstates the bifurcation of "good" and "bad" melancholy by associating the perpetrator figure with "bad" melancholy. Hildesheimer mobilizes the Elizabethan melancholy hero, Hamlet, as a version of the ethical memory of the victim survivor. His narratives, however, undermine the nobility of this melancholy figure that is, in the end, eclipsed by the more powerful figure of the slothful sinner. In this way he provides an original account of the syndrome of survivor guilt and makes a case for a radical melancholy poetics of negativity. His stance is thus politically more challenging than Grass's vision of moderation and compromise. Weiss uses Albrecht Dürer's iconic engraving of Renaissance genius, *Melencolia I*, allegorically to explore the problem of ethical memory, the risk and necessity of identification with the victim experience. In contrast to the other male writers discussed in this study, an incisive critique of the problem of melancholy and gender frames his consideration of the problems of Holocaust memory and representation. His portrayal of the feminine Holocaust reminds us of the danger of cultural amnesia, already a problem during the Holocaust, and the necessity of remembrance. Like Hildesheimer and especially Grass, Sebald is interested in a bombastic poetics of melancholy that swings between illness and empowerment. Melancholy underscores the obligation to ethical memory throughout his work, yet it is not without parody. His use of the *Weltschmerzler* figure as a means of talking about post-Holocaust German self-consciousness drives this home. Equally, however, he weaves melancholy iconography into a panoramic, global vision of genocide in the nineteenth and twentieth centuries.

In Hanika we encounter a new development: the parody of melancholy to bid farewell to a particular mnemonic type, ethical melancholy man, and to the era of postwar memory politics that informed West Germany of the 1960s, 1970s, 1980s, and 1990s. Since the start of the new millennium German memory culture has entered a new phase beyond normalization: one of big business, growing indifference, and waning commitment. Hanika marks this decline via the gendered signifier of *acedia*. Gone is the figure of genius. In its place is the fallen nation that Frambach and Graziela embody.

None of these writers succumb to melancholy as the expression of an authentic poetics of affect. Indeed, the exploitation of melancholy traditions in order to create a literary language of remembrance marked by distance and disharmony is the common trait across this diverse group of writers. While the appeal of certain melancholy icons, such as the figure of Renaissance genius, proves irresistible to the writer who wishes to don the robes of contrition yet maintain his artistic credentials, the very performativity of melancholy imagery means that few images may be taken literally. The melancholy performative, as suggested in the introduction, overstates the conventional, as opposed to the authentic, nature of melancholy. The divided scholarly positions on the condition reflect this ambivalence, as does the theoretical discourse on the deceitful and ghostly qualities of the evasive melancholy object. Yet this very ambivalence, alongside the diversity of melancholy traditions in culture and history, means that melancholy offers writers a unique poetics for the considered portrayal of post-Holocaust ethical memory and, beyond that, of its gradual, endemic demise.

Notes

[1] Hanika, *Das Eigentliche* (Graz: Droschl, 2010). Hereafter cited in text as *DE*.

[2] On *acedia* see Siegfried Wenzel, *The Sin of Sloth*. On "Shoah business" see Norman Finkelstein, *The Holocaust Industry: Reflection on the Exploitation of Jewish Suffering* (London: Verso, 2000). In coining the term "Vergangenheitsbewirtschaftung" Hanika put her finger on the pulse of contemporary critical thinking about Germany's formulaic and commercialized memory culture among literary scholars and historians. See Erhard Schütz, "Zweitgeschichte? Gegenwartsliteratur zwischen Vergangenheitsbewirtschaftung und Geschichtsermunterung," *Zeitschrift für Germanistik* 23, no. 3 (2013): 592–606. Hanika's novel inspired the title of Christoph Kühberger and Andreas Pudlat (eds.), *Vergangenheitsbewirtschaftung: Public History zwischen Wirtschaft und Wissenschaft* (Innsbruck, StudienVerlag: 2012).

³ Theodor W. Adorno, *Jargon der Eigentlichkeit: Zur deutschen Ideologie* (Frankfurt am Main: Suhrkamp, 1964). See also Gillian Rose, *The Melancholy Science: An Introduction to the Thought of Theodor W. Adorno* (London: Macmillan, 1978), 70–75.

⁴ Santner, *Mourning, Memory, and Film in Postwar Germany*, 28.

⁵ On mourning work and "working through" see Dominick LaCapra, *Writing History, Writing Trauma*, 65–66. Hildesheimer, *Tynset* and *Masante*.

⁶ Other references to the melancholy type include his obsession with numerical order and his preference for dark clothes, respectively: *DE*, 29, 86–87, 65, 104.

⁷ Theunissen, *Vorentwürfe von Moderne*. Barthes, *Wie zusammen leben: Simulationen einiger alltäglicher Räume im Roman; Vorlesung am Collège de France, 1976–1977*, ed. Éric Marty, trans. Horst Brühmann (Frankfurt am Main: Suhrkamp, 2007).

⁸ Theunissen, *Vorentwürfe von Moderne*, 12–13.

⁹ Theunissen, *Vorentwürfe von Moderne*, 15, 26–27.

¹⁰ Theunissen, *Vorentwürfe von Moderne*, 28, 32.

¹¹ Eliot, "The Love Song of J. Alfred Prufrock," in *The Norton Anthology of English Literature*, 2 vols., 6th edition, ed. M. H. Abrams (New York: Norton, 1993), 2:1971–76.

¹² Barthes, *Wie zusammen leben*, 62–65. Agamben, *Stanzas*, 25.

¹³ On the slothful person of Dame Melancholy see *SM*, 329.

¹⁴ Julia Schiesari, *The Gendering of Melancholia*.

¹⁵ Gumbrecht, *Stimmungen lesen*, 7–34.

Bibliography

Abraham, Nicolas, and Maria Torok. "Mourning *or* Melancholia: Introjection *versus* Incorporation." In Abraham and Torok, *The Shell and the Kernel: Renewals of Psychoanalysis*, vol. 1, 1:125–38.
———. *The Shell and the Kernel: Renewals of Psychoanalysis*. Vol. 1. Edited and translated by Nicolas T. Rand. Chicago: University of Chicago Press, 1994.
Adorno, Theodor W. *Jargon der Eigentlichkeit: Zur deutschen Ideologie*. Frankfurt am Main: Suhrkamp, 1964.
———. "Kulturkritik und Gesellschaft (1951)." In Adorno, *Gesammelte Schriften*, edited by Rolf Tiedemann, 20 vols., 10:1:11–30. Frankfurt am Main: Suhrkamp, 1977.
Agamben, Giorgio. *Homo Sacer: Sovereign Power and Bare Life*. Translated by Daniel Heller-Rozen. Stanford, CA: Stanford University Press, 1998.
———. *Stanzas: Word and Phantasm in Western Culture*. Translated by Ronald L. Martinez. Minneapolis: University of Minnesota Press, 1993.
Albes, Claudia. "Porträt ohne Modell: Bildbeschreibung und autobiographische Reflexion in W. G. Sebalds 'Elementargedicht' *Nach der Natur*." In Niehaus and Öhlschläger, *W. G. Sebald: Politische Archäologie und melancholische Bastelei*, 47–75.
American Psychiatric Association. *Diagnostic and Statistical Manual of Mental Disorders*. 4th ed., text revision, *DSM-IV-TR*. Washington, DC: American Psychiatric Association, 2000.
———. *Diagnostic and Statistical Manual of Mental Disorders*. 5th ed. *DSM-5*. Washington, DC: American Psychiatric Publishing, 2013.
Améry, Jean. "Ressentiments." In Améry, *Jenseits von Schuld und Sühne: Bewältigungsversuche eines Überwältigten*, 102–29. 2nd ed. Stuttgart: Klett-Cotta, 1977.
Andersch, Alfred. *Efraim*. Zurich: Diogenes, 1967.
Arendt, Hannah. *Eichmann in Jerusalem*. Munich: Piper, 1964.
Aristotle. *Aristotle: Problems II, Books XXII–XXXVIII*. Translated by W. S. Hett. Cambridge, MA: Harvard University Press, 1957.
———. "Brilliance and Melancholy." In Radden, *The Nature of Melancholy: From Aristotle to Kristeva*, 55–60.
Arnold, Armin. "La salade mixte du chef: Zu *Aus dem Tagebuch einer Schnecke* und *Kopfgeburten oder die Deutschen sterben aus*." In Manfred Durzak, *Zu Günter Grass: Geschichte auf dem poetischen Prüfstand*, 130–41. Stuttgart: Ernst Klett, 1985.

Arnold, Heinz Ludwig. "Gespräche mit Günter Grass." In *Text + Kritik* 1 (1978): 1–39.
Assmann, Aleida. *Der lange Schatten der Vergangenheit: Erinnerungskultur und Geschichtspolitik.* Munich: Beck, 2006.
Austin, J. L. *How to Do Things with Words.* Edited by J. O. Urmson and Marina Sbisa. Oxford: Clarendon Press, 1975.
Babb, Lawrence. *The Elizabethan Malady: A Study of Melancholia in English Literature from 1580 to 1642.* East Lansing: Michigan State College Press, 1951.
Bachmann, Ingeborg. *Das Buch Franza / Requiem für Fanny Goldmann: Texte des Todesarten-Projekts.* Edited by Dirk Göttsche and Monika Albrecht. Munich: Piper, 2004.
———. "Drei Wege zum See." In *Simultan: Erzählungen,* 94–165. Munich: DTV, 1974.
Bakhtin, Mikhail. *Rabelais and his World.* Translated by Hélène Iswolsky. Bloomington, IN: Indiana University Press, 1984.
Badenberg, Nana. "Kommentiertes Verzeichnis der in der *Ästhetik des Widerstands* erwähnten bildenden Künstler und Kunstwerke." In Honold and Schreiber, *Die Bilderwelt des Peter Weiss,* 163–230.
Bandmann, Günter. *Melancholie und Musik: Ikonographische Studien.* Cologne: Westdeutscher Verlag, 1960.
Barthes, Roland. *Wie zusammen leben: Simulationen einiger alltäglicher Räume im Roman. Vorlesung am Collège de France, 1976–1977.* Edited by Éric Marty. Translated by Horst Brühmann. Frankfurt am Main: Suhrkamp, 2007.
Barzilai, Maya. "Facing the Past and the Female Spectre in W. G. Sebald's *The Emigrants.*" In Long and Whitehead, *W. G. Sebald: A Critical Companion,* 203–16.
———. "Melancholia as World History: W. G. Sebald's Rewriting of Hegel in *Die Ringe des Saturn.*" In Fuchs and Long, *W. G. Sebald and the Writing of History,* 73–89.
Baumgart, Reinhard. *Deutsche Literatur der Gegenwart: Kritiken—Essays—Kommentare.* Munich: Hanser, 1994.
———. "Schlaflos schluchzend." *Der Spiegel,* Mar. 3, 1965.
Beck, John. "Reading Room: Erosion and Sedimentation in Sebald's Suffolk." In Long and Whitehead, *W. G. Sebald: A Critical Companion,* 75–88.
Benjamin, Walter. "Eduard Fuchs, der Sammler und der Historiker." In Benjamin, *Gesammelte Schriften,* 2.2:465–505.
———. *Gesammelte Schriften.* 7 vols. Edited by Rolf Tiedemann and Hermann Schweppenhäuser. Frankfurt am Main: Suhrkamp, 1977.
———. "Linke Melancholie: Zu Erich Kästners neuem Gedichtbuch." In *Gesammelte Schriften,* 3:279–83.
———. *Das Passagenwerk.* 2 vols. Frankfurt am Main: Suhrkamp, 1982.
———. *Ursprung des deutschen Trauerspiels.* 1928. Reprint, Frankfurt am Main: Suhrkamp, 1972.

Binswanger, Ludwig. *Melancholie und Manie: Phänomenologische Studien.* Pfullingen, Germany: Günther Neske, 1960.
Birkmeyer, Jens. *Bilder des Schreckens: Dantes Spuren und die Mythosrezeption in Peter Weiss' Roman "Die Ästhetik des Widerstands."* Wiesbaden: Deutscher Universitätsverlag, 1994.
Blamberger, Günter. *Versuch über den deutschen Gegenwartsroman: Krisenbewußtsein und Neubegründung im Zeichen der Melancholie.* Stuttgart: J. B. Metzler, 1985.
Bloomfield, Morton W. *The Seven Deadly Sins: An Introduction to the History of a Religious Concept with Special Reference to Medieval English Literature.* Ann Arbor: Michigan State College Press, 1952.
Bock, Wolfgang. *Walter Benjamin—Die Rettung der Nacht: Sterne, Melancholie und Messianismus.* Bielefeld: Aisthesis, 2000.
Böhme, Hartmut. *Albrecht Dürer: Melencolia I; Im Labyrinth der Deutung.* Frankfurt am Main: Fischer, 1989.
———. "Zur literarischen Rezeption von Albrecht Dürers Kupferstich *Melencolia I.*" In *Polyperspektivik in der literarischen Moderne: Studien zur Theorie, Geschichte und Wirkung der Literatur,* edited by Jörg Schönert and Harro Segeberg, 83–123. Frankfurt am Main: Lang, 1988.
Böhme, Hartmut, Peter Matussek, and Lothar Müller. *Orientierung Kulturwissenschaften: Was sie kann, was sie will.* Hamburg: Rowohlt, 2000.
Bohrer, Karl Heinz. *Der Abschied: Theorie der Trauer; Baudelaire, Goethe, Nietzsche, Benjamin.* Frankfurt am Main: Suhrkamp, 1996.
———. "Möglichkeiten einer nihilistischen Ethik." In Heidbrink, *Entzauberte Zeit,* 42–78.
Böll, Heinrich. *Ansichten eines Clowns.* Cologne: Kiepenhauer & Witsch, 1963.
Bond, Greg. "On the Misery of Nature and the Nature of Misery: W. G. Sebald's Landscapes." In Long and Whitehead, *W. G. Sebald: A Critical Companion,* 31–44.
Borchmeyer, Dieter, ed. *Melancholie und Heiterkeit.* Heidelberg: Winter, 2007.
Braese, Stephan. *Die andere Erinnerung: Jüdische Autoren in der westdeutschen Nachkriegsliteratur.* Berlin: Philo, 2001.
Braun, Rebecca. *Constructing Authorship in the Work of Günter Grass.* Oxford: Oxford University Press, 2008.
———. "Günter Grass as a World Author." In Braun and Brunssen, *Changing the Nation: Günter Grass in International Perspective,* 194–209.
Braun, Rebecca, and Frank Brunssen, eds. *Changing the Nation: Günter Grass in International Perspective.* Würzburg: Königshausen & Neumann, 2008.
Breuer, Ulrich. *Melancholie und Reise: Studien zur Archäologie des Individuellen im deutschen Roman des 16–18. Jahrhunderts.* Münster: LIT, 1994.
Brockmann, Stephen. *Nuremberg: The Imaginary Capital.* Rochester, NY: Camden House, 2006.

Brode, Hanspeter. "Von Danzig zur Bundesrepublik: Grass' Bücher *örtlich betäubt* und *Aus dem Tagebuch einer Schnecke*." *Text + Kritik* 1 (1978): 74–87.
Brook, Peter. *The Melodramatic Imagination: Balzac, Henry James; Melodrama and the Mode of Excess*. New Haven, CN: Yale University Press, 1976.
Brunner, Berthold. *Der Herakles / Stahlmann-Komplex in Peter Weiss' Ästhetik des Widerstands*. St. Ingbert, Germany: Röhrig, 1999.
Büchsel, Martin. *Albrecht Dürers Stich Melencolia I: Zeichen und Emotion; Logik einer kunsthistorischen Debatte*. Munich: Fink, 2010.
Bürger, Peter. "Der Ursprung der ästhetischen Moderne aus dem *ennui*." In Heidbrink, *Entzauberte Zeit: Der melancholische Geist der Moderne*, 101–19.
Burton, Robert. *The Anatomy of Melancholy*. Edited by Thomas C. Faulkner, Nicolas K. Kiessling, and Rhonda L. Blair. 3 vols. Vol. 1. Oxford: Clarendon, 1997.
Catling, Jo. "*Bibliotheca abscondita*: On W. G. Sebald's Library." In *Saturn's Moons: W. G. Sebald. A Handbook*, edited by Jo Catling and Richard Hibbit, 265–97. Oxford: Legenda, 2011.
Cepl-Kaufmann, Gertrude. *Günter Grass: Eine Analyse des Gesamtwerkes unter dem Aspekt von Literatur und Politik*. Kronberg: Scriptor, 1975.
Cheyne, George. *The English Malady; Or, a Treatise of Nervous Diseases of All Kinds, as Spleens, Vapours, Lowness of Spirits, Hypochondriacal, and Hysterical*. Cambridge: Cambridge Scholars, 2010.
Cohen, Robert. *Bio-Bibliographisches Handbuch zu Peter Weiss' "Ästhetik des Widerstands."* Hamburg: Argument, 1989.
Cosgrove, Mary. "The Anxiety of German Influence: Affiliation, Rejection, and Jewish Identity in W. G Sebald' Work." In Fuchs, Cosgrove, and Grote, *German Memory Contests: The Quest for Identity in Literature, Film, and Discourse since 1990*, 229–52.
———. "Austerlitz." In *The Novel in German since 1990*, edited by Stuart Taberner, 195–210. Cambridge: Cambridge UP, 2011.
———. "Erinnerungsethik und Dürerdiskurs im Werk von W. G. Sebald, Peter Weiss, Günter Grass und Jean Améry." In *W. G. Sebald: Intertextualität und Topographie*, edited by Irene Heidelberger-Leonard and Mireille Tabah, 153–68. Berlin: LIT, 2008.
———. "From Nobility to Sloth: Melancholy Self-Fashioning and the Hamlet Motif in Wolfgang Hildesheimer's *Tynset* and *Masante*." In *Wolfgang Hildesheimer und England: Zur Topologie eines literarischen Transfers*, edited by Rüdiger Görner and Isabel Wagner, 79–101. Bern: Peter Lang, 2012.
———. "Introduction: Sadness and Melancholy in German-Language Literature from the Seventeenth Century to the Present; An Overview." In *Edinburgh German Yearbook 6: Sadness and Melancholy in German-Language Literature and Culture*, edited by Mary Cosgrove and Anna Richards, 1–17. Rochester, NY: Camden House, 2012.

———. "Netzwerk und Erinnerung in Wolfgang Hildesheimers *Tynset*." In *Netzwerke: Ästhetiken und Techniken der Vernetzung 1800—1900—2000*, edited by Jürgen Barkhoff, Harmut Böhme, and Jeanne Riou, 251–61. Cologne: Böhlau, 2004.

Davis, Mike. *Late Victorian Holocausts: El Niño Famines and the Making of the Third World*. London: Verso, 2001.

De Man, Paul. "The Rhetoric of Temporality." In *Interpretation: Theory and Practice*, edited by Charles S. Singleton, 173–209. Baltimore, MD: Johns Hopkins University Press, 1969.

Dean, Carolyn J. *The Fragility of Empathy after the Holocaust*. Ithaca, NY: Cornell University Press, 2004.

Derrida, Jacques. *Limited Inc*. Translated by S. Weber. Evanston, ILL: Chicago University Press, 1988.

———. *Without Alibi*. Translated by P. Kamuf. Stanford, CA: Stanford University Press, 2002.

———. *Writing and Difference*, Translated by A. Bass. London: Routledge, 2005.

Diner, Dan. "Negative Symbiose: Deutsche und Juden nach Auschwitz." In *Ist der Nationalsozialismus Geschichte? Zu Historisierung und Historikerstreit*, edited by Wolfgang Benz and Dan Diner, 184–97. Frankfurt am Main: Fischer, 1987.

———. ed. *Zivilisationsbruch: Denken nach Auschwitz*. Frankfurt am Main: Fischer, 1996.

Dölling, Irene. "Frauen im Klassenkampf: Klassenkampf und Geschlechterfrage in Peter Weiss' *Die Ästhetik des Widerstands*." In *"Die Ästhetik des Widerstands": Erfahrungen mit dem Roman von Peter Weiss*, edited by Norbert Krenzlin, 45–63. Berlin: Akademie, 1987.

Dunker, Axel. *Die anwesende Abwesenheit: Literatur im Schatten von Auschwitz*. Munich: Fink, 2003.

Dwars, Jens-Fiejte. *Und dennoch Hoffnung: Peter Weiss; Eine Biographie*. Berlin: Aufbau, 2007.

Eaglestone, Robert. *The Holocaust and the Postmodern*. Oxford: Oxford University Press, 2004.

Ecker, Gisela. "'Heimat' oder die Grenzen der Bastelei." In Niehaus and Öhlschläger, *W. G. Sebald: Politische Archäologie und melancholische Bastelei*, 77–88.

———. ed. *Trauer tragen—Trauer zeigen: Inszenierungen der Geschlechter*. Munich: Fink, 1999.

———. "Trauer zeigen: Inszenierung und die Sorge um den Anderen." In Ecker, *Trauer tragen—Trauer zeigen: Inszenierungen der Geschlechter*, 9–25.

Eitz, Thorsten, and Stötzel Georg. *Wörterbuch der Vergangenheitsbewältigung: Die NS-Vergangenheit im öffentlichen Sprachgebrauch*. Hildesheim: Georg Olms, 2007.

Eliot, T. S. "The Love Song of J. Alfred Prufrock." In *The Norton Anthology of English Literature*, 6th edition, vol. 2, edited by M. H. Abrams, 1971–76. New York: Norton, 1993.

Emmerich, Wolfgang. *Kleine Literaturgeschichte der DDR: Erweiterte Neuausgabe.* 1996. Reprint, Leipzig: Gustav Kiepenhauer, 1997.

Erbel, Kunibert. *Sprachlose Körper, körperlose Sprache: Studien zu 'innerer' und 'äußerer' Natur in Die Ästhetik des Widerstands.* St Ingbert, Germany: Röhrig, 1991.

Eshel, Amir. "Against the Power of Time: The Poetics of Suspension in W. G. Sebald's *Austerlitz.*" *New German Critique* 88 (Winter, 2003): 71–96.

Feusthuber, Birgit. "Najaden und Sirenen: Weiblichkeitsbilder in der *Ästhetik des Widerstands.*" In Heidelberger-Leonard, *Peter Weiss: Neue Fragen an alte Texte*, 97–110.

Ficino, Marsilio. "Learned People and Melancholy." In Radden, *The Nature of Melancholy: From Aristotle to Kristeva*, 87–93.

———. *Three Books on Life.* Translated by Carol Kaske and John Clark. Binghampton, NY: Center of Medieval and Renaissance Studies, 1989.

Finch, Helen. *Sebald's Bachelors: Queer Resistance and the Unconforming Life.* Oxford: Legenda, 2013.

Finkelstein, Norman. *The Holocaust Industry: Reflection on the Exploitation of Jewish Suffering.* London: Verso, 2000.

Fischer, Torben, and Matthias N. Lorenz, eds. *Lexikon der "Vergangenheitsbewältigung" in Deutschland: Debatten- und Diskursgeschichte des Nationalsozialismus nach 1945.* Bielefeld: transcript, 2007.

Flashar, Hellmut. *Melancholie und Melancholiker in den medizinischen Theorien der Antike.* Berlin: de Gruyter, 1966.

Flatley, Jonathan. *Affective Mapping: Melancholia and the Politics of Modernism.* Cambridge, MA: Harvard University Press, 2008.

Fletcher, Angus. *Allegory: The Theory of a Symbolic Mode.* Ithaca, NY: Cornell University Press, 1964.

Földényi, László F. *Melancholie.* Translated by Nora Tahy. Berlin: Matthes & Seitz, 2004.

Foster, Edgar J. *Unmännliche Männlichkeit: Melancholie—Geschlecht—Verausgabung.* Vienna: Böhlau, 1998.

Foucault, Michel. *Discipline and Punish: The Birth of the Prison.* Translated by Alan Sheridan. London: Penguin, 1991.

———. *The History of Sexuality, Volume I: An Introduction.* Translated by Robert Hurley. London: Penguin, 1990.

———. *Madness and Civilisation: A History of Insanity in the Age of Reason.* Translated by Richard Howard. London: Routledge, 1999.

Freud, Sigmund. *Gesammelte Werke: Chronologisch geordnet.* Edited by Anna Freud, E. Bibring, W. Hoffer, E. Kris, and O. Isakower, with the collaboration of Marie Bonaparte. 18 vols. Frankfurt am Main: Fischer, 1940–68.

———. "Trauer und Melancholie." In *Gesammelte Werke: Chronologisch geordnet*, 10:428–46.

———. "Über Deckerinnerungen." In *Gesammelte Werke: Chronologisch geordnet*, 1:529–54.

———. "Das Unbehagen in der Kultur." In *Gesammelte Werke: Chronologisch geordnet*, 14:419–506.

———. "Das Unheimliche." In *Gesammelte Werke: Chronologisch geordnet*, 12:227–68.

Frye, Northrop. *The Anatomy of Criticism: Four Essays*. Princeton, NJ: Princeton University Press, 1957.

Fuchs, Anne. "'Ein Hauptkapitel der Geschichte der Unterwerfung': Representations of Nature in W. G. Sebald's *Die Ringe des Saturn*." In Fuchs and Long, *W. G. Sebald and the Writing of History*, 121–38.

———. "A *Heimat* in Ruins and the Ruins as *Heimat*: W. G. Sebald's *Luftkrieg und Literatur*." In Fuchs, Cosgrove, and Grote, *German Memory Contests: The Quest for Identity in Literature, Film, and Discourse since 1990*, 287–302.

———. *Phantoms of War in Contemporary German Literature, Films and Discourse: The Politics of Memory*. 2nd ed. Basingstoke, UK: Palgrave Macmillan, 2010.

———. *Die Schmerzensspuren der Geschichte: Zur Poetik der Erinnerung in W. G. Sebalds Prosa*. Cologne: Böhlau, 2004.

Fuchs, Anne, and Mary Cosgrove. "Introduction: Germany's Memory Contests and the Management of the Past." In Fuchs, Cosgrove, and Grote, *German Memory Contests: The Quest for Identity in Literature, Film, and Discourse since 1990*, 1–21.

Fuchs, Anne, Mary Cosgrove, and Georg Grote, eds. *German Memory Contests: The Quest for Identity in Literature, Film, and Discourse since 1990*. Rochester, NY: Camden House, 2006.

Fuchs, Anne, and J. J. Long, eds. *W. G. Sebald and the Writing of History*. Würzburg: Königshausen & Neumann, 2007.

Gadamer, Hans-Georg. *Wahrheit und Methode: Grundzüge einer philosophischen Hermeneutik*. Tübingen: Mohr, 1960.

Ganzfried, Daniel, and Sebastian Hefti, eds. *Alias Wilkomirski: Die Holocaust Travestie; Enthüllung und Dokumentation eines literarischen Skandals*. Berlin: Jüdischer Verlag, 2002.

Garde, Barbara. "'Die Frauengasse ist eine Gasse, durch die man lebenslang geht': Frauen in den Romanen von Günter Grass." *Text + Kritik* 1 (1978): 101–7.

Garloff, Katja. "Expanding the Canon of Holocaust Literature: Traumatic Address in Hubert Fichte and Wolfgang Hildesheimer." In "Memory and the Holocaust," special issue, *New German Critique* 96 (2005): 49–74.

———. *Words from Abroad: Trauma and Displacement in Postwar German Jewish Writers*. Detroit, MI: Wayne State University Press, 2005.

Gellrich, Jesse M. "Allegory and Materiality: Medieval Foundations of the Modern Debate." In "Reformulating Allegory: Literature, Theory,

Film," edited by Susanne Knaller, special issue, *Germanic Review* 77, no. 2 (2002): 146–59.

Gerlach, Rainer, and Matthias Richter, eds. *Peter Weiss im Gespräch*. Frankfurt am Main: Suhrkamp, 1986.

Giehlow, Karl. "Dürers Stich 'Melencolia I' und der maximilianische Humanistenkreis." *Mitteilungen der Gesellschaft für vervielfältigende Kunst* 26, no. 2 (1903): 29–41; 27, no. 3 (1904): 6–18; 27, no. 4: 57–78.

Gilman, Sander L. *Disease and Representation: Images of Illness from Madness to AIDS*. Ithaca, NY: Cornell University Press, 1988.

Glas, Gerrit. "A Conceptual History of Anxiety and Depression." In *Handbook of Depression and Anxiety: Second Edition, Revised and Expanded*, edited by Siegfried Kasper, Johan A. den Boer, and J. M. Ad Sitsen, 1–46. New York: Marcel Dekker, 2003.

Glaser, Herman, ed. *Am Beispiel Dürers: Reden von Jean Améry, Günter Grass, Richard Friedenthal, Hartmut von Hentig, Wilhelm Fucks, Adolf Portmann, Arnold Gehlen, Carlo Schmid*. Munich: Bruckmann, 1972.

Goethe, Johann Wolfgang von. *Die Leiden des jungen Werther*. Ditzingen: Reclam, 2001.

Goll-Bickmann, Dietmar. *Aspekte der Melancholie in der frühen und mittleren Prosa Wolfgang Hildesheimers*. Münster: LIT, 1989.

Gombrich, Ernst. *Aby Warburg: An Intellectual Biography with a Memoir on the History of the Library by F. Saxl*. Oxford: Phaidon, 1986.

Grass, Günter. *Aus dem Tagebuch einer Schnecke*. Munich: DTV, 1998.

———. *Beim Häuten der Zwiebel*. Göttingen: Steidl, 2006.

———. *Die Blechtrommel*. Darmstadt: Luchterhand, 1959.

———. *Die bösen Köche: Ein Drama in fünf Akten*. Darmstadt: Luchterhand, 1982.

———. *Der Butt*. Göttingen: Steidl, 2007.

———. *Günter Grass: Werkausgabe in zehn Bänden*. Edited by Volker Neuhaus. 10 vols. Darmstadt: Luchterhand, 1987.

———. *Im Krebsgang*. Göttingen: Steidl, 2002.

———. *Kopfgeburten oder die Deutschen sterben aus*. Göttingen: Steidl, 2003.

———. "Die melancholische Koalition." In *Günter Grass: Werkausgabe in zehn Bänden*, 9:176–81.

———. *örtlich betäubt*. Göttingen: Steidl, 1969.

———. "Rede über das Selbstverständliche." In *Günter Grass: Werkausgabe in zehn Bänden*, 9:136–54.

———. *Schreiben nach Auschwitz: Frankfurter Poetik-Vorlesung*. Frankfurt am Main: Luchterhand, 1990.

———. *Das Treffen in Telgte: Eine Erzählung*. Göttingen: Steidl, 2007.

———. "Über die Toleranz." In *Günter Grass: Werkausgabe in zehn Bänden*, 9:650–58.

———. "Unser Grundübel ist der Idealismus." In *Günter Grass: Werkausgabe in zehn Bänden*, 9:392–94.

———. "Vom mangelnden Selbstvertrauen der schreibenden Hofnarren unter Berücksichtigung nicht vorhandener Höfe." In *Günter Grass: Werkausgabe in zehn Bänden*, 9:153–58.

———. "Vom Stillstand im Fortschritt." In Glaser, *Am Beispiel Dürers: Reden von Jean Améry, Günter Grass, Richard Friedenthal, Hartmut von Hentig, Wilhelm Fucks, Adolf Portmann, Arnold Gehlen, Carlo Schmid*, 82–97.

Gumbrecht, Hans Ulrich. *Stimmungen lesen: Über eine verdeckte Wirklichkeit der Literatur*. Munich: Hanser, 2011.

Hamlin, Cyrus. *Hermeneutics of Form: Romantic Poetics in Theory and Practice*. New Haven, CT: Schwab, 1998.

Hanenberg, Peter. *Geschichte im Werk Wolfgang Hildesheimers*. Frankfurt am Main: Peter Lang, 1989.

Hanika, Iris. *Das Eigentliche*. Graz, Austria: Droschl, 2010.

Hegel, Georg Wilhelm Friedrich. "Letter to Friedrich Immanuel Niethammer, Oct. 13 1806." In *Briefe von und an Hegel, Vol. 1, 1785–1812*, edited by Johannes Hofmeister, 119–21. Hamburg: Felix Meiner, 1961.

Heidbrink, Ludger. ed. *Entzauberte Zeit: Der melancholische Geist der Moderne*. Munich: Hanser, 1997.

———. *Melancholie und Moderne: Zur Kritik der historischen Verzweiflung*. Munich: Fink, 1994.

Heidelberger-Leonard, Irene. *Jean Améry: Revolte in der Resignation*. Stuttgart: Klett-Cotta, 2005.

———. "Jean Amérys Selbstverständnis als Jude." In *Über Jean Améry*, edited by Irene Heidelberger-Leonard, 17–21. Heidelberg: Winter, 1990.

———. "Jüdisches Bewußtsein im Werk von Peter Weiss." In *Literatur, Ästhetik, Geschichte: Neue Zugänge zu Peter Weiss*, edited by Michael Hofmann, Karl Richter, Gerhard Sauder, and Gerhard Schmidt-Henkel, 49–64. St. Ingbert, Germany: Röhrig, 1992.

———. "'Die Kunst zu erben' oder Der Gebrauchswert der 'Divina Commedia' für Peter Weiss." In Höller, *Hinter jedem Wort die Gefahr des Verstummens: Sprachproblematik und literarische Tradition in der 'Ästhetik des Widerstands' von Peter Weiss*, 21–37.

———. "Melancholie als Widerstand." *Akzente* 48, no. 2 (2001): 122–30.

———. ed. *Peter Weiss: Neue Fragen an alte Texte*. Opladen, Germany: Westdeutscher Verlag, 1994.

Heidelberger-Leonard, Irene, and Mireille Tabah, eds. *W. G. Sebald: Intertextualität und Topographie*. Berlin: LIT, 2008.

Hell, Julia. "Eyes Wide Shut: German Post-Holocaust Authorship." *New German Critique* 88 (Winter 2003): 9–36.

———. "From Laokoon to Ge: Resistance to Jewish Authorship in Peter Weiss's *Ästhetik des Widerstands*." In *Rethinking Peter Weiss*, edited by Jost Hermand and Marc Silberman, 21–44. New York: Peter Lang, 2000.

———. "Rosa oder die Sehnsucht nach einer Geschichte ohne Stalin: Zur Logik einer vergeschlechtlichten Textproduktion in der *Ästhetik des Widerstands*." In *Peter Weiss Jahrbuch 6*, edited by Martin Rector and Jochen Vogt, 138–63. Opladen, Germany: Westdeutscher Verlag, 1997.

Hermann, Ingo, ed. *Wolfgang Hildesheimer: Ich werde nun schweigen; Gespräch mit Hans Helmut Hillrichs in der Reihe "Zeugen des Jahrhunderts."* Göttingen: Lamuv, 1995.
Hildegard of Bingen. "Melancholia in Men and Women." In Radden, *The Nature of Melancholy from Aristotle to Kristeva*, 81–85.
Hildesheimer, Wolfgang. "Antworten über *Tynset*." *Dichten und Trachten* 25 (1965): 7–12.
———. "Arbeitsprotokolle des Verfahrens 'Marbot.'" In *Das Ende der Fiktionen: Reden aus fünfundzwanzig Jahren*, 139–50.
———. "Bleibt Dürer Dürer?" In *Das Ende der Fiktionen: Reden aus fünfundzwanzig Jahren*, 27–46.
———. "Büchners Melancholie." In *Das Ende der Fiktionen: Reden aus fünfundzwanzig Jahren*, 87–101.
———. "Das Ende der Fiktionen." In *Das Ende der Fiktionen: Reden aus fünfundzwanzig Jahren*, 229–50.
———. *Das Ende der Fiktionen: Reden aus fünfundzwanzig Jahren*. Frankfurt am Main: Suhrkamp, 1984.
———. "Hamlet." In *Exerzitien mit Papst Johannes*, 9–25. Frankfurt am Main: Suhrkamp, 1979.
———. "'Ich kann über nichts schreiben als über ein potentielles Ich': Gespräch mit Wolfgang Hildesheimer." In *Gespräche über den Roman*, edited by Manfed Durzak, 271–95. Frankfurt am Main: Suhrkamp, 1976.
———. *Interpretationen: James Joyce, Georg Büchner; Zwei Frankfurter Vorlesungen*. Frankfurt am Main: Suhrkamp, 1969.
———. *Marbot: Eine Biographie*. Frankfurt am Main: Suhrkamp, 1981.
———. *Mary Stuart: Eine historische Szene / Anmerkungen zu einer historischen Szene*. In *Spectaculum: Sechs moderne Theaterstücke*, 261–332. Frankfurt am Main: Suhrkamp, 1971.
———. *Masante*. Frankfurt am Main: Suhrkamp, 1973.
———. "Mein Judentum." In *Das Ende der Fiktionen: Reden aus fünfundzwanzig Jahren*, 213–28.
———. *Mozart*. Frankfurt am Main: Suhrkamp, 1977.
———. "Die Subjektivität des Biographen." In *Das Ende der Fiktionen: Reden aus fünfundzwanzig Jahren*, 123–38.
———. *Tynset*. Frankfurt am Main: Suhrkamp, 1965.
———. "Über das absurde Theater." In *Das Ende der Fiktionen: Reden aus fünfundzwanzig Jahren*, 9–26.
———. *Vergebliche Aufzeichnungen*. Frankfurt am Main: Suhrkamp, 1962.
———. "Vita." In Jehle, *Wolfgang Hildesheimer*, 17–19.
Hirsch, Marianne. *Family Frames: Photography, Narrative and Postmemory*. Cambridge, MA: Harvard University Press, 1997.
Hirsch, Wolfgang. *Zwischen Wirklichkeit und erfundener Biographie: Zum Künstlerbild bei Wolfgang Hildesheimer*. Hamburg: LIT, 1997.

Hofmann, Gert, Rachel MagShamhráin, Marko Pajević, and Michael Shields, eds. *German and European Poetics after the Holocaust: Crisis and Creativity*. Rochester, NY: Camden House, 2011.
Hofmann, Michael. "Antifaschismus und poetische Erinnerung der Shoah." In *Peter Weiss Jahrbuch 3*, edited by Rainer Koch, Martin Rector, Rainer Rother, and Jochen Vogt, 122–34. Opladen, Germany: Westdeutscher Verlag, 1994.
Hofmannsthal, Hugo von. "Ein Brief." In *Der Brief des Lord Chandos: Schriften zur Literatur, Kultur und Geschichte*, edited by Mathias Mayer, 46–59. Stuttgart: Reclam, 2007.
Hohmann, Joachim S., ed. *Melancholie: Ein deutsches Gefühl*. Trier: editions trèves, 1989.
Höller, Hans, ed. *Hinter jedem Wort die Gefahr des Verstummens: Sprachproblematik und literarische Tradition in der 'Ästhetik des Widerstands' von Peter Weiss*. Stuttgart: Akademischer Verlag, 1988.
Hollington, Michael. *Günter Grass: The Writer in a Pluralist Society*. London: Marion Boyars, 1980.
Honold, Alexander. "Das Gedächtnis der Bilder: Zur Ästhetik der Memoria bei Peter Weiss." In Honold and Schreiber, *Die Bilderwelt des Peter Weiss*, 100–113.
Honold, Alexander, and Ulrich Schreiber, eds. *Die Bilderwelt des Peter Weiss*. Berlin: Argument, 1995.
Hopkins, Terence K., and Immanuel Wallerstein. *World-Systems Analysis: Theory and Methodology*. London: Sage, 1982.
Horn, Giesela, and Haike Wirrmann. "Der weibliche Widerstand." *Wissenschaftliche Zeitschrift* 36, no. 3 (1987): 433–38.
Horwitz, Allan V., and Jerome C. Wakefield. *The Loss of Sadness: How Psychiatry Transformed Normal Sorrow into Depressive Disorder*. Oxford: Oxford University Press, 2007.
Huyssen, Andreas. "Gray Zones of Remembrance." In *A New History of German Literature*, edited by David E. Wellbery and Judith Ryan, 970–75. Cambridge, MA: Harvard University Press, 2004.
———. "On Rewritings and New Beginnings: W. G. Sebald and the Literature about the *Luftkrieg*." *Zeitschrift für Literatur und Linguistik* 31 (2001): 72–90.
Ilsemann, Mark. "Going Astray: Melancholy, Natural History, and the Image of Exile in W. G. Sebald's *Austerlitz*." In *W. G. Sebald: History—Memory—Trauma*, edited by Scott Denham and Mark McCulloh, 301–14. Berlin: Walter de Gruyter, 2006.
Isenschmid, Andreas. "Melencolia: W. G. Sebalds *Schwindel: Gefühle*." In *W. G. Sebald: Porträt*, edited by Franz Loquai, 70–74. Eggingen, Germany: Isele, 1997.
Jackson, Stanley W. *Melancholia and Depression: From Hippocratic to Modern Times*. New Haven, CT: Yale University Press, 1986.
Jaques-Bosch, Bettina. *Kritik und Melancholie im Werk Max Frischs: Zur Entwicklung einer für die Schweizer Literatur typischen Dichotomie*. Bern: Peter Lang, 1984.

Jaspers, Karl. *Philosophische Logik I: Von der Wahrheit*. Munich: Piper, 1958.
———. *Die Schuldfrage*. Zurich: Artemis, 1946.
Jehle, Volker, ed. *Wolfgang Hildesheimer*. Frankfurt am Main: Suhrkamp, 1989.
———. *Wolfgang Hildesheimer: Werkgeschichte*. Frankfurt am Main: Suhrkamp, 1990.
Jens, Walter. "Appell und Anmut: Wolfgang Hildesheimer." In *Von deutscher Rede*, 214–25.
———. *Herr Meister: Dialog über einen Roman*. Munich: Piper, 1963.
———. "Melancholie und Moral." In *Von deutscher Rede*, 200–213.
———. *Von deutscher Rede*. Munich: Piper, 1983.
Kahl, Michael. "Der Begriff der Allegorie in Benjamins Trauerspielbuch und im Werk Paul de Mans." In van Reijen, *Allegorie und Melancholie*, 292–317.
Kemper, Hans Georg. *Deutsche Lyrik der frühen Neuzeit: Band 6 / 1 Empfindsamkeit*. Tübingen: Niemeyer, 1997.
Kessler, Achim. *"Schafft die Einheit!": Die Figurenkonstellation in der Ästhetik des Widerstands von Peter Weiss*. Hamburg: Argument, 1997.
Kiedaisch, Petra, ed. *Lyrik nach Auschwitz: Adorno und die Dichter*. Stuttgart: Reclam, 1995.
Klein, Kerwin Lee. "On the Emergence of Memory in Historical Discourse." *Representations* 69 (2000): 127–50.
Klibansky, Raymond, Erwin Panofsky, and Fritz Saxl. *Saturn and Melancholy: Studies in the History of Natural Philosophy, Religion, and Art*. London: Nelson, 1964.
———. *Saturn und Melancholie: Studien zur Geschichte der Naturphilosophie und Medizin, der Religion und der Kunst*. Translated by Christa Buschendorf. Frankfurt am Main: Suhrkamp, 1992.
Koebner, Thomas. "Entfremdung und Melancholie." In Rodewald, *Über Wolfgang Hildesheimer*, 32–59.
Krankenhagen, Stefan. *Auschwitz darstellen: Ästhetische Positionen zwischen Adorno, Spielberg und Walser*. Cologne: Böhlau, 2001.
Kristeva, Julia. *Black Sun: Depression and Melancholia*. Translated by Leon S. Roudiez. New York: Columbia University Press, 1989.
Krueger, Merle Curtis. *Authors and the Opposition: West German Writers and the Social Democratic Party from 1945 to 1969*. Stuttgart: Heinz, 1982.
Krylova, Katja. "Melancholy, Topography and the Search for Origin in Ingeborg Bachmann's 'Drei Wege zum See.'" *German Life and Letters* 62, no. 2 (2009): 157–73.
Kühberger, Christoph, and Andreas Pudlat, eds. *Vergangenheitsbewirtschaftung: Public History zwischen Wirtschaft und Wissenschaft* (Innsbruck: StudienVerlag, 2012).
Kuhn, Reinhard. *The Demon of Noontide: Ennui in Western Literature*. Princeton, NJ: Princeton University Press, 1976.
LaCapra, Dominick. *Writing History, Writing Trauma*. Baltimore, MD: Johns Hopkins University Press, 2001.

Langer, Renate. "Der Sohn als Guerillero: Imaginationen von Klassenkampf und präödipalem Drama in der *Ästhetik des Widerstands*." In Honold and Schreiber, *Die Bilderwelt des Peter Weiss*, 64–76.
Langston, Richard. "Affective Affinities: Sebald and Kluge on Feeling History." Special issue on W. G. Sebald, *Gegenwartsliteratur* 6 (2007): 44–68.
Lawlor, Clark. "Fashionable Melancholy." In *Melancholy Experience in Literature of the Long Eighteenth Century: Before Depression, 1660–1800*, ed. Allan Ingram, Stuart Sim, Clark Lawlor, Richard Terry, John Baker, and Leigh Wetherall-Dickson, 44–46. Basingstoke, UK: Palgrave Macmillan, 2011.
———. *From Melancholia to Depression: A History of Depression*. Oxford: Oxford University Press, 2012.
Lea, Henry A. "Hildesheimers Weg zum Ende der Fiktionen." In Jehle, *Wolfgang Hildesheimer*, 45–57.
———. "Wolfgang Hildesheimer and the German-Jewish Experience: Reflections on *Tynset* and *Masante*." *Monatshefte* 71 (1979): 19–28.
———. *Wolfgang Hildesheimers Weg als Jude und Deutscher*. Stuttgart: Akademischer Verlag, 1997.
Leader, Darian. *The New Black: Mourning, Melancholia and Depression*. London: Penguin, 2008.
———. *Strictly Bipolar*. London: Penguin, 2013.
Lemke, Anja. "Figurationen der Melancholie: Spuren Walter Benjamins in W. G. Sebalds 'Die Ringe des Saturn.'" *Zeitschrift für deutsche Philologie* 2 (2008): 239–67.
Leonardy, Ernst. "Das Sterben der Mutter und Heilmanns Abschiedsbrief: Beobachtungen zur Figurengestaltung im Epilogband der *Ästhetik des Widerstands*." In Heidelberger-Leonard, *Peter Weiss: Neue Fragen an alte Texte*, 111–23.
Lepenies, Wolfgang. *Melancholie und Gesellschaft: Mit einer neuen Einleitung; Das Ende der Utopie und die Wiederkehr der Melancholie*. Frankfurt am Main: Suhrkamp, 1998.
Levene, Mark. "A Dissenting Voice: Or How Current Assumptions of Deterring and Preventing Genocide May Be Looking at the Problem through the Wrong End of the Telescope, Part I." *Journal of Genocide Research* 6 (2004): 153–66.
———. "A Dissenting Voice: Part II." *Journal of Genocide Research* 6 (2004): 431–45.
Levi, Primo. *The Drowned and the Saved*. Translated by Raymond Rosenthal. London: Abacus, 2002.
Lindner, Burkhardt. "Allegorie." In *Benjamins Begriffe*, edited by Michael Opitz and Erdmut Wizisla, 50–94. Frankfurt am Main: Suhrkamp, 2000.
Löffler, Sigrid. "'Melancholie ist eine Form des Widerstands': Über das Saturnische bei W. G. Sebald und seine Aufhebung in der Schrift." *Text + Kritik* 158 (2003): 103–11.

Long, J. J. "Time and Narrative: Wolfgang Hildesheimer's *Tynset* and *Masante*." *German Life and Letters* 52, no. 4 (1999): 457–74.

———. *W. G. Sebald: Image, Archive, Modernity*. Edinburgh: Edinburgh University Press, 2007.

———. "W. G. Sebald's Miniature Histories." In Fuchs and Long, *W. G. Sebald and the Writing of History*, 111–20.

Long, J. J., and Anne Whitehead, eds. *W. G. Sebald: A Critical Companion*. Edinburgh: Edinburgh University Press, 2004.

Loomba, Ania. *Colonialism / Postcolonialism*. London: Routledge, 1998.

Loquai, Franz, ed. *Hamlet und Deutschland: Zur literarischen Shakespeare-Rezeption im 20. Jahrhundert*. Stuttgart: Metzler, 1993.

———. *Künstler und Melancholie in der Romantik*. Frankfurt am Main: Peter Lang, 1984.

Loraux, Nicole. *Mothers in Mourning: With the Essay "Of Amnesty and Its Opposite."* Translated by Corinne Pache. Ithaca, NY: Cornell University Press, 1998.

Loxley, James. *Performativity*. London: Routledge, 2007.

Maier, Anja. "'Der panische Halsknick.': Organisches und Anorganisches in W. G. Sebalds Prosa." In Niehaus and Öhlschläger, *W. G. Sebald: Politische Archäologie und melancholische Bastelei*, 111–26.

Maier, Charles S. "A Surfeit of Memory? Reflections on History, Melancholy and Denial." *History & Memory* 5, no. 2 (1993): 136–51.

Mann, Heinrich. *Die Jugend des Königs Henri Quatre*. Reinbek bei Hamburg: Rowohlt, 1994.

Mann, Thomas. *Doktor Faustus: Das Leben des deutschen Tonsetzers Adrian Leverkühn, erzählt von einem Freunde*. Frankfurt am Main: Fischer, 2007.

Martens, Wolfgang. *Bild und Motiv im Weltschmerz: Studien zur Dichtung Lenaus*. Cologne: Böhlau, 1957.

Mason, Ann L. "The Artist and Politics in Günter Grass' *Aus dem Tagebuch einer Schnecke*." In *Critical Essays on Günter Grass*, edited by Patrick O'Neill, 159–74. Boston, MA: Hall, 1987.

———. *The Skeptical Muse: A Study of Günter Grass' Conception of the Artist*. Bern: Lang, 1974.

Mattenklott, Gert. *Melancholie in der Dramatik des Sturm und Drangs*. Stuttgart: J. B. Metzlersche, 1968.

Mayer-Iswandy, Claudia. *"Vom Glück der Zwitter": Geschlechterrolle und Geschlechtsverhältnis bei Günter Grass*. Frankfurt am Main: Lang, 1991.

Mehnert, Henning. *Melancholie und Inspiration: Begriffs- und wissenschaftsgeschichtliche Untersuchungen zur poetischen "Psychologie" Baudelaires, Flauberts und Mallarmés*. Heidelberg: Winter, 1978.

Menninghaus, Winfried. *Ekel: Theorie und Gefühl einer starken Empfindung*. Frankfurt am Main: Suhrkamp, 1999.

Meyer-Sickendiek, Burkhard. *Tiefe: Über die Faszination des Grübelns*. Munich: Fink, 2010.

Miles, Keith. *Günter Grass*. London: Vision, 1975.

Mitscherlich, Alexander, and Margarete Mitscherlich. *Die Unfähigkeit zu trauern: Grundlagen kollektiven Verhaltens*. Munich: Piper, 2007.
Moeller, Robert G. *War Stories: The Search for a Usable Past in the Federal Republic of Germany*. Berkeley: University of California Press, 2001.
Montaigne, Michel de. *The Essays of Michel de Montaigne*. Translated and edited by M. A. Screech. London: Penguin, 1991.
———. "On Idleness." In *The Essays of Michel de Montaigne*, 30–31.
———. "On Moderation." In *The Essays of Michel de Montaigne*, 222–27.
———. "On Sadness." In *The Essays of Michel de Montaigne*, 7–10.
———. "On the Power of the Imagination." In *The Essays of Michel de Montaigne*, 109–20.
———. "To Philosophize Is to Learn How to Die." In *The Essays of Michel de Montaigne*, 89–109.
Morgan, Peter. "The Sign of Saturn: Melancholy, Homelessness and Apocalypse in W. G. Sebald's Prose Narratives." *German Life and Letters* 58 (2005): 75–92.
Moritz, Karl Philipp. *Anton Reiser: Ein psychologischer Roman*. Frankfurt am Main: Insel, 2006.
Mosbach, Bettina. *Figurationen der Katastrophe: Ästhetische Verfahren in W. G. Sebalds Die Ringe des Saturn und Austerlitz*. Bielefeld: Aisthesis, 2008.
Moses, A. Dirk. "Conceptual Blockages and Definitional Dilemmas in the 'Racial Century': Genocides of Indigenous People and the Holocaust." *Patterns of Prejudice* 36 (2002): 7–36.
———. *German Intellectuals and the Nazi Past*. Cambridge: Cambridge University Press, 2007.
———. "The Holocaust and Genocide." In *The Historiography of the Holocaust*, edited by Dan Stone, 533–55. Basingstoke, UK: Palgrave Macmillan, 2004.
Mundt, Hannelore. *Doktor Faustus und die Folgen: Kunstkritik als Gesellschaftskritik in deutschen Romanen seit 1947*. Bonn: Bouvier, 1989.
Neuhaus, Volker. *Günter Grass*. Stuttgart: Metzler, 1993.
———. ". . . über Menschen als Tiere, die kochen können: Kulinaristik bei Günter Grass." In Neuhaus and Weyer, *Küchenzettel: Essen und Trinken im Werk von Günter Grass*, 9–19.
Neuhaus, Volker, and Anselm Weyer, eds. *Küchenzettel: Essen und Trinken im Werk von Günter Grass*. Frankfurt am Main: Peter Lang, 2007.
Neumann, Peter Horst. "Hamlet will schlafen." In Jehle, *Wolfgang Hildesheimer*, 205–11.
New Larousse Encyclopaedia of Mythology. London: Hamlyn, 1970.
Niehaus, Michael. "W. G. Sebalds sentimentalische Dichtung." In Niehaus and Öhlschläger, *W. G. Sebald: Politische Archäologie und melancholische Bastelei*, 173–87.
Niehaus, Michael, and Claudia Öhlschläger, eds. *W. G. Sebald: Politische Archäologie und melancholische Bastelei*. Berlin: Erich Schmidt, 2006.

Nietzsche, Friedrich. *Also sprach Zarathustra.* In *Werke in drei Bänden*, 2:273–561.
———. *Ecce Homo.* In *Werke in drei Bänden*, 2:1063–159.
———. *Die Geburt der Tragödie.* In *Werke in drei Bänden*, 1:7–134.
———. *Jenseits von Gut und Böse.* In *Werke in drei Bänden*, 2:563–759.
———. *Werke in drei Bänden.* Edited by Karl Schlechta. Munich: Hanser, 1966.
———. *Zur Genealogie der Moral.* In *Werke in drei Bänden*, 2:761–900.
Obermüller, Klara. *Studien zur Melancholie in der deutschen Lyrik des Barock.* Bonn: Bouvier, 1974.
O'Dochartaigh, Pól, ed. "Jews in German Literature since 1945: German-Jewish Literature?" Special issue, *The German Monitor* 53 (2000).
O'Driscoll, Anna. *Constructions of Melancholy in Contemporary German and Austrian Literature.* Oxford: Peter Lang, 2013.
Öhlschläger, Claudia. *Beschädigtes Leben: Erzählte Risse; W. G. Sebalds poetische Ordnung des Unglücks.* Berlin: Rombach, 2006.
———. "Der Saturnring oder Etwas vom Eisenbau: W. G. Sebalds poetische Zivilisationskritik." In Niehaus and Öhlschläger, *W. G. Sebald: Politische Archäologie und melancholische Bastelei*, 189–204.
Panofsky, Erwin, and Fritz Saxl. *Dürers Melencolia I: Eine quellen- und typengeschichtliche Untersuchung.* Studien der Bibliothek Warburg 2. Leipzig: B. G. Teubner, 1923.
Pensky, Max. *Melancholy Dialectics: Walter Benjamin and the Play of Mourning.* Amherst: University of Massachusetts Press, 1993.
Pfau, Thomas. *Romantic Moods: Paranoia, Trauma and Melancholy, 1790–1840.* Baltimore, MD: Johns Hopkins University Press, 2005.
Pietsch, Timm Niklas. *"Wer hört noch zu?": Günter Grass als politischer Redner und Essayist.* Essen: Klartext, 2006.
Poore, Carol. "Mother Earth, Melancholia, and Mnemosyne: Women in Peter Weiss's *Die Ästhetik des Widerstands.*" *German Quarterly* 58, no. 1 (1985): 68–86.
Pourciau, Sarah. "Infernal Poetics: Peter Weiss and the Problem of Postwar Authorship." *Germanic Review* 82, no. 2 (2007): 157–78.
Prager, Brad. "The Good German as Narrator: On W. G. Sebald and the Risks of Holocaust Writing." Special issue, *Memory and the Holocaust*, *New German Critique* 96 (Fall, 2005): 75–102.
Preece, Julian. "Günter Grass, His Jews and Their Critics: From Klüger and Gilman to Sebald and Prawer." In "Jews in German Literature since 1945: German-Jewish Literature?" *German Monitor* 53 (2000): 609–24.
———. "Kann die Nahrung Sünde sein? Schonkost und Festessen im Barock: Von Grimmelshausen zu Grass." In Neuhaus and Weyer, *Küchenzettel: Essen und Trinken im Werk von Günter Grass*, 95–107.
Puknus, Heinz. *Wolfgang Hildesheimer.* Munich: Beck, 1978.
Radden, Jennifer. "From Melancholic States to Clinical Depression." In Radden, *The Nature of Melancholy: From Aristotle to Kristeva*, 3–51.

———. *Moody Minds Distempered: Essays on Melancholy and Depression.* Oxford: Oxford University Press, 2009.

———. ed. *The Nature of Melancholy: From Aristotle to Kristeva.* Oxford: Oxford University Press, 2000.

Rector, Martin. "Fünfundzwanzig Jahre *Die Ästhetik des Widerstands*: Prolegomena zu einem Forschungsbericht." In *Diese bebende, zähe, kühne Hoffnung: 25 Jahre Peter Weiss Die Ästhetik des Widerstands*, edited by Arnd Beise, Jens Birkmeyer, and Michael Hofmann, 13–47. St. Ingbert, Germany: Röhrig, 2008.

Reed, Amy Louise. *The Background of Gray's Elegy: A Study in the Taste for Melancholy Poetry, 1700–1751.* New York: Russell & Russell, 1962.

Ribó, Ignasi. "The One-Winged Angel: History and Memory in the Literary Discourse of W. G. Sebald." *Orbis Litterarum* 64, no. 3 (2009): 222–62.

Riordan, Colin. "Ecocentrism in Sebald's '*After Nature*'." In Long and Whitehead, *W. G. Sebald: A Critical Companion*, 45–57.

Rodewald, Dierk, ed. *Über Wolfgang Hildesheimer.* Frankfurt am Main: Suhrkamp, 1971.

Rose, Gillian. *The Melancholy Science: An Introduction to the Thought of Theodor W. Adorno.* London: Macmillan, 1978.

Rose, William. *From Goethe to Byron: The Development of "Weltschmerz" in German Literature.* London: Routledge, 1924.

Rothenberg, Jürgen. *Günter Grass: Das Chaos in verbesserter Ausführung.* Heidelberg: Carl Winter Universitätsverlag, 1976.

Ruehl, Martin. "A Master from Germany: Thomas Mann, Albrecht Dürer, and the Making of a National Icon." *Oxford German Studies* 38, no. 1 (2009): 61–106.

Santner, Eric L. *Mourning, Memory, and Film in Postwar Germany.* Ithaca, NY: Cornell University Press, 1990.

———. *On Creaturely Life: Rilke, Benjamin, Sebald.* Chicago: University of Chicago Press, 2006.

Sartre, Jean Paul. *Nausea.* Translated by Robert Baldick, with an introduction by James Wood. London: Penguin, 2000.

Scheffer, Bernd. "Transposition und sprachlich erzeugte Situation: Zur dichterischen Verfahrensweise Wolfgang Hildesheimers." In Rodewald, *Über Wolfgang Hildesheimer*, 17–31.

Scheffler, Markus. *Kunsthaß im Grunde: Über Melancholie bei Arthur Schopenhauer und deren Verwendung in Thomas Bernhards Prosa.* Heidelberg: Winter, 2008.

Schiesari, Juliana. *The Gendering of Melancholia: Feminism, Psychoanalysis, and the Symbolics of Loss in Renaissance Literature.* Ithaca, NY: Cornell University Press, 1992.

Schings, Hans-Jürgen. *Melancholie und Aufklärung: Melancholie und ihre Kritiker in Erfahrungsseelenkunde des 18. Jahrhunderts.* Stuttgart: J. B. Metzler, 1977.

Schleiner, Winfried. *Melancholy, Genius, and Utopia in the Renaissance.* Wiesbaden: Harrasowitz, 1991.

Schley, Fridolin. *Kataloge der Wahrheit: Zur Inszenierung von Autorschaft bei W. G. Sebald*. Göttingen: Wallstein, 2012.

Schmitt, Maria C. *"Die Ästhetik des Widerstands": Studien zu Kontext, Struktur und Kunstverständnis*. St. Ingbert, Germany: Röhrig, 1986.

Schmitter, Sebastian. *Basis, Wahrnehmung und Konsequenz: Zur literarischen Präsenz des Melancholischen in den Schriften von Hugo von Hofmannsthal und Robert Musil*. Würzburg: Königshausen & Neumann, 2000.

Schnabel, Anja. *"Nicht ein Tag, an dem ich nicht an den Tod denke": Todesvorstellungen und Todesdarstellungen in Peter Weiss' Bildern und Schriften*. St. Ingbert, Germany: Röhrig, 2010.

Schoenfeldt, Michael. *Bodies and Selves in Early Modern England: Physiology and Inwardness in Spenser, Shakespeare, Herbert, and Milton*. Cambridge: Cambridge University Press, 1999.

Schopenhauer, Arthur. *Die Welt als Wille und Vorstellung in zwei Teilbänden*. Edited by Arthur Hübscher. Zurich: Diogenes, 1977.

Schulte, Susanne. *Standpunkt Ohnmacht: Studien zur Melancholie bei Günter Eich*. Hamburg: LIT, 1993.

Schuster, Peter-Klaus. "Das Bild der Bilder: Zur Wirkungsgeschichte von Dürers Melancholiekupferstich." *Idea: Jahrbuch der Hamburger Kunsthalle* 1 (1982): 72–134.

Schütte, Uwe. "'In einer wildfremden Gegend': W. G. Sebalds Essays über die österreichische Literatur." In *The Anatomist of Melancholy: Essays in Memory of W. G. Sebald*, edited by Rüdiger Görner, 63–74. Munich: Iudicum, 2003.

Schütz, Erhard. "Zweitgeschichte? Gegenwartsliteratur zwischen Vergangenheitsbewirtschaftung und Geschichtsermunterung." *Zeitschrift für Germanistik* 23, no. 3 (2013): 592–606.

Schwarz, Anette. *Melancholie: Figuren und Orte einer Stimmung*. Vienna: Passagen, 1996.

Screech, Michael A. *Montaigne and Melancholy: The Wisdom of the Essays*. London: Duckworth, 1983.

Sebald, W. G. *Die Ausgewanderten: Vier lange Erzählungen*. Frankfurt am Main: Fischer, 1994.

———. *Austerlitz*. Frankfurt am Main: Fischer, 2001.

———. *Die Beschreibung des Unglücks: Zur österreichischen Literatur von Stifter bis Handke*. Vienna: Residenz, 1985.

———. "Konstruktionen der Trauer: Günter Grass und Wolfgang Hildesheimer." In *Campo Santo*, edited by Sven Meyer, 101–27. Munich: Hanser, 2003.

———. "Konstruktionen der Trauer: Günter Grass und Wolfgang Hildesheimer." *Der Deutschunterricht* 35, no. 5 (1983): 32–46.

———. *Luftkrieg und Literatur: Mit einem Essay über Alfred Andersch*. Munich: Carl Hanser, 1999.

———. *Nach der Natur: Ein Elementargedicht*. Frankfurt am Main: Fischer, 1995.

———. *Die Ringe des Saturn: Eine englische Wallfahrt*. Frankfurt am Main: Fischer, 1997.
———. *Schwindel. Gefühle*. Frankfurt am Main: Fischer, 2003.
Sickels, Eleanor M. *The Gloomy Egoist: Moods and Themes of Melancholy from Gray to Keats*. New York: Columbia University Press, 1932.
Sillem, Peter. "'der du gedeihen läßt und zerstörst': Melancholie, Karneval und die zwei Gesichter des Saturn." *Zeitsprünge: Forschungen zur Frühen Neuzeit* 5, no. 1/2 (2001): 9–23.
———. *Melancholie oder vom Glück, unglücklich zu sein: Ein Lesebuch*. Munich: DTV, 1997.
———. ed. "Saturns Spuren: Aspekte des Wechselspiels von Melancholie und Volkskultur in der Frühen Neuzeit." *Zeitsprünge: Forschungen zur Frühen Neuzeit* 5, no. 1/2 (2001).
Söllner, Alfons. "Peter Weiss' *Die Ermittlung* in zeitgeschichtlicher Perspektive." In *Deutsche Nachkriegsliteratur und der Holocaust*, edited by Stephan Braese, Holger Gehle, Doron Kiesel, and Hanno Loewy, 99–128. Frankfurt am Main: Campus, 1998.
Sontag, Susan. *Illness as Metaphor and AIDS and Its Metaphors*. London: Penguin, 1991.
Stallmann, Klaus. "'Von der Beschaffenheit des Abgrunds': Nachwort zu den Gesprächen mit Günter Grass." In Grass, *Günter Grass: Werkausgabe in zehn Bänden*, 370–87.
Stanley, Patricia H. "Sum, ergo spero? Wolfgang Hildesheimer's Tentative Absurd Hope." *Seminar* 31, no. 1 (1995): 50–65.
———. *Wolfgang Hildesheimer and His Critics*. Rochester, NY: Camden House, 1993.
Starobinski, Jean. *Histoire du traitement de la mélancolie des origines à 1900*. Basel: Acta psychosomatica, 1960.
———. "L'encre de la mélancolie." In *Mélancolie: Génie et folie en occident*, edited by Jean Clair, 24–30. Paris: Gallimard, 2005. Exhibition catalogue.
Steinmann, Holger. "Zitatruinen unterm Hundsstern: W. G. Sebalds Ansichten von der Nachtseite der Philologie." In Niehaus and Öhlschläger, *W. G. Sebald: Politische Archäologie und melancholische Bastelei*, 145–56.
Stolz, Dieter. *Vom privaten Motivkomplex zum poetischen Weltentwurf: Konstanten und Entwicklungen im literarischen Werk von Günter Grass (1956–1986)*. Würzburg: Königshausen & Neumann, 1994.
Taberner, Stuart. *Distorted Reflections: The Public and Private Uses of the Author in the Work of Uwe Johnson, Günther Grass, and Martin Walser, 1965–1975*. Amsterdam: Rodopi, 1998.
———. "German Nostalgia? Remembering German-Jewish Life in W. G. Sebald's *Die Ausgewanderten* and *Austerlitz*." Special issue on W. G. Sebald, *Germanic Review* 3 (2004): 181–202.
———, ed. *The Novel in German since 1990*. Cambridge: Cambridge University Press, 2011.

Taberner, Stuart, and Karina Berger, eds. *Germans as Victims in the Literary Fiction of the Berlin Republic*. Rochester, NY: Camden House, 2009.
Tellenbach, Hubertus. *Melancholie: Problemgeschichte, Endogenitaet, Typologie, Pathogenese, Klinik; Mit einem Exkurs in die manisch-melancholische Region*. Berlin: Springer, 1961.
———. *Melancholy: History of the Problem, Endogeneity, Typology, Pathogenesis, Clinical Considerations*. Translated by Erling Eng. Pittsburgh, PA: Duquesne University Press, 1980.
Teresa of Avila. "Melancholy Nuns." In Radden, *The Nature of Melancholy: From Aristotle to Kristeva*, 109–17.
Theissen, Bianca. "A Natural History of Destruction: W. G. Sebald's The Rings of Saturn." *Modern Language Notes* 121 (2006): 563–81.
Theunissen, Michael. *Vorentwürfe von Moderne: Antike Melancholie und die Acedia des Mittelalters*. Berlin: de Gruyter, 1996.
Tiedemann, Rolf, ed. *Theodor W. Adorno: Gesammelte Schriften*. 20 vols. Frankfurt am Main: Suhrkamp, 1977.
Torok, Maria. "The Illness of Mourning and the Fantasy of the Exquisite Corpse." In Abraham and Torok, *The Shell and the Kernel*, 107–24.
Tuchel, Johannes. "Das Ende der Legenden: Die Rote Kapelle im Widerstand gegen den Nationalsozialismus." In *Der 20. Juli: Das andere Deutschland in der Vergangenheitspolitik*, edited by Gerd R. Ueberschär, 347–65. Berlin: Elefanten Press, 1998.
Turner, Graham. *British Cultural Studies: An Introduction*. London: Routledge, 2002.
Ure, Michael. "Sympathy for the Devil." In *On Jean Améry: Philosophy of Catastrophe*, edited by Magdalena Zolkos, 235–62. Plymouth, UK: Lexington, 2011.
Valk, Thorsten. *Melancholie im Werk Goethes: Genese—Symtomatik—Therapie*. Tübingen: Niemeyer, 2002.
Van Ingen, Ferdinand. *Vanitas und Memento Mori in der deutschen Barocklyrik*. Groningen, Netherlands: J. B. Wolters, 1966.
Van Reijen, Willem, ed. *Allegorie und Melancholie*. Frankfurt am Main: Suhrkamp, 1992.
———. "Einleitung." In van Reijen, *Allegorie und Melancholie*, 7–16.
Vogt, Jochen. *Peter Weiss*. Hamburg: Rowohlt, 1987.
Völker, Ludwig, ed. *"Komm, heilige Melancholie": Eine Anthologie deutscher Melancholie-Gedichte*. Stuttgart: Reclam, 1983.
———. *Muse Melancholie—Therapeutikum Poesie: Studien zum Melancholie-Problem in der deutschen Lyrik von Hölty bis Benn*. Munich: Fink, 1978.
Von Engelhardt, Dietrich, Horst-Jürgen Gerigk, Guido Pressler, and Wolfram Schmitt, eds. *Melancholie in Literatur und Kunst*. Hürtgenwald, Germany: Guido Pressler, 1990.
Wagner, Isabel. *Textklänge und Bildspuren: Zur musikalischen Selbstreflexivität im Werk von Wolfgang Hildesheimer*. PhD dissertation, Queen Mary University of London, 2012.

Wagner-Egelhaaf, Martina. *Die Melancholie der Literatur: Diskursgeschichte und Textfiguration.* Stuttgart: Metzler, 1997.
Wallenborn, Markus. "Tell us what the children eat . . . Kinderlose Mütter und mutterlose Kinder im 'Butt.'" In Neuhaus and Weyer, *Küchenzettel: Essen und Trinken im Werk von Günter Grass*, 109–21.
Walter, Lutz, ed. *Melancholie.* Leipzig: Reclam, 1999.
Warburg, Aby. *Heidnisch-antike Weissagung in Wort und Bild zu Luthers Zeiten.* Heidelberg: Sitzungsberichte der Heidelberger Akademie, 1920.
Watanabe-O'Kelly, Helen. *Melancholie und die melancholische Landschaft: Ein Beitrag zur Geistesgeschichte des 17. Jahrhunderts.* Bern: Francke, 1978.
Weber, Andrew. *Günter Grass's Use of Baroque Literature.* London: W. S. Maney & Son, 1995.
Wegmann, Nikolaus. *Diskurse der Empfindsamkeit: Zur Geschichte eines Gefühls in der Literatur des 18. Jahrhunderts.* Stuttgart: J. B. Metzler, 1984.
Weigel, Sigrid. "'Generation as a Symbolic Form': On the Genealogical Discourse of Memory since 1945." *Germanic Review* 77 (2002): 264–77.
Weiss, Peter. *Abschied von den Eltern.* Frankfurt am Main: Suhrkamp, 1961.
———. *Die Ästhetik des Widerstands: Roman.* Frankfurt am Main: Suhrkamp, 1983.
———. *Die Ermittlung.* Frankfurt am Main: Suhrkamp, 1965.
———. *Fluchtpunkt.* Frankfurt am Main: Suhrkamp, 1962.
———. "Gespräch über Dante." In *Rapporte*, 142–69.
———. *Hölderlin.* Frankfurt am Main: Suhrkamp, 1971.
———. "Laokoon oder Über die Grenzen der Sprache." In *Rapporte*, 170–86.
———. "Manfred Haiduk im Gespräch mit Peter Weiss über *Die Ästhetik des Widerstands.*" In Gerlach and Richter, *Peter Weiss im Gespräch*, 208–15.
———. "Meine Ortschaft." In *Rapporte*, 113–24.
———. *Notizbücher, 1960–1971.* 2 vols. Frankfurt am Main: Suhrkamp, 1982.
———. *Notizbücher, 1971–1980.* 2 vols. Frankfurt am Main: Suhrkamp, 1981.
———. *Peter Weiss: Die Notizbücher; Kritische Gesamtausgabe*, ed. Jürgen Schutte, Wiebke Amthor, and Jenny Willner. CD-Rom. Berlin: Digitale Bibliothek, 2007.
———. *Rapporte.* Frankfurt am Main: Suhrkamp, 1968.
———. *Rapporte 2.* Frankfurt am Main: Suhrkamp, 1971.
———. *Rekonvaleszenz.* Frankfurt am Main: Suhrkamp, 1991.
———. "Vorübungen zum dreiteiligen Drama divina commedia." In *Rapporte*, 125–41.
———. "10 Arbeitspunkte eines Autors in der geteilten Welt." In *Rapporte 2*, 14–23. Frankfurt am Main: Suhrkamp, 1971.
———. "Zwischen Pergamon und Plötzensee oder die andere Darstellung der Verläufe: Peter Weiss im Gespräch mit Burkhardt Lindner." In Gerlach and Richter, *Peter Weiss im Gespräch*, 263–89.

Wenzel, Siegried. *The Sin of Sloth: Acedia in Medieval Thought and Literature*. Chapel Hill: University of North Carolina Press, 1960.
Wetzel, Heinz. "Namen in Hildesheimers *Masante*: 'Schall und Rauch' oder 'Schachte des Schreckens?'" *Seminar* 15 (1979): 148–62.
Wheeler, Kathleen, ed. *German Aesthetic and Literary Criticism: The Romantic Ironists and Goethe*. Cambridge: Cambridge University Press, 1984.
Wilms, Winfried. "Taboo and Repression in W. G. Sebald's *On the Natural History of Destruction*." In Long and Whitehead, *W. G. Sebald: A Critical Companion*, 175–89.
Wilson, Eric. G. *Against Happiness: In Praise of Melancholy*. New York: Farrar, Straus, & Giroux, 2008.
Wirtz, Thomas. "Schwarze Zuckerwatte: Anmerkungen zu W. G. Sebald." *Merkur* 6 (2001): 530–34.
Wittkower, Rudolf, and Margot Wittkower. *Born under Saturn: The Character and Conduct of Artists; A Documented History from Antiquity to the French Revolution*. London: Weidenfeld & Nicolson, 1963.
Zeller, Franz. "Hölderlin in der *Ästhetik des Widerstands*." In Höller, "*Hinter jedem Wort die Gefahr des Verstummens*": *Sprachproblematik und literarische Tradition in der "Ästhetik des Widerstands*," 79–102.
Zilcosky, John. "Lost and Found: Disorientation, Nostalgia, and Holocaust Melodrama in Sebald's *Austerlitz*." *Modern Language Notes* 121, no. 3 (2006): 679–98.
Zimmerer, Jürgen. "The Birth of the *Ostland* out of the Spirit of Colonialism: A Postcolonial Perspective on the Nazi Policy of Conquest and Extermination." *Patterns of Prejudice* 39 (2005): 197–219.
Zimmermann, Harro. "Skepsis und Melancholie: Über das Lichtenbergische bei Günter Grass." *Die Horen* 44, no. 1 (1999): 126–40.
Žižek, Slavoj. "Melancholy and the Act." *Critical Inquiry* 26 (2000): 657–81.

Index

Abel, 96
absence, constitutive, 2, 4, 6, 21, 22; of authentic feeling, 187–88; from historical event, 103–4; and loss, 85–87, 92–93, 155, 194
absurd, 3, 79, 82–84, 86–94, 98, 100, 103–5, 107, 148, 196
acedia, 16, 22, 32, 49, 51–53, 57–58, 79, 81–82, 94–99, 102–3, 108–9, 174, 185, 187–89, 191–97, 199. *See also* boredom; *ennui*; sloth; *taedium vitae*
Adorno, Theodor W., 2, 8, 24–25, 83–84, 91, 107, 185, 200; works by: *Jargon der Eigentlichkeit*, 185, 200; "Kulturkritik und Gesellschaft," 25, 107
affect, 5, 18, 20–21, 64, 67–68, 100, 103, 113–19, 122, 124–26, 128, 135–36, 138, 141, 145, 152–54, 157, 160–62, 179, 181–82, 186–88, 191, 193–96, 198–99. *See also* emotion
Agamben, Giorgio, 10, 22, 32–33, 73, 194, 200; works by: *Homo Sacer*, 73; *Stanzas*, 32, 33, 200
ahistoricism, 84
Alkyoneus, 127–28
allegory, 6, 41, 45, 47, 49–50, 60–67, 72, 74, 96, 98, 113, 119, 124, 170
Allied area bombings, 148
ambivalence, 6, 14, 19, 51, 54, 82, 85, 92–93, 110, 114, 121, 129, 145, 155–56, 160, 198–99
Améry, Jean, 6, 26, 66, 69, 80, 105–6; works by: "Ressentiments," 74, 105, 108–9, 80. *See also ressentiment*

amnesia, 60, 80, 92, 113, 136, 139, 198
amor vacui, 91
anthropology, 154
anti-fascist resistance, 110, 120, 126, 128, 134, 136–37, 141
antiquity, 7–10, 15–17, 25, 31, 68, 110, 188, 192
APO (*Außerparlamentarische Opposition, die*, West Germany), 52
Aquinas, Thomas, 189
Aristotle, 8, 10, 28–29, 32, 109, 144, 181; pseudo-Aristotle, 10, 14–17, 29, 99, 137, 150, 188; works by: *Aristotle: Problems II, Books XXII–XXXVIII*, 16, 29, 32, 109, 144
art history, 12
asceticism, 16, 48, 94–95, 98, 100, 102, 196. *See also* Christianity; desert monasticism
Assmann, Aleida, 154, 182; works by: *Der lange Schatten der Vergangenheit*, 182
astrology, 9, 12, 17, 147
astronomy, 49, 78, 88, 94, 99, 164, 174–75
Augustine, 100
Aurach, Max, 169, 175
Auschwitz, 1–5, 7, 9–10, 13–14, 24–25, 37, 72, 80–81, 83–85, 88, 92–93, 107, 140, 186–87, 191–96. *See also* Final Solution; Holocaust
Austin, J. L., 4, 26; works by: *How to Do Things with Words*, 26
Austrian literature, 30, 145, 149, 167
authenticity, 21, 143, 154, 157; jargon of, 185–86, 193, 196. *See also* Adorno, Theodor W.

autobiography, 35–36, 38–39, 65–66, 72, 74, 104, 140–43, 183

Bachmann, Ingeborg, 10, 28–29, 105, 122, 143; works by: *Das Buch Franza*, 29, 143

baroque, 11, 13, 16, 30, 38, 60, 69; baroque allegory, 60, 63, 74; baroque literature, 70–71, 73, 78–79; baroque tragic drama, 11, 30, 60. See also allegory; Benjamin, Walter; melancholy

Barthes, Roland, 188, 193, 200; works by: *Wie zusammen leben*, 200

Barzilai, Maja, 161, 163, 181, 183

Baumgart, Reinhard, 81, 106

Benjamin, Walter, 11, 22, 29, 30–31, 33, 60–63, 74, 108, 144, 145–46, 165, 169, 179, 181, 183; works by: "Linke Melancholie," 33; *Das Passagenwerk*, 74; *Ursprung des deutschen Trauerspiels*, 29–30, 33, 74, 108–9, 144, 146, 179, 183

bereavement, 18, 122

bereavement exclusion, 27. See also *DSM V*

Berlin Republic, 10, 24, 185–87, 192, 194–97

Bible, 96–97, 103, 175

Bingen, Hildegard of, 52, 73; works by: "Melancholia in Men and Women," 73

biography, 31, 35, 37, 45, 64, 67, 72, 83, 95, 102, 104, 106, 108–9, 140, 149, 192, 195

biology, 16, 32, 44, 47–48, 55–56, 119, 195

biopolitics, 55, 73

Bischoff, Lotte, 121, 141–42

black bile, 15–17, 52–53, 78, 99, 110–11, 119, 121, 168, 188, 192. See also humoral theory; temperaments, theory of

Blamberger, Günter, 13, 24, 28, 30–31, 71, 82, 105–6, 108

Böhme, Hartmut, 6, 27, 31, 49, 63, 70, 72, 74, 108, 143, 183–84; works by: *Albrecht Dürer: Melencolia I*, 27, 183; (with Peter Matussek and Lothar Müller) *Orientierung Kulturwissenschaften*, 31; "Zur literarischen Rezeption von Albrecht Dürers Kupferstich," 27, 70, 143

Bohrer, Karl-Heinz, 84, 88, 107–8

Bond, Greg, 152, 181

boredom, 95, 98, 108, 186, 191. See also *acedia*; *ennui*; *sloth*; *taedium vitae*

Boye, Karin, 113, 117, 121, 124–27, 129, 131–32

Braese, Stephan, 81–82, 84, 104, 106–7, 140

Brandt, Willy, 36

Braun, Rebecca, 45, 66, 70, 72, 74

Brook, Peter, 159, 182. See also melodrama

Browne, Thomas, 145, 166, 178

Burton, Robert, 7, 17, 27, 32, 35–36, 38, 40–41, 53, 58–59, 63, 68, 70–71, 73; works by: *The Anatomy of Melancholy*, 7, 27, 32, 35, 68, 70–71, 73–74, 176. See also melancholy

caesura in representation, 1–2, 78–79, 83–84, 93, 112, 124, 191. See also Holocaust; *Zivilisationsbruch*

Cain, 96–97, 103, 109

Canis Major, 165

capitalism, 48, 63, 113, 135, 145, 153, 162, 164–65, 170–73, 177–78, 183–84. See also world systems analysis

carnival, 51–53, 59, 73

castration, 100, 128; castration anxiety, 124, 127, 143, 163

Cheynes, George, 78; works by: *The English Malady*, 78

Christian Democrats, 36, 57

Christianity, 13, 16, 57, 79, 81, 94, 100, 102–3, 140, 185, 187, 191. See also asceticism; desert monasticism

Chronos, 17, 121, 167–68

citationality, 4–5, 7, 37–38, 94, 188, 191. *See also* conventionality; iterability; performative
Cold War, 36, 80
colonialism, 169–70, 183–84
commemoration, literary, 1–2, 9, 49, 189–91; ethics of, 50, 79, 149, 160, 186, 196; Holocaust, 192, 192
communism, 113, 115, 120
Communist Party, 113, 120, 141
Conrad, Joseph, 170
contingency, 84, 90, 92
conventionality, 4, 8, 21, 24, 60, 63–64, 135, 155–58, 188, 199. *See also* citationality; iterability; performative
Coppi, Hans, 120
Cultural Studies, 12, 30–31

Dakyns, Janine, 162–63, 168–69
Dame Melancholy, 11, 200
dandy, 3, 26
Dante, 117–19, 139–40, 142, 156
Danzig, 39, 44–48, 72
Davis, Mike, 177, 184
de Man, Paul, 61, 64, 74; works by: "The Rhetoric of Temporality," 74
decadence, 81, 83, 95, 98. See also *fin-de-siècle*
deconstruction, 2, 4–6, 197
demon of noontide, 16, 94, 96, 98–99, 108–9
demonic possession, 14, 16, 40
depression, 8–9, 12, 16–18, 27–29, 31–33, 43–44, 53, 63, 70, 85, 105, 107; endogenous, 18, 126; female, 50, 53, 110, 114, 116–17, 119, 122–24, 126, 130–32, 138, 144, 151, 162, 164; manic, 16, 43. *See also* melancholy
Derrida, Jacques, 4–6, 26–27; works by: *Limited Inc.*, 26–27; *Without Alibi*, 26
desert monasticism, 79, 94–97, 99, 103, 187. *See also* asceticism; Christianity

desertification, 169, 173, 177. *See also* environment; flooding; weather systems
deus absconditus, 79, 105. *See also* baroque
Diner, Dan, 2, 25, 182. *See also* negative symbiosis; *Zivilisationsbruch*
Dionysian, 57–58, 101–3
Dog Star, 165
drought-famine, 177. *See also* environment; Holocaust: late Victorian
DSM IV, 27–28, 32
DSM V, 27
Dunker, Axel, 1–2, 25, 143
Dürer, Albrecht, 3, 26–27, 29, 36, 70, 72, 74, 78, 114, 143, 162, 183–84, 198. See also *Melencolia I*
Dutch East Indies Company, 171

early modern period, 12–13, 17, 40–41, 49, 151
Ecker, Gisela, 11, 29, 160, 182
ecocentrism, 177–78, 184. *See also* environment
ecstasy, 41, 43, 52, 54, 73, 113
Edict of Nantes, 38
Ekel, 43–44, 53, 56, 62, 71, 100; *Ekel-Erkenntnis*, 57, 59
ekphrasis, 162
Eliot, T. S., 191, 200; works by: "The Love Song of J. Alfred Prufrock," 191, 200
Elizabethan period, 17, 33, 57, 79, 105, 187, 198
emotion, 6, 8, 18–19, 21, 23, 29, 60, 80, 86, 99, 113, 115–16, 122, 125, 136, 138, 140–41, 145, 150, 154, 157–62, 186–87, 190, 193, 198. *See also* affect
empathy, 4, 20, 53, 58, 96, 99, 110, 112, 114, 116, 119, 134–37, 153, 160, 176, 186, 190. *See also* mimesis
Empfindsamkeit, 153–54, 181–82. *See also* enthusiasm; melancholy: sweet; *Schwärmer*, sentimentality

Enlightenment, 22, 31, 35–36, 38–39, 48, 70, 146, 154, 157–58, 179
ennui, 95, 97–98, 100, 104, 108–9. See also *acedia*; boredom; sloth; *taedium vitae*
enthusiasm, 71, 137, 154, 158, 181. See also *Empfindsamkeit*; melancholy: sweet; *Schwärmer*; sentimentality
environment, 23, 153, 163, 165, 167–68, 173, 177–78. See also desertification; drought-famine; ecocentrism; flooding; weather systems
epistemology, 2, 6, 12, 17, 44, 63, 88–89, 91, 93–94, 123, 157, 162–65, 175–76, 178
Eros, 82, 106, 108
Eshel, Amir, 172, 179, 183
exhaustion, 134, 136, 144
exile, 35, 76, 80, 104, 112, 114, 120, 126–27, 140, 179
Existentialism, 13, 105

fall of man, 52–53, 57, 59, 62–63, 96–97, 99–100, 196. See also *acedia*; Cain; Christianity
fanaticism, 70, 99, 154
fascism, 113, 116, 121, 137, 143
Ficino, Marsilio, 17, 32, 122, 162; works by: *Three Books on Life*, 32
Final Solution, 47, 128, 133–36. See also Auschwitz; Holocaust
fin-de-siècle, 95, 145. See also decadence
First World War, 178
Fitzgerald, Edward, 166, 170
Flaubert, Gustave, 26, 169
flooding, 49, 120, 168–69, 177, 183. See also desertification; environment; weather systems
Foucault, Michel, 143, 157, 162, 182; works by: *Discipline and Punish*, 182; *The History of Sexuality, Volume I*, 143; *Madness and Civilization*, 182
Frankfurt School, 2
French Revolution, 9, 25

Freud, Sigmund, 4, 10, 18–21, 26, 29, 33, 85, 93, 98, 99, 100, 103, 107–9, 112, 139, 143, 145, 150, 179, 181; works by: "Trauer und Melancholie," 4, 10, 18–21, 26, 29, 33, 85, 99–100, 103, 107, 109, 112, 139, 145, 150, 179, 181; "Über Deckerinnerungen," 108; "Das Unbehagen in der Kultur," 109; "Das Unheimliche," 143
Fuchs, Anne, 34, 146–47, 177, 178–82, 184

Gadamer, Hans Georg, 61, 74; works by: *Wahrheit und Methode*, 74
Galen, 15
Ge, 127–28, 131, 135
gender, 9–11, 23, 29, 32, 50, 56, 72, 96, 99–101, 110, 114–15, 117–18, 122–24, 126, 128–30, 132, 134, 136, 139, 161, 163, 191, 196–200. See also under memory
generation, 37, 42, 70, 180, 191, 195; student, 39, 41, 51
Genesis, 96
genocide, 23, 86, 90, 100, 111, 124, 129, 136, 148, 162, 177–78, 184, 199
geometry, 88–89, 91, 94, 166, 174–76, 183–84
German self-hatred, 160, 193
German Studies, 12
German-Jews, 1, 71, 79, 86, 94, 101, 103–4, 140, 146, 182
Gestapo, 120
Ghent, Henry of, 89, 108
globalization, 23, 153, 170
Goethe, Johann Wolfgang von, 73–74, 108, 154, 181–82; works by: *Die Leiden des jungen Werther*, 154
Goll-Bickmann, Dieter, 82, 106
Grand Coalition, 36, 52
Grass, Günter, works by: *Aus dem Tagebuch einer Schnecke*, 6–7, 11, 26, 29, 35–75, 104, 109, 122, 147; *Beim Häuten der Zwiebel*, 23, 34, 35–70; *Die Blechtrommel*, 74; *Die bösen Köche*, 69; *Der*

Butt, 69–70, 73; *Im Krebsgang*, 74; *Kopfgeburten oder die Deutschen sterben aus*, 72; "Die melancholische Koalition," 36, 69; *örtlich betäubt*, 73; "Rede über das Selbstverständliche," 71; *Schreiben nach Auschwitz*, 72; *Das Treffen in Telgte*, 69; "Über die Toleranz," 36, 68; "Unser Grundübel ist der Idealismus," 70; "Vom mangelnden Selbstvertrauen der schreibenden Hofnarren," 71; "Vom Stillstand im Fortschritt," 69
grief, 10, 19, 28, 44, 51, 103–4. See also mourning; *Trauer*
grotesque, 41, 50, 55, 135, 169, 197
Guillaume Affair, 36
guilt: German, 3, 20, 44, 59, 77, 88, 93, 103, 149, 160, 186–87, 191, 193–95 (*see also* perpetrator); survivor, 7, 23, 79, 86, 94, 98, 99–101, 103, 118, 198 (*see also* Holocaust)
Gumbrecht, Hans Ulrich, 33, 197, 200
Graveyard Poets, 43, 71

Hades, 118, 167
Hamlet, 1, 3, 8, 10, 24, 28, 57–58, 73, 77–79, 81–82, 86, 94, 98–101, 103–5, 108–9, 187, 191, 198
Hanika, Iris, works by: *Das Eigentliche*, 24, 185–200
Harnack, Arvid, 120
Hegel, Friedrich, 39–40, 43–44, 55, 62, 70–71, 181; works by: *Briefe von und an Hegel, 1785–1812*, 71
Heilmann, Horst, 120, 125, 128, 137, 139, 144
Hell, Julia, 139–40, 144, 151, 181–82
Henri IV, 35, 68
Heracles / Hercules, 16, 125, 128–29, 137
Herbeck, Ernst, 149–50, 157, 166
Hesse, Hermann, 119
Hildesheimer, Wolfgang, works by: "Antworten über *Tynset*," 104; "Arbeitsprotokolle des Verfahrens 'Marbot'," 108; "Bleibt Dürer Dürer?" 108; "Büchners Melancholie," 108; "Das Ende der Fiktionen," 106; "Hamlet," 24, 105; "Ich kann über nichts schreiben als über ein potentielles Ich," 104; *Interpretationen: James Joyce, Georg Büchner; Zwei Frankfurter Vorlesungen*, 107; *Marbot*, 95, 102, 106–9; *Mary Stuart*, 107; *Masante*, 7, 23, 76–109, 111, 180, 187, 200; "Mein Judentum," 104; *Mozart*; "Die Subjektivität des Biographen," 108; *Tynset*, 7, 23, 76–109, 111, 180, 187, 200; "Über das absurde Theater," 105; "Vergebliche Aufzeichnungen," 24, 105
Hippocrates, 15, 53; works by: *Corpus Hippocraticum*, 15
Hitler, 20, 26
Hitler Youth, 37
Hofmannsthal, Hugo von, 95, 108; works by: "Ein Brief," 95, 108
Hölderlin, 118–19, 142
Holocaust, 39, 64, 66, 84, 88, 100, 110, 114, 124, 129, 135, 144, 146, 160, 178, 186, 193–94; gendered memory of, 117, 125, 129–30, 163, 196–98; historical event of, 7, 22, 66, 83, 103, 111, 147–48, 158, 178, 187, 193–94; imagination after, 89–92, 95, 97, 125, 193–94, 196; Jewish memory of, 66, 160; knowability of, 91, 93, 133, 136; late Victorian, 177, 184; memory of, 10–11, 18, 26, 28, 42, 49–50, 59, 79, 86, 101, 107, 110–11, 113, 117, 124, 137–39, 150, 153, 160, 180, 186–88, 191–92, 194–95, 198; post-Holocaust affect, 20–21, 117, 187, 195–96, 198; post-Holocaust literary work, 83, 142; post-Holocaust memory, 18–23, 33, 50, 68, 78, 122, 136, 145, 155, 191, 195–96; post-Holocaust world, 8, 19, 90, 93–94; pre-Holocaust

Holocaust—*(cont'd)*
world, 5, 24; representation of, 1–2, 7, 12, 42, 77–79, 82–85, 93, 110–12, 114, 119, 129, 132, 147; survivors of, 6–7, 22, 23, 66, 77, 79, 80, 94, 103, 190, 198; testimony, 25, 133; travesty, 33; uniqueness, 139; victims of, 3–4, 6, 25, 37, 51, 54, 59, 77, 79–80, 82, 86, 101, 103, 111, 113, 116, 122, 124, 127, 129, 136, 140, 149, 152, 167, 188, 193; witnessing of, 113, 131. *See also* Auschwitz; caesura; commemoration; Final Solution; memory; remembrance; *Vergangenheitsbewältigung*
homme intérieur, 100
homo melancholicus, 3, 190
homo timiditas, 190
Hopkins, Terence, 172, 183–84
Huguenots, 35, 38
Humanities, 12–13, 30, 116
humoral theory, 15–17, 41, 52, 99, 111, 168. *See also* black bile; temperaments: theory of
Huyssen, Andreas, 146, 180
Hydra, 128–29, 135
hysteria, 157–58

iconography, 12, 36, 78, 88, 96–97, 120, 145–47, 151, 160, 187, 199. *See also* melancholy
iconological method, 9, 11–12
idealism, 39, 45, 59, 68, 70, 73
idée fixe, 111
identification, 19, 21, 55, 97, 112–14, 116, 135, 137, 155, 158, 160, 178, 182, 191, 198. *See also* empathy; mimesis
ideology, 39, 42–43, 51–52, 54, 84, 123, 185, 200
idleness, 41, 69, 88, 95, 98, 101–2, 175, 186
Iliad, 167
imperium, 171
inability to mourn, 53, 66–67, 107, 122, 135, 149, 151. *See also*

Mitscherlich, Alexander, and Margarete Mitscherlich
insanity, 15, 40–41, 127, 133, 182; manic-depressive, 16. *See also* madness
insomnia, 76, 81, 93, 100
introjection, 19–20, 33, 141
irrationality, 22, 91, 132, 154, 157–58, 161
iterability, 4–5, 64. *See also* citationality; conventionality; and performative

Jargon, 185, 193, 200. *See also* Adorno, Theodor W.; authenticity
Jaspers, Karl, 3, 25, 103, 109; works by: *Philosophische Logik I*, 25, 109; *Die Schuldfrage*, 25
Jens, Walter, 1–5, 11, 24, 28, 78, 89, 100, 105–6, 108–9; works by: *Herr Meister*, 1–5, 8, 11, 24, 78, 89, 105, 108–9; "Melancholie und Moral," 28

Kafka, Franz, 155
Klibansky, Raymond, 12, 25, 29, 31, 37, 88, 94–95, 117, 122, 174, 176, 183; works by: (with Erwin Panofsky and Fritz Saxl) *Saturn und Melancholie*, 12, 25, 29, 31, 37, 88, 94–95, 117, 122, 174, 176, 183. *See also* Panofsky, Erwin; Saxl, Fritz
Koeppen, Wolfgang, 6, 28
Kraepelin, Emil, 15, 18, 143
Kristeva, Julia, 6, 10, 22, 27, 32–33, 114, 141; works by: *Black Sun*, 27, 33, 141

LaCapra, Dominick, 2, 20–22, 25–26, 33, 85, 107, 141, 154, 182, 200; works by, *Writing History, Writing Trauma*, 20, 25–26, 33, 107, 141
laesa imaginatio, 40
language crisis, 79
language skepticism, 79, 112
Laokoon, 118–19, 139, 140, 142
Lawlor, Clark, 10, 28–29, 31–32
Lenz, Siegfried, 25, 42, 45

Lepenies, Wolfgang, 26, 29, 68, 72, 98, 108–9, 146, 179; works by: *Melancholie und Gesellschaft*, 26, 30, 68, 109, 179
Levene, Mark, 177, 184
Leverkühn, Adrian, 6, 26, 42
Levi, Primo, 25, 86, 107; works by: *The Drowned and the Saved*, 107
Lichtenberg, Georg Christoph, 38, 43, 47, 70
Long, J. J., 92, 107–8, 153, 157, 162, 179–84
Loquai, Franz, 24, 30–31, 103, 105, 108–9, 179
loss, 6, 18–22, 29, 44, 92–93, 116, 119, 155, 189, 191, 193–94; concrete/historical loss, 22, 85, 92, 147, 149; loss of sadness, 27, 33; male loss, 10–11; narrative of, 85–87; pseudo-loss, 22. *See also* absence
Lord Chandos, 95, 108
lost object, 6, 18–19, 22, 79, 84, 86, 101, 103, 112–13, 125, 155, 194–96
Loxley, James, 4–5, 8, 26–27
Luther, Martin, 42, 79, 154

madness, 41, 112, 115, 119, 132–37, 142–43, 165, 182; feminine, 123; melancholy, 99; sweet, 43. *See also* insanity; mania; mental illness
Maier, Charles S., 22, 33, 141
mania, 17, 137, 139, 150, 189. *See also* insanity; madness; mental illness
Mann, Heinrich, 35, 68; works by: *Die Jugend des Königs Henri Quatre*, 68
Mann, Thomas, 6, 26, 42; works by: *Doktor Faustus*, 47, 26, 42, 71
Marxism, 120, 139
Mason, Ann L., 42, 69, 71, 73
mathematics, 89, 91–92, 94, 108, 174
medicine, 12, 15–16, 123, 129, 150; Greek, 12, 35
melancholia, 9, 27–29, 31–33, 70, 72, 122, 140, 144, 181, 200
melancholy: affect, 67; allegorist, 62, 64–65; *Anatomy of Melancholy*, 7, 27, 32, 35, 68, 70–71, 73–74, 176 (*see also* Burton, Robert); artist, 38, 50, 95, 151; autumnal, 37; baroque, 11, 38, 78, 92; Christianity and, 13, 16, 79, 185; defeatist, 149; dialectics, 17, 30, 32, 34, 77, 89, 105, 122, 150, 181, 198; discourse, 1–12, 21, 23, 29, 35, 37, 45, 77, 81–82, 122, 148, 161, 180, 189, 192; divine, 41; Elizabethan, 17, 33, 57, 187, 198; endogenous, 67 (*see also* depression); enthusiast, 154, 181 (*see also* enthusiasm); food, 40, 56; Freud and, 103, 112, 145 (*see also* Freud, Sigmund); gender and, 10–11, 32, 50, 72, 100–101, 110, 117, 122–24, 161, 191, 196–98 (*see also* gender); genial, 8–9, 23, 41–42, 57, 77, 79, 138, 188–89; genius, 7–8, 12, 17, 37, 40, 42, 50, 52, 58, 95, 114, 116, 121–22, 124, 130, 138, 160, 163–64, 185, 187–89 (*see also Vergangenheitsbewältigung*: genius of); graveyard, 37; hermit's, 185; heroic, 17, 122–23; humor, 99; icon, 4–5, 49, 78, 166, 198–99; iconography, 36, 88, 145–47, 151, 160, 199; intellectual history of, 12, 14, 18, 31, 36, 122; landscape, 49, 72; literary, 2, 13, 198; love, 37, 52, 70; madness, 99; and mourning, 19, 21, 33, 149; nihilism, 82; nun's, 99, 109; and patriarchy, 11, 126, 189; performative, 4, 63, 77, 79, 89, 124, 189, 191, 199; and psychoanalysis, 13, 18, 29, 82, 145, 150; religious, 79, 83; Renaissance, 17, 116, 121, 150; Romantic, 9, 13, 17, 26–28, 31, 33, 71, 86, 122–23, 153; sentimentality, 158, 160 (*see also Empfindsamkeit*; enthusiasm; melancholy: sweet; *Schwärmer*); sweet, 23, 43, 153, 156; time, 92, 94; traditions, 1–13, 23–24, 28, 35, 37–38, 43, 50–51, 64, 77–78, 82, 124, 145, 151, 162, 198–99

Melencolia I, 3, 5–6, 11–12, 26–27, 29, 31, 36, 48, 63–64, 69–70, 72, 78, 88, 94, 105, 111, 114, 116–17, 125, 130–31, 134, 138, 143, 162, 168–69, 174, 183, 198
melodrama, 148, 155, 157–59, 161, 176, 180–83
memento mori, 16, 32, 78, 92, 105, 108. See also *vanitas*
memory: collective, 4, 114, 118, 190; contests, 23, 34, 180, 182; cultural, 26, 136, 139; ethical, 3–5, 10, 19, 23, 44, 65, 72, 77, 85–86, 111–16, 122, 125, 130, 132, 136–38, 161, 163, 185, 189, 198–99; gender and, 10, 23, 100–101, 110, 114, 117, 122, 124, 136, 139, 161, 163, 198; German, 13, 18, 139, 185, 192, 194, 199; Jewish, 66; politics, 60, 65, 161–62, 199; subjective, 190; traumatic, 101; West German, 77, 82. See also commemoration; Holocaust; postmemory; remembrance; *Vergangenheitsbewältigung*
mental illness, 14, 118, 125, 150–51, 154, 161, 166, 181. See also insanity; madness; mania
Merkel, Angela, 195
messianism, 30, 54
metaphysics, 60, 88–89, 176
Meyer-Sickendieck, Burkhard, 13, 31
Middle Ages, 15–16, 51, 162, 166, 168, 185, 188–89
mimesis, 113, 160, 172. See also empathy; identification
Mitscherlich, Alexander, and Margarete Mitscherlich, 3, 20–21, 25, 33, 75, 107, 113, 134, 141, 144, 149, 180; works by: *Die Unfähigheit zu trauern*, 20, 33, 75, 107, 141, 144, 180. See also inability to mourn
modernism, 79, 141, 145
modernity, 13–14, 146, 153, 157–58, 181–83

Montaigne, Michel de, 35–36, 38–41, 43, 69–71; works by: *The Essays*, 36, 39, 41, 69, 71
Moses, A. Dirk, 70, 109, 178, 184
mourning, 11, 18–22, 30, 32–33, 79, 82, 85, 101, 103, 112, 125, 141, 145–46, 149–50, 152, 161, 187, 200; mourning woman, 138, 144; mourning work, 11, 19–21, 82, 112, 138, 146, 148–51, 160, 187, 200. See also *Trauerarbeit*
mythology, 56, 110, 120–21, 125, 127–28, 137, 146–47, 151, 165, 167, 173, 178, 180, 183

Napoleon, 44
narcissism, 19–21, 113–14, 134, 137
National Socialism, 3–4, 6, 26, 31, 39, 42, 44–46, 48, 51, 66–68, 80, 89, 93, 100, 111–13, 120–21, 129, 136, 149
Nazi past, 1, 6, 10, 12–13, 42, 44, 50, 60, 67, 69–70, 74, 109, 190
negation, 82, 189
negative sacralization, 2
negative sublime, 21, 116, 154, 161, 182, 191
negative symbiosis, 158–60. See also Diner, Dan
negativity, 79, 82, 86, 91–92, 95, 101, 112, 189, 198
Neoplatonism, 9, 12, 17
Neuhaus, Volker, 54, 67–68, 72–73
Nietzsche, Friedrich, 44, 57–60, 62, 67, 71, 73–75, 80–81, 98, 100–102, 106, 108–9; works by: *Also sprach Zarathustra*, 74–75, 100–103, 109; *Ecce Homo*, 73; *Die Geburt der Tragödie*, 73; *Jenseits von Gut und Böse*, 73
nihilism, 77, 107, 82, 84–85, 87–88, 93, 102
Nimrod the Hunter, 165
nostalgia, 146, 156, 162, 180, 182
Nuremberg Trials, 82

Öhlschläger, Claudia, 170, 179, 181–84

Opium Wars, 164, 168, 171, 174
Orion, 165

Panofsky, Erwin, 5–6, 11, 37; and Saxl, 25, 31, 69, 78, 105; works by: (with Fritz Saxl) *Dürers Melencolia I*, 29, 31, 69, 78, 105; (with Raymond Klibansky and Fritz Saxl), *Saturn und Melancholie*, 12, 25, 29, 31, 37, 88, 94–95, 117, 122, 174, 176, 183. *See also* Klibansky, Raymond; Saxl, Fritz
pathetic fallacy, 170
patriarchy, 11, 56, 113, 115, 123–26, 131–33, 135–36, 140–41, 143, 189
Pensky, Max, 17, 23, 30, 32, 34, 105
performance: of remembrance, 23, 37, 122, 139, 189; of sadness and affect, 21, 146
performative, 2, 4–8, 11, 13–14, 23–24, 35, 37–38, 61, 63–64, 77, 79, 89, 124, 155, 165, 188–89, 191, 199. *See also* citationality; conventionality; iterability
Pergamon Altar, 127–28, 137, 140, 143
peripheralization, 171–74, 178
perpetrator, 3, 35, 37–38, 66–68, 77, 80, 82, 88, 90–94, 96, 98, 101–2, 113, 198; collective, 7, 13, 23, 113, 148, 160
pessimism, 48, 64, 68, 84, 102
Pfau, Thomas, 5–7, 26–27, 33–34, 74, 182
Pietism, 154
Plato, 41, 54, 57, 73
politics, 6, 16, 21, 23, 39, 41–43, 45–46, 55–60, 65–69, 71–73, 77, 80–84, 91, 112–16, 118–20, 122, 137–38, 140–42, 158, 161–62, 171, 173, 178, 180, 185, 188, 190, 198–99; memory, 60, 65–66, 161–62, 199; reform, 36–37, 49–51, 56, 67, 69
postmemory, 23, 139, 186, 190, 195–96
Preece, Julian, 48, 69, 71–72

psychiatry, 15–16, 18, 27, 30, 32–33, 122–23, 126, 145
psychoanalysis, 11, 13, 18, 29, 33, 37, 82, 115, 145, 150
psychology, 8, 15, 31, 85–86, 91, 93, 145–46, 150–51, 176, 181; eighteenth-century and nineteenth-century, 122; moral, 154

Qing Emperors, 168

Radden, Jennifer, 11, 17–18, 29, 31–33, 73, 109, 122–23, 143, 183; works by: *Moody Minds Distempered*, 29, 31, 33, 143; *The Nature of Melancholy*, 32, 109, 183
Ranicki, Marcel Reich, 45
rationality, 18, 128, 136, 157–58, 176
reason, 22, 124, 128, 132, 134, 136, 143, 182. *See also* patriarchy; rationality
Reformation, 14
reification, 114, 186
religion, 16, 25, 31, 35–36, 39–40, 47, 51, 61, 71–72, 79, 84, 88–89, 94, 97, 99–103, 154–56, 185, 193, 195
Rembrandt, 176
remembrance: decline of, 191; ethical, 137, 196; Holocaust, 122; literary, 1, 4, 8, 13, 82, 189, 199; melancholy performance of, 23; necessity of, 198. *See also* commemoration; Holocaust; memory; *Vergangenheitsbewältigung*
Renaissance, 2–3, 5–7, 9–11, 14, 16–17, 22, 29, 35, 40–41, 94, 105, 122–23, 145, 147, 151, 162, 166, 170, 188; episteme, 5, 7, 26, 79, 86, 124, 147, 163; genius, 13, 17, 32, 70, 78, 89, 116–17, 138, 198, 199 (*see also* melancholy: genial; melancholy: genius); humanism, 3, 6, 10
repression, 18–20, 59, 77, 86, 111, 115, 127, 129, 138, 140, 148, 180

ressentiment, 74, 80–82, 87, 92, 94, 101–2, 105, 108–9, 148. See also Améry, Jean
Riordan, Colin, 177, 184
Romantic symbol, 61–62
Romanticism, 9, 13, 17, 26–28, 31, 33–34, 60–62, 64, 71, 74, 86, 95, 122–23, 153, 182
Rote Kapelle, 120, 142
Rothenberg, Jürgen, 66, 69–70, 75
Ruehl, Martin A., 6, 26
Ruisdael, Jakob van, 175–76

SA (*Sturmabteilung, die*, National Socialists), 167
sadness, 5–6, 8–10, 14, 43, 46, 48, 66, 68, 69, 149, 150–51; authenticity of, 150; as commemoration, 149, 151; "good" and "bad," 14, 21–22, 68, 198; and loss, 27, 33, 193; and melancholy, 28; "normal" and "abnormal," 18, 27, 33; pathological, 18, 27, 32–33, 66–68, 95, 145; performance of, 4, 146; subjective experience of, 68, 103–4; without cause, 18, 21, 27, 43, 68
Saint Sebaldus, 165
Saint Simeon, 100
sanguine type, 14, 41, 48, 124
Santner, Eric, 20–21, 33, 181, 187, 200; works by: *Stranded Objects*, 20–21, 33, 200
Sartre, Jean-Paul, 105, 150, 181; works by: *Nausea*, 105, 181
Saturn, 3, 9, 11–12, 17, 25–26, 28–29, 31–32, 49, 53, 73, 78, 81, 106, 121, 147, 150–52, 160, 162–84
Saxl, Fritz, 11–12, 25, 29, 31, 37, 69, 78, 105, 183; works by: (with Erwin Panofsky) *Dürers Melencolia I*, 29, 31, 69, 78, 105; (with Raymond Klibansky and Erwin Panofsky) *Saturn und Melancholie*, 12, 25, 29, 31, 37, 88, 94–95, 117, 122, 174, 176, 183. See also Klibansky, Raymond; Panofsky, Erwin

Scheub, Wolfgang, 45
Schiesari, Julia, 10, 29, 32, 72, 200; works by: *The Gendering of Melancholia*, 29, 32, 72, 200
Schings, Hans-Jürgen, 22, 30, 31, 33, 71, 154, 181; works by: *Melancholie und Aufklärung*, 30–31, 33, 71, 181
Schopenhauer, Arthur, 28, 48, 64, 72, 102, 109; works by: *Die Welt als Wille und Vorstellung*, 72
Schulze-Boysen, Harro, 120
Schütte, Uwe, 150, 180
Schwärmer, 137. See also *Empfindsamkeit*; enthusiasm; melancholy: sweet; sentimentality
Schwärmerroman, 181
Sea Battle of Southwold, 168
Sebald, W. G., works by: *Die Ausgewanderten*, 160–61, 163, 167, 169, 175, 181–83; *Austerlitz*, 158–61, 166, 168–69, 175, 179–82; *Die Beschreibung des Unglücks*, 145, 149–50, 179–81, 183; "Konstruktionen der Trauer," 71–72, 74–75, 149, 180–81; *Luftkrieg und Literatur*, 180; *Nach der Natur*, 147, 160, 164, 166, 180, 183; *Die Ringe des Saturn*, 11, 29, 81, 106, 151–52, 160, 162–70, 172, 175–79, 181, 183–84; *Schwindel. Gefühle*, 150, 155–57, 159–60, 165–70, 179, 181–82, 184
Second World War, 31, 39, 44, 110, 146–48, 167
sentimentality, 43, 48, 71, 125, 146, 152–62, 165–66, 170, 176, 179, 182. See also *Empfindsamkeit*; enthusiasm; melancholy: sweet; *Schwärmer*
Seven Cardinal Sins, 49, 95, 185
Screech, M. A., 41, 69, 71
Shakespeare, 1, 24, 70, 76, 78, 81, 86, 103–5; works by: *Hamlet*, 1, 8, 28, 77–79, 104–5, 109
Shoah business, 185–86, 190, 194, 199

sleep, 76, 96, 98, 109
sloth, sin of, 7, 9, 16, 22, 24, 32, 73, 76, 79, 82, 94–102, 105, 108, 191, 196, 198–99. See also *acedia*; boredom; *ennui*; *taedium vitae*
solipsism, 45, 65, 82, 98, 115, 130, 141, 148, 151
Sontag, Susan, 23, 34; works by: *Illness as Metaphor*, 34
Spanish Civil War, 120
SPD (*Sozialdemokratische Partei Deutschlands*), 36–37, 50, 57–58, 62, 64, 67, 69
Stalin, 115, 125, 137, 140, 144
Stalinism, 112–13, 120, 137
Starobinski, Jean, 17, 30, 32, 139; works by: *Histoire du traitement de la mélancolie*, 30, 32; "L'encre de la mélancolie," 139
status corruptionis, 52
Stifter, Adalbert, 149, 179
Stolpersteine, 195
Stolz, Dieter, 48, 69–70, 72–74
Swinburne, Algernon, 170

Taberner, Stuart, 45, 72, 74, 182
taedium vitae, 16, 59, 95, 187, 189. See also *acedia*; boredom; *ennui*; sloth
Tartaros, 167
Tatmensch, 41, 47, 72
teleology, 39, 47, 51, 69, 84–85, 88, 146, 173
Tellenbach, Hubertus, 30, 43, 71, 89, 108–9; works by: *Melancholy: History of the Problem*, 30, 40, 108–9
temperaments, theory of, 15–17, 40–41, 52, 71, 78, 124, 151, 168, 188. See also humoral theory
Temple of Jerusalem, 174–76
Thanatos, 77, 82, 106, 129
theology, 14, 38, 51–52, 94–95, 102–4, 185, 187
Theunissen, Michael, 109, 188–89, 192, 200; works by: *Vorentwürfe von Moderne*, 109, 188–89, 192, 200

Third Reich, 6, 39
transcendence, 50, 58, 61, 84, 90–92, 97, 99, 101–2, 116, 137, 189
transposition, 83, 107
Trauer, 26, 29, 33, 69, 71–72, 74–75, 107–10, 139, 146, 149, 179–81. See also grief; mourning
Trauerarbeit, 11, 146. See also mourning: mourning work
trauma, 20, 25–26, 33, 103, 107, 110, 118, 119–21, 130–31, 140, 154–55, 157, 180, 182, 200; and history, 2, 66, 86, 90–94, 112, 126, 136, 138, 150, 178; Holocaust, 85, 129, 146; and memory, 101, 187; transgenerational, 147, 180; victim's, 77, 79, 82–83, 126; working through, 146
tristitia, 95. See also sadness
typus Acediae, 94, 174
typus Geometriae, 88, 94, 174–75
typus melancholicus, 89

Übermensch, 65, 67
uncanny, 91, 124, 128, 132, 135–36, 161
unconscious, 18–20
United Nations, 167
Ure, Michael, 80
Ustasha regime, 178
utopia, 27, 30, 32, 43–44, 47, 50, 55–56, 60, 62, 70–71, 101, 105, 141

vanitas, 7, 16, 32, 38, 63, 78, 105, 108. See also *memento mori*
Vergangenheitsbewältigung, 9, 24–25, 28, 37–38, 50, 53, 66–67, 77, 185, 195; degraded, 188; deficits of, 42; genius of, 1, 10, 122, 191 (*see also* melancholy: genius); literary, 1, 44; West German, 66, 80–81
Vergangenheitsbewirtschaftung, 185–86, 190–91, 199
Verinnerlichung, 98
Victorian era, 123, 170–71
vita activa, 123
vita contemplativa, 123, 136

Waffen-SS, 23, 37–38, 48
Wagner, Isabel, 24, 77, 79, 82, 104–6, 108
Wagner-Egelhaaf, Martina, 13, 30–31, 105, 108, 181
Waldheim, Kurt, 167
Wallerstein, Immanuel, 172–73, 183–84
Wandervogelbewegung, 167
Warburg, Aby, 12, 31
weather systems, 49, 78, 162, 165, 168, 177–78. See also desertification; environment; flooding
Weber, Andrew, 38, 69–71, 73–74
Weiss, Peter, works by: *Abschied von den Eltern*, 140; *Die Ästhetik des Widerstands*, 23, 110–44, 148, 163, 180, 183; *Die Ermittlung*, 140; *Fluchtpunkt*, 140, 142; "Gespräch über Dante," 142; *Hölderlin*, 118, 142; "Laokoon oder Über die Grenzen der Sprache," 140, 142; "Meine Ortschaft," 140; *Notizbücher, 1960–1971*, 142; *Notizbücher, 1971–1980*, 29, 139, 142; *Rapporte*, 140, 142; *Rapporte 2*, 141; *Rekonvaleszenz*, 114–15, 141; "Vorübungen zum dreiteiligen Drama divina commedia," 142; "10 Arbeitspunkte eines Autors in der geteilten Welt," 141; "Zwischen Pergamon und Plötzensee," 140, 143
Weltgeist, 44
Weltschmerz, 71, 81, 145, 148, 152–58, 162, 165, 167–68, 176, 182, 199
Werther, 154, 181
West Germany, 36–37, 39, 42, 45, 60, 77, 80, 86, 91, 93, 112, 186, 191, 199; economic miracle, 59; inability to mourn, 53, 66; intellectual milieu, 81, 106; literature, 24, 69; memory, 26, 37, 66, 77, 82, 92; state, 77; West German collective, 3, 20, 37, 65, 67–68, 113, 135
Wilkomirski, Binjamin, 22, 33
Wittkower, Rudolf, and Margot Wittkower, 9, 25–26, 28–29, 151, 180–81; works by: *Born under Saturn*, 9, 26, 28–29, 147, 151, 180–81
world systems analysis, 172, 183–84. See also capitalism

Zarathustra, 74–75, 100–103, 109
Zeus, 167
Zionism, 45, 104
Zivilisationsbruch, 2, 25. See also caesura; Diner, Dan
Žižek, Slavoj, 22, 33, 182; works by: "Melancholy and the Act," 33, 182